copyright ©2016 by Christopher Broschell.

All rights reserved. No part of this book may be reproduced of transmitted in any form or by any means, electronic or mechanical, including photocopying, recording or by any information storage and retrieval system without permission in writing from the publisher.

Printed in the United States of America

ISBN: 978-0-9948396-3-3

Second Edition

PROLOGUE
The root causes of Germany's war

Nazi Germany's rise and subsequent declarations of the need for *lebensraum* – breathing room – can be diluted down to three words: lust for vengeance.

By this statement, you may think it was just Hitler and the Nazis who were responsible for World War II, but it was also the Allies at the end of World War I who were looking for blood and this was one of the greatest causes for the conflict. This vengeance even goes back to 1871 and the Franco-Prussian War. Emperor Napoleon III was informed by his military advisers the French army could handily beat the Prussian army and seeking to bolster his reputation at home, Napoleon III attacked.

The Prussians had superior numbers as well as a superior general army staff, which proved disastrous for France. The rapid and overwhelming victory of the German states under the leadership of von Bismarck and von Moltke made possible the creation of a unified German Empire and brought about the fall of the French empire. The Germans were divided culturally and politically, but they were united in their hatred for France since the Napoleonic Wars, when France had looted the German states and pressed an estimated 250,000 Germans into the French armies. As part of the peace settlement in 1871, the territory of Alsace-Lorraine was taken by Germany, which it held on to until after World War I. The German army also occupied the north of France until reparations of five billion francs were paid.

Fast forward to 1914; the French still had the loss as a thorn in its side. When World War I ended the Allies, with the French at the head, went after their pound of flesh. Originally, U.S. President Woodrow Wilson put out a peace plan which was more conducive to a rebuilt Europe. British Prime Minister David Lloyd George also was not looking for outrageous reparation sums, but his tone changed after he decided to dissolve Parliament and call an election, hoping to ride a wave of postwar euphoria. This euphoria changed quickly when the question of who was going to pay for the war started making the rounds.

The Prime Minister was warming to his work: "When Germany defeated France (in 1871) she made France pay. That is the principle which she herself has established. There is absolutely no doubt about the principle we should proceed upon – that Germany must pay the costs of the war up to the limit of her capacity to do so."[1]

Read closely into this: Germany must pay up to the limit of her capacity. A vague term, though what wasn't considered at the time is if Germany were to lose a large chunk of its industrial base, as well as overseas colonies, its merchant shipping, not to mention the two million men killed during the war, it was going to have a hard time surviving, let alone paying a stipend.

Germany had to give all merchant ships over 1,600 tons, half the vessels between 1,000 and 1,600 tons, and 25% of all trawlers and other fishing boats; these were not just the ones owned by the German government – **it was also privately-owned shipping**. Germany was also required to build up to 200,000 tons of shipping for the Allied powers yearly for five years – the equivalent of about 4.5 Iowa-class battleships a year. Germany also had to give up all of its overseas territories – private and public – and Germany had to pay for all improvements done in these territories *afterwards*. Imagine selling a house and getting a bill from the new owners for their kitchen renovation! Germany also had to send coal to various countries, including seven million tons to France a year for ten years and eight million each to Belgium and Italy each year for ten years.

Unfortunately, the loss of these resources meant Germany had little money left over to pay for imported products it needed to survive, including food. The Allies knew there was no way Germany could pay its reparations, yet continued to push. In Great Britain, the newspaper *The Times* wrote under the headline *Making Germany Pay*: "There is too much suspicion of influences concerned to let the Germans off lightly, whereas the only possible motive in determining their capacity to pay must be the interests of the Allies."[2]

With this in mind, Lloyd George had no alternative but to continue pressing for reparations, making public speeches which were inflammatory, but nonetheless necessary for him to continue as prime minister. Sir Eric Campbell-Geddes, former First Lord of the

Admiralty, was not to be outdone by Lloyd George stating: "We will get out of her all you can squeeze out of a lemon and a bit more. I will squeeze her until you can hear the pips squeak." Campbell-Geddes wanted as reparation all public and private property belonging to Germans in neutral and Allied countries as well as all of its gold, silver and jewels and the contents of its libraries and art galleries.[3] In other words, he wanted Germany to hold one massive garage sale and the Allies were to benefit from it. It was under this veil of vengeance the British election was held and under which David Lloyd George won.

Lloyd George never said he believed Germany could pay the whole cost of the war, but that didn't matter because that is precisely what everyone wanted to hear. Though it helped David Lloyd George win the general election, it did nothing to help the fortunes of Europe. The prime minister is looked upon as a moderating influence at the subsequent peace conference, one where French Prime Minister Georges Clemenceau wanted more than his pound of flesh. Clemenceau had only one thought in mind – vengeance against the godless Hun which raped his land and killed his people. From Keynes:

Clemenceau's aim was to weaken and destroy Germany in every possible way, and I fancy that he was always a little contemptuous about the Indemnity (reparations); he had no intention of leaving Germany in a position to practise a vast commercial activity [4]

This was written in 1920, well before the hyperinflation of 1923 and the Depression of 1929 would crush the German economy and it is unfortunate Keynes was so farsighted, yet the politicians of the day were not. Keynes pointed out the balancing of budgets in France was done with the express hope of reparation payments filling in the deficit, though the Allies knew the payments were well beyond the reach of the German economy they even wrote it in the Treaty of Versailles!

The Allied and Associated Governments recognise that the resources of Germany are not adequate, after taking into account permanent diminutions of such resources…to make complete reparation for all such loss and damage.

The Allied and Associated Governments, however, require, and Germany undertakes, that she will make compensation for all damage done to the civilian population of the Allied and Associated Powers and to their property during the period of the belligerency.

We know you can't pay, but we are going to make those pips squeak anyway. Brilliant thinking on the part of the people who were running the world at the time, though I can't help but wonder how many times the Germans sighed and shook their heads as they signed the document with the equivalent of a gun to their heads – the threat of invasion loomed over them if the Germans did not sign the punitive treaty. There was no choice in the matter, and Georges Clemenceau had taken his country's revenge and then some.

There were people even then who knew the peace terms were untenable. Keynes famously walked out of the conference, where he served as Britain's financial adviser. Keynes noted in his 1920 book he felt reparations should be set at $15 billion for damages and, if the Allies were quite adamant about the subject, a further $25 billion for pension payments to widows of servicemen killed during the conflict. Keynes felt this was perhaps over and above what was required, yet he included it in his estimates anyway, being fair to all parties. So from the foremost economist of the time we have a figure of $40 billion; the reparations commission set the figure at $63 billion anyway and this figure did not include the values of the Alsace-Lorraine region, the Saar coalfields and the lands lost to Denmark and the newly created Poland. As well, this didn't include the railways, airplanes and shipping taken, all of which would have helped reduce the burden on the country.

From the graph on the previous page, even if Germany's entire economic output was put toward reparations, it would take three years to pay it back – assuming nobody ate, had a house or did anything else to survive. In perspective, it would be like asking the United States to pay $51,000,000,000,000 to a foreign government, or over three times the current national debt.

So Germany is stripped clean, and now it needs to pay. Clemenceau now has about forty pounds of flesh, but it didn't even stop there. When Germany failed to make its reparation payments in 1922, the French and Belgians responded by arguing for the occupation of the Ruhr valley, which was the industrial heartland of the country. The British wanted moderation and a lowering of payments, but in January

1923 when Germany failed to deliver a timber payment, the French and Belgian troops moved in. France especially was looking for payment in goods such as iron and coal to satisfy its industrial needs. The Germans had other thoughts.

Led by Fritz Thyssen and others, the men and women of the Ruhr valley started a campaign of passive resistance – if the French wanted the goods, they were going to have to get at them themselves. Thyssen was joined by the other steel companies in the region and everyone refused to deliver coal to the French. The French took what they wanted anyway, though the Germans frustrated them at every turn by striking and being obstinately disobedient. The unfortunate by-product of the resistance was the shutdown of the Ruhr valley and the beginnings of hyperinflation. To pay for the striking workers and also for people the French had thrown out of their homes, the German government started to print money; lots of money.

A basic economics lesson – a government can't just print money to cover expenses, otherwise it can lead to spiralling inflation or a collapse in confidence in the government (a good lesson can be learned from the debt ceiling debate and subsequent debt downgrade in the United States in 2011). This is precisely what happened in Germany – confidence in the government waned, both inside and outside of the country and inflation began. The inflation, however, was outrageous and never before seen – and never since – in the history of the world. An excellent example of price inflation was a loaf of bread would cost 163 marks in 1922; the price rose to 200,000,000,000 (yes, billion!) marks by October 1923. Savings were wiped out, workers would rush to the stores after getting paid before the prices went up, often demanding they get paid daily. Many people took to bartering; the most extreme cases were housewives who would sell their personal sexual services in exchange for food for their families.

There was a lot of anger and resentment in Germany over the treaty – much of which was the wholesale pillaging of the land by the victors. One point which really stuck in their craw was Article 231 of the treaty, the aptly named "war guilt" clause:

> *The Allied and Associated Governments affirm and Germany accepts the responsibility of Germany and her allies for causing all the*

loss and damage to which the Allied and Associated Governments and their nationals have been subjected as a consequence of the war imposed upon them by the aggression of Germany and her allies.

By this, Germany alone was responsible for the actions of itself and its allies. This hurt German pride badly and it was under this guise political extremism took the country by storm. Fritz Thyssen for his part was arrested by the French authorities and placed on trial before a military tribunal. Though acquitted of the charges, Thyssen was subject of a heavy fine and this, along with the terms of Versailles, were a thorn in his side – a thorn which was being tugged out by a blustery former army corporal in Munich. Politicians were assassinated in the streets regularly, communists espoused Bolshevism as the proper route and one extremist in particular was very vocal in claiming the treaty was the bane of Germany's existence.

Adolf Hitler, an Austrian-born German soldier, fought in the trenches, was disliked by his fellow soldiers and was wounded twice including a mustard gas attack. He was convalescing in a military hospital from the gas attack when the armistice was signed. Angered by the German surrender, he started his anti-Semitic rants blaming the Jews for the surrender. The end of the war was a personally emotional disaster for Hitler as well. It brought the threat of demobilization, tearing him from the only community in which he had ever felt at home and returning him to a civilian life in which he had neither direction nor career prospects. Hitler did find employ with the army as an informer, in which he infiltrated many organizations, including the nascent German Workers' Party.

Hitler attended his first meeting of the German Workers' Party on September 12, 1919 listening to the speakers. When one of the attendees spoke in favor of the German state of Bavaria breaking away from Germany and forming a new South German nation with Austria, Hitler was enraged and he spoke out forcefully against the man for the next fifteen minutes uninterrupted. This was enough for Anton Drexler, one of the party's founders, to take Hitler aside after the meeting and give him a pamphlet entitled *My Political Awakening*. Since much of the writing followed Hitler's own political agenda, specifically a solid German nationalism and a strong anti-Semitic flow, Hitler was intrigued and joined the party. On September 16, 1919, Hitler issued his first written comment on the so-called Jewish Question. He defined the Jews as a race and not a religious community, characterized the effect of a Jewish presence as a "race-tuberculosis of the peoples," and identified the initial goal of a German government to be discriminatory legislative against Jews. The "ultimate goal must definitely be the removal of the Jews altogether."[5]

The party changed its name in 1920 to include the term National Socialist and became the *Nationalsozialistische Deutsche Arbeiterpartei*, usually shortened to Nazi. Over the next couple of years, the party grew in strength, particularly in the atmosphere of shrinking national fortunes. When the Ruhr was occupied in 1923, nationalist sentiment grew and when the German government resumed reparation payments to the Allies, they were considered traitors to the Republic. It was under this guise Hitler initiated his abortive coup in November 1923, the Bierkeller Putsch. With his famous line "The National Revolution has begun!" Hitler stormed a Munich beer hall where local businessmen and government officials were having a meeting.

The coup fizzled out quickly and afterwards Hitler was arrested, though what he said struck a chord with many, including Fritz Thyssen. The country seethed and boiled for years until Hitler's election in 1933 as Chancellor, then went on the route of rearmament and its own plan for vengeance. The revenge the Third Reich exacted over the course of the war was well known, in taking land it felt was misappropriated from it, including Alsace-Lorraine and Poland, as well as taking as much gold, goods and machinery as the Reich felt it needed to wage war as well as to compensate its people for the embarrassment it felt from the punitive Treaty. It is under these auspices much of the corporate profiteering, plunder and pillage fell and it is easy to see why so many businessmen felt it was their right to reclaim what was – they felt – wrongfully taken from them after World War I.

1
Ford & General Motors

The Ford Motor Company is one of the most iconic corporations in the world. In World War II, Ford turned out 8,600 B-24 Liberator bombers; in 1963, their Philco division developed the Mission Control Centre in Houston for the Apollo missions. Through Philco, they manufactured radar systems, color TVs, washers and dryers.

Though great, Henry Ford was legendary in his anti-Semitic views. He was partially a product of his times – in the late nineteenth and early twentieth century, anti-Semitism was rampant, the result of increased Jewish immigration from Europe. Ford would take camping trips with close friends including Thomas Edison and U.S. Presidents Harding and Coolidge. During one in 1919, he credited "all evil to Jews or to the Jewish capitalists. The Jews caused the war, the Jews caused the outbreak of thieving and robbery all over the country, the Jews caused the inefficiency of the navy…" To push this point home, Ford had bought his hometown newspaper *The Dearborn Independent* and began publishing a series of articles claiming a vast Jewish conspiracy was infecting America. The series ran in the following ninety-one issues. Ford bound the articles into four volumes titled *The International Jew* and distributed half a million copies to his vast network of dealerships and subscribers.[6]

Again, Ford wasn't alone in his views; he grew up Episcopalian, learning the Jews had crucified Christ. For 2,000 years, they have been paying for that and history is replete with examples:

- The First Crusade was as much an anti-Jewish crusade as it was an anti-Muslim one
- Jews were persecuted for being Jews during the Inquisition
- In 1215 the Fourth Lateran Council of Rome forced Jews to wear the "badge of shame" in all Christian countries
- In 1264 The Council of Vienna forced Jews to wear dunce caps and thousands were murdered.
- In 1290 King Edward I of England banned all Jews.

Even the great and revered Martin Luther had to get in on the action with his publication of *The Jews & Their Lies* in 1543. A little taste of Luther's work:

Therefore, be on your guard against the Jews, knowing that wherever they have their synagogues, nothing is found but a den of devils in-which sheer self-glory, conceit, lies, blasphemy, and defaming of God and men are practiced most maliciously and veheming his eyes on them and also Moreover, they are nothing but thieves and robbers who daily eat no morsel and wear no thread of clothing which they have not stolen and pilfered from us by means of their accursed usury[7]

Now we see where Henry Ford gets it from. A visit to church and you are blasted by a sermon quoting Martin Luther. Ford, and the business he built, were and still are very well-respected. If he is publishing anti-Semitic writings, that would be acceptable to the great mass of non-Jewish Americans – it was, after all, Henry Ford and if one of the nation's greatest industrialists had something to say, most people want to hear it. It was also quite acceptable to his most vociferous foreign follower: Adolf Hitler.

Hitler had an interesting and long connection to Henry Ford. It is not known how the two came to know of each other, but according to a *New York Times* article from 1924, Ford played an instrumental part in Hitler's Bierkeller Putsch. Ford funded Hitler's coup attempt, according to Interior Minister Erhard Auer of the Bavarian Diet (Parliament):

The Bavarian Diet has long had the information that the Hitler movement was partly financed by an American anti-Semitic chief, who is Henry Ford. Mr. Ford's interest began a year ago when one of Mr. Ford's agents came in contact with Diedrich Eichart. Eichart asked Mr. Ford's agent for financial aid. The agent returned to America and immediately Mr. Ford's money began coming to Munich[8]

Auer was Hitler's political adversary in Bavaria at the time and Ford Motor Company has always denied any money going from company coffers to Hitler. Henry Ford biographer Vincent Curcio points out there is no evidence substantiating Auer's claim and it would not be out of the realm of probability a politician would lie about an opponent. There was a conversation with government officials in 1922 about the sale of Ford tractors to the German Ministry of Agriculture, but nothing concrete. Any claims of further finance are repudiated by Kurt Ludecke, who on behalf of Hitler had actually called on Henry Ford in 1924. Ludecke was a German nationalist, international playboy, bon vivant and Nazi Party fundraiser. He joined the party in 1922 after hearing the "slight, pale man, his brown hair parted on one side and falling again and again over his sweating brow. Threatening and beseeching, with small pleading hands and flaming steel-blue eyes, he had the look of a fanatic."[9] That didn't matter as much to Ludecke as what Hitler said. Ludecke was enamored with National Socialism and joined the party the day after sitting in on a rally. Hitler spoke to him about fundraising outside of Germany which brought Ludecke, in his words, many headaches and few results. One of those meetings was with Henry Ford.

Ludecke landed in New York in January 1924 and met up with Siegfried and Winnifred Wagner. Siegfried was a well-known conductor and the son of Hitler's favorite composer Richard Wagner. At the time, Siegfried was on a tour of the United States. The Wagners managed to arrange an evening with Henry and Clara Ford at their Fair Lane estate on January 31, 1924. Mrs. Wagner recalled Ford speaking after dinner and the tone was set: "the philosophy and ideas of Ford and Hitler were similar."

Ludecke started his sales pitch the next morning at Ford's office in Dearborn. Hitler could put into place the "social program which *The Dearborn Independent*'s articles provided such suggestive material." Ford's response was "Yes the Jews, these cunning Jews."[10] However, that was the end of it and Ford politely sent Ludecke on his way, empty-handed.

Hitler still admired Ford and purportedly, a life-sized portrait of Ford hung on the wall of Hitler's office. On July 30, 1938, Ford celebrated his 75th birthday by receiving the Grand Cross of the German Eagle, the most important honor Germany could offer a non-citizen. He received the award — a golden Maltese cross embraced by four swastikas — in his office and he received it with a personal note from Hitler, thanking Ford for his devotion to peace and humanitarian ideals.[11] To be fair to Ford, Hitler also bestowed the award on James Mooney over at General Motors for his "distinguished service to the Reich."

The International Jew was one of the source materials for *Mein Kampf* and Hitler's admiration of Henry Ford is so impressive that Ford is the only non-German mentioned in Hitler's diatribe *Mein Kampf*:

> *Jews are the regents of the stock exchange power of the American Union. Every year they manage to become increasingly the controlling masters of the labor power of a people of 120,000,000 souls; one great man, Ford, to their exasperation still holds out independently there even now.*[12]

Ford is an easy target – his articles in *The Dearborn Independent*, packaged up neatly and published in *The International Jew,* have cemented his hatred and contempt for Jewish people. Hatred of Jews does not make Ford someone who profited personally from the Third Reich. So what exactly did Ford Motor Company do to help the Nazis, and make a profit in the process?

In the interwar period, German nationalism continued to be a problem for Ford. They were considered the German government's supplier of last resort, due to their foreign ownership. In 1939 amid growing pressure, they reorganized and changed the name of the company to Ford-Werke.[13]

It didn't stop there. According to a *Washington Post* article, under pressure from the Nazi government, Ford-Werke sent a 50,000 Reichsmarks birthday present to the Führer on his 50th birthday in 1939. Ford Motor Company in Dearborn would have had some knowledge of this, as the U.S. parent still owned 52% of the company as late as 1941. But the Reich government was against Ford divesting itself of Ford-Werke, as it "would deprive German Ford of 'the excellent sales organization' of the parent company and make it more difficult to bring 'the remaining European Ford companies under German influence'."[14] Truly, Ford-Werke was one of the only unmolested enemy companies in the Reich.

It may have had "an excellent sales organization," but the sales force was not much of a concern to the company, since Ford-Werke had already started making tracked vehicles for the Wehrmacht in 1938. By 1941 the company had completely ceased production of passenger vehicles in favor of military trucks, of which it is estimated Ford-Werke produced 35% of the trucks used by the Nazis in World War II. A U.S. Army report, written by Henry Schneider in 1945 claimed just three years earlier 100-120,000 Wehrmacht trucks were Ford-built. The study commissioned by Ford itself in 2001 puts that number at a slightly more conservative 87-92,000.[15] So how did Ford-Werke make this many trucks? As with most manufacturing concerns in World War II Germany, Ford faced massive labor shortages. These were, not surprisingly, filled by slave labor. Elsa Iwanowa was one of these slave laborers. At the age of 16, she was abducted from her home in the southern Russian city of Rostov by German soldiers to work at the Ford plant at Köln (Cologne).

> On October 6, 1942, Nazi troops abducted Iwanowa and transported her to Germany with approximately 2,000 other adolescents. When Iwanowa arrived in Wuppertal, Germany, a representative of Ford-Werke purchased her, along with thirty-eight other adolescents from Rostov. Ford-Werke's representative had Iwanowa, and the other adolescents, transported to Ford-Werke's plant in Cologne. Once in Cologne, Ford-Werke placed Iwanowa with approximately sixty-five Ukrainian deportees in a wooden hut, without heat, running water or sewage facilities. They slept in three-tiered bunks without bedding and were locked in at night. From 1942-1945, Ford-Werke required Iwanowa to perform heavy labor at its Cologne plant. Iwanowa's assignment consisted of drilling holes into the motor blocks of engines for military trucks. Ford-Werke security officials supervised the forced laborers, at times using rubber truncheons to beat those who failed to meet production quotas.[16]

Iwanowa launched a class action lawsuit against Ford in the late 1990s. The case was dismissed by Judge Joseph Greenaway Jr. in September, 2000 on the basis the statute of limitations had expired. Greenaway also agreed with Ford's rationale they had lost control of

Ford-Werke and compensation should be taken care of by the German government as the successor to the Nazi regime. According to Ford spokeswoman Lydia Cisaruk at the time "We did not do business in Germany during the war. The Nazis confiscated the plant there and we lost all contact."[17]

That's not entirely true. As stated earlier, Ford still owned 52% of the plant in 1941 and profited still from Ford-Werke throughout the war. In fact, the U.S. Treasury Department wrote at the time "There would seem to be at least a tacit acceptance by Mr. Edsel Ford of the reliance...on the known neutrality of the Ford family as a basis of receipt of favors from the German Reich."[18] Ford-Werke stayed marginally in U.S. Ford's hands throughout the war, being placed in trusteeship by the Köln Supreme Court in 1942.

By 1943, it is estimated at least half of those working at the Ford-Werke plant in Köln were slave laborers, working twelve hour days under harsh conditions, much like those attested to in Iwanowa's class action suit. This practice began as early as 1940, according to Robert Schmidt, the Nazi general director who ran Ford-Werke from 1937. Schmidt, an ambitious man, set about consolidating his European Ford empire with the Nazi conquests. He became administrator of Ford plants in Holland and Belgium, seized assets from Ford SAF's plant in the Asnières suburb of Paris and set about implementing a Reich program of uniform production for all Ford plants in occupied Europe, to be directed by Ford-Werke. The factories in France, Belgium and Holland would coordinate with Ford-Werke to make interchangeable parts to be used in all trucks manufactured by Ford-Werke – which is something done today by automotive manufacturers around the world, but was a novel concept then. These collaborations were relayed by Schmidt to Henry Ford's son Edsel, who was Chief Executive Officer of Ford Motor Company in Michigan at the time.

U.S. Ford was quite happy to see Ford-Werke prosper and did whatever they could to help. Around 1935, they ordered parts from the facility in Köln to be delivered to Ford plants in Latin America and Japan. In 1936, the Nazi government started to block the German Ford from buying raw materials, which makes sense considering Ford was still only making passenger vehicles and the rearmament process had begun. U.S. Ford, realizing production delays of this sort could shut down the German subsidiary, shipped rubber and other raw materials in exchange for German-made parts. With the blessing of U.S. Ford, the Nazi government took 25% of the imported raw materials destined for German Ford and gave them to other manufacturers.[19]

When Ford AG was set up in 1925, its board was entirely made up of Americans for the first two years, including Henry Ford. By 1929, Henry wanted Germans to sit on the board, so he issued instructions to find "the best farmer, the best lawyer and the best industrialist" in Germany.[20] These men were the farmer Alwin Schurig; the lawyer Heinrich Albert and the industrialist Carl Bosch. The farmer was just that; Heinrich Albert was a well-known World War I German spy, later setting up a law practice in the United States; Carl Bosch was the chair of IG Farben, the largest chemical conglomerate in the world at the time. Farben retained 15% of Ford AG and as a reward, Edsel Ford sat on the board of IG Chemical Corporation, Farben's US subsidiary.[21] IG Chemical (US) became General Aniline & Film (GAF) and went on to manufacture photo film and asphalt shingles.

Throughout the 1930s, Ford AG claimed it was constantly being attacked by Nazi Party officials, due mostly to its foreign ownership. This claim can be disputed however. At the 1936 International Automobile Exhibit in Berlin, Hitler proclaimed the assembly-line method of manufacture used by Ford to be a model for German industry. A few days later, Hermann Göring purchased a Ford Eiffel for his personal use. And it didn't stop there. The Luftwaffe started sending contracts Ford's way; the Wehrmacht changed direction from its previous anti-foreigner stance and gave Ford a contract in 1938 for troop carriers, to be built to Ford's standards. Ford's U.S. production chief – and member of Ford AG's board – was on hand for a board meeting which finalized plans for the armored personnel carriers. He sent a telegram stateside saying "German plans are turning out very satisfactory."[22]

By the time war was declared in 1939, Ford-Werke – as it was now called – was producing a great deal of trucks and troop carriers, but the Wehrmacht needed something else. The Nazis needed munitions and approached Schmidt and Heinrich Albert about the possibility of the company diversifying. Nothing could have been worse for Ford than having German munitions recovered by the Allies with a Ford nameplate on it. However, Albert was up to the unscrupulous task. He set up a shell company, with the principal investor being the banking house of Spolz & Co. Ford was under a different name making parts for flamethrowers and rockets for the Germans – think of it as a Mercury, not a Ford. Ford-Werke profited to the tune of 1.5 million Reichsmarks a year until the war ended, but there is no conclusive proof Ford in the United States condoned, or even knew of the scheme.[23]

Ford-Werke did, however, keep Ford Motor Company in the loop about other dealings with the Nazi government. Executives in Dearborn, Michigan were briefed on Ford-Werke's work on Luftwaffe lifeboats, Junkers landing gear and the myriad of trucks and personnel carriers coming out of the plant in Köln. The flow of information continued until the German declaration of war on the United States in 1941, but before that, Ford vice-president Charles Sorensen received at least 180 reports from Ford-Werke chairman Heinrich Albert and general director Robert Schmidt.

After the fall of France, Ford-Werke proudly placed an advertisement in the Frankfurter Zeitung stating "German Ford vehicles were the dependable servants of the brave soldier."

Imagine though, being an Allied serviceman coming off the beach on D-Day and seeing Ford-branded trucks on the Nazi side. "Ford trucks prominently present in the supply lines of the Wehrmacht were understandably an unpleasant sight to the men in our Army."[24] Henry Ford himself wanted his company to remain officially neutral in all matters of war. In 1940, Edsel Ford was approached by the U.S. government with a contract to manufacture 6,000 Rolls Royce engines for the RAF. Edsel took this back to his father, who was still in ultimate control of the company. When Ford senior found out it was for the British, he flatly refused, stating he would not support the war machine of one country. At this exact time, Ford-Werke was already manufacturing trucks and armored personnel carriers for the German Army which were already rolling over the plains of France towards Paris.

Did this refusal come from Ford's long-standing neutrality stance, or was there something else behind it? J. Edgar Hoover had his doubts – he had Ford's Dearborn headquarters monitored since World War I when Ford's personal secretary Ernest Liebold was thought to be a German spy. His surveillance paid off when Gerhart Westrick, who was also thought to be a World War I German spy, came to visit two weeks after Ford cancelled the Rolls Royce contracts.

Dr. Gerhart Westrick conferred with Mr. Henry Ford in an endeavor to persuade Mr. Ford to use his influence in keeping the United States Government from furnishing any materials of war to Great Britain. Westrick stated if Britain's war supply was cut off, the war would be over in 90 days...[25]

The FBI dismissed the matter, but perhaps should have looked closer – both Liebold and Westrick were purported German spies, as was Westrick's business partner in the law firm of Westrick & Albert, the same Heinrich Albert who was chairman of Ford-Werke. Albert was well known to an American who would go on to head the Office of Strategic Services branch in Switzerland. Allen Dulles would lead the OSS in the postwar years, when it became the CIA.

Meanwhile, the Wehrmacht and Ford-Werke continued its work. In May, 1940, the Wehrmacht moved into France exploiting new equipment, most notably armored vehicles and aircraft and creating and utilizing tactics which maximized their effects. The greatest of these tactics was the blitzkrieg or "lightning war," a tactic the Americans called Shock and Awe in Iraq. On May 10, 1940 Germany commenced Operation Sichelschnitt (Sickle Cut) led by airstrikes against Allied airfields. Holland surrendered after five days, Belgium held on with the help of 35 Allied divisions until the 28th, two days after the Allied evacuation at Dunkirk. By the third of June, the Germans had started bombing Paris and then entered the city on the 14th. A week later, the French government surrendered.

After the fall of France, Ford-Werke proudly placed an advertisement in the *Frankfurter Zeitung* stating, "German Ford vehicles were the dependable servants of the brave soldier."[26] Ford-Werke gained control of Holland and Belgium, but France was a much harder prospect. Maurice Dollfuss, Ford France's general manager, was adamant about his company still reporting to the U.S. and managed to persuade Schmidt to relent. Dollfuss told his American overlords the Germans were treating Ford France better than most other companies and that he had been "selling considerable quantities of spare parts, trucks and cars to the German authorities."[27] In other words, while Henry Ford was refusing to make Rolls Royce engines for the RAF so they could win the Battle of Britain, Ford France was making a "brilliant" profit from the Wehrmacht.

Dollfuss wrote to Edsel in July of 1940 after the fall of France to inform him Ford of France had delivered a large number of spare parts as well as trucks and passenger vehicles to the German authorities, who had "shown clearly their wish to protect the Ford interest as much as they can."[28] This is mind-boggling, since Ford's Dearborn head office was still refusing to build the Rolls-Royce engines for the RAF

Robert Schmidt, meanwhile, indicated in a letter to the United States he was "safeguarding the interests of the Ford plants in the occupied territories."[29] Dollfuss was quite happy to oblige the Nazi government, and indicated Ford's neutrality credo had served them well in Germany – except what was good for Herr Goose was not good for the British Gander. Ford France, under the generous auspices of Ford-Werke and the Nazi regime, remained free to continue to produce; just now they were producing for the Wehrmacht. The Nazis were so pleased with the work of Ford they made it clear in a letter to Edsel Ford:

At this stage I would like to outline the importance attached by high officials to respect the desires and maintain the good will of "Ford" – and by "Ford," I mean your father, yourself and the Ford Motor Company, Dearborn.[30]

This goodwill extended to Nazi expropriations after the United States entered the war. Whereby almost all of the 250 American companies with interests in Germany were taken over and folded into the Hermann Göring Werke, the company Göring formed to take care of the Nazi's Four Year Plan, Ford-Werke was spared. In 1940, Carl Bosch died and was replaced by Carl Krauch at both IG Farben and

Ford-Werke. Krauch personally went to Göring in 1942 to plead Ford's case:

> *I myself knew Henry Ford and admired him. I went to see Göring personally about that. I told Göring if we took Ford independence away, it would aggrieve friendly relations with American industry in the future. I counted on a lot of success for the adaptation of American methods in Germany's industries. Göring listened then said, "I agree. I shall see to it that the German Ford Company will not be incorporated into the Hermann Göring Company.*[31]

Schmidt continued his work as general director, prodding the company to churn out more and more armored cars and trucks. When the Köln Supreme Court demanded Ford-Werke appoint a trustee to excise the company's "enemy" influence, the Nazis appointed…Robert Schmidt. Profits from Ford-Werke were placed in escrow until after the war, at which point Ford in the United States would be entitled to its share. Considering the thousands upon thousands of trucks Ford-Werke produced for the Reich, it must have been a sizable amount indeed (Unfortunately, as Ford was a private company until 1956, it is impossible to ascertain the exact amount).

Since Schmidt was producing more vehicles for the Wehrmacht, he had to address his growing labor problem, which by 1943 was 37% foreign, including Russian, French, Dutch, Belgian and Polish PoWs. The Western Europeans were treated somewhat well, but the Russians and the Polish were considered subservient to the Aryan race and tended to beaten, threatened, starved and all around poorly treated. Even in 1940, before the United States entered the war, Ford used French PoWs in the manufacturing plant in Köln. All of this contravenes the Geneva Convention which states:

> *Work done by prisoners of war shall have no direct connection with the operations of the war. In particular, it is forbidden to employ prisoners in the manufacture or transport of arms or munitions of any kind, or on the transport of material destined for combatant units.*[32]

Ford-Werke wasn't the only company doing this: IG Farben, Siemens, Nestlé and General Motors' Opel division were just a few companies also engaging in the use of prisoner labor. As a common claim after the Nuremberg trials, most companies claim they were forced into using slave labor by the Nazis – Ford is one of these companies. However, Robert Schmidt had on many occasions solicited the use of slave labor at the Ford-Werke plant. Ford Motor Company commissioned a report in 2001, and though you must applaud the company for airing its dirty laundry, it was nonetheless damning:

From 1939 to 1945, millions of non-Germans were registered to work, usually forcibly, in factories, farms, mines and construction sites throughout the German Reich, as military conscription worsened an existing labor shortage. Most industrial companies in Germany applied for and used foreign workers during this time...Large-scale use of foreign workers started almost immediately after the war began in September 1939 and was expanded after Germany occupied Western Europe in the spring of 1940. Extensive recruitment in the occupied territories of the Soviet Union began in early 1942, and evolved into a more coercive system. Forced workers were distributed to industries that requested workers through government labor offices...In August 1944, the automotive industry was permitted to apply for concentration camp labor...Wartime use of foreign and forced labor at Ford-Werke generally followed the pattern described. **Foreigners from Eastern and Western Europe, Italian PoWs and men from the Buchenwald concentration camp were put to work at Ford-Werke.**[33]

Note the words "applied for and used foreign workers." Schmidt had to make applications to the government to use these forced recruits and also had to apply for concentration camp labor. U.S. Ford would not have known this, but since the company was able to receive the escrow profits after the war, the company most certainly profited from the use of slave labor. The above report also mentions a 1943 U.S. government investigation into correspondence between U.S. Ford and Ford France. The letters in question came from Maurice Dollfuss. As the territory was occupied by the Germans, any information, specifically company information, would be considered a violation of the *Trading with the Enemy Act*. Dollfuss sent the letters through the American embassy in neutral Vichy so as to avoid any overt suspicion. The letters were sent to Edsel Ford, then CEO of Ford Motor Company and are mentioned in the report tabled by J. John Lawler of the Office of the General Counsel to the Treasury Department.

> *On May 25, 1943, (Treasury Secretary) Morgenthau forwarded a copy of the Lawler report to President Roosevelt, directing attention to what he calls the "amazing and shocking correspondence" between Edsel Ford and Dollfuss.*[34]

The Justice Department continued the investigation and they believed there was the basis for a case against Edsel Ford for violations of the *Trading with the Enemy Act*. The Justice Department concluded it did not have a case for two reasons: The Treasury Department assessment contained "a good deal in the way of opinion, argument and conjecture"[35] but the case was dropped mainly due to the untimely death of Edsel Ford on May 26, 1943 from stomach cancer. According to the Lawler report, Edsel had informed Ford executives, specifically his father and Charles Sorensen of the communiques. The report commissioned by Ford did unearth in the National Archives that Edsel and Dollfuss knowingly exchanged correspondence regarding the health of Ford France in 1942, after the United States had entered the war and in direct violation of the *Trading with the Enemy Act*. Until October 1942, the U.S. State Department facilitated messages between the two through the embassy in Vichy.

Again, this is semantics. If the State Department allowed it, it must be all right. They would be acting upon the orders of the President, would they not? Doubtful, as at this point, Ford-Werke had manufactured tens of thousands of personnel carriers and trucks for moving the Wehrmacht around Europe, a fact that was known to Ford Motor Company and must have been evident to representatives of the United States government. After the U.S. Embassy was closed in Vichy in 1942, there was no further communication between Edsel and Dollfuss before Edsel died and none between anyone at Ford and the Nazi-occupied plants.

Ford, to this day, denies complicity in the Nazi operations at Ford-Werke. They repurchased the outstanding shares in 1951 with the dividends from Ford-Werke that were held in escrow by the Nazi government and the company becomes a division of Ford Motor Company. The company is now Ford-Werke GmbH and is the centre of Ford's European operations. Robert Schmidt was banned by the Allies from working at Ford-Werke after the war, but was officially cleared of wrongdoing in October 1947. It was not until 1950 Ford Motor Company allowed Schmidt to rejoin the company as a technical adviser and member of the board. He died in 1962. In the words of U.S. Army investigator Henry Schneider Ford-Werke "had, with Dearborn's consent, become an arsenal of Nazism".[30] It had made upwards of 92,000 trucks and personnel carriers for the Wehrmacht, made munitions under a secret company, even manufactured the jet turbines used in the V-2 rockets which rained terror down on London.

Like Ford, General Motors would not escape the pull of the Nazis and the company is today embarrassed by what it did in Germany during World War II. After the publication of an article by Edwin Black, who also wrote the book *IBM and the Holocaust*, General Motors released a statement saying it wished it could "hit the rewind button and change some of the things Mr. Sloan thought and said." The Mr. Sloan in question was Alfred P. Sloan, the CEO of General Motors and the most formative man in the company's history.

General Motors' roots go back to 1899 when David Dunbar Buick founded the Buick Auto-Vim and Power Company. The company was sold to James Whiting who brought in William Crapo Durant to manage his new holding. Durant used Buick as the first building block in General Motors and added the inventions of Ransom Eli Olds and Louis Chevrolet in the ensuing years. These names are undoubtedly familiar: Buick, Olds(mobile) and Chevrolet. That is in North America. In Europe, the names are different, but the company is the same. By 1923, Sloan was 48 and the new president of General Motors; by 1937 he was Chairman of the Board, a position he held until 1956.

In Germany, 35 years before Buick began his company, Adam Opel invented his first sewing machine in Rüsselsheim. Fifteen years later, Opel branched out into bicycles. By the turn of the century, Opel had produced its first car. By 1910, the company started using rudimentary assembly-line manufacturing, and Opel began putting prefabricated bodies on to premade chassis and engines. The next year a fire destroyed a large portion of the plant and the company made its last sewing machine, focusing on cars, motorcycles and bicycles. The result of the fire was not all bad though – the company designed a fire engine to service the factory and began selling it to towns and cities in Germany. During World War I, the company made heavy trucks for the military and in 1917 the family was rewarded for their service to the Kaiser by being elevated to the peerage.

Opel moved on after World War I, and by the middle of the 1920s was the largest automobile manufacturer in Europe. In 1925, the company built a state-of-the-art plant using true assembly lines. This allowed the company to lower prices on the Opel *Laubfrosch* – the Tree Frog, so named for its green lacquered finish – from 4,500 marks down to 1,990. For the everyday man to finance his purchase, Opel opened the Opel Bank. It was at this time General Motors turned a covetous eye towards the company. Towards the end of the 1920s, Opel's share of the German automobile market was just under thirty-eight percent and after talks with GM, the company converted into a corporation, Opel AG. Just before the Depression, GM purchased eighty percent of the company from the Opel family for $26,000,000.

Now back to Alfred Sloan. Sloan was, according to journalist Edwin Black, not a real big fan of President Roosevelt. Roosevelt advocated what to some would equate with socialism at best and communism at worst. His New Deal plan called for a Social Security program, government regulation and support for labor unions, things taken for granted today, but after the Roaring Twenties, this interference by government in big business was blasphemous to the industrialists of the day. Men like Ford, Sloan, J. P. Morgan and the duPonts despised what Roosevelt was proposing. As now, businessmen espoused loss of jobs, profits and possibly even moving manufacturing to jurisdictions which are friendlier to business.

From Black's article:

Sloan's disdain for the American government went beyond ordinary political dissent. The GM chief so hated the president and his administration that he co-founded a virulently anti-Roosevelt organization, and donated to at least one other Roosevelt-bashing group. Moreover, Sloan actually pressured GM executives not to serve in government positions, although many disregarded his advice and loyally joined the government's push for war preparedness.

At one point, Sloan's senior officials at GM even threatened to launch a deliberate business slowdown to sabotage the administration's recovery plan, according to papers unearthed by one historian. At the same time, Sloan and GM did not fail to express admiration for the stellar accomplishments of the Third Reich, and went the extra mile to advance German economic growth.

Indeed, Sloan felt that GM could — and should — create its own foreign policy, and back the Hitler regime even as America recoiled from it. "Industry must assume the role of enlightened industrial statesmanship," Sloan declared in an April 1936 quarterly report to GM stockholders. "It can no longer confine its responsibilities to the mere physical production and distribution of goods and services. It must aggressively move forward and attune its thinking and its policies toward advancing the interest of the community at large, from which it receives a most valuable franchise."[36]

These are inflammatory words, so research had to be done. Did Alfred Sloan hate Roosevelt? Three reliable sources backed up this claim, including the book *Alfred P. Sloan: Critical Evaluations in Business and Management*, which states: "GM officials encouraged workers hatred of New Deal intervention. They castigated the 'present attitude of the government and its experiments'."[37] David Farber in his book *Sloan Rules: Alfred P. Sloan and the Triumph of General Motors* also goes into detail of Sloan's revilement of FDR's New Deal. Finally, *The New York Times*, in Sloan's obituary wrote "When Franklin D. Roosevelt took office in 1933, Mr. Sloan at first cooperated with the New Administration, becoming a member of the Industrial Advisory Board of the National Recovery Administration. When the dollar was devalued, however, the New Deal lost a friend and gained a persistent critic."[38]

Let's get back to Farber though – he raised some points about Sloan which are disturbing. Sloan was one of the founding members of the Liberty League, a short-lived group of mainly high-echelon businessmen whose main goal was to dismantle the New Deal. The Liberty League was involved in questionable activities leading up to the 1936 election, including funding the anti-Semitic Sentinels of the Republic. The Sentinels' main goals were smaller government and stopping the spread of communism. They believed they could do this by lobbying against child labor laws and the New Deal. The lobbying started even before FDR became president. During Herbert Hoover's presidency, the Sentinels wanted to abolish the Sheppard-Towner Act (enacted by Harding in 1921 to lower infant mortality rates), opposed the creation of the Department of Education and the Department of Welfare.[39]

Sloan was a supporter of the Liberty League, as well as the Sentinels financially. Farber accounted for at least $10,000 Sloan donated to the groups ($144,000 in 2016 dollars). Giving money to a group like this is not criminal – misguided, but not criminal.

Now the big question – did Sloan express admiration for the Third Reich? Since Sloan kept no private papers, and his corporate papers were destroyed by General Motors, and I could find no evidence stating this directly, I can neither confirm nor deny this claim, but it is obvious Sloan wanted to profit from whomever was in power. In March 1939, Sloan said the Opel business would continue, as it was "highly profitable," and "The internal politics of Nazi Germany 'should not be considered the business of the management of General Motors,' Sloan explained in a letter to a concerned shareholder dated April 6, 1939. 'We must conduct ourselves [in Germany] as a German organization…We have no right to shut down the plant.'[40] So then, did General Motors participate in the buildup of Nazi Germany or profit from it?

Opel was a General Motors subsidiary run by James D. Mooney until almost 1942. Mooney was the president of General Motors Export Company when the offshore division purchased Opel. In his position, Mooney met and would have negotiated with various Nazi leaders, including Hjalmar Schacht, Chancellor Heinrich Brüning, and after a rally at the Berlin Templehof Airport, Adolf Hitler. Mooney, along with Ronald K. Evans and R.A. Fleischer of Opel, met Hitler on May 2, 1934. Though he never learned to drive, Hitler was a car enthusiast and was always chauffeured around in a Mercedes limousine. However, his dream of a car for the people was evident at the meeting. Hitler told the men the Opel P-4 was his concept of a true *Volkswagen* – a people's car. This was welcome news to both the Opel men and to Sloan.

Opel would have been favored by Hitler for a few reasons – it was the largest producer in the country; it produced affordable cars, it had industrial capability which would have been useful for rearmament and it was a proud old German automaker (though in the hands of Americans now). Mooney told Hitler Opel could and would produce an inexpensive car with the mass appeal of Henry Ford´s Model T. All Opel needed was the Reich to guarantee sales of 100,000 cars a year and control the price of raw materials. The people's car was a dream of Hitler – which led to Volkswagen's creation – but Opel was probably the best bet for an operation to get off the ground almost immediately.

Hitler was excited – so much so the original fifteen-minute meeting went for ninety minutes and the Führer had Wilhelm Keppler contact Mooney the next day with more questions. Mooney spent most of the day writing answers to Hitler's queries. A few weeks after the meeting, the company publication *General Motors World* recounted it saying, "Hitler is a strong man, well fitted to lead the German people out of their former economic distress... He is leading them, not by force or fear, but by intelligent planning and execution of fundamentally sound principles of government."[41] This puts both Mooney and Sloan in a bad light – at least from the point of history. In 1934, the world was only starting to get an inkling of Hitler's fanaticism – there was still two years until the Berlin Olympics. So while GM in general and Mooney and Sloan in particular look like Nazi sympathizers, it only shows the writer of the company newsletter's ignorance of current affairs in Germany. It is also unfair of Black to proclaim this showed how Mooney and GM were willing to make the equivalent of billions of dollars off Hitler's desire to rearm. It does show General Motors was willing to make money off Hitler's desire to market an affordable car to the German people, since rearmament only openly started in Germany the next year.

Black quotes a *New York Times* article written on March 26, 1933 entitled *Hitler a Menace*. In it, Princeton professor John Hibben is quoted as saying: "Adolf Hitler is a menace to the world's peace, and if his policies bring war to Europe, the United States cannot escape participating." Again, this is two years before the Germans began rearming, so to use this as evidence of Mooney's implicit Nazism is misleading.

According to Black, the impetus for Sloan's actions was his hatred for Roosevelt and the New Deal. In contrast, Adolf Hitler was showing an iron determination to get Germany back on its feet, out from the punitive measures of the Versailles Treaty, and he was going to enlist industry to do that. Hitler was reining in trade unions and though his party was the National Socialists, there was very little to do with socialism in Hitler's agenda.

Mooney has been criticized for his role in Germany, so let's look at his time as head of GM's international division. Mooney began his time as vice-president and general manager of General Motors Export Corporation on New Year's Day 1922 with almost 100 countries to service. By November, Mooney was the president. He attended various functions and met with several dignitaries during his tenure. In 1924, Mooney attended attended galas with King George V. Though this evidence does not make Mooney a monarchist, the same logic is used by some internet wags as to Sloan and Mooney being Nazi collaborators. It does mean General Motors was feeling out possible acquisitions in the United Kingdom, one of which came to fruition a 18 months later when GM purchased Vauxhall. Mooney stated how great the purchase was for General Motors and how the British working man was "always willing and have always been willing to do a good day's work for a fair day's pay." This led to European growth for the company, which led it to Opel.

Opel was the crown jewel of the German auto industry and a plum pick for GM. Originally, Opel built economical little cars for the European and eventually South African markets, areas which General Motors couldn't otherwise penetrate. Help was given by Hitler's Reich, in the form of assurances Germany would "allow no discrimination against foreign capital invested in legitimate business pursuits in Germany. That also applies, despite the special German interest in advancing the German motor vehicle industry, to the capital of General Motors and similar companies."[42] Hitler's promise was not broken and Opel was treated as though it was a German company.

So this business model worked for a couple of years. By 1939, with Opel still as a wholly-owned subsidiary of General Motors, the company started making engines for the JU 88 medium-ranged bomber. GM's board were aware of this, making subtle comments in its 1940 annual report:

In manufacturing countries at war normal peacetime production was subordinated to the demands for the materials of war. In other areas curtailment of distribution facilities prevented goods and services from reaching their normal markets. Governments at war have taken over the responsibility of directing production and distribution of essential commodities and have subordinated the comfort and even the health of the civilian population to the needs of defense[43]

Opel AG was still a profit centre for GM and the company had not divested itself of the asset, according to the 1940 Annual Report. GM was not giving up on Opel, as GM reported the earnings it expected to garner from the company – just over $15.6 million or $0.36 per share in the same annual report. General Motors seemed unwilling to shy away from business in Germany – or anywhere else for that matter – as the Opel division was still making the company a substantial amount of money.

Mooney, as the president of the international arm of GM, negotiated with governments for many reasons, including trying to avoid war and trying to guarantee the employment of his workers. War is generally bad for business, with employees getting themselves conscripted, or killed in bombing raids. In Germany, 26,000 people worked for Opel and the Reich was keenly interested in keeping the concern going. Hjalmar Schacht, the head of the Reichsbank, continually met with Mooney to make sure Opel was running smoothly, which by 1940 meant it was making the prerequisite Junkers engines needed for bombers to bomb Paris.

Mooney also met with Franklin Roosevelt in 1935 and it is certain talks were not just about the newest Opel or Vauxhall coupe. Mooney had internal knowledge of the workings of the German government, having met with Hitler, Göring, Schacht and others and would have been able to supply Roosevelt with his own "automotive diplomacy."

Mooney knew war was coming – just perhaps not in 1934 when he met with Hitler. In an address to the Economic Club of New York in 1937 he said:

> There is a great war threatening in Europe. When this great war will come, whether it will come at all, I do not even pretend to be able to say. But I do know that the Germans will not starve. They will be on the march again before they starve. America and her recent allies could make an intelligent gamble toward halting this march and the war by putting up the food for Germany in exchange for guarantees for peace.[44]

In 1938 the War Office in Great Britain also saw the impending conflict, and when General Motors contacted officials from the War Office to offer the company's assistance, there was a great amount of interest. With this interest in mind, General Motors froze all production overseas of heavy trucks in anticipation of a large order from the British. When Prime Minister Chamberlain signed the Munich Agreement with Hitler, it was assumed peace had been achieved and the War Office fell back. But in gratitude for the work the company did, the British government ordered 500 trucks, which were manufactured at the company's plant in Alexandria, Egypt. Also in 1938, and also like Henry Ford, James Mooney was presented with the Reich's highest decoration for foreigners, the Grand Cross of the German Eagle for meritorious service to the German people and government. A lapse in judgment by both Ford and Mooney? History is replete with bad choices like this – Queen Elizabeth II knighted brutal Romanian dictator Nicolae Ceausescu in 1978.

As with Ford, GM was pressured into exporting rubber to Germany. The American parent had to put up $1 million as part of a government ruling, and as with Ford, part of the rubber went to the Wehrmacht. General Motors only agreed to this after receiving assurances the expenditure would be bartered for the export of Opel cars and trucks. It was further agreed the German government would assume the financing responsibility for crude rubber in about a year.[45]

Mooney visited Berlin in March of 1939 after receiving disturbing news. Upon arriving in Southampton, England he was met by Vauxhall executives and Wilhelm von Opel, who told him several engineering executives of the company had been taken into custody by the Gestapo. Mooney went straight to Berlin to request their release. After a week of negotiations, which included pressure exerted by the American charge d'affaires Raymond Geist and German foreign minister Joachim von Ribbentrop, the men were released. Now Mooney could concentrate on the rubber subsidy. He advised Opel president Dr. Carl Lüer he did not want to continue financing rubber coming into Germany. Lüer arranged for a dinner meeting with Emil Puhl of the Reichsbank and the departmental chief of the Four Year Plan. Mooney argued the rubber plan had met its goal and had continued on for longer than the year originally planned; he also went on to say exporting Opel cars would do more for Germany's trade deficit than rubber subsidies.

"Automotive Diplomacy"

But Mooney had one more ace up his sleeve – with the assembled dignitaries listening, Mooney made the following suggestion: if the Germans could negotiate some form of gold loan, would they be willing to stop subsidizing their exports, a practice which was the thorn in the side of foreign traders. Puhl readily agreed to this proposal, which would help the Germans resume normal trading arrangements. Also, gold was the hard currency the Reich was severely lacking – exports were all well and good, but if the Nazis could secure gold, it could be used to purchase raw materials in Spain and Turkey such as chromium and tungsten for steel production.

The gold loan was also of interest to the Americans and British – when Mooney met with the American Ambassador to Great Britain, he put the concept to him. Ambassador Joseph Kennedy – the same whose son would become president one day – suggested a meeting with Emil Puhl in Paris. Mooney also met with Francis Rodd, who was a partner at Morgan Grenfell – the British affiliate of J.P. Morgan. Rodd agreed with Mooney's assessment, as did many of his compatriots in London's financial district, and thought a loan arranged through British and American channels could possibly stave off a war. Puhl was unable to attend in Paris, sending a director from the Four Year Plan. Mooney waited in Paris, only to find out Roosevelt had nixed the plan. Mooney flew back to London and confronted Kennedy with a new plan, which in exchange for a loan of between $500 million and $1 billion of gold, as well as access to former German colonies and a cut in trade embargoes against Germany, the Germans would continue making reparation payments, cut rearmament and sign non-aggression treaties. To Mooney and Kennedy, this made perfect sense – to Roosevelt it did not and he refused approval for the plan for a second time. This was the end of Mooney's diplomacy for now.

Mooney continued his travels, heading back and forth across the Atlantic, eventually going back to Germany in May 1939. Mooney travelled to Berlin to confer with his business associates about the status of GM's properties in the event of war, about the evacuation of GM non-German personnel, and about the various measures possible for the protection of GM's investments within the Reich. On September 1, 1939, just as the Wehrmacht was blazing across Poland, Mooney sat down for lunch with Helmuth Wohlthat of the Four Year Plan. Two weeks later he headed for the Opel plant to examine the works, at which point some of the plant would have already been retooled for armament production. Though there is no official word on this, it must be assumed Mooney would have known this, as it would have been extremely hard for the management of the plant to hide this fact from him.

Around September 21, he headed to Switzerland to send a cable to General Motors in the United States to apprise them of the situation. Two days earlier a meeting was held in Berlin between Göring, Luftwaffe Generals Udent and Milch, Junkers CEO Heinrich Koppenburg and General von Schell of the Wehrmacht. At the meeting it was agreed the Brandenburg Opel plant should continue producing Blitz trucks for the Wehrmacht leaving the Rüsselsheim plant for the Junkers parts production program. Immediately after the meeting Rüsselsheim began converting to war production and then two days after Mooney left for Switzerland, Opel allegedly purchased RM 10 million in German equities. This is interesting, as it should to have been approved by the Corporation's Policy Committee of which Mooney was a member.[46]

GM spokesman John F. Mueller said General Motors lost day-to-day control over its German plants in September 1939 and "did not assist the Nazis in any way during World War II."[47] This is a hard thing for General Motors to disprove, considering the in-depth negotiations Mooney was having with higher-ups in the German government. Mooney met with Göring and Wohlthat in Berlin on October 19, 1939. Mooney was acquainted with Göring, as they had met three years previously. Was this a secret meeting? Doubtful, as Hugh Wilson, the American Ambassador to Germany suggested to Mooney he wear his Grand Cross of the German Eagle. According to Mooney's personal papers, Göring said if the British Empire didn't bother Germany, Germany would reciprocate in kind. Göring then urged Mooney to go back to Great Britain and find out whether the British wanted to fight. He even went so far as to agree to a meeting in a neutral country, and Göring agreed to go if necessary. After the meeting, Mooney found out the meeting was with the full knowledge and concurrence of Hitler.

Mooney headed to Paris to meet with the American ambassador to France William Bullitt. Bullitt was a close friend of Roosevelt's and was told of the meeting with Göring. Bullitt informed the president, though his take on it was a little different from Mooney's – he was dead set against it going any further. Bullitt telephoned Joseph Kennedy in London before Mooney arrived in Paris and by the time the GM executive met with him, Kennedy was also against the plan. Mooney managed to meet with members of the British Foreign Office and was earnestly looked at until the morning of November 11, 1939. On that day, Mooney met with Sir Robert Vansittart, the Chief Diplomatic Adviser to His Majesty's Government. Vansittart, who was also the brother of GM executive and Mooney's associate Nick Vansittart, read a statement to Mooney, which said the British government was interested in listening to the Germans – as long as it wasn't the Germans who were currently in power.

Mooney was unable to secure a peace between Germany and the Allies, which frankly would have been better for business than a war would have. He returned to Germany in February 1940 and was met by Cyrus R. Osborn, General Manager of Opel and Fritz Belitz, a member of the Opel Aufsichtsrat (Supervisory Board). At the same time, engines, cockpits and canopies for the Junkers Ju 88 were being made under licence at Rüsselsheim, so again, for a GM spokesman to say the company did not assist the Nazis in any way, or the company had no control over operations at Opel is patently false. For Mooney to meet with the manager of the plant and a member of the supervisory board, yet have no control over – or any idea about – the workings of the subsidiary is absurd. Not only that, but Opel still listed Mooney, Alfred Sloan and Graeme Howard on its Aufsichtsrat up until 1941.

Understandably, Opel had a special place for the Führer as well as the German people – a true success story. But why was General Motors still allowed leeway with ownership, when by this point many non-Aryan companies had been compromised or nationalized? The answer may be Mooney himself. The self-appointed diplomat had made many overtures to peace, acting as a liaison between the German and Allied governments, with varying degrees of success. He is one of the few individuals in history who would have spoken with both Roosevelt and Hitler and one of his final meetings with Hitler came on March 4, 1940.

Hitler shook hands with Mooney and Dr. Paul Schmidt joined the two as interpreter – the only other person in the room was a uniformed bodyguard. Hitler referred back to the last conversation they had back in 1934, and then indicated his readiness to hear what Mooney had to say. Mooney told Hitler President Roosevelt had offered his services as a moderator between Germany and the Allies and this intrigued the Chancellor. When the discussion turned to Great Britain, Hitler became angry and berated the British Government for its attitude towards Germany. He insisted Britain and France should come to their senses and stop talking so loud, saying "Who is England to talk to me this way?" Hitler, Mooney felt, was ready to accept Roosevelt as a moderator and his general attitude was that he had no axe to grind with the United States. Hitler said "Germany regarded it as inadmissible two countries like Britain and France should endeavour to rule the whole world by means of their Empires and to reserve to their exclusive use the whole of the economic resources of the world. For Germany's economic security it was imperative she get out of the position where Britain by one means or another could take steps every ten years or so to throttle or impede this flow of essential foodstuffs and necessary materials and goods."[48]

Was Mooney realistic and was Hitler about to come to a peace? This is doubtful, considering Hitler's past record and his need for both *lebensraum* and his aggressive anti-Semitic stance. Had Hitler continued the extermination of the Jews in a negotiated peace, it is possible the Allies would not have sat idly by and watched – though there is historical precedent for great governments to sit on their hands while tyrants exterminated those they considered undesirable including:

- The Armenian genocide at the hands of the Turks in 1922;
- Stalin's pogroms throughout the 1920s and 1930s;
- The Kurdish population in Iraq through the 1980s and 1990s;
- The Serbian "ethnic cleansing" in the 1990s and,
- The Rwandan genocide in 1994

All clear examples of world governments sitting and watching. It's quite possible a German peace in 1940 would have been substantially worse for the Jews than World War II itself was.

Many sources claim Mooney was pro-German and wanted a peace achieved – this is partly true. Mooney did advocate a peace, but to say he was pro-German makes it sound as if he was pro-Nazi – this is not true. Mooney continued his peace initiative, though by this point, he was told it was in the hands of the British. He returned to Rüsselsheim for a board meeting of Opel on March 19, 1940, the last he would attend.

One of the major sources of General Motors alleged pro-Nazi sentiment comes from a 1974 United States Senate report by Bradford Snell, a young attorney with the State Department. The basis of the report was Snell's belief the Big Three automakers had conspired to destroy public transit in the United States in order to affect greater profits. This should have been the crux of the report; however, Snell continually brought up General Motors involvement in World War II:

GM is a major force in international affairs. During World War II, for instance, it maximized global profits by supplying both the Axis and Allied powers with armaments. Its auto plants in Germany built thousands of bomber and jet propulsion systems for the Luftwaffe at the same time that its American plants produced aircraft engines for the U.S. Army Air Corps.[49]

All true, yet nothing to do with public transit in Cleveland. It does get the public thinking GM is shady – they made bombers for the Nazis, so they must be trying to destroy public transit and the American Way. Shame on General Motors!

Back in Germany, Opel started to come under attack from Nazi officials. A local official, in a report to the area Gauleiter, stated the company reeked of treason and espionage and was an American "plutocratic complex."[50] The focus for this talk was Cyrus Osborn, who was tagged by the Nazi official as a British spy and who had already fallen out of favor with the local Gauleiter. By the end of 1940, Osborn was out and Heinrich Wagner was in. The basis for much of this was growing animosity towards the Americans – American authorities were seizing German ships in port; and there was the uncertainty of the Americans position in the war. By now it was well known the United States was funnelling war materials to the British and Soviets and acting negatively towards the Nazis. This did not bode well for the American managers left at Opel.

Meanwhile, the Nazis looked to appoint their own managers at Opel – the one they seized on was Eduard Winter. Winter was an Opel dealer in Berlin and well known to GM, yet when he tried to gain an appointment to Opel's Aufsichtsrat, GM vice president Graeme Howard mistrusted his ambitions. Opel bought out Winter's dealership and severed all ties. This was a poor tactical maneuver on Howard's part though, as Winter had many friends in high places. When the Germans occupied Belgium and France, he was appointed administrator of General Motors operations in the two countries. General Motors advised its Opel managers to cooperate with Winter, but by the following year, it became obvious even to the Gestapo Winter was looting what he was administering. Opel's lawyer Heinrich Richter was alarmed when talk turned to Winter acting as manager of Opel's German operations, a situation exacerbated by the information the Nazis were looking to buy out GM.

Richter acted quickly, getting the support of the Gauleiter to work against Winter. In his stead, Richter was able to get Carl Lüer appointed as general manager of Opel's operations. Richter had Lüer swear an oath of allegiance to General Motors over the Third Reich before taking the job and insisted that, even though the climate was a little frigid toward American businesses, General Motors was the owner of the German-based company. At a rally at the plant, no speakers mentioned Opel's ownership and the local Gauleiter went on to denounce the Bolsheviks, the plutocrats and the Jews – a triumvirate of evil headed by Stalin, Churchill and Roosevelt.[51] Richter acted with due diligence throughout this, calling his American employers as much as possible, though the last trans-Atlantic call came on July 28, 1941. At this time, he received approval to formally remove Cyrus Osborn from the Aufsichtsrat to placate the Nazis. Richter's plan was to reconfirm membership on the Aufsichtsrat of the American members Alfred Sloan, James Mooney and Graeme Howard, but Howard refused to approve this move and the Americans were dropped from the supervisory board in late 1941. Richter continued to give updates to GM through diplomatic pouches which were sent via the American State Department until the end of 1941, though most were vague as Richter still feared Nazi intervention.

Richter had made an enemy of Winter, and this showed when Johannes Krohn was made Commissar of Enemy Property. Krohn was a career bureaucrat and not a Nazi, but he felt pressure from all sides as to who to appoint as head of Opel. Winter was still favored by General von Schell, who went to great lengths to discredit Lüer. Winter, on the other hand, tried to discredit Richter by alluding to a Jewish connection with the lawyer. General von Schell formalized his request to have Winter appointed by Göring, though without written consent from the Reichsmarschall, Krohn was unwilling to act. For his part, Richter tried to persuade Krohn there was no need at all to appoint a custodian of Opel, saying GM had placed German managers of irrefutable ability in charge, and that James Mooney was pro-German, given his overtures at diplomacy at the start of the war. But by this point, General Motors had no control over the workings of the company.

The final words GM had on Opel before communication was cut was their hand-picked manager Carl Lüer was in charge and the plants were running well. By the time of Krohn's appointment though, Lüer had lost the confidence of his deputy Heinrich Wagner and the remaining members of the Aufsichtsrat – Wilhelm von Opel and Franz Belitz – as well as Richter himself. Lüer's high-handedness was his undoing, as was his arrogant optimism. In May of 1942, Lüer had pledged to triple production at the Brandenburg truck plant, a completely unrealistic idea considering the acute shortages of building materials, raw materials and labor. Thankfully Hitler put an end to the idea as well, stating it would be unwise to increase production at a plant which would be subject to Allied bombings.

The other reason Lüer had fallen out of favor with Richter was the former's acquaintance with Jakob Werlin, to whom Lüer had made those outrageous claims about truck production at Brandenburg. Werlin was also a close associate of Heinrich Himmler, a man Richter was not keen on. Rumors abounded about the SS taking over Opel and infusing it with slave labor. These were rumors, but what wasn't a rumor was a plan by Himmler to open a truck factory in Poland under the Opel name using slave labor from concentration camps nearby. This disgusted Richter, if for no other reason than it gave Himmler a great say in the operations of the entire company.

Hitler decided to go with the tried and true – Himmler did not get his truck factory, but Daimler-Benz did receive a contract to produce the Opel Blitz truck. This infuriated Richter, and he charged Lüer had allowed the fortunes of the company to get away from him, as well as confidential truck designs, which were now in the hands of a competitor. It was at this point Richter changed sides and backed Eduard Winter as custodian of the company. An untimely move, since Winter was being investigated by the Gestapo for being a little too much of a free spender.

The inner fighting at Opel reached Göring, who decided to remove Lüer from his position and replace him with Heinrich Wagner. Göring did not stop there though – he wanted the company added to his empire. Hermann Göring Werke could easily swallow Opel, but Johannes Krohn stepped into the breach this time. Since the company had not been declared confiscated, Krohn was unwilling to hand the keys over to Göring. Remember, Krohn was a career bureaucrat, not a Nazi, and so paperwork which was properly processed and following the letter of the law was the only way for Göring to get his hands on Opel, and this was not forthcoming – it would seem Göring was not one for delving into his paperwork.

Back in Michigan, GM had decided their investment was gone – at least for tax purposes. In 1942 General Motors was allowed to write off its investment in Opel and keep the shares on the books at a value of one dollar. General Motors still left Opel on its books either out of hope or because they knew the assets had been sequestered and ownership was still nominally in GM's hands. Sequestration meant the government could do nothing to economically harm the enterprise and Krohn again adhered to the letter of the law. Since the company was of vast importance both to the Reich war effort and to the general German economy itself, Krohn appointed a supervisory council to continually review the business. On the council were Wilhelm von Opel, Fritz Belitz, Richter and IG Farben executive Wilhelm Avieny, who was appointed chair of the council.

In Brandenburg, the Opel Blitz was rolling off the assembly line and straight to the Russian front. The truck was favored in the poor conditions in the Soviet Union as it could be outfitted with four-wheel drive or a halftrack in place of the rear drive wheels. Production of the three-ton truck, as well as buses and ambulances for the military, continued at a blistering pace – 2,600 a month by 1944 or 86 per day. Production at the Brandenburg plant was headed by Heinz Nordhoff – a man who was legendary in the German car industry for resurrecting Volkswagen after the Second World War and for churning out record numbers of the Volkswagen Beetle. But production of this level at Opel was only achieved by changing the work week to sixty hours and running the plants twenty-four hours a day, seven days a week.

Once the American GM managers left Opel, they were replaced by Nazi thugs who were carefully selected by the local Gauleiter. These henchmen zealously enforced Nazi ideology as well as punishing those who voiced an opinion opposite that of the Führer. Those they found particularly unhelpful were turned over to the Gestapo for interrogation or prison sentence – one was even convicted of treason and executed for voicing a dissenting opinion against the war. The Nazis moved, as with every other concern in Germany, to have anyone who was racially impure removed from their position; this included their wives as well. When it was found the heads of the legal, statistical and tax departments had wives who *may* have had Jewish blood in their background, Carl Lüer received notification they should be dismissed from their positions. Lüer did not follow these directives and one man credited protection from Heinrich Wagner for saving his position; another claimed he was saved by Wilhelm von Opel. Other lesser employees were not so lucky, as they were dismissed or demoted.[52]

Opel made use of slave labor, as did other major German concerns. General Motors head office was still nominally in charge of the company when French prisoners of war were used at the Rüsselsheim plant in 1941. Though the percentage of foreign forced workers seems lower at Opel than its competitors Daimler-Benz and BMW, there were still about 7,000 foreign workers employed at the Rüsselsheim plant alone. The Slavic workers, many of whom were forced into labor, were treated as poorly as at any other German company. Paid piteously, from which food, shelter and taxes were deducted, these workers were also denied air raid shelters when Allied bombs rained down on the works. In one particular air raid, 115 workers were killed and 260 injured, though no German workers were killed in the same attack.

Henry Ashby Turner, who wrote an internal GM audit of their wartime works, asserts no concentration camp workers were used at Opel plants and other historical documents seems to back up this belief. However, the repair shops set up in Latvia and Poland did use Jewish forced labor which came from the ghettos set up by the Nazis. These were not concentration camps in the truest sense but the living conditions and squalor in the ghettos would have been similar to the concentration camps.

And what about assertions made by other students of General Motors and Opel? Bradford Snell has made many accusations about GM's involvement in Adam Opel AG during World War II – some substantiated, others not. For example, Snell claimed fifty percent of Junkers Ju 88 bomber engines were made at Rüsselsheim, as were ten percent of the legendary Me-262 jet engines. These claims are most likely true. Some claims which Snell has made which have been disputed are more inflammatory. Let's take those item by item:

1. In an essay excerpted from his Senate testimony, Snell maintained Alfred Sloan, James Mooney, John T. Smith and Graeme Howard all served on the Adam Opel AG board "throughout the war."

VERDICT: Not entirely true. Smith was gone by 1938 and the other three were off the Opel board by the end of 1941.[53]

2. Snell said in his testimony "GM continued to operate its Opel plants after the United States formally declared war on Germany without any apparent interference by the German government up until Nov. 25, 1942...The GM-appointed directors and management remained. The management during the war remained essentially the same as prewar, with the exception of American personnel."[54]

VERDICT: Somewhat true, yet very misleading. His statement about General Motors operating the Opel plants "without any apparent interference" by the Nazis makes an implicit assumption that GM was controlling the plants from Michigan, in direct violation of the American *Trading with the Enemy Act* – a link Snell attempts to tenuously make.

By Snell alleging Alfred Sloan and James Mooney still sat on the Aufsichtsrat and then by quoting the Darmstadt Court which installed Lüer, he makes it sound like the Americans still had ultimate authority – which is again untrue, since only Germans sat on the board by the time Carl Lüer was appointed. Snell attempts to obscure facts by stating them in a blatantly anti-General Motors slant. By saying the managers appointed by GM remained makes it sound like GM was complicit in anything which happened at the plant. With this flow of logic, anyone who hired John Wayne Gacy as a clown would have been complicit in the murders he committed. In GM's 1939 annual report, the company clearly stated what it was doing with the outbreak of war:

> As a result of the declaration of war, and in the line with the Corporation's operating policies, with full recognition of the responsibility that the manufacturing facilities of Adam Opel A. G. must now assume under a war regime, the Corporation has withdrawn the American personnel formerly in executive charge of this operation, and has turned the administrative responsibility over to German nationals. Its relationship is now limited to representation on the Board of Directors.[55]

As it should be said of almost all foreign companies doing business in Germany, General Motors had two choices: refuse to make parts for bombers, jet fighter engines and three-ton trucks or not to refuse. This is a great question for armchair historians – GM could have very easily refused to make any war armament. This would have led to either Opel being shut down and 26,000 people put out of work (unlikely) or the Reich government taking over the operation and doing it anyway. With every other manufacturing endeavor doing the same, it would have been incredibly difficult for Opel to make a stand – and possibly would have meant imprisonment, torture or death for the managers and probably some of the employees of the company. This is exactly what General Motors would not want.

That is not to say GM is some massive humanitarian organization – it was just doing what it had to do to survive. To be blunt, here is how James Mooney summed it up when he, Sloan and Howard were under investigation in 1941 by the FBI for possible treasonous activity:

Mooney said immediately after the medal from Hitler was presented, sent it down to the U. S. Navy for instructions, and that the Navy up to then had given him no instructions about it.

I then asked him whether he would now (meaning at the time of our conversation — about mid-October, 1940) give back the medal to Hitler. He said he would not. He thought it might jeopardize General Motors chances of some day getting part of that $100,000,000 of stockholders' money invested Nazi Germany. Moreover, he said he thought Hitler was right and he wasn't going to do anything to make him mad. "I know," he said, "Hitler has all the cards."

He went on this way at some length, the general argument being that although his sympathies were with the British people, he thought Hitler was sure to win the war; that there was justice in Hitler's general position; that Germany needed more room, etc.; that German people were more aggressive, vigorous, etc., and that if we tried to prevent the expansion of the German people under Hitler, it would be just too bad for us, etc.[56]

Was Mooney a traitor or a pragmatist? Yes, Hitler is the devil incarnate and yes, he did give Mooney a medal but to give it back would be a slap in the face, and Mooney wouldn't take the brunt of it –

his workers would. Sometimes, it's better to take one for the team, but again, some would look at that as a blatant sign of treason. Historian Henry Ashby Turner summed up the position of all men involved very well:

Some of the GM executives charged with responsibility for Opel have been unjustly branded as pro-Nazi. But with the exception of Graeme Howard, none had any particular interest in Germany or its politics. Howard initially admired the peacetime successes of Hitler's regime, as did many other foreigners. Personal exposure to Nazi methods soon dispelled his illusions, although he continued to believe that Germany had legitimate territorial grievances as a result of Versailles. Howard's chief, James Mooney, refused to take seriously ideological politics of any kind, including Nazism. For him, Hitler was just another of the foreign potentates he had to cope with in running GM's far-flung overseas operations.[57]

Did Opel help the German war effort? Absolutely and unequivocally – between Ford and GM, Snell estimated 90% of the three-ton trucks the Wehrmacht used were produced by the two companies. Up until the Germans declared war on the Americans, the United States was neutral. As a neutral, it is hard to support one side and not the other – otherwise you run the risk of not being neutral. That being said, GM's Vauxhall division in England produced the Churchill tank for the British as well as the MW lorries produced by Bedford, a division of Vauxhall, well before the Americans joined the war. It must be pointed out that, if the British lost the war, the gist of this book would take a substantially different tone – GM would be rebuked for its role in Vauxhall, but not Opel!

So did General Motors profit from the Nazis? Directly and indirectly, yes they did. Directly, the write off of the Opel assets benefited the company come the 1942 tax year. As well, the company recouped its assets at the end of the Second World War, though not without significant thought. Alfred Sloan was quoted as wondering if it was worth rebuilding the plant, considering the chaos in postwar Germany. The industriousness of the German employees made up his mind for him. By July 26, 1946, the first of the new Opel Blitz 1½-ton trucks left the assembly line. General Motors did take the dividends Opel accumulated during the war, which were presented to Michigan after Opel was reacquired by GM. Indirectly, GM profited from the Nazis. If it wasn't for Hitler going on his mad rampage, many of these companies would not have been able to pull out of the Depression and continue on during the postwar boom, since many companies made large profits from Nazi aggression. Many more, especially in Europe, paid dearly for the war, in plants, materials and lives.

The final way both Ford and General Motors profited from the war took place many years after the fact. Claiming war reparations and damages, both companies took advantage of tax write offs and federal payouts – General Motors to the tune of $33 million by 1967 and Ford around $1 million.[58]

2
The German Automakers

Although the manufacture of aircraft engines only made a minor contribution to sales before the First World War, Archduke Franz Ferdinand's body was barely cold when both Daimler and Benz started making complete aircraft in great numbers. Of the over 13,800 fighters built by the German and Austro-Hungarian empires in World War I, about 10,000 used either Mercedes or Benz engines and all 1,223 bombers made for the Central Powers used Mercedes or Benz engines. Fokker produced about 1,500 fighters, all using engines from Oberursel – which is now part of Rolls Royce Plc; Hannoversche Waggonfabrik mainly used Argus engines in its Hannover-series fighters, though switched to the BMW IIIa late in the war and Siemens produced its 288 fighters with its own engines. DMG and Benz & Cie. developed into the biggest aircraft engine manufacturers in Germany and among the largest in the world.

The needs of the German Imperial Army overtook any needs for consumer vehicles and production was almost totally geared to the war. World War I was revolutionary for trucks for both companies. The Prussian army issued regulations for military motor vehicles as early as 1898. In 1908, a program calling for subsidy trucks began, whereby the army subsidized truck purchasers, so long as the buyers made these vehicles available to the army in times of war. When war finally did come, the German army had around 5,000 subsidized trucks at its disposal, though most of these never made it back to their original owners. Even with the strides made in truck manufacture, market share for DMG and Benz & Cie actually decreased. The reason for this was the huge number of start-ups in this segment before and during the war.

BMW was one such start-up, or that is two separate aircraft engine manufacturers – Rapp Motorenwerke GmbH and Bayerische Flugzeug-Werke AG (BFW). In 1913 Karl Rapp set up a plant in Munich to manufacture aircraft engines. Rapp wasn't a great designer, and the company ended up enlisting Franz Josef Popp at the behest of the Austrian Navy. Popp originally worked for AEG-Union in Vienna and when World War I started he was asked to develop aircraft engines for AEG and Austro-Daimler. When it was decided capacity at either company wasn't enough for the Austrian demands, Popp traveled to Germany to solicit manufacturers to make Austro-Daimler engines under contract. Popp supervised the manufacture of a 12-cylinder Austro-Daimler design engine at Rapp, then managed to secure the talents of DMG engineer Max Friz. Friz designed a new aircraft engine in short order, and when the drawings were shown to the Deutsches Luftstreitkräfte – the Imperial German Air Service – they immediately liked what they saw. Enraged, Karl Rapp left the company that bore his name and on July 21, 1917 the name was changed –to Bayerische Motoren Werke GmbH. Subsequently, Max Friz's engine acquired the name by which it has been known ever since: the BMW IIIa.

The BMW IIIa was 185hp, one of the higher producing engines of the period. It was used primarily in the Fokker D.VII, starting in June 1918. One man who would fly it was German ace Hermann Göring who took over the Jagdgeschwader 1 squadron, after the death of the Red Baron. After World War I, almost all of the Fokker aircraft were confiscated as war reparations and many were sent to the United States to be refitted with the 215hp Liberty L-6 engine. The end of the war was crunch time for BMW – the Luftstreitkräfte (German Air Force) was its only customer, and under the conditions of the Treaty of Versailles, the Luftstreitkräfte was dissolved completely on 8 May 1920 and its remaining airplanes completely destroyed. The Allies also barred all German firms from manufacturing aircraft and aircraft engines. There was now zero demand for a BMW, Daimler or Benz aircraft engine. Since the economy was collapsing in Germany, there was no need for civilian aircraft – people couldn't afford bread, let alone a flight from Frankfurt to Hannover.

There were other major problems faced by the German manufacturers as well. Since almost all resources were poured towards the war effort, there was next to no research and development done on civilian vehicles. The Treaty of Versailles allowed foreign producers like the Ford Motor Company to get a foothold in Germany, cutting profits further. Daimler decided to branch out, making Mercedes bicycles in 1923 and tried its hand at Mercedes typewriters as well. But this did not stop Mercedes from competing in grand prix events in

Europe and they won great prestige for themselves and for their team sponsor, Adolf Hitler.[59]

At BMW, railway brakes and inboard engines were manufactured following the prohibition on the production of aircraft. The Allied ban on manufacturing remained in force until 1923, when BMW resumed production, starting with the BMW IIIa and IV engines. BMW manufactured its first complete land vehicle – the R32 motorcycle and in 1928 after purchasing manufacturer Fahrzeugfabrik Eisenach built its first car, the Dixi, under license from Austin Motor Company.

The dire financial situation meant the collapse of many companies in Germany. Fokker avoided this by moving to the Netherlands in 1919. Albatros Flugzeugwerke merged with Focke-Wulf in 1931, others were not so lucky. Aviatik, Hannoversche Waggonfabrik, Pfalz Flugzeugwerke and Luft-Fahrzeug-Gesellschaft were all bankrupt by 1933. The only companies to survive were Luftschiffbau Zeppelin which continued making dirigibles with Goodyear; Siemens, which only made a smattering of aircraft; Junkers and the three engine makers – Daimler; Benz & Cie and Bayerische Motoren Werke GmbH, which itself had been sold to brake manufacturer Knorr Bremse AG. Knorr sold the BMW engine works to financier Camillo Castiglioni and Daimler and Benz merged in 1926 and moved its offices to Stuttgart, but this wasn't Daimler's first choice. In 1920 an overture to armaments manufacturer Krupp was rebuffed. A subsequent attempt to merge with steelmaker Otto Wolff Eisengroßhandel also failed when both companies realized – to use 21st century parlance – there would be no synergies realized. Ironically, Wolff is now a subsidiary of ThyssenKrupp.[60] This was not the first time Daimler and Benz considered merging – ten years earlier, a large block of Benz shares was offered up to DMG by a third party, but this failed on the advice of board member Dr. Ernst Berge.

Daimler-Benz shied away from aircraft engines in the interwar years, but not BMW. Head designer Max Friz went ahead and developed the BMW VI 12-cylinder aircraft engine, capable of producing 650hp. The only engine close at the time was the V-12 Curtiss V-1570 Conqueror, also a 650hp engine. This engine had the distinction of making a larger contribution to company profits than any other BMW product of the 1920s and 1930s. The BMW VI was also the first BMW aircraft engine which had international demand, with licensing agreement with Mikulin in the Soviet Union and Kawasaki in Japan.

In 1932, Junkers unveiled a state-of-the-art civil transport aircraft, the Ju 52. Deutsche Luft Hansa (not today's Lufthansa) asked for the new aircraft to be fitted with radial engines from BMW. The airline eventually got its way and BMW was awarded a contract to supply air-cooled engines for the Ju 52. Shortly after, BMW renewed its licence agreement with American aircraft engine manufacturer Pratt & Whitney and proceeded to market the latest version of the Hornet engine in Germany under the name BMW 132. This meant that, from 1933 onwards, BMW was the leading German manufacturer of both air-cooled and water-cooled aircraft engines and ensured BMW had access to major aeronautical engineering knowledge. This was quite important for BMW's next evolutionary step.

Nineteen thirty-three saw the newly formed Reich Ministry of Aviation launch an all-out effort to rebuild the newly-named Luftwaffe. Soon major orders were rolling in for BMW, now one of the largest German aircraft engine manufacturers alongside Junkers and Daimler-Benz. Construction of the BMW aircraft engine factory in Allach (1935), expansion of the manufacturing facilities in Eisenach (1937) and acquisition of the Brandenburg Motor Works (Bramo) in Berlin-Spandau enabled BMW to expand capacities for aircraft engine manufacture under Popp's leadership. Increasingly the aircraft engine division dwarfed the two other BMW product divisions – cars and motorcycles. Acting as aircraft engine supplier to the Reich Ministry of Aviation eventually resulted in a close dependency on the Nazi regime and led to a step-by-step restructuring of the company around a single market sector: aviation. Following the acquisition of Bramo in 1939, BMW enjoyed a monopoly for the production of air-cooled aircraft engines in Germany. This made BMW a key strategic company for the German aviation industry as the Third Reich rearmed.

In 1939 the company tested its new BMW 801 engine. This 14-cylinder 2,000hp was by far its most advanced and was mainly used in the Focke-Wulf Fw-190 Würger fighter and the Junkers Ju-88night fighter variant. Following the German attack on Poland, the Reich

Ministry of Aviation wanted the company to start supplying BMW 801 engines as quickly as possible. The new engine was rushed into production too quickly, which inevitably resulted in technical problems. It wasn't until 1942 various fundamental development issues were sorted out. The BMW 801 then went on, by the end of the war, to become one of the biggest-selling German aircraft engines, spawning countless different versions which powered a wide range of German aircraft.[61]

Daimler-Benz was deeply involved with Hitler and the Nazis, even before Hitler came to power. "Leading managers of Daimler-Benz lent valuable assistance to the National Socialists before Hitler became Chancellor in 1933. The corporation even claimed it was responsible for 'helping to motorize the movement.'"[62] From 1937, Daimler-Benz AG increasingly produced armaments such as the LG 3000 truck and aircraft engines such as the DEUTSCHE 600 and DEUTSCHE 601. Daimler built another plant in Genshagen south of Berlin in 1936 in addition to the Marienfelde plant to create additional capacity for aircraft engine production. Hitler loved Mercedes – his private vehicles were all made by Daimler-Benz and he even held Daimler-Benz stock in his portfolio.[63]

About 450km northeast of Daimler-Benz, Adolf Hitler believed the German people (die Volk) needed a car (ein Wagen) they could afford. "It is for the broad masses that this car has been built. Its purpose is to answer their transportation needs, and it is intended to give them joy."[64] The result was the Ford Volkswagen, to be sold for 1,990 Reichmarks, or about $796. This may seem like a fabrication, but it isn't entirely untrue; in the 1930s, Ford did produce a vehicle in their German division for this price. The truth of the matter is Hitler did want a car the ordinary person could afford, much as he saw was happening in the United States, thanks to his Übermensch Henry Ford and the Model T. The Berlin auto shows in the 1930s showcased Volkswagens, though it was then a concept, not an actual vehicle brand. Other manufacturers like Daimler-Benz, Opel, Ford and BMW were beginning to market "Volks-wagens;" today we would call them compact cars. NSU Motorenwerke commissioned renowned auto designer Ferdinand Porsche and his Porsche Büro to design a

"Volkswagen." NSU could not follow through and the gauntlet was picked up by the Reichsverband der Deutschen Automobilindustrie – or the Reich Auto Industry Association – on June 22, 1934. Again, Porsche was asked to design the car, but this time the Reich was footing the bill.

Porsche was 59 and was helped on the design by his son, also Ferdinand. The senior Porsche was already well renowned for his design and engineering skill, having developed the first electric car in 1897. In World War I, he designed aircraft engines for the Austro-Hungarian army and tractors for heavy artillery; and had been employed at Daimler-Benz as technical manager and executive board member. Porsche left Daimler in 1930 to open his own shop and become intricately involved in the People's Car. In 1932, Stalin invited him to the Soviet Union for an informational visit. "At first we thought the invitation was so improbable that we had trouble taking it seriously," Ferdinand Jr. later wrote in his autobiography. "But soon it was made very clear to us that everything was perfectly serious."[65] Stalin wanted to advance industrial development in the Soviet Union and made him an offer to become general director of the development of the Soviet auto industry. Porsche turned Stalin down – not because he feared Stalin or a dislike of communism – but because he could not speak Russian.

Along with Porsche, the *Deutsche Arbeitsfront* – German Labor Front – also became deeply involved. As it was Hitler's pet project, it's perfectly logical the Nazi trade union would be running the factory. Porsche ran the Volkswagenwerke plant until 1941 when his son-in-law, Anton Piëch took over. This allowed Porsche to concentrate on his position as head of Hitler's tank commission. As Chair of the Panzer Committee, Porsche was the innovator behind the introduction of the Tiger and the Ferdinand heavy tanks and also was vital in the development and manufacturer of the V1 flying bombs.[66] Porsche joined the Nazi Party as well as the SS, both of his own free will, though he would claim later this was as a matter of business pragmatism, not philosophy.

Over at Volkswagen, the altruistic dream of a People's Car vanished with the advance of the Second World War. Instead of churning out the round little Beetles, the Volkswagen plant in Wolfsburg manufactured mines, tank chains and a small ATV. Only

630 Beetles were produced during the war, and those were made for the privileged few. Anton Piëch began managing the plant in 1941. "In the summer of 1943, Piëch bluntly declared that he had to use cheap Eastern workers in order to fulfill the Führer's wish that the Volkswagen be produced for 990 Reichsmark."[67] This did not worry Hitler though. He still dreamed of his People's Car, sketching it out and talking about it endlessly during his nightly tea sessions. One of Hitler's secretaries claimed he used to drive around Berghof in the specially made black VW cabriolet Ferdinand Porsche gave him on his 50th birthday in 1939, always telling everyone how Porsche was a genius.

BMW itself was classified as an armaments and war materials manufacturer, and devoted its resources almost exclusively to building aircraft engines for the Luftwaffe. Other plants were opened in addition to those in Munich and Eisenach. BMW began using foreign workers in 1940, employing them on the factory floor. Starting in 1942 convicts, Eastern European PoWs, and Western European forced laborers were made to work at BMW alongside concentration camp prisoners from Dachau. By 1944, more than 17,000 people or 90% of BMW's workforce[68] were slaves working at the aircraft engine plant in Munich-Allach.

If BMW was an arms maker – Daimler-Benz was *the* leading arms manufacturer in Germany in World War II. The company's plants made airplane motors and spare parts, tanks and armored vehicles, heavy trucks and sections of the V-2 rocket. In order to cope with the volume of requisitions from the Luftwaffe and Wehrmacht, Daimler-Benz initially recruited women. However, as staff numbers were still too low, Daimler-Benz also used forced laborers. These prisoners of war, abducted civilians and detainees from concentration camps were housed close to the plants. Forced laborers from Western Europe lived in guest houses, private accommodation or schools. The *Ostarbeiters* and Eastern PoWs were interned in barrack camps with poor, prison-like conditions. Female concentration camp inmates from Sachsenhausen and Ravensbrück were monitored by the SS under inhumane conditions. Daimler worked under the same deal as Volkswagen, paying the SS 4RM a day for the use of its prisoners. In 1944, almost half of Daimler-Benz's 63,610 employees were civilian forced laborers, prisoners of war or concentration camp detainees.

At all three manufacturers, the forced laborers were mainly *Ostarbeiter* – the eastern workers of the Soviet Union and Poland, as well as Soviet PoWs. Piëch at VW wasn't kidding when he said cheap laborers. Volkswagenwerke paid the Wehrmacht 48 pfennig a day – the equivalent of about 2½ cents – for the privilege of using Soviet PoWs, and paid the PoWs themselves 20 pfennigs in "camp money"[69] to be used at the labor camp at inflated prices. Even at that, the Soviets were no bargain. Most arrived at the camp malnourished, diseased and severely underweight:

The use of Russian prisoners of war is merely a question of nutrition. At present the ratio is still two of them to one German worker. Russian prisoners of war cured of their typhus and once again made available to the firms weigh only 40 kilograms (88 pounds) on an average, and must therefore first be cared for before they can be put to work. Russian prisoners of war are, without exception, willing to work, and able to perform well when they have had enough to eat.[70]

The irony of this is they may have been able to perform well if they had enough to eat – they never did though. The Soviets weren't the only ones who were considerably malnourished and mistreated. After Mussolini surrendered in 1943, the Italian army was taken prisoner wholesale by the Wehrmacht. Of these, 1,000 soldiers and 200 officers ended up working at Volkswagenwerke. The Italians were considered equal to the Soviets, not by birth and racially, but due to what the Germans considered their treason against the Axis. From Cesare Pilesi, a former Italian military internee:

This work with pick and shovel was arduous, and the food was meager. My body quickly suffered from this so much that, with the help of a nasty bout of diarrhea, my weight fell to 45 kilos. Under these conditions, with this work and a temperature of between –15° and –18°, I would soon be dead.[71]

Of course, it was not only men who suffered. Volkswagenwerke had acquired many Jewish women from Auschwitz and their job was manufacturing mines and bazookas. Mortality rates were much lower for the 649 women who came to Volkswagenwerke, with only five of them dying at the camp operated by the company. Volkswagenwerke paid the SS 4RM a day for their use; the women received nothing. Until December 1942, those who were either already or had become pregnant were returned to their homes. At the beginning of 1943, with the routs the Wehrmacht suffered on the Russian front, it became impossible to try to return these women, so the children were born in the camp. Volkswagenwerke had only up to this time cared for around twenty infants; this number increased dramatically and there were 120 babies under the care of the Polish and Soviet nurses in the camp by 1944. According to at least one camp account, the infant mortality rate was 100%:

> *Not far from Wolfsburg there was a children's home or a nursery for infants in which the mothers had to leave their children, and be sent back to work themselves, of course. The parents or the mothers were able to visit their children every Sunday, but unfortunately the children survived for only a few months there, no child longer than six months; after that they died 'for various reasons.'*[72]

Volkswagenwerke tried to lessen the effects of the war on the children, moving them off-site to Rühen in the summer of 1944. Their efforts were not in the best interests of the children however; mother and child were separated immediately after birth and the mothers sent back to the camp. Camp doctor Hans Körbel contented himself with sending memos to Porsche and other managers regarding both the malnutrition of the Soviet prisoners though mentioned nothing of the mortality rate at the children's camp. The rations for the Soviets were purportedly increased; Körbel ended up visiting the Rühen camp only once a week, mainly to issue death certificates. He did not want to admit any wrongdoing on his part in regards to the treatment – or lack thereof – of the children. As a result of this and poor treatment by the doctors, 365 children had died of malnourishment and insufficient care. Körbel was sentenced to death by the British and executed in March 1947.

Though it was generally thought men were more productive workers than women, the women at Volkswagenwerke received better care and food. They had hot and cold running water and received an allotment of one pound of bread, butter and meat.[73] This contradicts a study revealed in *Der Spiegel* in 1987: "The girls who worked there were forced to work without coats, stockings and protection from the cold, and came to me for paper for the soles of their shoes," according to another prison doctor at the time.[74]

The Nazis had a different regard for their western European conquests. French, Dutch and Belgian PoWs were afforded better pay, better housing and better food. By the spring of 1943, over 1,000 French PoWs were working at the Volkswagen plant. As for the civilian guest workers, they were paid equivalent to the German workers, and are shown in pictures wearing suits on Sunday, smoking cigarettes, and looking the part of the jaunty men about town. However, even towards the end of the war, the western European position became untenable. French PoWs had their meal allowances slashed and when this was pointed out, Volkswagenwerke claimed there must be a mistake used in the calculations for food allowances. Plant managers said they were overall "quite satisfied" with the French PoWs output, especially the French gentleman who served as payroll administrator to the 17,000 camp inmates. The 750 Dutch – guest and forced – labor at the plant were regarded as equals to the Germans, as they were *Volksdeutsche* – Germans outside of Germany. As such, they were afforded many more freedoms than the Slavic *Ostarbeiter* who the Germans considered *Untermenschen* or sub-human. The Dutch, however, were also prone to the Nazi punishments and in 1943, 40 of them were sent to a re-education camp in Salzgitter-Watenstedt. As with the French, pictures show the Dutch wearing suits, smoking pipes and looking generally comfortable with their surroundings.[75]

In July 1944, work started on the Laagberg work camp at Volkswagenwerke, using Soviet, French, Dutch and Polish PoWs under the auspices of the SS. The commanders in charge, SS-Hauptscharführer Johannes Pump and his deputy SS-Unterscharführer Anton Peter Callesen, treated the PoWs with exceptional cruelty. By 1945, 130 of the original 800 prisoners had died due to mistreatment, malnourishment or work-related injuries. As is almost always the case, Pump and Callesen survived the war – Pump died while on trial in West Germany in 1955. Callesen was arrested by the Danish authorities in

1945, sentenced to death in 1950 and was pardoned and released in 1951. He died in 1979.

Volkswagenwerke did not usually employ the use of the SS and had its own security, the Werkschutz, which worked in conjunction with the Gestapo. The Werkschutz was charged with the discipline and punishment in the camp and factory, looking for incidents of non-conformism, supposed sabotage or refusal to work. Master craftsmen and foremen would either carry out corporal punishment themselves or called in the Werkschutz to help. Beatings in the camp and plant were a daily occurrence, as was the denial of food to inmates. Plant managers would send offence reports to the Gestapo, but when they found their inmates were sent to penal or work education camps and came back in poor health or worse, didn't come back at all, the practice was avoided. This did not stop them from using concentration camp prisoners.

Starting in the first days of 1942, the SS started suggesting the use of the labor pool it had "acquired" in concentration camps. Himmler and Volkswagenwerke management agreed to this readily and the company started accepting these forced laborers from the Neuengamme camp in April. They were tasked with building a light metals foundry, which would be used mainly after the war for production of Volkswagen personal vehicles.

The prisoners lived in the foundry's windowless air raid shelters, which it was almost impossible to ventilate. They were so damp that the condensation dripped from the ceiling. The prisoners had to carry out heavy construction work. Due to the inadequate construction equipment and the driving work pace imposed by the SS guards, there were numerous accidents at work.[76]

The company stopped using concentration camp inmates at the foundry in October 1942, when Armaments Minister Albert Speer declared it redundant to the war effort. The inmates were sent off to the Sachsenhausen camp until May 1944, when the labor shortage again threatened production. Until the end of the war, approximately 5,000 more inmates were used at Volkswagenwerke.

As the German war machine continued to deteriorate, plans were made to move manufacturing underground to avoid Allied bombing. Volkswagenwerke began by moving production to the iron mine at Tiercelet, on the French side of the Luxembourg border. Up until then, the company's main output was fuel tanks, mines, bazookas and the Kübelwagen, but this changed in 1944 when production started on the V-1 flying bomb. Plant engineer Arthur Schmiele traveled to Auschwitz in May 1944, where he assembled a group of 300 Hungarian Jews who were skilled metalworkers. The men were intended to become the core workforce in the underground production and assembly plant in Tiercelet. When they arrived, they had their own beds and sheets as well as shower facilities in rooms close to the air-raid shelters. These skilled workers were regarded as difficult to replace and so punishments were rare. This changed once they actually arrived at the underground factory a month later, when they joined another 500 Jewish prisoners who had also arrived from Auschwitz. The conditions in Tiercelet were much worse than at the main plant but by September 1944, with the advance of the Allies through France, Tiercelet was abandoned and work on the V-1 had been transferred to Mittelwerk GmbH. The inmates were sent to the Mittelbau-Dora concentration camp to die.[77]

Volkswagenwerke became frantic by August 1944 after Allied bombing raids on the main plant. Strangely, it was decided to move production to an asphalt pit near Eschershausen and again concentration camp workers, this time from Buchenwald, were drafted. Almost 500 workers came from Buchenwald, 35 of these to replace those who had died on the job and as always, workers who were unable to continue were sent back to the concentration camp for extermination.

With neither power nor raw materials, manufacturing ceased at Volkswagenwerke in April of 1945. On April 7, the SS ordered the company's labor camp evacuated and the female inmates were taken to Salzwedel by freight car. They were liberated by the Allies within the week; the men were not so lucky. They were forced to march to Ludwigslust, a distance of 130 kilometres. Many died en route, many more at the internment camp until that camp was liberated on May 2, 1945.

In the postwar era, Volkswagen was almost completely destroyed. As a truly Nazi organization, it was deeply distrusted by the Allies. It fell under the British sphere of control after the war and because it was only pushing out armaments – and was Hitler's baby– the British felt it had no value to reconstruction efforts. The company – plants, machinery and workforce – was offered up to Ford Motor Company for free. In March 1948, Henry Ford II – Henry senior had died a year earlier – and Ford Executive Vice President Ernie Breech traveled to West Germany to assess Ford-Werke when British representatives approached them about Volkswagen. Breech already had a reputation for turning around businesses and as a trouble shooter. He was hired at Ford in 1946 by Henry II to cut the corporate fat at the company, which was contributing a net loss of $10 million a month. The next year, Ford made an annual profit of $60 million. This time, Breech did not see any value – his assessment of Volkswagen, even at the bargain price of zero, was "Mr. Ford, I don't think what we're being offered here is worth a damn!"[78] Breech was wrong of course and the company came under the management of Heinz Nordhoff. Nordhoff was a senior manager at Opel and though he was working as a mechanic at the time, he was offered the position by Major Ivan Hirst, the British officer in charge. Nordhoff managed to rebuild the company and by the time he died in 1968, he had made the front cover of *Time*, was considered the greatest manager in postwar Germany and had produced 14 million Volkswagens. All three – Ford II, Breech and Nordhoff – are members of the Automotive Hall of Fame.

After the Second World War, Allied soldiers requisitioned and occupied the BMW plants. Since BMW had been classified as an armaments company, the machines and tools were dismantled. From 1945 onwards stopgap production, mainly of kitchen utensils, was started in Milbertshofen – as was also the case at the Berlin plant. In October 1945, the US military government issued a command for dismantling the BMW plants in Munich and Allach. A large proportion of the intact machines were dismantled at the Munich-Milbertshofen plant and shipped all over the world as reparations.

BMW was purchased in 1960 by Herbert Quandt when he sold his shares in Accumulatoren Fabrik AG (AFA) to acquire the automobile manufacturer. Quandt and his father Günther were both shareholders in BMW and Daimler-Benz during the war. Günther sat on the Aufsichtsrat of Daimler-Benz as well as Deutsche Bank and after the war his son Herbert started accumulating shares in BMW. For its part, AFA made industrial-sized batteries for the Wehrmacht, Nazi U-Boats and V-2 rockets and also employed slave labor. The company became Varta AG and has sold off all assets now.

Günther was an interesting character – during World War I, he supplied the Imperial German Army with uniforms and with the fortune he made he acquired AFA shortly after the end of the war. In World War II, Quandt used forced laborers at AFA with his son Herbert as head of personnel. Günther was married twice – the second time to Magda Ritschel in 1921.

Günther divorced Magda in 1929 after she had an affair with the Zionist leader Chaim Vitaly Arlosoroff. Magda then took up with her new employer, Doctor Josef Göbbels. Magda married the propagandist in 1931 with Adolf Hitler as their best man. Günther died in 1954 and was not charged with any crimes after the war. Magda died in Hitler's bunker in 1945 after helping her husband poison their six children. Today the Quandt family owns a substantial part of BMW – Herbert's daughter Susanne Klatten owns 12.6% of the company; his son Stefan 17.6% and is deputy chair of the Aufsichtsrat. Susanne sits on the board as well – both are listed as "independent entrepreneurs." Their mother Johanna, who was Herbert's third wife, holds 16.7% of the company – combined in 2014 the Quandt holdings are worth just under €24 billion or 46.7% of BMW.

Daimler-Benz pursued the war effort until the bitter end. Even as the Reich was going down in flames, the proud company that made Hitler's staff cars was making due "with huddled foreign inmates assembling motors for no pay"[79] All the work Gottlieb and Paul Daimler and Carl Benz had done to acquire foreign markets was for naught – war reparations stipulated foreign subsidiaries and assets were forfeit. The Soviets took what they wanted out of their zone of influence. Daimler-Benz had four heavily damaged factories left to its name. Otto Hoppe, who had been terminated because of his Jewish wife in 1942, rejoined the board in May 1945 before the Nazis surrendered. Daimler-Benz began fixing US army vehicles when the war ended and was able to begin manufacturing cars and trucks by 1947 and made a profit in 1948.

For all, this was a very embarrassing period in the histories of these companies. From BMW:

The use of forced labour is tacitly approved and accepted. During the Third Reich, forced labourers must work in deeply distressing conditions. Today, BMW is painfully aware of the great human suffering caused by this, and deeply regrets the fate of the forced labourers.[80]

Daimler-Benz offers this curt appraisal of their World War II work:

Daimler-Benz admitted its links with the Nazi regime, and also became involved in the German Industry Foundation's initiative "Remembrance, Responsibility and Future", whose work included the provision of humanitarian aid for former forced labourers.[81]

3

The Food Companies

As research progresses, I can't stop but think all of these companies are American as apple pie – Ford, General Motors and Coca-Cola. Coca-Cola has to be the most honest, integrity-driven company in world – I mean, they invented the modern connotation of Santa Claus, didn't they?

Coca-Cola was perhaps the greatest marketer of World War II. Rationing of sugar meant most companies had to cut back on production, but not Coke and that was mainly because of Robert Woodruff. Woodruff's father Ernest led a consortium of businessmen which purchased the Coca-Cola Company in 1919 for $25 million. Back then, Coke wasn't the international brand it is today – there were about 400 licensed factories in the United States, mostly mom-and-pop operations and only a minor presence in five countries. What should have been a great purchase turned into a white elephant when the company was forced to honor sugar purchase contracts which were made at higher prices during World War I. While their competitors were able to buy sugar cheaply after the war, Coke was tied to their previous agreements and it almost sank the company.

By 1923 they needed help, and this came in the form of Robert Woodruff. At the tender age of 32, he was already vice president of the White Motor Company, the parent company of Western Star trucks. Ernest Woodruff and Coca-Cola chairman W. C. Bradley convinced Robert to take a $50,000 a year pay cut – a monumental amount in 1923 – and join the company as president. His biggest innovation was going global – in seven years, Woodruff had increased the number of countries under the Coke umbrella from five to 30, including Germany which was added in 1929. Woodruff was an excellent businessman, realizing the need for comfort during the Dirty Thirties. While many companies disappeared during the Great Depression, Coca-Cola flourished with its five-cents-a-bottle product. By the time World War II started, Coke was firmly entrenched in 44 countries.

There were issues for the company when the war started, not the least of which was the rationing of sugar once again. This is where

Woodruff came upon a brilliant idea: Coca-Cola would be available to American GIs worldwide for a guaranteed price of five cents a bottle for the duration of the war. Eisenhower approved of the plan personally and this had a double down effect for Coke – it was deemed an essential for servicemen, so the company was exempt from sugar rationing. The other upside was Coke set up many wartime plants in countries that had no presence before, which gave it a worldwide footprint by the time the war was over.

The German-born Max Keith took the reins of Coca-Cola GmbH in 1938 when its American-born director died. Keith was an endless promoter, always looking for ways to enhance the brand; in effect, the perfect company man. Before the war he would send out salesmen with large briefcases which were tin-lined, filled with ice and ten bottles of Coke. He would send these men to taverns whose owners would try to throw them out – the salesmen would persist, proffering a cold Coke to the purveyors of beer. That was the sales pitch and it worked – many of the innkeepers hadn't tried a cold bottle and anyone who's had a Coke knows the warm version is not so tasty. After this, the owners would start to sell it.[82] By the start of the Second World War, Coca-Cola GmbH had 39 plants across Germany bottling the product. Keith's ability to have Coca-Cola omnipresent in Germany was impressive:

> *In early 1945, a group of German prisoners of war debarked in Hoboken, New Jersey, apprehensive and lonely in a foreign land. When one of them pointed to a Coca-Cola sign on a nearby building, the prisoners began excitedly gesticulating and talking among themselves. Taken aback, the guard yelled for order, demanding an explanation from a prisoner who spoke English. "We are surprised," he answered, "that you have Coca-Cola here too.*[83]

All was well at Coca-Cola GmbH until 1941 when it did not have the supply of Coca-Cola syrup the rest of the world had thanks to the Allied blockade. This is where Keith had to improvise and a new product was born: Fanta.

Keith did what anyone in his position would do – find alternative raw materials. When the syrup was gone, he needed something else to make his drink and the results, though bizarre, actually worked. After consultations with Coca-Cola GmbH chemist Dr. Scheteling to develop an alternative, Keith started by gathering together the apple fibers left behind by the cider-making process; then added whey, a dairy by-product; sweetened it with saccharin which was a relatively available coal-tar derivative and added whatever fruits he could import from Italy. The result was Fanta.[84] At the time, Keith had limited communication with the Atlanta head office of Coca-Cola – the only time he could communicate was through the Swiss subsidiary, but he had no way of getting the syrup via the neutral country. The saccharin was dropped relatively quickly when Coke GmbH was allowed to use beet sugar.

Fanta was derived from the German word for fantasy and after a while, it *was* quite a fantasy. With foodstuffs scarce, Germans were actually using it as a soup base during the war.[85] This kept the factories open and the staff employed and since Fanta was not as essential to the German war effort as Coca-Cola was to the American, there is no indication Coke used slave or forced labor at its plants in Germany until the latter years of the war. Keith's hands were full when the Wehrmacht moved – the Nazis placed him in charge of Coca-Cola's properties in the occupied countries, and he sent word through Coca-Cola's bottler in neutral Switzerland he would try to keep the enterprises alive, which he did with Fanta.[86]

Does this make Keith a Nazi or does this mean Coke supported the Nazi regime? No. Keith steadfastly refused to join the Nazi party, which actually harmed his reputation in the Reich, though it was very prescient for the end of the war – there was no stigma attached to him or Coke.

Keith was integral to both advertising and distribution of product at the 1936 Berlin Olympics. Again, we see pictures of Coca-Cola advertising next to the swastikas, or perhaps we envision Hitler or Göring swigging back a Coke from its distinctive bottle. Does this make Coke a Nazi drink? If that's the case, then we must say it is an Al-Qaeda drink if Osama bin Laden liked to have one as well. And if the presence of Coke (and other American companies) at the Berlin Olympics is an implicit sanction of Nazism or anti-Semitism, then isn't the presence of VISA, McDonalds and Coca-Cola at the 2014 Sochi

Olympics an implicit sanction of anti-homosexuality? Robert Woodruff was being entertained by Göring and propaganda minister Josef Göbbels during the Olympics and his only complaint with the proceedings was the caveat the Nazi health ministry put on the bottles – "contains caffeine."

Coca-Cola GmbH's largest issue came from one of its competitors, strangely called AfriCola. It is interesting that a product named after what the Nazis would consider a sub-species would make head roads against the good ol' boys from Atlanta, but Karl Flach, the head of Afri-Cola was both a prominent Nazi and not one to stray from smear campaigns. In 1936 while visiting the United States, he arranged to have a tour of the Atlanta bottling plant of Coca-Cola. While there, he absconded with some bottle caps, which providentially for him were printed with the Hebrew inscription for kosher.

At this point you say "hold on a minute, Coca-Cola is kosher?" Rabbi Tobias Geffen was the dean of Southern Jewish Orthodoxy and served Atlanta's Congregation Shearith Israel. As Jewish immigration increased after World War I, many of the children born in the United States, though Jewish, wanted to partake in the new American lifestyle – and this meant drinking Coke. Rabbi Geffen's colleagues around the country posed the question of him – is Coke kosher? The rabbi took it upon himself to contact Coca-Cola and see. Sworn under strict secrecy, Rabbi Geffen was allowed to see the formula for Coke.

Rabbi Geffen came back and said no, it was not kosher because of one ingredient: beef tallow – fat – which was in glycerin. The chemist at the time replied it was only present in one part per thousand, which the rabbi replied was still unacceptable and Coca-Cola was deemed not kosher. The executives at Coke realized the growing Jewish population was also a growing demographic for the company, so for such a tiny ingredient, why couldn't there be an alternative? The chemists went back to the drawing board and found out Procter & Gamble had been working on a cottonseed oil-based glycerin which would pass muster. The rabbi approved, but then noted a second problem, which pervades today in a different form.

Back in the 1930s, there was minute traces of alcohol from the grain-based sugars used in the formula. This would make Coke inconsumable at Passover, when they considered anything *kitniyot* forbidden. For Eastern European Jews, this would include corn.. Coca-Cola came to a solution which still stands today: for several weeks before Passover, Coke is available in a kosher form, made from beet sugar. The rabbi was quite pleased and here is his response:

> *Because Coca-Cola has already been accepted by the general public in this country and Canada and because it has become an insurmountable problem to induce the great majority of Jews to refrain from partaking of this drink, I have tried earnestly to find a method of permitting its usage. With the help of God, I have been able to uncover a pragmatic solution in which there would be no question nor any doubt concerning the ingredients of Coca-Cola.*[87]

Great for the burgeoning Jewish population across North America, but being kosher was not kosher with Karl Flach and the Nazis. He spirited some of the kosher-stamped bottle caps back to Germany and started printing thousands of leaflets with a picture of the bottle cap, claiming his competitor was a Jewish-American business run by the Jew Harold Hirsch. Hirsch was an attorney for Coca-Cola and had filed the trademarks for both Coke's logo and bottle design, but that was it. It was enough to almost kill Coca-Cola GmbH. Robert Woodruff had prohibited Keith from defending Coke, because he thought it denigrated the brand. Woodruff preferred talking about the positives and not rehashing the negatives.[88]

Sales in Germany were crippled and the Nazi party headquarters canceled all orders. Keith responded by the only way he could: he kept on advertising at key events – like the Berlin Olympics – and giving out free samples. The next year, Keith wanted to showcase the mighty Coca-Cola machine, which he did at the 1937 Working People Exhibit in Düsseldorf. With a fully functioning bottling plant at the centre of the fair next to the Propaganda Ministry's booth, Coke took centre stage at the Nazis' salute to industry and technology. A company photographer managed to get a shot of Hermann Göring stopping by the booth and having a Coke and it is said – though this remains apocryphal – Hitler the health nut enjoyed the occasional bottle of Coke.[89]

In his book *For God, Country & Coca-Cola*, Mark Pendergrast claims "Far from expressing horror at Nazi aggression, Keith and his men swiftly followed the troops into Austria,"[90] following the Anschluss in 1938. Sometimes, time and history give a better perspective on events, but here is what the Encyclopaedia Britannica says on the Anschluss:

In February 1938 Hitler invited the Austrian chancellor Kurt von Schuschnigg to Germany and forced him to agree to give the Austrian Nazis virtually a free hand...The German Nazi minister Hermann Göring ordered the Austrian Nazi leader Arthur Seyss-Inquartt to send a telegram requesting German military aid, but he refused, and the telegram was sent by a German agent in Vienna. On March 12 Germany invaded, and the enthusiasm that followed gave Hitler the cover to annex Austria outright on March 13. A controlled plebiscite of April 10 gave a 99.7 percent approval.

We know all the facts today, but the German people in 1938 would have known what the Nazi newspapers told them – the Austrian people, gripped by recession, restless, resentful and alienated from Europe after World War I, yearned to be joined with their Aryan brethren.[91] It is very patriotic to follow your country's army into another nation to liberate it from the tyranny of despair; so how is this different from companies such as Halliburton, which profited from the liberation of Iraq? It is very easy to proselytize about the evils of Hitler and Nazism 70 years on, but one must look at it from the point of view not of history, but of the current. Before the war, Keith and others would have acted in the company's best interest, though unfortunately it was easy for the masses to turn a blind eye to the acts of the SA and the virulent anti-Semitism; that is, until Kristallnacht.

Kristallnacht – or the Night of Broken Glass – was the culmination of Hitler's anti-Jewish pogroms. On the night of November 9-10 1938, Nazi Party officials, members of the SA and Hitler Youth rampaged through the streets of Germany, Austria and the Sudetenland of Czechoslovakia destroying synagogues, homes, and Jewish-owned businesses, burning, plundering and murdering as they went. Kristallnacht started after the assassination of low-level German diplomat Ernst vom Rath by a 17-year-old Polish Jew in Paris. The Nazis responded with Propaganda Minister Göbbels claiming "'World Jewry' had conspired to commit the assassination and announced 'the Führer has decided that ... demonstrations should not be prepared or organized by the Party, but insofar as they erupt spontaneously, they are not to be hampered.'"[92] In other words, go nuts boys.

But once again, we are presented with the bias of history. It is easy to show the horrors of Kristallnacht today, how it was carefully orchestrated by the Nazis, but if you were in Germany and read the local paper the next day, you would see how *"the population protests against the murderous Jewish attack"* of vom Rath and *"The people marched through the streets, demonstrating their indignation at this vicious murder."*[93] Even in Great Britain, the *Daily Express* headline on the 11th was:

Note the last sentence: NOT EVEN THE PROCLAMATION OF DR. GOEBBELS – THE PROPAGANDA MINISTER – BROADCAST THIS AFTERNOON AND AGAIN TONIGHT – ORDERING THE STOPPAGE OF THE POGROMS COULD CURB THE MADNESS OF THE MOBS. So if the foreign press at the time is fooled by the moves of the master propagandist, why shouldn't the ordinary German? Max Keith would probably look at the morning paper, sipping his coffee (or perhaps a cold bottle of Coke) and think "Stupid rioters, they are bad for business."

Wholesale mob rioting didn't deter Keith, nor did it stop him when the supply of Coca-Cola syrup dried up in 1942. Fanta was created by Coca-Cola GmbH for the German consumer, and not as the Internet rumor mill would attest by the Nazis and for the Nazis. Yes, Nazis would drink it, but that is guilt by association. Keith kept the taps running at Coke through skill and bravado. He squirreled away the last bottles of Coke in Germany to be given to wounded German soldiers in hospitals, which much like Woodruff's manoeuver with the American armed forces, was a move to make someone who was far from home and injured feel comfort from something familiar – and an excellent marketing move.[94]

Did Keith collaborate with the Nazi regime, as Pendergrast attests, or was he just a businessman? Nobody died from ingesting a bottle of Coke or Fanta; they did not make armaments for the

Wehrmacht; they were not in bed with the SS. They *did* use forced labor at their plants, though it was convicts at first, then refugees. According to Keith "people would come from anywhere in Europe – the war brought them from everywhere."[95] The SS did not actively seek out an American soft drink bottler for prison or concentration camp labor – it just doesn't make sense, and there is no indication Coca-Cola GmbH did either. As Klaus Pütter, retired senior vice president at Coca-Cola and someone who worked with Keith said, "Max Keith tried not to offend those in power. When you live in a country governed by a dictatorship, you have to watch your tongue and be very careful. If your neighbor heard you say anything against Hitler, they came at night and fetched you and off you went. One false step, one false remark would have been fatal."[96]

Keith went out of his way to prove his mettle to the company, and not Nazi Germany. When he was summoned in 1945 and told to change the name of Coca-Cola to anything else "Call it Max Keith GmbH if you want, but change it within two days, or you will be placed in a concentration camp,"[97] he actually refused, but within the two days, the general who gave him the directive died in an air raid, and so did his directive.

Keith survived the war and sent a telegram to Atlanta: "Coca-Cola GmbH still functioning. Send auditors." He was only too happy to send the wartime profits back to the United States to show how well he had run the business. So yes, Coca-Cola did profit from Nazi Germany, but not really on the backs of the oppressed, the Jewish population or at the detriment of the Allied servicemen. On the contrary, Coca-Cola technical observers were able to start bottling Coke in Germany by April of 1945 a few weeks before the war ended.

So Hitler liked sipping on a Coke while watching *Gone with the Wind* and perhaps he nibbled on a chocolate – does that make Warner Brothers a Nazi supporter? Since the Warners were Polish Jews and Jack Warner openly criticized the Nazi regime, that's a definite "no." Does that make Nestlé a Nazi company? No, but Nestlé did have its Nazi ties.

Nestlé: the largest food company in the world; over US$88 billion in sales, a market cap of US$246 billion in 2016, just behind

Johnson & Johnson. A remarkable company known for Nescafé and Taster's Choice coffees, 74 different water brands, Carnation milk and Nestea, Haagen-Dazs, Gerber baby food, Boost nutritional supplements, Maggi seasoning, Stouffer's, Lean Cuisine, Toll House cookies, Baby Ruth, Butterfinger, Oh Henry, Alpo, Purina and it owns 30% of L'Oréal which produces Maybelline, Garnier and Lancôme. In other words, a really, really big company – so how did they get involved with the Nazis? First a little history.

Nestlé was founded in 1866 by its namesake Henri Nestlé, who developed an infant formula for a neighbor's sick child. The company entered the German market in 1874 with its infant formula. From there, it purchased a Norwegian condensed milk company in 1898 and opened factories in the United States, Great Britain and Germany in the early 1900s. In 1906, Nestlé bought the Cressbrook Dairy Company in Brisbane, Australia giving it a foothold in the Far East.

Fresh milk supplies dwindled during World War I, causing shortages for factories and most fresh milk was sold almost immediately to local towns. Trade embargoes, increased costs, and restrictions on the use of production facilities added to Nestlé's wartime difficulties.[98] Nestlé combated this by purchasing and building factories in countries largely unaffected by the war so by 1921 it had over doubled its prewar capacity and set up shop in Brazil.

Nestlé expanded into chocolate at the turn of the century and in 1929 merged with Peter, Cailler, Kohler Chocolats Suisses S.A. and bought German chocolatier Sarotti AG in the same year. Sarotti has since been sold off to Stollwerck GmbH, but during World War II, Nestlé made the Sarotti plant in Hattersheim available to the Nazis for armament production and the plant in Berlin kept making chocolates – for consumption only by the military.[99]

As war loomed in Europe, Nestlé realized the neutral Switzerland would not be a safe haven as had happened in World War I. The company divided its management team between Vevey, Switzerland and Stamford, Connecticut until 1945. This served the company well as it was able to play both sides of the field during the war. Its powdered and evaporated milk as well as instant coffee were essential to the Allied armed forces and this gave Nestlé a great foothold in the United States. In 1936, Nestlé set up the holding company that would service most of the world after the outbreak of war. Fully 75% of the firm's revenues were generated away from the German sphere of influence under the brand Unilac.[100]

Nestlé managed to continue manufacturing chocolate for the Wehrmacht and interestingly, Nescafé was also considered an essential to the war and the Wehrmacht procured the manufacture of the product – for its use only. It continued working with the help of forced laborers, as did many companies at the time. At Nestlé's factory in Kappeln, 38 people were fit snugly into just under 640 square feet, or the size of about five small bedrooms; at Lonza in Waldshut in the summer of 1944, nearly 800 foreigners lived in 17 barracks with a total of 64 rooms.[101] Food, as always, was an issue – the irony is they were in the business of food; and again, it was the Soviet PoWs who suffered the most from malnourishment. At the Maggi GmbH plant in Singen:

The work was hard and the food was pitiful: there was soup swimming with maggots. Begging for more bread or better food resulted in merciless beating from the camp commander.[102]

To be fair, Maggi was acquired by Nestlé in 1947. Prior to this, it was a spirited supporter of the Third Reich. At the Singen plant, there was no need to go through an Aryanization process as there were no Jewish managers; they were ardent supporters of the new regime and were very vocal about it.[103] Maggi had gone through tough times after World War I, with many larger competitors such as Knorr nipping at their heels. The company was accused of being run by foreigners, was defamed and boycotted. The only thing they could do was support the new regime, which back in 1933 wouldn't have seemed like a bad idea. The firm complied fully with the new ideology with all the consequences this entailed (discipline, internal propaganda, exclusion of Jewish employees, appointing Party members to the board, etc.). In turn it was rewarded with advantageous production conditions – a head office in Berlin (1938) and a plant in Singen (1940) – and granted the title of "exemplary Nazi firm" in 1940. It was the desire to survive rather than any ideological convictions which forced these subsidiaries into the arms of Nazism.[104] This led the company to do some less than exemplary things, including the use of forced labor at its plants, many of whom, as noted above, were beaten on a regular basis.

As Maggi aligned its ideology with the Nazi party, certain aspects became clear:

> *As early as spring 1933, Maggi declared, "Not a single share of our company capital is in Jewish hands." In 1935, a statutory declaration was made concerning the Aryan character of the firm and in 1936 the Board assured the authorities that only 3 people out of a total staff of 3200 were not Aryans.*[105]

Good Nazi business on Maggi's part. At the time, it would be akin to claiming "Made in the USA" as a selling feature. It was also a way of taking that one arrow away from competitors; an arrow which struck at many Swiss firms – it was claimed they were foreign, Jewish companies. One of the defaming competitors was C. H. Knorr AG, known for their soups.

> *Aryanization (German: Arisierung) is a term coined during Nazism referring to the forced expulsion of so-called "non-Aryans", mainly Jews, from business life in Nazi Germany and the territories it controlled. It entailed the transfer of Jewish property into "Aryan" hands in order to "de-Jew the economy".*

In Germany and the occupied Austria, the period of Aryanisation of businesses had begun and Nestlé was not immune:

> *In Austria, The Danzas Company (now DHL) experienced this first-hand at the end of 1941, when rivals informed the authorities that it was in "Jewish and freemasonic hands" and was working for the British Secret Services. In this manner, some Jewish firms were "Aryanised," particularly in Austria after the Anschluss. Bally, Nestlé, and Geigy played along, while Roche refused.*[106]

In May, 1938 Hans Schenk, a long time Nestlé employee, signed a purchase agreement with the Jewish chocolatiers Altmann &

Kühne. Unfortunately, the Nazi regime in Austria didn't agree, believing the three shops in the chain would provide employment for three Germans, not act as a conduit for a Swiss company. Schenk continued negotiating with the administrators for Altmann & Kühne, whose namesakes had fled Vienna for New York. By November, an agreement was reached, based on Schenk's assurances no corporate money was used and it would not be a division of Nestlé. Schenk had secured an advance from Nestlé, though by the end of the war, the company had written off the money and claimed they wanted no part of it. Schenk contacted Nestlé after the war, but Nestlé refused to respond, saying Schenk had not acted as a representative of the company, but rather in his own personal interests.[107] This is not true, considering there is ample evidence the managing director of Nestle informed the board of the purchase, and that a price of 100,000 Reichsmarks would be acceptable.[108] The Nazi regime in Austria went ahead and liquidated Altmann anyway.

The Anschluss provided an opportunity for Nestlé to expand, but as a foreign company, it's supervisory board believed it would be unable to carry out any purchases. Therefore, the Nestle story ends here.

In the Netherlands and Great Britain, what would become Maggi competitor G. H. Knorr's parent company was also well placed for the advent of war. That company was Unilever and before 1929, Unilever was two separate entities – Lever Brothers in Great Britain and Margarine Unie N.V. in the Netherlands. The founding companies of Margarine Unie started in Holland in 1872; Lever Brothers started manufacturing Sunlight soap in the U.K. 12 years later. The companies' fortunes would start to intertwine by 1909, when both groups purchased palm plantations – palm oil being essential to both margarine and soap production. Since palm oil was easily interchangeable, Lever Brothers was approached at the beginning of the war by the British government to begin producing margarine. Lever readily agreed, considering the minimal difference in chemistry and manufacture.

By 1927, the owners of four manufacturers joined to form Margarine Unie NV. Margarine Unie also had facilities in Great Britain which were in competition with Lever Brothers. In a strange twist not normally seen in the corporate world, both companies realized it was smarter to amalgamate than compete and in 1929 Unilever was born. It was – and remains – a unique company in that it is two separate companies operating as one: Unilever PLC in Great Britain and Unilever N.V in the Netherlands.

As World War II approached, Unilever was in a position of exceptional strength. Knorr was still a middling-sized soup manufacturer whose fortunes were still tied to Germany. Aryanisation and Nazi oversight figured heavily into Knorr's corporate ideology, as with most major enterprises. Local Nazi party boss Richard Drauz requested a seat on Knorr's board but was denied, a wise decision on their part. Drauz was later to become infamous for his violent behavior and his scorched earth policy, having told the local authorities in Heilbronn to leave the fires burning from air raids as well as shooting the local civil defense leader, brandishing him a traitor. Drauz ordered local inhabitants shot for displaying white sheets outside their homes as the Wehrmacht retreated and the Allies moved closer. He was captured after the war and executed by the Americans for war crimes.

Unilever's German holdings were amalgamated into Margarine-Verkauf-Union in the late 1920s. By 1932, the company controlled 70% of the margarine industry in Germany, which produced one-third of the world's annual 1.5 million tons of margarine production. The company controlled all aspects of the manufacturing process – not only producing margarine, but also owning packaging, trucking and retail concerns. MVU, like other concerns, were forced to remove Jewish employees and managers. Albert van den Bergh, Dr. Treitel and Dr. Friedman were all forced to resign from the Aufsichtsrat of MVU in 1933.[109]

With a one-third ownership, MVU was also able to control the Nordsee Deutsche Hochseefischerei AG, the dominant fish processor in Germany. Nordsee owned at least 167 large fishing vessels, processing facilities and 240 retail stores in Germany and Austria. After the occupation of Norway, the company opened a frozen fillet factory in Trondheim, which only shipped product back to Germany. This led to another opportunity for Unilever – shipbuilding. While the company was not allowed to take money out of the country directly, it was allowed to build ships and sell them to foreign interests, thereby supplying the Reich with hard currency. Starting in 1934 and with the

German government's help, the company supplied money to shipyards in Kiel, Hamburg and Bremen, which in turn built ships for Unilever. The company used some of the ships itself and sold off the rest. During the term of the agreement, Unilever built 550,000 tons of shipping, which it paid for both with blocked Reichsmarks and raw materials. This supplied the Reich not only with employment for the shipyards but also raw materials such as palm and whale oils.[110] Unilever did lose these ships after the war when the Allies confiscated them

By the end of the agreement in 1936, the Nazis proposed to Unilever it invest in an artificial wool concern. The government guaranteed against any losses on the business over a period of seven years as well as five percent interest on the investment during the same period. This appealed to the soap division of Unilever, since it could test detergents on these new fibres. In February 1937 the Westfälische Zellstoff A.G. was established with a total equity capital of RM 2.2 million, of which Unilever contributed RM 800,000.[111] This led to Unilever's Aryanization of Jewish property. Unilever did, from the accounts researched, conduct business in a manner which was much better than most other companies, but as pointed out by Wubs in his research, it was not charitable by any stretch.

Fritz Cohen Tuchfabrik AG was a cloth manufacturer in MönchenglaDeutscheach. Unilever, after researching the firm, made an offer to Felix, Fritz and Paul Cohen in 1935. The Cohens emigrated to the United States and acted as advisers to the company as well as an agency in their new homeland. After the war they claimed they were satisfied with the way they had been treated by Unilever.

J. Wertheimer & Co. in Bielefeld was acquired in 1937. Wertheimer was an artificial silk manufacturer and the family asked for RM 3 million. Unilever proposed RM2.3 million, which was slightly more than the value of the liquid assets of the company. Wertheimer finally settled for RM2.5 million plus profit sharing up to RM1.4 million before leaving for Great Britain. The company was renamed Ravensberger Seidenweberei GmbH and was marginally profitable for Unilever. The Werth family wanted back 50% of Ravensberger after the war. Unilever came back with an offer of 25% and settled with the family in 1949 for £20,000 and a debenture worth one million Deutschmarks.[112]

The last company Unilever acquired was Aluminium Foil Works D. Morgenstern, which it purchased in 1938 for 400,000 Reichsmarks, a fraction of the RM 1 million book value. To their credit, Unilever did come good on its investment in Morgenstern as it did with

> *The Keppler Kreis – or Keppler Circle – was an group of German industrialists who were intent on influencing economic policy in the Third Reich. Besides Kaselowsky, the group included Rudolf Bingel of Siemens, Karl Blessing who would later be chair of the Bundesbank, Karl Ritter von Halt of Deutsche Bank, Karl Lindemann, Emil Meyer and Karl Rasche of Dresdner Bank and Kurt Schmitt of Allianz, among others*

the Werth family. After the war, Unilever reached an agreement with Herr Morgenstern's widow and paid her an annuity in American dollars.

In 1939 at the behest of Reichsmarschall Göring, the company invested in frozen foods. As Unilever had the technology available through its Nordsee division, Göring wanted it expanded to include vegetables and fruit to supply the Wehrmacht. Just before the invasion of Poland, Solo Feinfrost began production with the Wehrmacht as its largest customer. By 1941, cigarette magnate Phillip Reemtsma decided he wanted Nordsee for himself and used his Nazi connections to acquire a 25 percent share of the company from Unilever. The Reich Secretary for Food and Agriculture complained bitterly about the acquisition and Reemtsma was forced to put his shares into the custody of the City of Hamburg.[113]

One company which freezes almost everything it sells now is Dr. Oetker. The good doctor was not a Nazi, having died in 1918, but some of his offspring were. Doctor August Oetker was born in 1862 and was a pharmacist by trade. In 1891 he founded his company and two years later came out with the product which would be a mainstay for well over a hundred years – single serving baking powder packets. As someone of German heritage, I grew up on my parents' Dr. Oetker cookbook, in which every recipe used the Oetker brand "Backin" or baking powder. A remarkable 96% of German consumers either know of, or have used the Oetker brand, a product dominance almost unequalled, save for McDonald's in the United States, Tim Horton's in Canada or Marks & Spencer in Great Britain.

As with all of these food companies, we must ask: how did a company which made baking powder get involved with the Nazis? How many cakes did the Luftwaffe need? It started when August died in 1918, two years after his only son Rudolf died at the Battle of Verdun. Rudolf's wife Ida was pregnant with their only son who was born six months after his father's death. After the end of World War I, Ida was a widow and single mother and not a businesswoman. Luckily, Richard Kaselowsky came to the rescue. Kaselowsky was a friend of her late husband and with Rudolf's uncle Louis, the two ran the company, starting in 1921. Kaselowsky and Ida married in 1919 and Ida's son Rudolf-August Oetker was raised by his mother and stepfather.

Louis and Richard built additional factories and diversified into other businesses in Germany, including sewing machines and phosphates. Louis Oetker died in 1931, leaving Richard Kaselowsky solely in charge. Kaselowsky was a devout Nazi, a member of the Keppler Kreis and was self-serving: "He was a Nazi by conviction, and interested in gaining a reputation and close contact with leading party officials," according to author Rudiger Jungbluth, who wrote the biography *Die Oetkers*.

Strange as it may seem, Dr. Oetker did contribute to the Nazi war effort by delivering pudding and baking powder to the troops during the war. At this point, many would say "big deal, baking powder and pudding don't kill people." I would tend to agree. Howitzers and machine guns do though. Remember that sewing machine manufacturer – it seems they switched production to howitzer grenades and parts for the MG 42 machine guns; and they were majority owned by Dr. Oetker. The company also used slave labor in its plants, much as every other major concern in the country did. "During World War II, no company was really clean," according to historian Joachim Scholtyseck "Everyone had to resort to slave labor when their own workers were fighting at the front." That even included adamant opponents of the regime like industrialist Robert Bosch.[114] Kaselowsky was either proud of Dr. Oetker's initiatives, or used it to his own advantage. One of the advertising snippets from the Second World War shows crates of baking powder lined up like soldiers with the words "Wehrmacht's Packung" emblazoned on them and underneath the tagline was: *Dr. Oetker Puddingpulver für die Wehrmacht* – **Dr. Oetker baking powder for the German Army.** Kaselowsky donated money to both the Nazi Party and the Keppler Kreis and kept on very good terms with the Nazis. Freundeskreis-Sekretär Fritz Kranefuß said of Kaselowsky: "Though he is not one of our old friends from the time before the seizure of power…he has extraordinarily proven himself" and that Kaselowsky "was always striving to participate in meetings"[115] of the Keppler Kreis. Kaselowsky was proud of his membership in the Keppler Kreis – he was the only member from a food company, surrounded by bankers and arms dealers.

While this was going on, young Rudolf-August had enrolled in the Waffen-SS officer training program and was very much influenced by his step-father.[116] After the war, Rudolf-August never spoke about his past to his children – they only found out from rumors at the Bielefeld riding club. It has been found out by researchers he volunteered for the Waffen-SS, if only to get an administrative job after the war and avoid frontline duty. His response to his children years after the fact was that he was a Nazi, but to leave him in peace.

Rudolf-August was ready to be stationed at the front when news came from home: his mother, stepfather and stepsisters had been killed in an Allied bombing raid. He was released from military service and sent home to run the family business. It is from here the business bloomed – the baking powder and pudding mixes were a start, to which Kaselowsky had added luxury hotels and a stake in Hamburg Süd Shipping. To this mix, Rudolf-August added a bank in 1949, the remaining stake in Hamburg Süd in 1955, Henkell Trocken champagne in 1958 as well as Radeberger Pilsner and OEDIV Oetker data and information processing. The Hamburg Süd is the largest division, taking in € 5.3 billion in 2013 and has 104 container ships plying the world's oceans, though to many, the Dr. Oetker brand today means frozen pizzas and lots of them.

4

How the world's banks stopped worrying and learned to love the Reichsmark

When we think of Nazi bankers today, the Swiss mainly come to mind. Turning a blind eye to the atrocities being committed around it, Switzerland was a haven for Nazi loot especially that confiscated from Jewish businesses, plundered lands, even the gold from the teeth of concentration camp casualties. There were many other banks around the world which helped the Third Reich on its way. The Swiss were Johnny-come-latelys on the war scene – their involvement didn't start until much later in the war. American banks, British banks and of course the German banks were involved in money-laundering schemes with the Third Reich as well as using money confiscated from Jewish families

The first two now form one of the largest banks in the world: Chase National Bank and J. P. Morgan and Co. Morgan was the banking agent responsible for the mergers that created General Electric, US Steel and International Harvester. In 1907 bailed out both the City of New York and the New York Stock Exchange and brought together the finances to build the Panama Canal. In September 1915, Morgan arranged a half-billion-dollar loan to the English and the French governments and was the purchasing agent of choice in the United States for the Allied Powers. The Allies purchased $3 billion worth of goods through Morgan during the war and this is what King George V had to say in a telegram to J. P. Morgan Jr.

> *I THANK YOU WITH ALL MY HEART FOR YOUR CONGRATULATIONS IN THE GLORIOUS VICTORY TO WHICH YOUR GREAT COUNTRY HAS SO MATERIALLY CONTRIBUTED. I KNOW HOW MUCH ALSO WE OWE TO YOUR OWN PERSONAL HELP*
>
> *-GEORGE R I*

In the 1920s, banks diversified into underwriting securities as well – two of the most prominent were Chase and Guaranty Trust.

Chase purchased five banks in the 1920s, including the Metropolitan Bank division of Metropolitan Life. Met Life was the largest single depositor at Chase in 1928, usually keeping around $20 million at the bank.[117] Chase opened its first branch in Europe in Berlin in 1928, then merged with The Equitable Trust Co. in 1930, acquiring the branches it had in Mexico, London, Shanghai, Hong Kong and Paris. That's a very brief history of Chase and J. P. Morgan before World War II.

Next is Guaranty Trust Co., which was established in 1864 and reorganized in 1894 as the Guaranty Trust Company of New York. The directors' list was a who's who of New York finance: Oliver Harriman, (grand uncle to Averell Harriman, Secretary of Commerce to Harry Truman), Frederick Vanderbilt, George Baker and J. Pierpont Morgan.[118] Baker is not widely known, but was one of the founders of the First National Bank as well as its largest stockholder; the third largest stockholder in the National Bank of Commerce, the largest stockholder in the Chase National, and the second largest in the Liberty National.[119] Guaranty merged with Morton Trust in 1911, adding Thomas Lamont to its board. Lamont was a partner at J.P. Morgan who would later secure a $100 million loan for Mussolini in 1926.

Guaranty merged with J.P. Morgan in 1959, which is why we bring the company into the conversation. Guaranty was not without controversy, underwriting a loan for $450,000 to purchase guns and ammunition for Pancho Villa during the Mexican Revolution, though this was dwarfed by the $3 million Chase National loaned. This might be a minor issue, had not the initial idea come from German spy Franz von Rintelen.

Rintelen was a banker by trade when World War I started, and German intelligence sent him to the still-neutral United States in 1915 to sabotage American ships carrying munitions and supplies to the Allies. Arriving in New York City, he posed as businessman Frederick Hansen and with Heinrich Albert set up a dummy corporation called Bridgeport Projectile Company. Through Bridgeport, he purchased gunpowder which he then destroyed. The goal was to create shortages of smokeless powder on the American market which was to prevent the Allies from purchasing munitions.[120] Rintelen joined a group of emissaries from Germany in 1915, which included:

- Ambassador Count Johann Heinrich von Bernstorff;
- Future chancellor Franz von Papen, superspy at large;
- The improbably named naval attaché Karl Boy-Ed;
- And someone who would have many future dealings with big business and the Third Reich, Heinrich Albert.

Franz von Papen and Boy-Ed established an espionage ring of epic proportions in the United States with two hopes: either get the United States into the war on the side of Germany, or blow them up so they couldn't enter with the Entente powers.

> *When von Papen was not roistering at Washington and New York night spots, he was busy in a "front" office at 60 Wall Street, in lower Manhattan, issuing false passports for German agents to England and France, and paying off a multitude of organizations and individuals spreading anti-Allied sentiment. There were many takers.*[121]

Heinrich Albert, meanwhile, was not the tactical master some may think. Albert was paymaster for the spy ring and committed a grievous error – in fact, the worst mistake a spy can make; he let his documents fall into enemy hands. In July, 1915 he left his offices with briefcase in hand and walked on to the Sixth Avenue subway. While he dozed, Frank Burke, a Secret Service agent who had been tailing him managed to abscond with the briefcase. Unbelievably, Albert placed an ad in the *New York Evening Telegram*:

> *Lost on Saturday. On 3:30 Harlem elevated train at 50th St. Station, Brown Leather Bag, Containing Documents. Deliver to G. H. Hoffman, 5 E. 47th St., Against $20 Reward.*[122]

James Bond he was not. Albert, von Papen and Boy-Ed were dispatched back to Germany. Count von Bernstorff now had two main agents, Wolf von Igel and von Rintelen. Rintelen liked to play both sides in Mexico. He negotiated both with Victoriano Huerta and supplied arms to Pancho Villa, hoping whichever side won would side with Germany and pre-emptively declare war on the United States. Huerta had staged a coup in Mexico in 1913 and though it was supported surreptitiously by U.S. Ambassador Henry Wilson, Huerta fell out of favor with U.S. President Woodrow Wilson due to his harshness. After losing in battle to Villa and finally resigning in 1914, Huerta traveled to New York to negotiate with von Rintelen about a possible return to power the following year. Again, not the tactical masters – the Secret Service knew about the meetings and had not only tapped von Rintelen's phone, but also followed Huerta. From von Rintelen:

I learned that Huerta was in the United States and made every effort to find where he was staying. He suddenly turned up in New York, and I went to his hotel, the Manhattan, to see him... I told him I was a German officer, mentioned the munition transports, and offered him my help there and then I expressed my readiness to do all I could to bring his party into power again in Mexico...Though I gave my reasons for visiting him, he was afraid of a trap and thought I might be an American agent...At last he believed me and was prepared to speak frankly...Huerta stipulated that I should procure the sanction of the German Government to the following conditions: German U-boats were to land weapons along the Mexican coast; abundant funds were to be provided for the purchase of armaments; and Germany should agree to furnish Mexico with moral support...

As I left the hotel I caught sight of two familiar faces. They were those of detectives who had frequently shadowed me in the past. I remained in the vicinity of the hotel until I saw Huerta come out, followed by two men, who were apparently guarding him. I went after them in order to make sure. Huerta entered a car, and the two detectives stopped a taxi and followed. There was no longer room for doubt that our interview had been observed...I was still waiting for the answer from Berlin which was to sanction my conspiracy with Huerta. It arrived eventually...Later I heard that Huerta had been poisoned by his cook in a country house on the Mexican border[123]

Throughout this, von Rintelen was also funding Huerta's foe Pancho Villa, securing $380,000 and paying through a network which included Guaranty Trust.[124][125] Guaranty was obviously a patriot company, funding a revolution against a Mexican despot who wanted war with the Americans so they could take back Texas, New Mexico and Arizona. That would be quite a stretch, especially after a coded telegram from German Foreign Secretary Arthur Zimmerman to Germany's ambassador to Mexico. It read (italics are my doing):

We intend to begin on the first of February unrestricted submarine warfare. We shall endeavor in spite of this to keep the United States of America neutral. In the event of this not succeeding, ***we make Mexico a proposal of alliance on the following basis: make war together, make peace together, generous financial support and an understanding on our part that Mexico is to reconquer the lost territory in Texas, New Mexico, and Arizona.*** The settlement in detail is left to you ... Signed, ZIMMERMANN[126]

The now infamous Zimmerman Telegram was deciphered by the British and handed over to the Americans. The American press had a field day with it, public opinion turned dramatically against the Germans and the United States Congress declared war six weeks later. Mexico stayed neutral for the balance of the war.

Was this all Guaranty did during the First World War? Not at all. Guaranty Trust was also involved in a scheme to fund the Russian government during World War I before the United States entered the war. This was a direct violation of American neutrality policy as well as international law, though that didn't seem to bother either Guaranty or the American ambassador to Russia. David Francis served as ambassador in 1916 and 1917, and through him a number of telegrams were transmitted using official government cipher, to be delivered to Guaranty Trust. One of these telegrams details the involvement of Olof Aschberg, head of the Stockholm bank Nya Banken, Rolph Marsh of Guaranty Trust and Samuel MacRoberts of National City Bank, who were together in Petrograd in 1916 to negotiate a deal. When Secretary of State Robert Lansing caught wind of this, his response was unequivocal:

Before delivering messages to Vanderlip and Guaranty Trust Company, I must inquire whether they refer to Russian Government loans of any description. If they do, I regret that the Department can not be a party to their transmission, as such action would submit it to justifiable criticism because of participation by this Government in loan transaction by a belligerent for the purpose of carrying on its hostile operations. Such participation is contrary to the accepted rule of international law that neutral Governments should not lend their assistance to the raising of war loans by belligerents.[127]

In other words, no money for the Russians. However, it could be a very profitable venture. In a circular published by *The International Monthly, Inc.* in 1916, brazenly entitled *The Imperial Russian Finances: Certain Important Points which the Guaranty Trust Company Neglected to Tell Prospective Investors in Russian Securities and Enterprises* the authors point out that Guaranty, in a syndicate with J. P. Morgan and others have closed a loan of $50 million to the Russian Imperial government. The circular also goes on to list certain anecdotes about the trustworthiness of the Russians, specifically the disappearance of 17 million bags of flour destined for Tarnopol; and the construction of a battleship which was paid for by the government, purportedly christened by the provincial governor and subsequently sunk a month later – the battleship was a fiction, the graft not so much.[128]

Whether this is true or not, one thing is certain – Guaranty, along with a syndicate including J.P. Morgan, Chase and many others organized loans for the Allied powers in World War I. Was this wrong? From our view of history, not at all. But for a truly legal standpoint, as Secretary of State Lansing pointed out, the United States was neutral – there was no playing sides in the war, even if we greatly sympathized with one group over another. Again, it would be interesting if Germany and Austria-Hungary had won the First World War, how differently people would look on this.

J. P. Morgan was the preeminent institution during World War I, bar none. Its ability to raise capital and secure financing was far and above even the Bank of England. In August 1914, mere days after the beginning of hostilities and around the same time Germany struck at France, the BoE appointed J. P Morgan as their financial agent and asked about a $100 million loan. The United States government denied the request, then backtracked two months later in hopes of both staving off a recession in the United States and German aggression. Morgan acted as an agency for purchases in World War I to stop war profiteering – Allied governments were competing against each other to purchase armaments in the United States and middlemen were jacking up the prices. Morgan was approached by the British government in hopes of stopping the practice. With the blessing of the Wilson administration, Morgan placed Edward Reilly Stettinius, formerly president of the Diamond Match Company in charge of this new Export Department.

Lord Horatio Kitchener, the British Secretary of State for War, foresaw a long war but only assumed purchases through the Export Department to amount to £10 million – about US$50 million. By the end of the war, the total purchases were in excess of £600 million. One percent of the total purchases went to J. P. Morgan as commission, $28.2 million or just under $500 million 2016 dollars.[129] Stettinius negotiated with every facet of American business, always aggressively sourcing out items as varied as corned beef, barbed wire, locomotives and artificial limbs, spending in excess of $10 million a day. Manufacturers flocked to the Morgan office on Wall Street in an effort to put their business in front of all others. When production did not match demand, Stettinius had Morgan and the British government make loans to companies such as Winchester Repeating Arms to build new factories. Stettinius himself was the object of death threats and spent most of the war on the *USS Margaret* moored in New York harbor.[130]

Jack Morgan was quoted as saying on July 31, 1914: "If the delicate situation can be held in abeyance for a few weeks, I should expect a rising tide of protest from the people who are to pay for war with their blood and property."[131] It was, after all, bad for business to be destroying this much of Europe. This earned J. P. Morgan the reputation as a war profiteer, a moniker it didn't deserve. In September 1915, Morgan underwrote a loan which was monstrously large at the time - $500 million – for use by the British and French governments to pay for more munitions and other wartime goods. The final tally for Morgan-negotiated loans was $1.5 billion – just under $24 billion in 2016 dollars.

Fast forward to the early 1920s. As we know, in Germany hyperinflation was sending the country into chaos, but J. P. Morgan was central to a plan to save it. By January 1923, Germany defaulted on its reparation payments and the French and the Belgian armies moved in and occupied the industrial Ruhr valley. The German government backed a plan for passive resistance and the situation worsened. In the United States, there was little interest in collecting war reparations, but there was a lot of interest in collecting outstanding loans to the Allies, a large portion of which J. P. Morgan had initially negotiated.

The Americans requested Chicago banker Charles Dawes look at the payment plan. Dawes came up with the eponymous Dawes Plan, which suggested lengthening the term of German payments and reducing the amount until such time as the German economy got back on its feet. The Dawes Plan effectively put Germany into receivership; the country was for mortgaged to the Allies and its railways and the Reichsbank were effectively put in foreign control.[132] Bank of England Governor Montagu Norman wanted to diffuse the situation and asked Jack Morgan, Tom Lamont and Hjalmar Schacht to come to London. Of floating the huge loans to Germany, Norman said: "It can only be accomplished, if at all, through the Bank of England and in New York, J. P. Morgan & Co."[133] An emergency $200 million loan was made to the German government, of which $110 million was underwritten by J. P. Morgan. Dawes won the Nobel Peace Prize in 1925 for his efforts, Morgan swallowed a substantial commission and the Dawes Plan failed as the terms were almost as unsupportable as the original treaty. There was upside to the Dawes Plan, even with its crippling repayment structure; unemployment plunged in Germany and American capital and companies streamed into the country to open up shop. These included Ford Motor Company, General Motors, DuPont, General Electric, Standard Oil of New Jersey and Dow Chemical.[134]

The upside was not so rosy to most in the financial industry. Russell Leffingwell, a partner at J. P. Morgan, had this to say about reparations in the mid-1920s: "My doubt about Germany is how long her people will consent to be seated for the benefit of her former enemies."[135] Norman and Chancellor of the Exchequer Philip Snowden agreed with Leffingwell's assessment. A new committee was chaired in 1928 by General Electric head Owen Young and also included Jack

Morgan and Morgan partner Tom Lamont. There were many rocks placed on the road to recovery and Young's plan was doomed as well. The French were obstinately opposed to lower reparations; France had paid reparations to Germany when they lost wars in 1819 and 1871 and now they wanted theirs in turn. Lamont suggested a new reparation amount of $40 billion; France still wanted $200 billion and Great Britain $120 billion. The reparations committee set as a final amount $32 billion, to be paid over 59 years – ending in 1988. Not one party to the plan, whether the United States, Great Britain, France, or even Germany, was happy with the result.[136] Reichsbank president Hjalmar Schacht, though an original signatory of the Young Plan, believed the reparations were still unsupportable and resigned his position in 1930 in protest. Two years later, he sided with the Nazi Party and prodded Deutsche Bank and Dresdner Bank to lend financial support to the government.

Lamont always felt, even throughout World War II, the Treaty of Versailles "was more than just to Germany and less than just to the Allies."[137] The European nations finally gave up on reparation payments from Germany in 1932 and the United States gave up on collecting their loans by 1934, as every country but Finland had defaulted.[138] In June 1933, Schacht officially announced a moratorium on long-term overseas debt repayments, causing investors to panic. Tom Lamont reminded Schacht that J. P. Morgan & Co. had supplied half of the money for the Dawes Plan and a third for the Young Plan.[139] Though surely Lamont was trying to sound magnanimous, the manoeuver backfired and the Americans were put towards the bottom of the repayment list, caused by the very dislike towards the two plans the Germans harbored. In other words, don't remind me about all the money I owe you.

Jack Morgan, though he virulently disliked the Hun, did have this to say about Hitler in 1933: "I should feel myself that we are all going to get along pretty well. Except for this attitude towards the Jews, which I consider wholesome, the new Dictator of Germany seems to me very much like the old Kaiser."[140] Morgan was anti-Semitic – of this there is no doubt. He used his position as an overseer at Harvard University to advise the president of the university to not fill a board position with either a Jew or a Catholic, as neither could be trusted to put the interests of the country ahead of their religions.[141]

Though the Young Plan failed, one of its members profited handsomely – Jack Morgan was not only on the Young Committee, his bank also underwrote the second set of loans to Germany, this time worth $100 million. But this was all history, and now we must move forward the the Second World War.

Meanwhile, in Paris…

The Guaranty offices in Paris were requisitioned for German military use during World War II, though this wasn't the first time Guaranty would figure in the war. As with Chase, J. P. Morgan, the Bank of the City of New York and American Express, Guaranty was implicated in freely handing over lists of Jewish clients *before* the Nazis requested them. Whereas 75,000 Jews were expelled from France and only 7,000 returned alive, Guaranty fared better; it "reopened its prewar quarters at 4 Place de la Concorde in the historic Hotel de Coislin, adjoining the American Embassy and fronting on the famous square"[142] in March 1945.

A French government commission, investigating the seizure of Jewish bank accounts during the Second World War, says the five American banks had moved quickly. It says their Paris branches handed over to the Nazi occupiers about 100 such accounts. Commission member Claire Andrieu said at the time, "the United States was not at war with Germany, and the American banks could have behaved differently."[143]

Chase Manhattan had branches in Paris when the Nazis rolled in and was particularly optimistic with the Nazi occupation. In a letter sent to the vice president of Chase in May 1942, Paris branch manager Carlos Niedermann gushed about their good relations with the Nazis. He urged that Chase continue doing business with the Third Reich and Niedermann would identify future business opportunities. These included making loans to German industries which were assisting the Nazi war effort. A U.S. Treasury report implicated Chase head office in New York of forward knowledge of Niedermann's doings, yet did nothing to stop him.[144] Chase *did* chose to freeze the assets of Jewish customers, anticipating the Nazis would want the money. By June of

1942, Niedermann was pulling the records of all Chase branches in France back to the main Paris branch and collating the data. In exchange for this help, the Nazis "donated" 15 million francs to Chase to offset the costs of this exhaustive gathering of information[145] as well as Chase being the bank of the German embassy in Paris. Albert Bertrand, who headed up Chase's branches in Vichy France, documented the actions of himself and Niedermann in a letter to Chase's vice-president for Europe, Joseph Larkin. With Larkin's consent, Bertrand transferred large amounts of Jewish cash and securities from the occupied state back to Germany.

From Chase to J.P Morgan: to endear itself to local Nazi officials, it boasted of anti-Semitic hiring practices and that none of the partners in New York were Jewish. The Nazis loved this, and designated J.P. Morgan an international Aryan organization.[146] Like Chase National, J. P. Morgan turned over the funds of Jewish clients to the Nazi government. Chase and J.P. Morgan denied any knowledge of the day-to-day operations at the Paris branches. To do so would have been in violation of the *Trading with the Enemy Act* – in effect corporate treason. Chase claimed only three Jewish bank accounts had been confiscated and eleven safety deposit boxes, which they found by an internal review. Morgan et Compagnie, as the French division was known, did manage to operate successfully in the Vichy regime, virtually unmolested. This was partly due to its close relationships with the French government before the war, acting as an agent for international loan agreements as well as its close ties with the Banque de France. The shroud of a coming war was known to the Morgan banks well before the invasion of France in 1940; it bought a rundown hotel southeast of Nantes, put safes in the basement and shipped out securities in the weeks before the Nazis entered Paris.

There was always a deep-seated thought Morgan & Cie. collaborated with the Vichy regime and with the Nazis. Mainly, this came from the ease with which the business ran throughout the war. But perhaps the more telling reason was its clientele. The leader of the Vichy government – the aged and highly decorated Marshal Petain – was a client of Morgan, and allowed the bank to act in a larger sphere of influence that was unavailable to other foreign banks. This was not to be carte blanche for the bank though – there were times even the Marshal could not protect them.

After the Nazis declared war on the United States in 1941, the company was branded an enemy and a Nazi overseer was placed in charge. The overseer insisted Morgan & Cie. accept accounts from Nazi banks and businesses. Maurice Pesson-Didion – who with Louis Tuteleers headed the bank's operations before the invasion – refused, saying they were instructed by Morgan in New York not to accept *any* new accounts and if they were forced into it, they would have to liquidate the bank.[147] This put off the overseer, but did not stop the Nazis from emptying Jewish accounts and safe deposit boxes. There were other times Morgan was not protected by Petain, the most notable was in 1944 when an SS officer strode into the bank and demanded the deposits of a certain client. When Tuteleers refused, the SS officer shoved a gun in his back and marched him to SS headquarters in the city telling him to either give up the money or go to a prison camp. He was released after a few hours when an $8,000 ransom was paid.[148]

And back in the USA...

Chase was not only engaging in less than stellar activities in Paris – it was also practicing dubious transactions at home. The Nazis used agents to purchase American dollars using Rückwanderer Marks – Rückwanderer literally means returning citizen – which could be sold by U.S. citizens of German descent. The scheme was to get hard currency the Germans could use to purchase items abroad where the Reichsmark was not particularly welcome. The United States National Archives, which is usually quite impartial, was very blunt:

It has been known since the war years that the Nazi government built dollar exchange in the United States until the June 14, 1941 Executive Order freezing German assets. The Germans sold special German Marks—known as Rueckwanderer [returnee] Marks—to U.S. residents of German descent. It has also been known that Chase National Bank (now J.P. Morgan Chase) was involved in these transactions. Newly declassified FBI records offer a far more detailed picture than ever before. Thanks to FBI sources within Chase National and the other businesses involved as well as documents subpoenaed for a Grand Jury investigation launched in August 1941, the Bureau was able to follow a money trail.

While the scheme to build dollar exchange for Germany through the sale of Rueckwanderer Marks originated with Germany, U.S. financial institutions were clearly implicated. They helped the Germans raise over $20 million between 1936 and 1941, and in return earned over $1.2 million in commissions. The financial houses understood that the German government paid the commissions through the sale of discounted, blocked Marks that came mainly from Jews who had fled Germany. In fact, these financial houses, especially Chase, were most eager to increase the scope of their business after the Nazi anti-Jewish pogrom known as Kristallnacht in November 1938, when Jewish emigration from Germany reached its height.

Using confidential sources with Chase National Bank, the FBI began to investigate the scheme in October 1940. This was more than four years after the scheme had begun, and the FBI's aim was to compile lists for further surveillance of German-Americans who had purchased blocked Marks. The sale of blocked Marks thus continued for nine months after the FBI investigation began, and the business was at its heaviest during that time. Chase National executives avoided federal prosecution for violations of the Johnson Debt Act of 1939, the Espionage Act of 1917, and the Foreign Agents Act of 1938 when Chase's lead lawyer, a former U.S. attorney from the same district office that had conducted the Grand Jury investigation, threatened to reveal FBI, Army, and Navy sources and methods in open court.[149]

Of the five permit holder banks which were allowed to exchange Rückwanderers, Chase held the lion's share – almost $9 million worth, the next closest was the Nazi front Robert C. Mayer Co., which processed $4.4 million.[150] The FBI was very interested in the Rückwanderer scheme, but since they could not prosecute Chase directly, J. Edgar Hoover wanted to know who was acting as agents in the United States. Up to 1943, the FBI had rounded up 5,977 Germans. "Some who have been taken into custody frankly admitted they would welcome an opportunity to fight against the United States," Director Hoover said. "It was necessary the FBI know the identity of such persons so that the proper steps could be taken to prevent them from committing acts detrimental to the security of the United States." According to the FBI at the time, of the 923 individuals who were purchasing Rückwanderer Marks, 433 were working in the manufacture of materials necessary for the war effort. Of these, 46 were fired by either the Secretary of War or the Secretary of the Navy. FBI investigators found that some of these purchasers were "violently pro-Nazi" and if given the chance, would fight for the Fatherland against the United States.[151]

One of these men was Heinrich Claus, who purchased $5,000 worth of Rückwanderer Mark from Hautz & Co. through Chase National. Claus was a foreman at Brewster Aeronautical, which made among others, the Brewster F2A Buffalo fighter. Chase officials chose not to connect the dots, though the FBI had.

Chase National's chairman Winthrop Aldrich, laid the blame squarely at the doorstep of the federal government. *"It is difficult, in the absence of action by the United States government to control assets owned by German, Italian and Japanese nationals."*[152] In other words, if we conduct our business in a treasonous manner, we need it in writing, please. Chase received it in writing in August of 1941 when they were subpoenaed by a grand jury investigating the Rückwanderer purchases. There was also consideration at the time to charge Chase management with violations of the *Espionage Act* and the *Conspiracy Act*. J. Edgar Hoover looked forward to the case being prosecuted claiming the amount of man hours spent was considerable. Hoover's wishes did not come to fruition in 1941, though the case was looked at again in 1944. The New York field office of the FBI went to the US Attorney's office and opined the case would be difficult to win. Hoover was livid – field agents do not get to decide who to prosecute. The agents had found out the lead attorney for Chase National was the former U.S. Attorney from the New York district where the grand jury was going to take place. Chase already knew how to win the case before the file folder was even open. The prosecution went back to Washington with its tail between its legs and the case died.

The "link" between the Nazis and George Bush

Brown Brothers Harriman is over 200 years old and as an investment house, has employed partners who have become: two Governors of the Bank of England, the governor of New York, and Senator Prescott Bush, father of George H.W. Bush and grandfather to George W. Bush.

Prescott Bush was the son of Samuel and Flora Bush. Sam was the president of Buckeye Steel, which manufactured gun barrels and railway parts and among its customers were Ned Harriman's Union and South Pacific railroad. Prescott graduated from Yale in 1917 and served in the American Expeditionary Force in World War I. After the war, Prescott started out small, working as a hardware clerk in St. Louis, but his connection to the Harriman family proved invaluable, when Ned's son Averell introduced Prescott to his partner George Herbert Walker. Later in 1919, George introduced Prescott to his daughter Dorothy. They married in 1921 and had five children, their second oldest being the future president George Bush Sr.

George Walker and Averell agreed to make Prescott vice-president of W. A. Harriman and Co. in 1926. Harriman had extensive business interests in Germany and the Soviet Union including negotiating manganese mining rights with Leon Trotsky; setting up the Hamburg-Amerika line and helping the Thyssen and Flick families set up both *Vereinigte Stahlwerke* and a Harriman-Thyssen joint venture called Union Banking Corporation. Remember, it was still the 1920s and both Thyssen and Flick were engaged in purely capitalist business interests and there was no real Nazi party yet. At the time, the Silesian coal fields were held by Poland as part of the reparations paid by Germany. Poland had the right to expropriate German property up to 1938, so it was next to impossible to develop any mines in the area. The idea was that a neutral third party could facilitate the problem; this is where W. A. Harriman comes in.

Harriman and Anaconda Copper – a Rockefeller company – contacted the Giesche Corporation who was seriously in debt. Giesche was the largest zinc producer and one of the largest coal producers in Poland, and it was owned by the German company *Bergwerksgesellschaft Georg von Giesches Erben*. The company was turned into Silesian Holdings, which was jointly owned by Anaconda and Harriman. Prescott became a director of Consolidated Silesian Steel and was brought in to specifically look after Thyssen and Flick. Harriman also acquired interests in *Vereinigte König und Laurahütte AG* and *Bismarckhütte*, both steel concerns. Consolidated Silesian Steel was formed in 1929 as an umbrella corporation for the steel companies and only Americans sat on its board, including Bush and Harriman.[153]

Union Banking Corporation was incorporated in 1924 and its shares were held by the *Bank voor Handel en Scheepvaardt N.V* a Dutch bank which was a subsidiary of the August Thyssen Bank of Germany. Of the 4,000 shares issued, *Bank voor Handel* owned all shares and they were registered to the seven American directors; Union chairman Roland Harriman – Averell's brother – held 3,991; Prescott Bush held one. The bank was closely affiliated with *Vereinigte Stahlwerke* according to an Oct. 5, 1942 report from the federal Office of Alien Property Custodian.[154] When Union Banking Corp. (UBC) was set up, this was not a big concern – Germany was emerging from the morass created by the Treaty of Versailles. Even when Germany invaded Poland, the American stance of neutrality meant BBH could probably press the boundaries. It's after December 11, 1941, when Hitler reluctantly declared war on the United States that it presented a problem. Unfortunately, Union Banking continued their business.

The problems with Union are many: ownership is nebulous, even to its own president. In a letter sent to John Pehle, the Assistant to the Secretary of the Treasury, it states UBC's president Cornelis Lievense did not know who owns *Bank voor Handel* "but believes it's possible that Baron Heinrich Thyssen, brother of Fritz Thyssen, may own a substantial interest."[155] An investigation at the time showed no wrongdoing by UBC, even making mention of a transfer of $3 million from a safe deposit box at UBC to the firm's account at BBH. The transaction was suitably accounted for, according to the investigation. Union Banking was seized by the United States government in 1942 for violations of the *Trading with the Enemy Act*.

Were Averell Harriman and Prescott Bush aware of the slave labor, the atrocities, the murder and exterminations? It's highly doubtful. They would have sat in their toney, wood-panelled offices in New York, blissfully unaware of what was happening; only collecting commissions and fees. Were they guilty of violations of the *Trading with the Enemy Act*? Most assuredly they were. Even their erstwhile partner Fritz Thyssen, though he initially supported the Nazis, broke ranks in 1938 when the persecution of Catholics and Jews became too much for him. He was arrested in France in 1941 and he and his wife were incarcerated first in Sachsenhausen and later in Dachau from 1943 until the end of the war. Thyssen paid for his values; it seems Harriman and Bush had none.

The Vichy Bankers

December 17, 1997: the lawyers for six French, two American and one English bank filed into a Brooklyn courtroom to begin a case with ramifications that would be felt throughout the European banking industry. In *Bodner v. Banque Paribas et al*, it was claimed the banks –

- Paribas,
- Credit Lyonnais,
- Societé Generale,
- Credit Agricole,
- Credit Agricole Indosuez,
- Banque Française du Commerce Extérieur,
- Barclays Bank,
- J.P. Morgan and
- Chase Manhattan

had looted "cash, records, art, jewelry, bank deposit…allegedly wrongfully taken and withheld from them and their families by …Defendant Banks during the German occupation in France, and by the Vichy government"[156] For over three years, negotiations and legal wrangling would take place with the class action lawyers, bank lawyers, American and French diplomats and American jurists.

It was a fluke meeting at a cocktail party between a Holocaust survivor and a lawyer which began the proceedings. The question was asked of the lawyer, in light of the cases pending against Swiss bankers, could the French banks be sued as well.[157] Class-action lawyer Ken McCallion, professor Richard Weisberg and Harriet Tamen, a former attorney for Citibank, Credit Lyonnais and Chase Manhattan were all brought in for the plaintiffs. Initially, it was thought the judge would dismiss the case, as his predecessors had in the past. Judge Sterling Johnson had a differing opinion from his peers though, and it came from one tidbit of evidence: the French Bank Association asked its members for lists of their Jewish account holders *before* their assets were frozen. This implied to Judge Johnson the Nazis and the French banks were conspiring together to steal assets from their Jewish clients.

It was determined all banks listed had agreed to the request from the bank association and had knowingly frozen, then transferred account balances, safe deposit box contents, investments and other items to the hands of the Vichy government, who forwarded the majority on to their Nazi overlords. It was not a minute number either – estimates average near 80,000 accounts held by 64,000 people. The Vichy government imposed the Aryanisation laws on the country swiftly and ruthlessly, confiscating Jewish art collections, residences and businesses, as well as what the banks forwarded. A total of at least 6.5 billion francs worth of property was taken by the Vichy government, plus another 7.2 billion francs taken from the 80,000 accounts (inflation adjusted $5.9 billion was confiscated).

From the fall of France in 1940 until his dismissal in May 1942, the Commissioner-General for Jewish Questions was Xavier Vallat. Though he was virulently anti-Semitic and wholeheartedly robbed French Jews of their possessions, Vallat would not submit to the Nazis more extreme measures, including deportation (which of course inevitably led to extermination).[158] His successor, Louis Darquier de Pellepoix, promoted extermination of the Jews and was instrumental in the deportation of 70,000 Jews to death camps. Vallat served two years in jail for his crimes, de Pellepoix was reportedly executed in 1945, but it was determined he fled to Spain and was protected by the government of Francisco Franco until his death in 1980.

In 1995 the French government of Jacques Chirac took responsibility for the actions of the Vichy regime. Chirac called for a commission to be set up to investigate and to right the wrongs of the Second World War. The commission, called *The Study Mission on the Spoliation of Jews in France*, was set up in 1997 and was headed by Jean Mattéoli, a French resistance fighter in World War II and also former government minister. Mattéoli was specifically chosen because he was not Jewish and as a former member of the resistance, could not be tied to the Vichy regime. The commission studied until the spring of 2000, when it released its results. According to the report, the spoliation of Jews in France affected at least 300,000 people and included:

- the liquidation of industries, companies and workshops
- the sale of securities deposited in financial institutions
- the deductions from bank accounts to pay the 1-billion franc fine levied by the Nazis
- theft of money and property from internees at French concentration camps.[159]

The French government has made attempts in the past to return stolen items. Starting in November 1944, the Artistic Recovery Commission began seeking out and returning pillaged works of art. In 1948, the government took responsibility to pay back the one-billion franc fine to those who paid it. The commission claimed 92% of the account balances taken had been restored to the banks, but no evidence of how much to their legal owners or heirs. The French government appointed Jacques Andreani ambassador-at-large for Holocaust issues and it was with him that the class action lawyers, the lawyers for the defendant banks and U.S. Deputy Secretary of the Treasury Stuart Eizenstat met in 2000 to discuss reparations.

Eizenstat was President Clinton's Secretary of State on Holocaust-Era Issues. He had already negotiated reparations with the Swiss and Germans and was finishing negotiations with the Austrians when the French approached him. A precedent had been set when J.P. Morgan had settled for $2.75 million and Barclays for $3.6 million so the plaintiff's lawyers had the upper hand in discussions and some were playing harDeutscheall. Harriet Tamen wanted $1 billion, though the other class action lawyers were more compromising. When the dust settled, everyone agreed to a $50 million revolving escrow fund for claims with proof and a $22.5 million fund for what they termed a "rough justice" fund or monies for people who, in good faith, believed their relatives had funds at the banks in question but no proof. There was a $3,000 ceiling payment for those claims.[160]

Were the French banks making profits from the Nazis? Not really. They conducted their business as they saw fit and followed the letter of the law – Vichy collaborationist law that is – when it served them. Mattéoli pointed out in 1942 "in the Southern zone, banks displayed little zeal when it came to meeting the demands of provisional company administrators. The following year, the 5% levy, particularly in the Southern zone, did not elicit a great deal of enthusiasm from the banking establishments." By 1944, resistance had seeped into the banking establishments and when required to hand over Jewish assets to the Nazis, "the Ministry of Finance and the professional Banking Association used delaying tactics requiring the most meticulous formalism."[161] Bureaucracy was a term invented by the French in the 1830s so it seems appropriate they would take bureaucracy to its highest level now.

The French banks only seemed to profit from day-to-day operations, not necessarily with dealings with the Nazis. The only French banking organization which engaged in spoliation was the Caisse des Dépôts et Consignations, which is a state-run agency. On the other hand, Barclays took an active role in collaboration with the Vichy regime according to allegations printed in the British newspaper *The Guardian*. The 325-year-old British bank enlisted as its French manager Marcel Cheradame, who "'volunteered' information about its Jewish employees to the Nazis and helped to arrange finance for projects to sustain Hitler's war machine."[162] One of these projects was the funding of a lime quarry which was expropriated from the de Wendel family by the Nazis. The Germans wanted the quarry to increase capacity of the lime, which was then sent to a steel foundry owned by Reichswerke Hermann Göring. "The U.S. investigators concluded: 'It is apparent from the letters that Cheradame saw no harm in being a party to a project, the aim of which was to lend British funds to a French enterprise for the purpose of making increased production for the German war machine.'"[163]

Barclays has asserted when war broke out, all British citizens employed by the bank left for Great Britain and when the Nazis invaded France, the banks northern French branches were closed and left for the south of the country. Clients withdrew their assets from Barclays, though the Bank of France blocked Barclays French accounts twice, once as a retaliatory measure for Great Britain blocking French assets under their *Trading with the Enemy Act*. It was at this point the bank fell under the control of Marcel Cheradame. Cheradame reopened the bank's operations in August of 1940 after assuring the Germans that no British staff was employed there. Cheradame sought guidance from Barclays in the U.K., but the telegram back was unequivocal: *We cannot advise you*. Barclays in Great Britain was cut off from Barclays France until the end of the occupation in 1944.[164]

Barclays has stood behind its managers, stating control was held by two Nazi-appointed commissars and Cheradame and others were forced to act as a depository for enemy assets frozen and confiscated by the Germans. The bank also received a large cash deposit from the Drancy transit camp in a north-east suburb of Paris, from which French Jews were sent across the border to die in concentration camps. The money was plundered from the Jewish prisoners bound for Auschwitz. When the allegations came out in 1997 and Barclays was named as a defendant in the class action suit, the bank sought to investigate the issue on its own.

Codenamed "lumiere" because they wanted to shed light on the dark years of the war, they commissioned constitutional lawyer Floyd Abrams of Cahill Gordon & Reindel to investigate. Barclays employed Abrams and his firm for almost two years. They found most documents were either missing or destroyed, some by malicious forethought, others by wartime destruction. Many items would not have been archived for the fifty years since the war since French law stipulates general banking records need only be kept for ten years. They did, however, find 650 boxes of archived data at both the Paris headquarters and at two external archives. Abrams' team also interviewed past and present Barclays France employees to glean whatever information they could. This led the team to look through archives in London and New York as well and to both the Jewish Contemporary Document Centre in Paris and the French national archives in the city.

The group widened their scope, also looking into the archives of the Caisse des Dépôts et Consignations, the French Ministry of Foreign Affairs, the Prefecture of Police, the Bank of France, the French Bankers' Association, the Paris Stock Exchange and the French National Library.[165] When French research was exhausted, they went abroad, searching the German National Archives as well as those at the Bundesbank, the German Foreign Office, the US National Archives, the New York Public Library, the Bank of England and the British Foreign Office. What the researchers found was not particularly startling, though it does show they were following the Vichy regime's laws. Jewish account holders were catalogued and were allowed to withdraw from their accounts no more than 15,000 francs a month for a living allowance, the equivalent of $4,600 in 2016. Barclays complied with these measures, although the research by Abrams group showed Barclays would often give the accountholders more.

When the billion-franc fine was imposed in 1941, Barclays and the other banks were ordered to deduct 50% of all Jewish bank accounts with a balance of 10,000 francs – or £57 – to pay the fine. Barclays claims only seven of their Jewish clients had monies deducted and these were less than the 50% rule stipulated. When the Germans came to empty out the safe deposit boxes of the Jewish clients, Barclays managers documented their protests. At the start of the war, Barclays had deposits on hand of around 900 million francs, of which just under 40 million francs belonged to the 350 Jewish customers Barclays believed they had. More than 37 million francs were returned to account holders after the war, either by the bank itself or by the French government's restitution efforts, with only 2.1 million francs worth of assets unaccounted for, or about $236,000 in 2016. Barclays maintains it holds no funds of Holocaust victims today, though they have contributed $3.6 million to a claims fund.[166] Kenneth McCallion, one of the class action lawyers in the case, lauded Barclays for their forthrightness. "Instead of moving to dismiss the case, Barclays engaged in a serious and extensive effort designed to shed light on the activities of its bank."[167] At the same time, Chase Manhattan acknowledged it had about 100 accounts which had been seized according to Nazi dictates.

The Swiss

Many banks in Switzerland took an active role in the Nazi war machine. Perhaps the most culpable was the Swiss National Bank. From 1940 until 1945, it acted as a clearing house for the Reichsbank's gold, swapping out over 1.6 billion in Swiss francs for the Third Reich – the equivalent of over $4.9 billion in 2016. This was sent to various groups, including the central banks of Portugal, Sweden, Romania, Slovakia and Spain. As well, commercial institutions laundered over 1.7 million ounces of German gold, including Swiss Bank Corp., Bank Leu & Co., Union Bank of Switzerland, Basler Handelsbank, Credit Suisse and Eidgenössische Bank.[168]

In 1939, there were 363 banks in Switzerland of varying sizes. The largest were Swiss Bank Corp., Credit Suisse, Swiss Volksbank, UBS, Leu & Co. AG and Basler.[169] Basler was purchased by Swiss Bank Corp. in 1945; Eidgenössische Bank also didn't survive the end of the war and was purchased by UBS in 1945. Leu was founded in 1758 and was one of the oldest banks in Switzerland, though two insider trading scandals in the 1980s cost it its reputation and it was acquired by Credit Suisse in 1990. Swiss Volksbank was established in 1869 to "provide financial services for the small saver;"[170] it merged with Credit Suisse in 1993. UBS traces its roots to 1747 with Bank Ragazzi and subsequently is a compilation of over 300 different institutions. An overview:

Individual gold bars were particularly well documented by the Reichsbank and this allowed for an in-depth forensic audit to be done. Bars which came from the National Bank of Belgium, for example, were easily identifiable, as were ones tagged "Melmer." Melmer was SS Hauptsturmführer Bruno Melmer and the ones he delivered were made from contraband coins, jewelry and dental fillings extracted from concentration camp casualties. Melmer delivered just over 3,800 ounces of gold to the Swiss National Bank, though this is minor compared to the over 77,000 ounces of Melmer gold sold through Deutsche Bank and Dresdner Bank.[171] The report commissioned by the Swiss government claims this is the surest evidence linking Swiss authorities with the proceeds of the Holocaust. At the time, the Swiss National Bank could not deny knowledge – it was even being printed in Swiss newspapers. The *Neue Zürcher Zeitung* published a report ***in 1942*** stating the gold had been stolen, though the SNB denied knowing this, saying it was second-hand reports and hearsay until the Allies advised the Swiss government of the possibility in January of 1943.

SNB was not the only bank responsible – the Central Bank of France also played a key role in turning over gold looted. The Bank of France acted as the emergency depository for the Central Bank of Belgium – in good faith. Pierre-Eugène Fournier, the French bank governor, refused to release the gold to the Nazis, so the Vichy government fired him. His replacement, Yves de Boisanger, was only too willing to help his German and Vichy collaborationist overlords, and sent the gold to Berlin, where the Prussian mint re-smelted it and sent it to Switzerland.[172] Even though the Allies had warned Switzerland about the gold being looted from the occupied countries, the SNB didn't seem worried – they were even able to justify it during meetings. Eight months after the Allied warning, SNB Director General Paul Rossy stated in a meeting the bank had *not* been informed Germans had looted any gold, and even if they did, international law permitted the authorities of occupying powers to seize gold reserves.

With the cautions spelled out in both Swiss newspapers and by the Allies, it seems unlikely the SNB was exercising good judgment – though there was some thought given to it at the time. SNB Governing Board Chairman Ernst Weber justified the bank's position throughout the allegations with two rationales: asking the Nazis top prove ownership of the gold would ruffle feathers and cast the "neutral" Swiss in a bad light – a brilliant don't ask, don't tell policy. The second rationale was since Switzerland was a neutral country, it must accept deposits from all countries, belligerent or otherwise.

International law may allow occupiers to seize government gold reserves, but it does not allow them to seize personal and private assets. It was known to the Swiss bankers a portion of the gold came from private citizens; and the Belgian national bank was privately owned, not a government agency. Therefore, the Swiss argument they were only following international law does not hold water. In fact, the Swiss National Bank was also privately owned which was in part because of this – the Swiss would never have to worry about their gold reserves falling into enemy hands. The Germans had set a precedent in the Franco-Prussian war in 1871 when they left the French gold reserves as they were in private hands at the time.

It was not just gold for which the Swiss created spurious transactions. *Schweizerische Bodenkreditanstalt* (SBKA), which was a mainly a mortgagor, enacted many trades and deals to liquidate Sperrmarks, which were hard-to-convert or "frozen" marks issued during the war. SBKA obfuscated and obscured its transactions in order to convert the marks into francs. SBKA agents such as Hermann Göring's confidant Wilhelm Öding and prominent Zurich lawyer Wilhelm Frick would import goods from Germany, then have the consignees pay in Swiss francs, a process which SBKA would have to pay bribes to the compromised officials.[173] Not only were the Sperrmarks converted into hard currency, they were also used by third parties to purchase munitions. SBKA became the clearing house for 3% of the total tungsten requirements for the Germans – tungsten being an important component is shell casings and armor-piercing weapons.

Looted securities were another way the Swiss banks profited during the war. The company Eisenhandelsgesellschaft Otto Wolff, for example, would act as an intermediary between officials and their Swiss banking counterparts. Wolff acted for, among others, Herman Göring and sold shares of Royal Dutch Shell which was one of the most liquid stocks available to the Germans. The trades had to use falsified affidavits to attest to their provenance. Credit Suisse issued orders to its people that trades of this type had to be scrutinized. This did not stop the trades, however. When the Allies issued their warning about Nazi looting, trading by the larger Swiss banks ceased; trading by the lesser ones continued. It is estimated by the end of the war, not less than 50 million Swiss francs worth of trades had been completed and this trading volume was included in restitutions afterwards, though the extent will never be known.[174]

How did the Swiss banks get themselves into this line of work? After the First World War, it was in Germany's best interests to not divulge certain financial transactions, in case the proceeds be confiscated by France, Belgium, Great Britain or the United States. So a black market developed in Switzerland for trading in securities that would "fall below the radar." It was therefore a natural extension for the Swiss banks to continue these operations throughout the Second World War. The Swiss sensed war was coming, so even if these transactions were profitable, there was nothing to say they would continue to be or if it would even be safe in Switzerland. They cast their eyes west to the United States.

The Swiss Bank Corporation – one of the founding companies of UBS – was the first to set up shop in New York, just six weeks after war was declared in September 1939. Credit Suisse had put out feelers even earlier – in December 1938 it started looking at the old banking house of Speyer & Co. The only problem was it was Jewish and that wouldn't go over well with their Aryan customers to the north. In a meeting of Credit Suisse's financial commission, the comment was made – unattributed, unfortunately – that Speyer & Co. had "an odour not easily effaced...even if the non-Aryan partners could be eliminated".[175] Credit Suisse was able to eliminate the odor, so to speak, as they purchased the assets of Speyer & Co. and set up a branch office in New York in 1940, though not without some rancor in the boardroom, specifically those fearing the alienation of their Italian and German clients by dealing with Jews.

The United States would become ripe grounds for the Swiss banks, with over half of their assets sequestered across the Atlantic. For Credit Suisse, 66% of their assets were held in the United States, and only two per cent in Germany. The question then remains – if only two per cent is in the Third Reich, why bother? Plain, unadulterated greed is the biggest reason – there was still a buck (or Swiss franc) to be made in Germany, so continue doing business there until the situation becomes untenable, which for the Swiss banks it never did. Politically, it would have been difficult for them to excise their German business, due to the close relationship developed with the Reichsbank, high members of the Nazi party and the German banks. Denial of banking services, in the Swiss' minds, would have been tantamount to asking the Germans to invade. It would therefore be better to keep their collective heads down and do as they were told.

But back to greed – there was a tiny bit of good that came out of the Swiss banks willingness to do business with Germany and Germans in general. Since they were willing to exchange Sperrmarks for Swiss francs and willing to act as a depository for Jewish customers who wanted to flee the Fatherland, it did make it easier for some people to get out of Germany before it was too late. Bergier in his report even states "despite the fact that Switzerland did not always prove to be an entirely safe haven, persecuted Jews were still well-advised to seek a safe destination for their assets if possible in or via Switzerland."[176]

Many of these accounts were inaccessible by their owners, so bank managers and lawyers tended to act as trustees, fully expecting their clients to come back after the war. Yes, it was profitable for the banks, but it was also good customer service. Also in the vein of good customer service: many Jewish companies which were "Aryanised" by the Nazis prior to the war would attempt to withdraw any capital from Swiss banks they could. As long as the signature of the Jewish owner matched the one on file, the Swiss complied. Unfortunately, many of these signatures were obtained in the basement of a Gestapo headquarters or during a beating. However, if a Jewish business owner survived and managed to get to Switzerland to protest, the withdrawal was quashed and the assets stayed with the court. This was the exception, not the rule. In one case,

> *in November 1939, the Polish bank Lodzer Industrieller GmbH asked Credit Suisse to transfer assets deposited with it to an account at the German Reichsbank in Berlin. The bank saw a fundamental problem in this procedure and asked its legal affairs department to examine the matter. The latter recommended not complying with the request since the customer's signature had most likely been obtained under duress by the occupying authorities. A further reason for refusing the request was that it had come from Berlin and contained incorrect information about the amount deposited with Credit Suisse... The Reichsbank agreed that...Swiss banks were not obliged to comply with requests from German administrators. Although there were legal and moral objections to transferring the funds, the consideration that they "still had important interests in Germany, and should avoid friction and unpleasantness whenever possible" prevailed at Credit Suisse. They complied with the request and opted for the principle of carrying out legally signed orders even when they were not received directly from customers, but via the Reichsbank in Berlin.*[177]

These dealings were minor compared to the increase in business the banks had through their dealings with the Reichsbank. UBS was asked by the Reichsbank in 1941 to act as intermediary between it and American dollar transactions. UBS politely declined, as it was policy to outsource questionable transactions, though not necessarily refuse to do them. Instead, UBS put the Reichsbank in touch with LombarDeutscheank AG, an Aryanised bank in Zurich. UBS would only ask for a small commission of 0.5%, but the Reichsbank had now politely declined in favor of Swiss Bank Corporation – also now part of UBS – who was only too happy to oblige the Germans at a lower fee. Swiss Bank's offices in Zurich became the clearing house for all dollar-to-Reichsmark transactions in 1941. Again, obfuscation was key and in order to disguise the origins of the Reichsmarks, Swiss Bank used Chase National in New York to transfer the money, which in turn transferred it to the Mexican Banco Germánico de la América del Sur, which was a subsidiary of Dresdner Bank.[178]

Why didn't the FBI or Department of the Treasury get involved when these transactions were taking place? The short answer is: they couldn't. American banking law allowed a certain anonymity to depositors. This didn't stop the Treasury Department from trying – it requested the names of clients in April of 1941. The information wasn't particularly forthcoming and the United States froze the assets of all banks from Europe by late summer. Again, ownership would have to be proven, though clients would have to wait until the end of the war. By 1944, the United Nations – not the same-named organization of today, but the name given to the Allies at the time – had met at the Monetary and Financial Conference at Bretton Woods to discuss the matters and their rebuke – though not mentioning Switzerland by name – was stinging:

enemy leaders, enemy nationals and their collaborators are transferring assets to and through neutral countries in order to conceal them and to perpetuate their influence, power, and ability to plan future aggrandisement and world domination[179]

In 1998, UBS AG and Credit Suisse settled the outstanding lawsuit for $1.25 billion, with the caveat that it indemnified all class actions against both of the banks and the Swiss government, the Swiss National Bank and all Swiss companies – including insurers, industry and the like. Every major Jewish organization in the world endorsed the settlement, as did the American and Swiss governments.[180]

5
German banks

The Internet is great for both divulging secrets and for spreading rumors. It is virtually impossible to hide any information that would have been safe only 20 years ago. So what is a company to do when rumors and secrets get out in the open? Hit them head on, reveal everything and hope people understand. That is the stance of Deutsche Bank.

A Brief History of Deutsche Bank

Deutsche Bank (Deutsche) started in 1870 when a group of private bankers led by Adelbert Delbrück joined together with an eye on foreign trade. At the time, French francs and the pound sterling dominated international imports and exports – the German Empire had just been founded and the mark was non-existent. Most of the member states of the Empire used different currencies, which was problematic on the international scene. The Goldmark made its debut in 1876, by which point Deutsche Bank had offices in Bremen, Hamburg and London. Deutsche has a history with J. P. Morgan going back to the 1880s, converting Deutsche Edison Gesellschaft into Allgemeine Elektricitäts-Gesellschaft (AEG), the German version of General Electric. Deutsche was a large investor in railways in the 1800s, securing funding with Morgan for the Northern Pacific Railroad in the United States, the Anatolian Railway, which linked Constantinople to Ankara and the Shantung Railway in northern China. It was also central to the bond issues of the steel company Krupp and the introduction of Bayer at the Berlin stock exchange.

Deutsche Bank held interests in AEG and the newly formed Deutsch-Überseeische-Elektricitäts-Gesellschaft (DUEG) which by 1908 was Argentina's major electricity supplier. In 1903, Deutsche purchased Steaua Romana, a Romanian oil company and the next year reorganized all of its oil interests into a holding company Deutsche Petroleum AG. DUEG was sold in 1919 to a Spanish consortium and Deutsche Petroleum was lost in the postwar reparations. Undeterred, Deutsche re-entered the petroleum industry three years later with their acquisition of Deutsche Petroleum-Aktien-Gesellschaft. In 1926, Deutsche acted as the agent for the merger of Daimler and Benz as well as IG Farben, Lufthansa, Zeiss Ikon and Thyssen.

The Anatolian Railway was of particular interest to Deutsche, as it opened up trade and relations with Turkey. Turkey was still part of the Ottoman Empire, but the Empire had been in decline since the loss of the Russo-Turkish War in 1878. Deutsche saw potential in the area as the empire crumbled, and this potential was seeded in the Anatolian and later the Baghdad Railway, with the goal of linking Constantinople (now Istanbul) with Baghdad and the Persian Gulf. In 1893, after visiting with Ulû Sultân Abd ūl-Hāmīd Khan, Kaiser Wilhelm secured the rights for Deutsche Bank to oil exploration in a twenty-kilometer radius around the rail line from Mosul to Baghdad. When France occupied Tunisia in 1881 and British Egypt the following year, the Ottomans realized their empire was at risk and turned to Germany, who had not made any hostile moves.

The Sultan requested – and the Kaiser accepted – that the Germans help modernize and reorganize both the Ottoman army and its finances. Of the latter, Deutsche was integral. In payment, the Sultan agreed to the concession for the Baghdad Railway, which by 1940 had become a line from the Persian Gulf to Istanbul and finally to Berlin. The British were also very interested in oil exploration in the area and when the Sultan was deposed during the Young Turk Revolution in 1908, they were in good stead with the new pro-British government. Seven years earlier, the Englishman William Knox D'Arcy negotiated with the Shah of Persia to oil rights through his country for 60 years. D'Arcy sent a team to Constantinople in 1903 to negotiate the same. D'Arcy's claim made the Sultan void the agreement with the Germans due to non-performance, but since the Sultan would not return monies owed to the Germans, they ignored him. Both D'Arcy and the Germans fought for eight years and the result was a split. In 1910, the National Bank of Turkey was formed to support British enterprise in Turkey and two years later, the Turkish Petroleum Company was founded with Deutsche Bank owning a 25% interest. When World War I broke out, the British confiscated Deutsche's holdings and after the war, they were given as reparations to the French government.[181] Turkish Petroleum

Co. became the Iraq Petroleum Co., which was nationalised by Ahmed Hassan al-Bakr in 1972.

Deutsche set up office in Constantinople in 1909, seeing the need to have an actual presence in the area. This was perceptive for the German Empire – during the war, the branch served as an impromptu embassy between Berlin and their Ottoman allies. The branch fell into Allied hands at the end of the First World War and a new branch wasn't opened again until 1923, then closed again in 1944 when diplomatic relations between Germany and Turkey were severed.[182]

Of Deutsche Bank, Baron Kurt von Schröder had this to say:

They had a very powerful influence with the (Nazi) Party and with the Government...the officials of the big banks would be consulted on practically every issue by the Reichsbank and other Government officials and very often what they said was considered the last word on the subject. Men like Abs, Rösler, Kimmich and Urbig of the Deutsche Bank were continuously consulted...[183]

How powerful? Deutsche Bank was the bank of choice for a number of people and organizations, including Reichsmarschall Göring, Field Marshall Keitel, Foreign Minister Ribbentrop, Reich Minister Lammers, Reichsleiter Rosenberg, Chief of the Reich Press Dietrich and the Head Office of the Nazi Party. Deutsche was a prime contributor to the *Hitler Spende* – the "Adolf Hitler Fund of German Trade and Industry," led by Gustav Krupp. The fund was to be at the disposal of the leadership to execute tasks for the Nazi Party, the SA and the SS, among others. Eventually, Deutsche contributed 75% of the donations to the fund, outstripping IG Farben, Krupp and rival bank Dresdner – donating RM900,000 per year.

Dresdner was Himmler's bank of choice for the SS, though irony of ironies, one of the founders in 1872 was the Jewish businessman Eugen Gutman. By the turn of the century, Dresdner had the largest branch network in Germany and in 1905 it joined with J. P. Morgan in international finance, particularly the purchase of American securities by German investors. By the end of World War I it had operations in the Far East, southern Europe, Africa, Mexico and Canada.[184] It was involved with Deutsche Bank in the building of the Ankara to Constantinople railway.

World War I and its aftermath were a disaster for Deutsche and Dresdner, both of which had profited by financing the government's astronomical war-time expenses. The German economy was unprepared for war, which coupled with the Allied blockade and the industrial might of the United States, crippled non-military industries. The war dried up all opportunities for continued expansion and placed a tremendous burden on German industry, forcing it to produce the materials necessary for war on an unprecedented scale. This stopped the expansion of the bank and cut off investment revenue. The burden of Germany's heavy war reparations hurt Dresdner even more than the lack of expansion during the war years had. Dresdner was a major shareholder in many German firms so it felt the pinch of the Treaty of Versailles worse than the rest of Germany. On top of this was the Allies' insistence all Allied countries be given the right to confiscate any German private property abroad.

At the beginning of the hyperinflation era, the banks faced a unique problem – they were running out of money. Not figuratively, but they were literally running out of paper money because the government couldn't print it fast enough to cover the devaluation of the mark. One story from the branch manager in Köln shows this:

"On one fine day, we were completely cleaned out. We closed the branch doors and put up a sign: 'Temporarily closed due to lack of currency.' When we went to take down the sign later in the day, it was covered with banknotes that had meanwhile already become worthless due to inflation. Although we could not resume business with these notes either, this assistance was proof that, despite everything, the people of Köln had not lost their sense of humour.[185]

At the high point of economic chaos in 1923, Dresdner held assets of 204 trillion marks, though remember, a postage stamp, such as the one at the left, cost five billion marks. Three years later, when the banking industry was stabilized by the introduction of the Rentenmark,

Dresdner's share capital and reserves totaled only 100 million Rentenmarks, or only about $24 million at the time.

Deutsche Bank prevailed when lesser institutions sank under the economic crisis. After the Wall Street crash in 1929, the German government had to step in and nationalize many of the banks which were still marginally solvent, including Dresdner Bank. Deutsche Bank avoided this, though they did have to deposit 50 million Reichsmarks into the government-run Deutsche Golddiskontbank as a reserve.

Before 1929, the economy's volume of business was 50% greater than it was before the war, due largely to the capital loans Dresdner and the other leading banks made to new and developing German industries. But the banks were too loyal to their customers and lent out too much money. When the effects of the American stock market crash hit Germany in 1931, there was little cash on hand to pay investors. By the end of 1931, the German government owned 66% and Deutsche Golddiskontbank owned 22% of Dresdner Bank shares. Hjalmar Schacht served as deputy director of the bank at the time and Dresdner was not reprivatized again until 1937. Dresdner did benefit from the government's plan to restructure the banks and keep credit rates down by buying up banks and giving them cash. In the year after the crash, Dresdner was able to buy another of the major Berlin banks, Darmstadter, making Dresdner for a time the largest bank in Germany.

Deutsche expanded through the interwar years through acquisitions, buying up banks throughout Germany – 14 banks from 1917 to 1929. The largest was a merger of Deutsche with *Direction der Disconte-Gesellschaft*, Germany's second-largest bank. The combined company had resources in excess of RM 5.5 billion – just over $18.4 billion in 2016 – and over 800,000 account holders. By 1944, through expropriation, Aryanization and just plain plunder and pillaging, Deutsche Bank's assets grew to RM 11.4 billion.

Commerzbank was the third of the big banks in Germany, behind Deutsche and Dresdner, though it was eclipsed in 1942 by the *Bank der Deutschen Arbeit* (which didn't survive the war). Commerzbank was founded in Hamburg in 1870 and by the end of World War I it had tripled its number of branches by buying eight smaller banks. In 1921 it merged with *Mitteldeutsche Privatbank AG*, which added 100 branches. At this point, Commerzbank was close to the volume of Deutsche, Dresdner and Disconto-Gesellschaft.

The years of hyperinflation were not especially severe for Commerzbank, since it took on the role of hunter. Commerzbank purchased seven more banks, giving it 300 locations across Germany. In 1927, Commerzbank made the acquaintance of Chase National Bank, obtaining a $20 million loan which it was then passing on to German industry. When Commerzbank brought *Mitteldeutsche Kreditbank* – not to be confused with *Mitteldeutsche Privatbank* – into the fold in 1932, it also brought a Nazi with it: Friedrich Reinhart. According to a military report on the bank issued in 1947, "Friedrich Reinhart of the *Mitteldeutsche Kreditbank* who…took over the position of chairman of the Aufsichtsrat was more than any one other individual instrumental in bringing the Commerzbank into the Nazi orbit"[186] and "Reinhart used the power of this office to make himself the virtual dictator of the bank."[187] Not just that, he was on the advisory council of the Reichsbank, councillor of state for Prussia and chairman of the Private Bank economic group, which formed policy for the banks at the government level.

Commerzbank executives Eugen Bandel, Eugen Boode, Carl Harter and Paul Marx joined the Nazi Party by 1934, but it was Reinhart who took the ideology to heart. Reinhart was not a fan of Chancellor Brüning's deflationary policies and believed National Socialism was a way out of the economic morass Germany was in. He joined the Nazi Party in 1932 and was a founding member of the Keppler Kreis. Reinhart was one of the signatories of a letter to President von Hindenburg asking him to appoint Hitler as chancellor.[188] Another signatory was Ewald Hecker, who was vice-chair of the Commerzbank Aufsichtsrat, as well as a member of the Keppler Kreis. According to fellow Keppler member Karl Lindemann of Dresdner Bank, Hecker was the strongest supporter of the group. Hecker was devoted to the cause of National Socialism and his ardent support of the Reich led to appointments as chief officer on the staff of Reichsführer Himmler and the rank of SS-Brigadeführer – the equivalent of brigadier general in the Nazi secret police. Hecker, not to be confused with the eminent psychiatrist of the same name, was important to the economics of the Nazi state, heading the Reich Chamber of Business and succeeded Gustav Krupp as head of the Reichsstand der Industrie, the Nazi industrial leadership group.[189]

Of all members of the Commerzbank Vorstand, only Josef Schilling did not join the Nazi Party. Once Harter and Boode retired and moved on to the Aufsichtsrat, their replacements on the Vorstand, Karl Hettlage, Hanns Deuß, Paul Hampf and Fritz Hoefermann were all Nazi Party members. Hettlage was a member of the SS when he joined Commerzbank in 1939, though he left three short years later to become the financial adviser to the Speer Ministry. This dissatisfied Reinhart, who felt Hettlage devoted himself to politics and self-serving endeavors as opposed to banking. Speer did not feel the same way, making Hettlage the head of financial administration in the ministry, giving him financial control of all Reich enterprises and price control for all government-owned factories which were rented to private concerns.[190] Paul Hampf was a fervent Nazi who owed his position to his party membership. In 1937 he was appointed a deputy Betriebsführer – the Nazi term for personnel manager and public relations officer. Hampf had numerous other appointments, including judge for the Reich Labor Court, member of the Labor Front committee for banks and insurance companies and member of the Labor Front court of honor

Hanns Deuß

On the Vorstand, we have Hanns Deuß (pronounced Doyss), formerly of the Dresdner Bank. Deuß managed the Frankfurt branch of Dresdner from 1932 to 1942 when he was appointed to Commerzbank's Vorstand. Deuß obtained his position at Dresdner through capability and through the attrition of his Jewish colleagues. He rose to the Vorstand at Commerzbank through both this same capability and through his Nazi connections. Deuß joined the party in 1933 and was a supporting member of the SS at the same time. While managing Dresdner's Frankfurt branch, Deuß was heavily involved in Aryanization activities, as Frankfurt was the center of many Jewish-owned businesses. By Deuß' own admission, the bank gave advice, assisted in the drafting of contracts and furnished suitable purchasers.[191] Aryanization also meant Deuß ended up sitting on the Aufsichtsrat of 17 different companies as their Jewish board members were forced out.

Deuß was handpicked for Commerzbank by Martin Bormann's banking committee and was endorsed by Friedrich Reinhart; he served on the Aufsichtsrat of the Dutch subsidiary Rhijnsche Handelsbank, as well as Heinkel Flugzeug. Heinkel had been nationalized by the Nazis in 1942, and at the time Commerzbank headed the syndicate to refinance the new concern. Heinkel was well known as user of both slave labor and prisoners of war,[192] which Deuß was well aware. At its height, Heinkel used 14,000 slave laborers at its plant, and Deuß would have observed this when visiting the Orianenburg concentration camp.[193]

Josef Schilling

Up until 1932, Josef Schilling was a branch manager for the Reichsbank, then joined the Vorstand of Commerzbank. As with other Vorstand members, Schilling formulated policy for using bank resources to support the Nazi rearmament program, as well as the exploitation of occupied territories. Though not a member of the Nazi Party or the SS, Schilling constantly voted in favor of donating RM50,000 a year to the Himmler Fund. Schilling owed his appointment to the Vorstand to the banking crisis which followed in the footsteps of the Depression. When Commerzbank was deemed "too big to fail," the Reichsbank stepped in and purchased 70% of its capital. As Schilling was a prominent manager at the Reichsbank, it requested his placement on the Vorstand of Commerzbank to watch over its investment. Schilling also sat on the Aufsichtsrat of 25 different companies, including eight different banks and 17 industrial concerns, many of which used slave labor. The amusing final word from the Military Government report on Schilling: "Schilling was hardly the driving force at the Commerzbank."[194]

As the years of hyperinflation were not severe, the years of the Depression were. Commerzbank had to recapitalize in 1931 with the help of the government. Afterwards, 55% of the company was owned by the federal Deutsche Golddiskontbank and 15% more by the Reich government. In return, representatives from the Nazi government sat on the Aufsichtsrat of the bank. Government ownership lasted until 1937 when the bank was allowed to put its shares back to the public. As with

Deutsche and Dresdner Banks, Commerzbank was a complete supporter of Nazi rearmament. This was in contradiction to its long standing business model of funding small to medium-sized enterprises; now Commerzbank focused on large companies and government schemes.

Dresdner also supplied financial support to both the Nazi Party and "semi-official" agencies of the party as well as loans. Loans were also made to the SS on a regular basis, even though Dresdner would have implicitly known the only way for the SS to repay was "the loot and blackmail extracted from Jews and political enemies of the Nazi regime, and later from inhabitants of the occupied countries."[195] Indifferently, the Vorstand reported on these loans in minutes from 1938 and 1939:

21-7-38. Dr. Meyer reports the leader of the SS Death's Head Band and concentration camp governing office advised...the amount in question RM20,000 per house has been listed. In his view, the procurement of mortgages will not present any difficulties.

19-6-39 The Gesellschaft zur Pflege Deutscher Kulturdenmaler (SS) has requested a loan of RM 2 million, with the usual guarantee of the Reichsführer of the SS (Himmler)

7-8-39 After Mr. Goetz has been consulted, the Gotha Lebensversicherungs AG and the Allianz were contacted...The Reichsführer of the SS agrees to pay 6% for this loan. It will be guaranteed by the usual declaration of the Reichsführer of the SS[196]

Deutsche Bank was the largest bank in Germany and by the end of the Second World War, the largest in Europe. By 1942 it had 490 branches around the world, including South America and Asia. Thirty percent of all stock transfers of major German corporations were done by Deutsche and the bank floated more stock and bond issues than any other. In proxy voting, it controlled 28% of the stock of AEG, 38% of IG Farben, 49% of DEMAG and 53% of Mannesmann.[197] In other words, it was a giant. The members of the Vorstand and Aufsichtsrat were also members on the boards of 376 different industrial enterprises, interlocking Deutsche with every facet of German economic life during World War II.

One of the great figures at Deutsche was Emil Georg von Stauß, Director General of the bank and the man behind the reorganization of the German aircraft industry after World War I. Stauß was instrumental in reorganizing BMW and Daimler-Benz, when both were struggling aircraft manufacturers. Deutsche Petroleum AG was an acquisition the bank made which was, though out of the realm of traditional banking, did add substantially to its cash and foreign exchange reserves. Though von Stauß retired from the Vorstand in 1933, his legacy of ardent nationalism and militarism stuck with Deutsche, and his strong and early ties with Nazi leaders meant his appointment as Vice President of the Reichstag in 1934. Stauß was instrumental before World War I in gathering Germany's oil interests in the Middle East together as General Manager of the Anatolian Railway as well as supporting German oil policy in Romania. He was elevated to the peerage in 1918 and also was chairman of Deutsche Luft Hansa A.G (not to be confused with its postwar successor Lufthansa), Daimler-Benz and BMW.

It was von Stauß who founded Luft Hansa as an outlet for the production of the German aircraft industry and as a means of developing German aviation. As chair of both the national airline and two of the largest aircraft companies in Germany, von Stauß was uniquely positioned to control the entire aviation industry in the Third Reich. Stauß was elected to the Reichstag in 1930 and was a member of the group of industrialists and financiers who supported Hitler financially before his rise to power. Through this, von Stauß became friends with World War I ace Hermann Göring and arranged the first meeting between the Reichsmarschall and Hjalmar Schacht. Stauß retired from the Vorstand of Deutsche in 1933 and joined the Aufsichtsrat, where he stayed until his death in 1942.

The Second Reich was the period of German history from the founding of the Empire in 1870 until the end of World War I and the abdication of Kaiser Wilhelm II.

Deutsche was a leader in many areas – it invested over a third of its total assets in government paper by 1938, contributing vast sums of credit to Germany's rearmament program. By 1942, 73% of its assets were in government bonds and loans, an astronomical number for any enterprise. One of Deutsche's first great ventures was when the Second Reich made the bank the exclusive agent for one billion marks worth of melted silver coins – $5.7 billion in 2016.

Plunder and pillage were not the only sources of income for Deutsche – just its most profitable. Government finance was increasingly important for the Reich, and Deutsche was at the forefront with Dresdner of this less-profitable business. In 1942, Deutsche distributed RM1.4 billion in treasury and industrial bonds[198] and owned 21% of all government securities held by all 653 banks in Germany. Direct lending was a secondary business during the war years, though new loans increased every year from 1932 to 1943 to over RM2 billion, an increase of 400%. Between Deutsche and Dresdner, the two accounted for two-thirds of all sales and purchases on the Berlin stock exchange, which handled more volume than all other German markets combined.

Deutsche Bank had to reorganize both the supervisory and management boards after the accession of the Führer, to better represent the needs of the Party. Newcomers to the board included: Carl Eduard Herzog von Saxe-Coburg und Gotha, who was the Duke of Saxe-Coburg and Gotha, and in England, the Duke of Albany. His grandmother was Queen Victoria; his uncle King Edward VII and his cousins included George V of Great Britain and Kaiser Wilhelm of Germany. Duke Carl Eduard was a Major General in the SA and President of the German Red Cross.

The duke was joined by Philipp Reemtsma, the cigarette tycoon and head of Reemtsma Cigarettenfabriken GmbH which made 80% of the cigarettes smoked in Germany, 42 billion in total by 1941. Reemtsma was no angel either – he had contributed one million Reichsmarks annually to "special projects close to the heart of Marshall Göring,"[199] and had also employed slave labor in the Crimean Peninsula, using the inhabitants to plant and pick tobacco and paying them in a miniscule ration of bread.[200] Reemtsma was appointed a Wehrwirtschaftsführer in 1939, as the Nazis saw the necessity for cigarette production (not being funny, actually quite serious). A Wehrwirtschaftsführer was an executive of a company deemed essential to the rearmament or war effort. Reemtsma's allegiance to Deutsche goes back to 1929, when several smaller cigarette companies were merged into Reemtsma's company, all under the guidance of Deutsche Bank.

Reemtsma also went on to join the Aufsichtsrat of Henkel, the largest soap manufacturer in Germany at the behest of Deutsche due to his close connections with Göring and to smooth over troubles Henkel was having with the Reichsmarschall. As well, the cigarette tycoon represented Deutsche when he joined the Aufsichtsrat of Vereinigte Glanzstoff Fabriken AG (VGF), the huge rayon manufacturer, though his interest was fleeting – by his own admission, he spent half a day every two years at the company. It did, however, give Deutsche access to what it considered an important industry. In a marginally legal practice, Deutsche asked Reemtsma to purchase RM5 million in stock in VGF, which Reemtsma later deposited at the bank and authorized it to represent him at meetings. In return, Deutsche guaranteed credit to cover customs and tax obligations on his tobacco products as well as floating the company a loan of 7.5 million Dutch florins to purchase the Dutch Caland Tobacco Company.

Further, Deutsche's presence in Turkey allowed Reemtsma access to tobacco in the country, and when the Reich made the tobacconist the exclusive purchasing agent for the Turkish tobacco for all of Germany, Deutsche extended another RM20 million in credit. When Reemtsma planned to expand into shipping, Deutsche sold him its 42% share of Hansa Steamship Co., after which he acquired 40% of Hamburg America Line and 28% of North German Lloyd.

With Reemtsma and the Duke of Albany was Hermann Schmitz, the head of IG Farben who was added to Deutsche's Aufsichtsrat in 1934. Wolfgang Andreas Reuter joined Schmitz and was already very powerful in the steel industry as the head of DEMAG. Fritz Springorum, a Nazi member of the Reichstag and chair of the Aufsichtsrat of steel manufacturer Hoesch AG and Carl Friedrich von Siemens rounded out the group. Siemens was the head of the Siemens group of companies and was a very close friend of von Stauß. Both von Siemens and Springorum died before the end of the war. As other members were purged and died off, they were replaced by even more ardent followers of Nazi doctrine. Men like Albert Pietzsch, who joined the Nazi Party in 1927 and was a personal friend of the Führer. Pietzsch also served on the Aufsichtsrat of Siemens and received the *Adlerschild des Deutschen Reiches* – the same award bestowed upon Henry Ford and James Mooney – with the following inscription: "To the Leader and Promoter of the German Economy".[201] Finally we have Wilhelm Zangen, head of Mannesmann, ardent Nazi, user of slave labor. Zangen served four months in jail after the war for Mannesmann's involvement in rearmament and for the use of forced labor, then went back to heading Mannesmann from 1957 to 1966.

Mannesmann was of particular interest to Deutsche, as it was the largest of the companies it controlled. From the report on Mannesmann by the Joint Special Financial Detachment of the United States Group Control Council after the war:

> *From 1933 onwards M/W was one of the small group of very large, vital German industries which...operated autonomously under the self-imposed discipline of the cartels, in the sphere of one or more of the largest banks and in cooperation with the Nazi government it helped to power. Over simplifying these elements, the man is Wilhelm Zangen, the cartel is the Röhrenverband, the bank is the Deutsche Bank.*[202]

Through the war years, Mannesmann became one of the most important suppliers of pig iron, raw steel, plates and tubing, churning out a combined tonnage of almost three million tons of steel product in 1943 alone. Mannesmann used its Deutsche Bank connection to expand into occupied territories. One such example is the addition of the aryanized Metallwalzwerk AG in Czechoslovakia, which was facilitated by Deutsche's subsidiary Böhmische Union Bank (BUB). Zangen's place in all this is significant, as he also sat on the coordinating committee between industry, the armed forces and the Speer ministry.

Mannesmann was extremely busy in expropriating, acquiring and otherwise pillaging and plundering corporate treasure – and Deutsche Bank was right there, holding the treasure map. In Austria, Deutsche's subsidiary Creditanstalt-Bankverein helped Mannesmann take over the majority of Trauzl AG in Vienna; in Czechoslovakia, it was Prager Eisen-Industrie, which had been partly Jewish owned. The

Jewish shares were in the safekeeping of BUB and amounted to 1.3 million Reichsmarks. Another Jewish company, Max Graber & Sohn AG fell into Mannesmann's hands after it was acquired by BUB as well. Two other companies of note in Czechoslovakia were Böhmische Montangesellschaft and the partially-Jewish Waagtaler Syenit Asbestzamentschieferfabrik & Bergbau AG (the very longwinded Waag Valleys syenite, asbestos cement, slate factory & mining company), its shares being held by Creditanstalt-Bankverein.

Mannesmann saw potential in three Luxembourg-Lorraine companies which were owned by the Jewish Dr. Alfred Ganz. Ganz sold his shares in 1936 to a Swiss national, but the sale was a sham in order to camouflage their origins. Mannesmann acquired the shares through the Deutsche subsidiary General Bank Luxembourg and Ganz was forced to renounce his right to repurchase the shares. Holland likewise had very little mining and steel interests, but Mannesmann found them through Deutsche subsidiary H. Albert de Bay. In 1942, Mannesmann bought the liquidated assets of the Jewish owner van Leer and Wilhelm Zangen acted as the trustee for liquidation. Mr. van Leer found it was safer to leave Holland than try his luck with the Nazis.

Synthetic fuel production was yet another area in which Deutsche invested and which Germany needed help to develop. Germany is rich in coal, but has no deposits of oil or gas and as soon as the Wehrmacht stepped over the Polish border, British naval blockades ended any flow of oil into German ports. The only solution available to the Nazis was the construction of facilities to produce synthetic gasoline from lignite – also known as brown coal. This was a natural fit for Deutsche Bank with its long standing relationship to the coal industry – risky yet a great prospect for huge profits and a great way to Deutsche to do its duty to the Reich. Dresdner also felt it was a great opportunity and was more aggressive in the field of development.

The Reich formed another monopoly for this endeavor, the Braunkohle-Benzin AG (Brabag). Brabag capitalized initially in 1934 with 100 million Reichsmarks which was funded not by the government, but by the Duty Association of the German Lignite Industry, a heavy-handed approach by the Nazis to strong-arm the coal producers into backing this venture. It was headed by SS General Baron Kurt von Schröder and Dresdner headed the syndicate of funding banks with a 25% investment; Deutsche followed with twenty. This syndicate added another RM130 million to Brabag's coffers. Brabag started production in 1936 and the following year had produced 320,000 tons of synthetic fuel.

Deutsche Bank would not sit on the sidelines for long – it had too deep of a relationship with the industry. In 1935, Ruhrbenzin AG was formed at the behest of the government by Ruhr valley coal miners, most of which were either Deutsche clients or under its control, including some of the largest names at the time: Vestag, Hoesch, Krupp and Mannesmann. The initial capacity of Ruhrbenzin was only going to be 30,000 tons a year of fuel and lubricants, to which the syndicate loaned RM9 million. Four million came from Deutsche, 2.8 million from Dresdner, 1.7 million from Commerzbank and the remainder from Berliner Handelsgesellschaft.[203] A further RM12 million loan was made the next year, with Deutsche again leading the syndicate, loaning half the money needed. What was great about the business model was the Nazi government was buying all production from Ruhrbenzin at a guaranteed price.

This guaranteed price must have whetted the appetites of the Ruhr colliers, because late the next year Vestag formed on its own Gelsenberg-Benzin AG to produce synthetic gasoline. Once again, Deutsche Bank was called on to fund this enterprise to the tune of RM30 million. Both Deutsche and Dresdner ponied up 10.5 million Reichsmarks, with Commerzbank following up with just over three million. The government was hedging its bets by requesting the founding of many synthetic fuel producers, and the very next month after Vestag's venture, colliers in the Rhineland founded Union Rheinische Braunkohle Kraftstoff AG – The Rhineland Union of Lignite Fuel Co. – with RM45 million in capital. Deutsche was particularly close to Union Rheinische due to its ties with two of its founding companies and provided loans throughout the war years of RM155 million – the equivalent of $863 million in 2016.

The last big company to be founded in this gold rush was Oberschlesische Hydierwerke AG in Upper Silesia. It was founded in December 1939 with Hermann Göring Werke owning over a quarter of the company. Share capital was increased in 1942 to a quarter of a billion Reichsmarks, of which Deutsche and Dresdner floated 28% of the issue and Commerzbank another twelve. This company was considered to be the jewel in the crown of the synthetic fuel industry in Germany, with an output of one million tons of fuel hoped for, and its main customers would be the Luftwaffe and the Kriegsmarine. Even with this, "the earning power of the hydrating works was decidedly questionable as they were experimenting with processes untested in quantity production. In spite of this fact, the banks agreed to place large bond issues with their customers," according to Dr. Hermann Jannsen, Vorstand member at the Reichs-Kredit-Gesellschaft.[204]

This didn't matter to any of the banks though, which is interesting in that bankers are generally a conservative lot and don't usually stray from their comfort zone. Deutsche Bank, Dresdner Bank and Commerzbank all definitely did with this operation. There was a certain amount of camaraderie between the banks during the war, and this is seen through the sharing of risk. Under normal circumstances, all three would have supplied loans to clients in good standing on their own. As the effects of the war continued to drain and change the German economy, it became necessary for all banks to ask for help, so to speak. This was because of the size of the loans, the extension of repayment terms and the risks involved; hence the syndicates to float loans. An example of this is Bubiag, a lignite producer in Niederlausitz, which though a Deutsche client, the size of a RM10 million loan was enough for Deutsche to share the risk, only extending 50% of the eight-year loan, with two other banks picking up the slack.

These large longer-term loans weren't just in risky synthetic fuel production – the government needed money to buy essentials, such as eggs, butter, grain and clothing from overseas. These loans, though guaranteed by the government, were of such a size – over half a billion Reichsmarks in total – that one bank could not float them on its own and hence the need for syndicates.

Deutsche's Vorstand officially remained aloof of the Nazi Party, though agreed to admit three members when others left. They included such characters as Karl Ritter von Halt, a former Olympic athlete and head of the Reich Sports Office, as well as being on the executive of the International Olympic Committee from 1937 to 1945. Halt was also a member of Himmler's Circle of Friends and made sure the annual donation of RM75,000 from Deutsche Bank made it into the SS Reichsführer's hands, as seen in this letter from him:

> *Dear Baron von Schröder:*
> *Thank you for your friendly letter of 15 March 1944; I hereby inform you that my bank again will make available the amount of RM 75,000 for the purpose described in your letter. The sum has already been transmitted to the Special Account "S" with your banking house in Köln.*
> *I remain with cordial greetings and*
> *Heil Hitler!*[205]

The account in question was at J. H. Stein, of with SS General von Schröder was a partner and the Special Account "S" was earmarked for Himmler.

The most bizarre appointment to the Vorstand was that of Dr. Heinrich Hunke. Hunke was a Nazi Party member since 1928 and had trained as a primary school teacher. Hunke later received his doctorate on the acoustic measurement of intensity. What is strange about Hunke's appointment was, though he served in the propaganda ministry and was in the Reichstag, he had also written a critical editorial in 1934 advocating the nationalization of the banks in Germany.[206] The Vorstand had no objections to the appointment of Hunke, as he was also a member of the Advisory Board of the Reichsbank and a member of Martin Bormann's banking committee, both of which gave Deutsche Bank voices in the Reich government.

And from the most bizarre to the most prominent of appointments was that of Hermann J. Abs, former partner of the banking house of Delbrück, Schickler and Co., the favorite personal bank of Hitler and Alfred Rosenberg. Abs replaced the deceased Gustav Schlieper in 1937 and took charge of Deutsche's foreign business. Abs was both Deutsche's most brilliant Vorstand member and the most adept contact the bank had with the Reich government.

Of Hermann J. Abs, Baron Kurt von Schröder had this to say:

> *Abs proved very valuable to the Party and to the Government by using his bank to assist the Government in doing business in the*

occupied countries and in other foreign countries. Abs enjoyed excellent relations with Funk, who was both president of the Reichsbank and head of the Ministry of Economics in recent years.[207]

Hermann Abs was in fact so powerful and so well versed in the banking industry both Hjalmar Schacht and Walther Funk believed he was one of the few men in the country who could explain the banking sector in Germany to the Allies after the war. His work for Deutsche was all encompassing and he sat on more than 40 management boards by 1941, including the Reichsbank, IG Farben, Zeiss Ikon AG and Creditanstalt-Bankverein Wien. Abs main concern was the expansion and domination of Germany over its occupied territories.

Hermann Abs was assisted in this by three men – the most important and active was Alfred Kurzmeyer, one of Deutsche's managers just below the level of the Vorstand. Kurzmeyer was integral to all of Deutsche's expropriations which had Belgian or French importance, including the Societé Generale de Belgique; the Banque de l'Union Parisienne and the Banque de Paris et des Pays Bas. This in turn gave control to Deutsche of holdings in the Balkans held by the Western Europeans previously unavailable to the bank.[208] Kurzmeyer became a Swiss citizen in 1943, further obscuring his ultimate goals and presenting himself as a neutral party. This allowed him to become intermediary between Deutsche and its operations in Argentina, Spain and Turkey without arousing suspicion.

Kurzmeyer was a devious man. He started work at Mendelssohn & Co. and moved to Deutsche when it liquidated the stock of Mendelssohn. After, he took an active interest in forced acquisitions and was instrumental in Deutsche's takeover of Banca Commerciala Romana, Romania's third largest bank, which was strongarmed into accepting Deutsche's offer. Kurzmeyer's own interests took hold and he started Transportgesellschaft Carmen, which he used as a shell company to divert gold to an account at Schweizerische Creditanstalt – now Credit Suisse.[209] After he left for Switzerland, he acted for Deutsche in Turkey, where the bank's Istanbul branch had been closed and its managers incarcerated as enemy aliens. Holding a Swiss passport, he could come and go as he pleased, though the Swiss were not easily fooled – the secret service tailed him after

December 1944 when he started selling jewelry, the source of which could not be ascertained.

Kurzmeyer set up shop in Zurich at the Hotel Savoy, a posh establishment, and acted as the de facto Deutsche Bank branch in the country. Kurzmeyer played the part of playboy, according to police reports. He had a "tendency to spend time on the shores of Lake Lucerne flirting with females," and haul huge suitcases filled with gold and jewelry around to garner hard currency and pay for services rendered to the bank.[210] The police referred to him as a *Schieber*, which has many meanings, including pusher, gun runner and gangster. One of the more disturbing stories concerning Kurzmeyer comes near the end of the war. Kurzmeyer was supposed to act as an intermediary between the SS and a Hungarian Jew named August Wild. Wild would be released if he paid a ransom of 239,000 Swiss francs. Kurzmeyer secured the money, took his cut and then transferred the money to SS General Oswald Pohl in Berlin. Pohl promptly had Wild shot.

Deutsche Bank had its finger in every facet of Germany banking, whether the companies liked it or not. Local commercial banks such as J. Wichelhaus P. Sohn AG, C. G. Trinkaus and Burkhardt & Co. were controlled by Deutsche either by complete possession of the capital (in the case of Wichelhaus) or by holding enough capital to make its voice heard (rather loudly).[211] Regional commercial banks, such as Niederlausitzer Bank AG, Mecklenburgische Depositen- und Wechselbank and Allgemein Deutsche Credit-Anstalt (ADCA) were controlled by Deutsche, sometimes with only a 10% shareholding and in the case of ADCA, just by supplying loan capital for larger endeavors. For this, Deutsche had three members on the ADCA board of directors.

By law, banks such as Dresdner and Deutsche were excluded from mortgage banking, though both exerted considerable power in the area anyway, mainly due to the banks placing mortgage bonds to cover the credit extended by these institutions. Deutsche Bank was affiliated with half of the 26 mortgage lenders in Germany either through stock ownership or interlocking directorships. Insurance companies, though separate entities, had close relationships with Deutsche, with the bank having executives on 23 different insurance companies in Germany. The relationship was mutual, with Deutsche and others directing business to insurance companies and the insurers keeping large deposits on hand.

Deutsche Bank's ability to parlay its influence over industry in Germany was above all other competitors, and it accomplished this in a variety of ways. One was interlocking directorships – though not uncommon, Deutsche used it extensively as a way of making sure its interests were taken care of. To become a director on a client firm, Deutsche either bought up considerable voting stock, or engaged in widespread loaning to the companies. Members of Deutsche's Vorstand, Aufsichtsrat and Direktoren der Bank were also directors on 707 company boards – this does not even include smaller companies or other bank officials, such as branch managers and department heads. This was a very lucrative position for many of these officials, with Vorstand member Hans Rummel sitting on the Aufsichtsrat of 18 companies and picking up an extra RM150,000 from these seats. Since the Corporations Law of 1937 limited the number of directorships to 20 per person, there was a certain amount of juggling done at Deutsche, hence why bank managers often sat on boards of smaller companies. Deutsche needed government permission for Abs and Rösler to sit on more than the legal limit of companies, specifically banks expropriated during the Anschluss. These interlocking directorships were the most important tool of Deutsche, as it let them control day-to-day operations of many of their clients, and by extension the German economy.

The second most important tool Deutsche had at its disposal was proxy voting of corporate stock. In some instances, Deutsche Bank used this as a means of getting directorships on companies; at other times, it used this leverage to control the outcome of certain financial decisions companies would be making. As indicated earlier, Deutsche voted 38% of the total stock voted in IG Farben, the largest chemical company in the world; 19% of Vestag, the largest steel combine in Europe and third-largest in the world, and 28% and 20% of AEG and Siemens respectively, the two largest electricity companies in Germany. Hans Rinn of Dresdner Bank explained why by saying the banks desired to maintain their voting strength to retain the corporation as a customer and retain their quota in syndicate transactions.[212]

As today, banks acted as proxy voters for shares which they were custodians. German law required proxies to be signed by individual shareholders, so banks would print proxy forms and circulate them to clients with a letter stating the bank could act in their interests in absentia. This allowed, for example, Deutsche Bank to vote 80% of Mannesmann shares in certain years and 50% of both Daimler-Benz and BMW without owning a tenth of the stock, though Deutsche did own all 259,000 preferred shares of Daimler, which had voting rights equivalent to 7.7 million common shares.

Loans issued by Deutsche allowed it control companies without looking too out of the ordinary. The debtor-creditor relationship is usually at arm's length, but Deutsche managed an inordinate amount of control over many of these companies, many times by insisting on a Deutsche director sitting on the board of the client company – so as to watch over the bank's interests, of course. Though Deutsche Bank expressed its concerns for financing a solely military economy, it did nothing to alleviate this. In fact, it consistently loaned money to munitions and arms manufacturers, such as aircraft makers Messerschmidt, Heinkel and Junkers.

Sometimes, Deutsche Bank was so deeply involved, it was almost impossible to ascertain who worked for whom. Daimler-Benz and BMW are excellent examples of this, since Deutsche dominated both companies in the interwar years. Emil Georg von Stauß engineered the reorganization of BMW and the merger of Daimler and Benz and sat as chairman of the Aufsichtsrat of both companies as well as that of Deutsche until his death in 1942. He was succeeded by Deutsche Vorstand member Hans Rummel, and between the two gave members of the Deutsche Bank board control over two of the most important aircraft manufacturing concerns in Germany for over 20 years. Both Rummel and von Stauß would make regular visits to both companies' headquarters, usually about once a month and likewise, officials from both companies would visit Deutsche head office to give updates on production figures, personnel and financials.

Stauß maintained a separate office in Deutsche Bank, Berlin, which he used to handle the affairs of BMW and Daimler-Benz. He took a great deal of interest in these companies and was responsible for extension of large credits to them. The other members of the Kredit Ausschuss were not in favor of these credits but could not intervene as von Stauß was obviously collaborating with the Reich government in these matters.[213]

Rummel and von Stauß weren't the only members in Deutsche's employ who sat on the boards of the two companies. Hermann Köhler, the manager of Deutsche's Stuttgart branch; Carl Jahr, the Chair of Deutsche's Advisory Council for Baden and Palatinate; Max Schmid, Günther Quandt and Werner Carp, all of the Aufsichtsrat of Deutsche also sat on Daimler's Aufsichtsrat, out of a total of fourteen members. At BMW, it was Rummel, Schmid and Victor von Rintelen, the manager of the Munich branch who sat on a ten-member board. Deutsche Bank controlled 50% of the stock of each company through direct or proxy votes and Dresdner controlled 15 and 22 percent. This allowed Deutsche unlimited power with both companies, and acted as primary agent during stock and bond issues for both companies, floating a total of RM218 million in securities.

Since Daimler-Benz was so active in the war effort, Deutsche Bank and its executives cannot claim ignorance of the rearmament of the Reich, especially since Deutsche was funding such activities. When Daimler enlarged its plant at Untertürkheim and built a new one at Berlin-Marienfelde, it was for the production of aircraft motors, which Deutsche implicitly knew was for the Luftwaffe. As well, since Deutsche Bank dominated the board of the company, men like Rummel would have known Daimler was producing tanks in 1937.

As Daimler-Benz's output increased from RM100 million in 1933 to almost ten times that amount ten years later, if Deutsche Bank was truly neutral to the war, alarm bells would have rung – how could Daimler be making ten times as many cars and trucks during the largest war in history? Deutsche Bank not only engaged in active management of the company, but also sent over nearly RM28 million in credit. Since Rummel took an active interest in the company, he would know that in the first eight months of 1944 Daimler delivered almost 8,500 aircraft engines and 796 Panzers.[214]

At BMW, they were more secretive of their war efforts. To hide the output of aircraft, the company set up four separate subsidiaries:

- BMW Flugmotoren GmbH;
- BMW Flugmoterenwerke Brandenburg GmbH,
- BMW Flugmotorenfabrik Eisenach GmbH and

- Giesserei und Machinenfabrik Bitschweiler GmbH.

The first three are BMW Aircraft Engines, BMW Aircraft Engine Plant and BMW Aircraft Engine Factory – not very original, but enough to discern a subtle difference. By being GmbH – limited liability corporations – they could hide their output volume as well as what they were making. A GmbH is not required to publish annual reports, whereas an AG is. By 1943, BMW AG was only cranking out less than ten percent of the total of the company, even though production, as at Daimler, increased ten-fold.

As with Daimler, Rummel had implicit knowledge of the workings of BMW, and knew full well that by 1943, 95% of production was for the Luftwaffe. This would have been envisaged by von Stauß, who when he drove BMW deeper into production of aircraft engines, the development of large production facilities would only have one major client – the German air force. Yes, von Stauß had founded Luft Hansa, which did ship 258 tons of cargo in its first year – but air travel was still in its infancy and unless von Stauß was an amazing futurist, military use would have been first and foremost on his mind.

Göring was not so psychic. From a secret conference in July 1938:

We are fully embarked on the way to mobilization...this is why I again beg of you with all my heart, gentlemen, consider yourself an industry which has the duty to create an Air Force and which is most intimately connected with that Air Force...Gentlemen, I have no reason, and this is gratifying to me, to complain of the airplane industry, but to praise, to acknowledge, and to thank. You went my way on the whole...and you did really wonderful work...Here the main task will be to produce Mercedes GOIs in large numbers. As to BMW, I put great hopes on the future.[215]

Every large bank in Germany was engaged in financing heavy industry, and Commerzbank was no different, even if there was an implicit knowledge this financing was going towards rearmament. A plea of ignorance is unfounded, considering Commerzbank Vorstand member Paul Marx was at the same meeting as Dresdner and Deutsche

Bank with the Reich Air Ministry in 1935. Commerzbank was expected to give RM15 million in loans to the companies engaged in building fighters and bombers for the Luftwaffe. One such company was Daimler-Benz, to which Commerzbank increased its loans from three to four million Reichsmarks even before the meeting. Other large loans (value in 2016 dollars in brackets) included:

- RM14.4 million to steel manufacturer Vestag ($101 million),
- RM6.1 million to aircraft maker Junkers ($43 million),
- RM3 million to steel and arms maker August Thyssen Hütte ($21 million),
- over RM13.7 million loaned to weapons makers including Mauser and Deutsche Waffen- und Munitionsfabriken ($96 million).[216]

Other industries covered by Commerzbank loans included almost RM18 million to shipbuilders by 1938 and Maschinenfabrike Augsburg-Nürnberg AG – now known as MAN and the truck building division of Volkswagen, though then it was the company that supplied diesel engines for submarines and Panzers, and parts for Mauser. As well, Commerzbank funded purchases of raw materials and food, though to be fair to Commerzbank, food it not considered an essential to the war effort. However, purchases by Brabag, Ruhrbenzin and IG Farben are.

Of IG Farben, less control was exercised, only because of the sheer size of the company. Farben was so big, it owned its own bank, but Deutsche did end up with some say in the company. Deutsche Bank was BASF's bank during the merger of Bayer, BASF and others which started IG Farben and so was naturally allowed to continue in some banking activities. As well, Hermann J. Abs sat on Farben's board, while Herman Schmitz of Farben sat on the Aufsichtsrat of Deutsche. For its subsidiaries, von Schinckel of Deutsche was chairman of explosive manufacturer Dynamit AG and Karl Kimmich sat on the board of Rheinische Stahlwerke which Farben also controlled. After the Anschluss, Farben's Max Ilgner sat on the board of Creditanstalt-Bankverein in Vienna, a soon-to-be subsidiary of Deutsche. Ilgner also sat on Deutsche Überseeische Bank (the German Overseas Bank), of which Deutsche owned 51%.

DEMAG AG was a heavy machinery producer which had Deutsche Vorstand members Kiehl and Kimmich serving on its Aufsichtsrat and DEMAG chair Wolfgang Reuter sat on Deutsche's Aufsichtsrat. Deutsche also held proxies for 50% of DEMAG's stock. Hoesch AG was a top coal and steel producer and in this instance, Kimmich sat as chairman and Bechtolf was a member of the Aufsichtsrat, whereas Erich Tgahrt, Chair of the Vorstand of Hoesch, sat on Deutsche's Aufsichtsrat. This led to certain animosity with Dresdner and one of its executives, Friedrich Flick. Flick was also a coal magnate and wanted control of a company which ended up going to Hoesch. It would seem that, if Flick sat on the Deutsche Bank board instead of the Dresdner board, these types of problems wouldn't creep up.[217]

All of this leads to Deutsche Bank helping to prepare the economy and the country for war. In 1933, the bank had to make up its mind whether it would support the Nazi regime and rearmament, or be relegated to second-class institution and quite possibly nationalized if it didn't comply. To say Deutsche Bank was an implicit provider of the means necessary for a war would be true, and there were choices to be made – but most of these choices were just varying shades of gray for the bankers. Once the bank started making loans to the Reich and financing the war industry and directing these industries into armaments production, there was no turning back.

One of the biggest investments Deutsche made in the Reich was placement of treasury bills and bonds. By 1942 Deutsche placed RM1 billion in bonds issued and the bank held on to an additional RM479 million – today's equivalent of $8.7 billion in bonds. Of T-bills, the bank held 23.1 percent of the issue, or almost RM4 billion by 1942, increasing to over RM 7.5 billion two years later. This accounted for 66% of the total assets of the bank, which is extraordinary; when you add in the bonds, promissory notes and loans extended to the government, this amount balloons to 82% of total assets. Of course, Deutsche Bank was proud of this, as seen in its 1940 annual report:

In this year, in which Germany's armed forces gained victories of historic proportions, the German war economy has measured up to what had been expected of it. The credit banks have contributed particularly in the successful execution of the short-term financing of the Reich.[218]

And that was just the orthodox measures used by the Nazis. The unorthodox ones are a little more interesting. Germany's full employment strategy and the Four Year Plan in 1933 needed an outlay of RM4.5 billion for public works, including the building of the Autobahn. Today we think of the Autobahn as a means to get somewhere fast in Germany in a Mercedes – back then its prime value was to get somewhere fast in Germany in a Mercedes armored personnel carrier or a Panzer. Deutsche funded these public works programs by granting credit on special bills and certificates issued by the Reich to fund them. The other very strange instrument was the Mefo bill.

After 1935, when Germany withdrew from the disarmament conference and reintroduced the draft, it meant the country went on a true war footing. This program was financed by Mefo bills, which were introduced by the Reichsbank in 1936. A Mefo bill was issued as payment from the Metallurgische Forschungsgesellschaft mbH – translated as the innocuous Institute for Metallurgical Research Ltd and Mefo for short– in lieu of a cash payment. The banks accepted these bills at a discount, issued cash to the depositor, then in turn returned them to the Reichsbank for payment. Mefo bills were discontinued in 1938 and the Reichsbank called in the debt. Of the RM12 billion outstanding, almost RM11 billion came from commercial banks. But the Reichsbank didn't hand over cash – it redeemed the bills for Mefo bill certificates, which matured between three months and a year. The main attraction for the banks is they could list them as commercial paper on their financial statements instead of government paper, concealing total Reich expenditures in the areas of rearmament. The Mefo certificates were actually redeemed starting in 1941, and finished in 1943.[219]

Besides loans, Commerzbank made a brisk business in Mefo bills, as did Deutsche and Dresdner. There was no risk in taking these payment guarantees from clients as they were guaranteed by the Reich. The Mefo bills were known to every member of the Commerzbank Aufsichtsrat when they were brought to their attention at a meeting on

February 25, 1937. This is important as the bank's participation in rearmament would have been known at this time. By the end of June 1938, Commerzbank still had RM175 million of Mefo bills still on its books. Other government guarantees, such as treasury paper, were heavily weighted on Commerzbank's balance sheet, taking up 68% of the RM5.155 billion in assets by 1944.[220]

After the Mefo bills, the Reichsbank started distributing delivery notes as payment for delivery of armament. The delivery notes were payable at the end of six months by the Reich treasury. This made them an attractive short term note and the banks gobbled them up, again as commercial paper. The Reichsbank and its director Walther Funk were amazingly original in the ways they sought to fund the rearmament of the Third Reich. In conjunction with this, the Reichsbank started issuing promissory notes of the Deutsche Golddiskontbank (Dego notes). As with the Mefo bills, banks could list them as commercial paper instead of treasury notes, making them attractive as window dressing on the banks' balance sheets. Deutsche Bank purchased large amounts of these notes, holding almost RM873 million by the end of 1944.[221]

Commerzbank was the number three bank in Nazi Germany, approximately half the size of either Deutsche Bank or Dresdner. Like its bigger brothers, Commerzbank increased assets dramatically during the war years, tripling from 1938 to 1944, mainly through the acquisition of government and industrial paper such as stocks, bonds, loans and promissory notes. The cooperation between bank and government goes back to the accession of Hitler in 1933. From Commerzbank's 1934 annual report (italics in all cases are my addition):

The German banking industry has regarded as its first duty, to support the efforts of the Reich Government according to its best efforts and to take the legitimate credit needs of all economic sectors into account.[222]

By 1936, this was the tone:

> *In 1936, systematic control of all monetary and economic factors has been more visible than any other year, and the **evidence shows that the correct path has been trodden**...The banks have used their great power to play a significant role in this success. The Reich has since 1932 increased tax revenues, and a decline in unemployment benefits has added about RM6-7 billion for additional expenses, which have been the financial basis for the substantial strengthening of the Reich economy.*[223]

And by 1938…

> *The year 1938 was a great challenge to the German economy. The Reunification of Austria and the Sudetenland with the German Reich – **this tremendous act of the Führer** – and the first efforts to rebuild the indigenous industry in these areas were of special interest. **The tasks of rearmament and the further expansion of national defense systems, the extensive production of the Four Year Plan as well as the further implementation of the construction of autobahns and the rest of government projects put an extraordinary stress on the German Economy**.*
>
> *Our own holdings of non-interest bearing Reich treasury notes from month to month increased with reductions in exchange portfolio. **Our involvement in the long-term supply of credit to the State was even more extensive than in the previous year** due to the further financing long-term Reich bonds. While in 1937 a total of RM3 billion Reich bonds were issued last year's, including the November bond, was around RM8 billion.*[224]

Note Commerzbank is not only holding non-interest bearing treasury notes, thereby loaning the Reich free money, it is also making note of the money it is loaning is for "urgent Four Year Plan investments," which would only be for rearmament before Hitler's declarations of war. By 1940, a swastika and German iron cross had been placed prominently in the annual report with the slogan *For our colleagues who gave their lives for the Führer and the Fatherland.*

In 1940, the war defined the tasks of the German banks. **Based on the overwhelming victory of the German forces in the west, all the resources of the nation could be used with determination for the continuation of the war. The monetary conditions of the economy were so fluid, that the financing of the war, with the involvement of the German banking proved no difficulty. The banks have successfully become the dedicated placers of medium-and long-term Reich Treasury bonds...**ature network of offices (at the close of the year 361) was expanded in 1940 by the construction of offices in the new western territories. We opened branches in Strasbourg, Alsace, Saarbrücken and Esch (Alzig) for the Moselle district of Luxembourg. In the Netherlands we created in the N.V. Rhijnsche Handelmaatschappij as a permanent representation[225]*

As with Deutsche Bank, Commerzbank revels in the victories of the first year of the war and that the war will continue. By 1942, the tone had changed somewhat:

The most important task of the German banks is the participation in the procurement of the necessary warfare agents. In our balance sheet this is shown by a substantial increase in inventory of Reich Treasury notes. In addition, credit was made available to the war economy, partly in consequence to a substantial increase in the funding of public works.

Our reduced workforce, due to conscription, has increased the workload of the staff, which has done this in an exemplary and dutiful devotion to their work. We thank and appreciate this. We especially care for the sense of belonging with our employees and their family members. In the course of the war, our branch network was reduced last year by 40 offices.[226]

And by 1944, it was positively grim:

Despite the ongoing war-related workforce reduction and consequent extraordinary additional work, our employees have shown exemplary devotion under an increasingly difficult air war. It is our sincere desire to repeat our heartfelt gratitude and our full recognition.

We convey our heart-filled emotion to our separated employees and their families. We take particular pleasure in the award of numerous bravery awards to our comrades, one of whom received another Knight's Cross this past fiscal year. In awe and gratitude we remember our 113 workmates who in 1944 in the battle for German honor lost their lives on the battlefield and on the home front. Their sacrifice is our sacred obligation. We also mourn the passing of 34 active members and 37 pension recipients. We will remember and cherish of all of us fallen comrades.[227]

In the first years of the Third Reich, the financial industry foresaw great investment opportunities. With Deutsche Golddiskontbank's support, in 1934 Deutsche wanted to form a German syndicate to exploit copper ore in Turkey and have all machinery for it manufactured and financed in Germany: "The enterprise constitutes a valuable asset to German economic activity abroad...*it assumes great significance in general, and, more particularly, for our armament economy*. It appears to us to be extremely important to secure and to strengthen the German influence in the enterprise."[228] Not only would this be good for financing the importation of copper into Germany, it was excellent for German manufacturers of equipment which would also need loans provided by the banks.

This was one of the few times Deutsche Bank engaged in external sources for war materiel before the beginning of hostilities. Usually, it invested heavily in domestic producers of munitions and developers of raw materials. By 1941, there were 544 new loans of over RM1 million to 160 separate clients at Deutsche Bank. Of course, Deutsche knew these loans were good – munitions manufacturers had only one customer and Deutsche could take that to the bank.

An area of Nazi – and bank – interest which is not well known is the rayon cartel in Germany. The Allgemeine Kunstzijde Unie and Vereinigte Glanzstoff-Fabriken joined together in a marriage of the Dutch General Rayon Union and the German United Rayon Factories. Vereinigte Glanzstoff-Fabriken (VGF), in its short history was the largest rayon manufacturer in Germany and had become the center of world-wide rayon interests prior to the Second World War. In 1929, VGF formed a cartel arrangement with its much smaller Dutch partner and the Dutch actually became the holding company. Cartel agreements were made around the world, including the United States, Japan, Great Britain and France, and through these, the company gained interests in South America, Eastern and Western Europe.

But why was rayon so important? Yes, it was used in clothing, but the more important use was as tire cord. With the intense shortage of natural rubber in Germany, ways had to be found to conserve the use of it. Every one thousand pounds of high grade rayon tire cord would save 670 pounds of rubber it didn't have to either import or attempt to synthesize. Deutsche Bank was VGF's bank and in 1942, four of the eight members of VGF's Aufsichtsrat were from Deutsche: Hermann Abs, Johannes Kiel, Werner Carp and Philip Reemtsma. Deutsche Bank had three members on the Allgemein Kunstzijde Unie board as well – in 1939 it was von Stauß, Kiehl and Schlitter. The cartel issued 48 "priority shares" in 1929, each with the voting power of control over the group. Twenty-four of these shares were in the hands of both the Dutch and German sides – The German side was controls by Abs, his hand-chosen CEO Dr. Ernst Vits and by Baron Kurt von Schröder. Deutsche Bank was commissioned by the Nazis to buy up as much of the Dutch stock as it could to put the majority of the cartel in German hands.

This wasn't the only way the Nazis had to wrest control from the Dutch. By 1940, a severe shortage of textiles and pressure from the Speer ministry and Dr. Hans Fischböck, the German Economic Commissioner for the Netherlands, had caused the cartel to consider building two new factories. Deutsche Bank was right there with its syndicate to finance the two plants and in exchange for loans, Deutsche Bank took possession of ten million guilder of Allgemein Kunstzijde Unie stock. This money passed through the Dutch clearing account for occupation costs and Reichsmarks were credited back…to the clearing account, where it was used to pay for machinery for the new plants. Between Deutsche and its subsidiary Albert de Bary & Co NV buying up shares in the company, Deutsche Bank accumulated 31% of the company.

Did Deutsche Bank engage in the use of slave labor? Not directly – hard to have loans officers who are chained to their desks. But indirectly, through the companies Deutsche controlled, there was most certainly a huge amount of slave labor used. Companies such as

Mannesmann, BMW and Daimler-Benz actively engaged in the use of prisoners of war, concentration camp inmates and forced labor from Slavic regions of Europe. Members of Deutsche Bank's Vorstand sat in the chairmanship of all three companies, so unless they drove to the works with bags over their heads, it would be difficult for any of them to say they knew nothing of it. Wilhelm Zangen, head of Mannesmann and member of the Vorstand of Deutsche, was kept apprised of goings-on at the plants, including these referred to in a US Military Government Report after the war:

*All instances of mistreatment, abuse and criminal neglect mention in this memorandum were taken from reports prepared by Mannesmann and their own field managers...the picture drawn on Mannesmann's summary...will show conclusively that **Mannesmann, and this includes the Vorstand, the directors of subsidiaries and their employees in charge of foreign workers, are guilty of: murder by starvation, forcible use, inhuman treatment, gross criminal neglect and abuse of foreign labor.***[229]

Particularly, the murder by starvation occurred at the Neanderthal lime quarries used by the company. There, Doctor Gilhaus was the specialist on site and his report mentions the food for PoWs was insufficient; some were suffering from famine oedema, a condition which caused intense pain and body parts to swell. If lucky, they may recover in one to three months, given the appropriate amount of food and nutrition. These men were not lucky, much to the dismay of Dr. Gilhaus, who asked for more food to be given to the PoWs. Eventually, many of them died, though exact numbers are not available. At Mannesmann's mines in Gelsenkirchen, it was found the 2,000 PoWs and 800 civilians being used as forced labor were inadequately fed, though the two meals a day of carrots, potatoes and sauerkraut was more than most were getting in German slave industry. In Mannesmann's Duisberg facility, 150 Italian PoWs were used to be point of exhaustion. Forty of the men had lost between 22 and 33 pounds from their already slight frames and "according to the company physician, most of the internees have no muscular tissue left...their recovery, according to the doctor, would take several months."[230]

Remember, Georg von Stauß and Hans Rummel of the Deutsche Vorstand led both Daimler-Benz and BMW for twenty years. As Rummel was deeply involved in personnel issues – von Stauß was already dead by this point – he would have implicitly known about the use of slave labor at both companies. At BMW, inmates from Dachau as well as PoWs and forced foreign labor were used. In this case, Rummel's own secretary Herr Wörner tells the tale:

The first time I learned of the employment of concentration camp inmates by the BMW was in the middle of 1943 from the so-called concern reports, which the BMW sent monthly to Mr. Rummel and which in addition to statistical material on the financial situation, turnover, orders, etc. contained data on the personnel; one day in these reports appeared "concentration camp inmates and SS prisoners." I cannot tell whether the number of these prisoners was stated in the reports or if it was occasionally mentioned by one of the managers. In any case I recall the number of 3-5,000...In February-March 1944 after a meeting of the board of directors the members visited the works Allach and saw at this occasion a fitting shed where concentration camp inmates and SS prisoners were put up...I seem to remember that Mr. Rummel was present. According to what I was told the inmates and prisoners did not receive any cash payment from the SS.[231]

Deutsche Bank also acted as a transfer agent for companies paying forced labor wages – not to the employees, but to the federal German Settlement Bank. Deutsche Bank management knew the money was not being given to the laborers, but held by the government, yet voiced no concerns. In 1943, the magazine *Die Deutsche Volkswirtschaft* published the following:

Germany's clearing debts have been further increased. However, this increase was due less to a change in the relation between imports and exports than to services in the field of war economics rendered by foreign countries. This applies first of all to the use of foreign workers in Germany; the savings from their wages, which have reached considerable amounts, have been transferred within the framework of clearing agreements.[232]

Very clearly, this states in a respected magazine foreign workers are being, if nothing else, paid substantially less than Germans, and have been paid through the clearing accounts of the occupation governments in Europe. So, not only was Germany getting cheap labor, any payment received was made by the country the worker was stolen from in the first place! Deutsche Bank administered all the transfers, save for the ones in Greece and Slovakia, which were handled by Dresdner. Deutsche Bank was the recipient of this plum contract thanks to the position of Vorstand member Dr. Kurt Weigelt, attorney at law. Weigelt, a Nazi Party and SS member also was an expansionist and colonialist – he owned a banana plantation in Cameroon up to the Second World War. After the success of Deutsche's work as transfer agent for Italian laborers in 1937, it added Bulgaria and Hungary in 1939; Belgium, Denmark and France in 1940; Finland, Norway, Serbia and part of Slovakia in 1941 and the province of Lubliana, Slovenia in 1944. Deutsche Bank charged 25 pfennig for each transfer at first, then increased it to 60 pfennig shortly thereafter. The bank netted RM7.5 million Reichsmarks for handling the money, which totaled 1.85 billion Reichsmarks by 1944.

The business of transfers was so big for Deutsche Bank, it actually set up a separate division for it, with 200 full time workers. Employers – including companies like Daimler-Benz, IG Farben and Opel – would remit directly to their local Deutsche branch. Workers who were allowed to come and go could purchase traveller's checks from Deutsche – the bank would even have employees accompany workers on their trains home, just in case. The payment would be made to a beneficiary back in the home country – wife, mother, etc.

As Germany was gearing up for its war economy, it was also exporting arms. Deutsche, Dresdner and the Reich Kredit Gesellschaft all engaged in funding these activities, extending over RM100 million to Portugal, Afghanistan and Turkey to purchase arms from companies such as Krupp and Daimler. Bulgaria, while also an Axis country, received half a billion in funds to build up defenses and its army. This money was also loaned by a syndicate led by Deutsche and Dresdner banks.

Richard Freudenberg, Vileda cloth man

Deutsche Bank employed the usual cast of black hats in its operations. Richard Freudenberg was a leather manufacturer and member of the Aufsichtsrat. Through his business interests, Freudenberg became part owner of the formerly Jewish concern Conrad Tack & Cie, and the Julius Hirsch Company, which were both aryanized by his company. Freudenberg only joined the Nazi Party in 1943, though he contributed RM 36,000 a year to the Adolf Hitler Spende for nine years previous to that.[233] Through his connections at Deutsche, he attempted to Aryanize Jewish shoe companies in Holland and Czechoslovakia. A successful businessman, he asserted to the military interrogators his business decreased during the war, though his income rose from RM38,000 in 1933 to 1.26 million Reichsmarks ten years later! Freudenberg was tagged by the U.S. Military Government as committing a crime against peace and was being held in internment camps for two years after the war, but he was acquitted of helping the Nazis and went on to become a member of the Bundestag and both head of his company and the Aufsichtsrat of the new Deutsche Bank. Freudenberg's company diversified after the war and started making Vileda cleaning cloths in 1948, shock absorbers in 1957 and lubricants in 1966. The family divested itself of its shares in 1984, forming a non-profit foundation.

Dr. Albert Pietzsch, Rocket Scientist

Albert Pietzsch was a close personal friend of Hitler's, going back to 1925 when he opened up an office for Hitler in Munich. His first contribution to the party was RM7,000 and Pietzsch continued to contribute every year at least one thousand marks more until 1932. After that, his contributions went directly to the Adolf Hitler Fund. Pietzsch sat in on various meetings with the Reich cabinet, including those dealing with rearmament back in 1934. In 1936, he was appointed president of the Reich Economic Chamber, of which only the president of the Reichsbank and Minister of Economics would have higher authority. Pietzsch was trained as an engineer, but had some very distinct economic views, as expressed in a 1938 pamphlet: *"The* *national socialist state claims the leadership in all walks of German life. Hence it is not possible for economy to go its own ways; it must subordinate itself to the state, its aims and needs."*²³⁴

Pietzsch served his master well, and as such was appointed vice-chairman of the Aufsichtsrat at Deutsche Bank. He also was a member of the board of the Reichsbank, on the Aufsichtsrat at Siemens, at Bubiag, Löwenbrau, Bayerischer Lloyd, Bavaria-Film and a member of the board of directors of Buffalo Electrochemical Works in Buffalo, NY.

This was not the good doctor's main claim to fame though – he was the founder of a company which produced concentrated hydrogen peroxide electrochemically. This was of intense interest for the German military as a propellant. Pietzsch convinced Helmuth Walter he could make a 100% pure concentration of hydrogen peroxide which would work as a rocket fuel. Walter was intrigued, as he had already started work on designs for a fast submarine, a wakeless torpedo and a jet engine. The submarine travelled twice as fast as any conventional submarine at the time, but storage problems with the hydrogen peroxide made the Germans abandon the program. Rocket propulsion tests started in 1937, mainly on the new V-1 rocket bombs and on the Heinkel He-176 jet plane, the first plane of the jet age which flew in 1939. These plans never went much further, though a jet-powered Luftwaffe would have probably changed the outcome of the war. Walter was captured by the British after the war; Pietzsch spent two and a half years in American internment camps, then was released and died in 1957.

Hans Rummel, CEO of Daimler-Benz and BMW (at the same time!)

Deutsche Vorstand member Hans Rummel joined the board in 1933 when it was aryanized and Theodor Frank and Jacob Wassermann were kicked to the curb. Although not a member of the Nazi Party, he did agree with the other members of the Vorstand to contribute RM75,000 annually to the Keppler Kreis. As well as sitting on the Vorstand at Deutsche, he was chairman of the Aufsichtsrat at BMW, Daimler-Benz, and seven other companies; he was vice-chair of Stock

& Co. and Deutsche Telefon & Kabelwerke and on the Aufsichtsrat of Deutsche Hypothekenbank and Allianz. While Rummel wasn't a card-carrying Nazi, he was integral to companies which supplied over a billion Reichsmarks worth of trucks, tanks and aircraft engines...in 1943 alone! As stated earlier, Rummel and Georg von Stauß before him exerted complete control over BMW and Daimler-Benz, so it can be fairly stated that Deutsche Bank had an iron grip over the operations of two of Nazi Germany's most prolific producers of war materiel. This would have included the use of slave labor in at least 15 different companies of which Rummel took an active role in the finances or operations.

Max Schmid, slave driver

Max Schmid, head of the Waldhof paper mill conglomerate, joined the Deutsche Bank Aufsichtsrat in 1940. As well as Deutsche, Schmid sat on the boards of Degussa, BMW, Daimler-Benz and 15 other companies. Schmid claimed not to be a member of the Nazi Party, but he was not adverse to the use of slave labor – his paper mills employed between 1-2,000 out of a force of 7,000 workers. He was not adverse to theft as well, acquiring a house in Vienna in 1939 which was confiscated from a Polish citizen. Schmid went back to Waldhof after the war, meeting up once again with Hermann J. Abs, who sat as chair of the Aufsichtsrat of the paper company.

Both the Aufsichtsrat and Vorstand at Commerzbank were "Nazified" by the start of 1940, but this didn't stop the Nazis interest in – and interference with – the top personnel there. Former officials of the bank blame this interference on *"the bank's antagonistic attitude in many fields and because its top personnel was not considered politically reliable after all."*[235] It would seem the real reason for this interference was more centred on the party's ideology. In 1942, Bormann's banking committee wanted Nazi economists working at the big banks – such as Commerz, Deutsche and Dresdner – to set up the banks for reorganization on a more municipal or "Gau" level. The Gau was to be headed by the Gauleiter, who would have had power over many aspects of the Gau, including financial institutions. The big banks were vehemently opposed to local control of their branch network, especially since it would have eventually led to the dismantling of the big banks.

This scheme was held in abatement at Commerzbank by Friedrich Reinhart's leadership – and his devout Nazism. When he died however, the banking committee insisted three economic advisers to Gauleiters – Emeran Amon, Walter Jander and Adolf Mittag – become members of the Aufsichtsrat. They joined ardent Nazi and industrialist Wilhelm Tengelmann. Tengelmann's father Ernst and brother Walter joined the Nazi Party in 1930 along with Wilhelm, who went further by becoming a member of the SS. Wilhelm became an Obersturmbannführer (lieutenant colonel) in the SS as well as a member of many economic advisory councils. At the Vorstand, Hampf and Höfermann were installed at the behest of Aufsichtsrat vice-chair Hans Harney.

As with the other big banks, Commerzbank followed the Wehrmacht into conquered territories, but instead of taking over other banks, it chose to mainly open up new ones under its name. Also unlike the other big banks, Commerzbank shares were widely held, as opposed to Deutsche Bank for example, which had large blocks of its stock placed in industrial hands such as Philip Reemtsma. Do not be deceived by this all-inclusiveness; in the 1942 annual meeting, 2½% of the outstanding shares were voted by their owners – the other 97½% was by an employee of Commerzbank.

Large contributions of any kind had to be approved by not just the working committee of the Aufsichtsrat, but the entire Vorstand; while Commerzbank was looked upon to contribute to the Party, it also made larger donations of its own free will. By 1944, Commerzbank was contributing RM175,000 to the Adolf Hitler Spende; RM50,000 annually to the Himmler account at J. Stein Bank, and various other contributions, including the welfare fund of the Gauleitung Berlin, sixth anniversary celebration of Hitler's ascension to power, even collaborating with other banks to collect funds to acquire a painting for Göring on his birthday. Commerzbank was the bank of choice for highly secretive accounts, including one opened by Rudolf Hess for the Adolf Hitler Spende. In one case Delbrück Schickler & Co and Deutsche Bank both contributed to this account, which showed a balance of 27 million Reichsmarks by the end of the war. Another was a secret account for the construction and maintenance of Party buildings at Berchtesgaden, near the Austrian border. That account had RM75 million in it by 1945.[236]

Again, as with Deutsche and Dresdner Banks, Commerzbank held large tracts of proxy votes for stockholders in various enterprises. While Commerzbank maintained at the end of the war they were "safeguarding the interests of innumerable small and otherwise inarticulate stockholders," the bank was also integral in determining business policy for the companies in which it proxy voted. Members of the Aufsichtsrat and Vorstand were also members of the boards of 125 important firms, 50 of which as chair or vice-chair.

6
Reich banks outside the Reich

It wasn't just the business inside Germany which was immensely profitable for Deutsche, Dresdner and Commerzbank – the newly occupied territories of the Reich presented an awesome possibility for growth, plunder and robbery. It is hard to imagine the staid, wool-suited, monocled bankers behaving like halberd-wielding Vikings, but that is just what they did.

Austria

Before the war, Deutsche Bank had limited penetration in foreign markets, mainly in the Netherlands, South America and Spain. After the Anschluss, its aggressive expansion began. In Austria, the highest levels of the German government acquiesced to Deutsche Bank's acquisition and control of Creditanstalt-Bankverein (CABV), the largest commercial bank in Austria. According to Reichsbank vice-president Emil Puhl, "the big banks made known to (us) their intentions and interests in Austrian banking and so the Deutsche Bank expressed their desire to acquire control of the CABV, the Dresdner Bank stated the same intentions to the Länderbank, Wien."[237] CABV was important to Deutsche's expansion not only for Austria, but it was also the most important bank in the Balkans. At the end of 1940, CABV had assets of RM780 million and 45 branches in Austria. It also controlled three regional banks in Austria, with combined assets of RM135 million.

Of the 78,267 kilograms of gold pilfered from Austria's Central Bank, just over 50 metric tons were returned after World War II. The remainder went into the International Fund for the Victims of National Socialism in 1998. The gold was valued at 470 million schillings in 1938 –or over $2.15 billion in 2016.

Deutsche Bank was extremely interested, holding talks with CABV prior to the Anschluss, though Germany's annexation of Austria proved pivotal in the negotiations.

Five days after the Wehrmacht crossed the Austrian border, CABV invited Hermann Abs to Vienna to discuss the matter. The result was a letter to the Ministry of Economics, proposing Deutsche take over the 120,000 shares of CABV held by the Austrian government, 20,000 held by the Austrian Central Bank, 50,000 held by Österreichische Industrie-Kredit AG and 43,000 held by the CABV pension plan.[3] Deutsche wanted CABV, and of course the Reich wanted its largest bank to control its first victim country's largest bank. At the time of the Anschluss, the federal Austrian government owned 76% of CABV's stock. Deutsche's plans hit a snag when the shares held by Austria (and its central bank) were put into the custody of VIAG and the Reichs-Kredit-Gesellschaft, both of which in turn were controlled by the Reich Ministry of Finance. The Austrian Central Bank was gobbled up by the Reichsbank in March 1938 and afterwards it was ordered liquidated by Germany. All of Austria's foreign currency reserves and gold reserves were turned over to the Reichsbank, whereas the industrial holdings were put under VIAG's control.[238] Hermann Abs and Karl Kimmich began negotiating with VIAG into late 1938 and by December of that year, Deutsche controlled 35% of the company and this went further: the agreement stated among other things:

- Deutsche and VIAG would jointly administer their shares – Deutsche owned 35%, VIAG 41%, but they would jointly administer the total.
- Deutsche and VIAG would exert their combined pressure on management during meetings to extend their joint agenda.
- Banking transactions in southeast Europe shall be done by a German bank, and they would find "an adequate place for Creditanstalt"

By the spring of 1942, Deutsche controlled a majority interest in CABV, but here's the catch: Deutsche was transferred another block of 25% ownership in exchange for various industrial holdings Deutsche held. CABV held these stocks, but wait – Deutsche now controlled

CABV! The smoke and mirrors used to obfuscate this transaction is amazing.

Even after this divestiture, CABV was still the premier holder of industrial stock in Austria, including three-quarter interests in four Austrian textile manufacturers, one paper mill and two leather tanneries. The importance is seen in the composition of the Aufsichtsrat of CABV, on which there were three representatives of Deutsche Bank – Abs as vice-chair, Rummel and Oswald Rösler, although Rummel was replaced by Ritter von Halt in 1943. CABV was given all of the minority holdings Deutsche Bank held in south-east Europe, including the branches it had opened in Cracow and Demberg in Poland. After, CABV added the Böhmische Union Bank (BUB) branch in Pressburg, Slovakia and 33% of the capital of BUB. In Bulgaria, CABV was given thirty percent of Deutsche-Bulgarische Kreditbank and in Romania, thirty percent of Banca Commerciala Romana. BUB was directed by CABV – and in turn by Deutsche – to conduct business as it saw fit in Hungary, Serbia and Croatia. Creditanstalt-Bankverein was immensely important to Deutsche Bank's growth in south-east Europe – so much so that the bank dispatched advisers trained in industrial finance and stock and foreign exchange trade to shore up the institution. Not that it needed it – CABV was already a strong bank, but Deutsche wanted to funnel all business in the south of Europe through CABV.

Länderbank, the second-largest bank in Austria, was forcibly merged with Dresdner after the Anschluss. The Vienna branch of the Czech bank Zivnostenska was also annexed. Commerzbank differed from its big brothers in its operations in occupied territories. While Deutsche Bank and Dresdner would go in and take over unsuspecting competitors, Commerzbank decided the honorable thing to do would be to go in and open up its own branches, which it did in the Sudetenland, Austria, Poland, Alsace, the Netherlands, Luxembourg, Belgium, Latvia, Estonia and Czechoslovakia. In all countries, the bank only opened one or two branches, except for nine branches in the Sudetenland. Commerzbank did find it profitable to invest in banks taken over by Deutsche and Dresdner, including a 14% holding in Societatea Banca Romana.

In Austria, there was one branch in Vienna, which mostly invested in Reich treasury paper. Its second largest commercial creditor was Heinkel with a RM5 million loan, but this was administered through the Berlin head office. Otherwise, Commerzbank participated in syndicate financing of Austrian industry as the third person to the party, as always behind the big two. In Czechoslovakia, of the nine branches opened in 1939, six were closed by 1942.

This merger and acquisition activity was only one thing condoned by the Nazi regime. Göring's Four Year Plan office gave Karl Rasche at Dresdner the order to "investigate the economic conditions of Sweden and Hungary; discover unused or inefficiently used productive powers; discover possibilities for business transactions in combination with third countries and additional export possibilities from occupied territories; to generally observe the economic activities of enemy countries and their representatives"[239] This would be straightforward for Dresdner – they already had branches in various countries and with occupation, more were added almost monthly.

Czechoslovakia

The acquisition of BUB made Deutsche Bank bubbly with excitement (sorry about the pun). In Deutsche's 1938 annual report:

the historically memorable year 1938, which brought to our Fatherland an increase of 10 million people and an area of some 110,000 square kilometres with the return of the Ostmark (Austria) and the Sudetenland, presented the German economy with a task of hitherto unknown magnitude...our taking over of the Sudeten business of the Böhmische Union Bank created the organizational foundation for our cooperation in the solution of the banking and credit tasks which will serve as the basis for our activity in the new areas and, closely connected therewith, in the South-Eastern regions...Through this (acquisition) our business connections in the Sudetenland received valuable addition.[240]

All German banks were invited to submit proposals to the Ministry of Economics as to how they would help Germany with their acquisition of these properties. Obviously Deutsche Bank's proposal was stunning, considering the letter the Reich Commissioner for Lending Friedrich Ernst sent to the bank in October 1938. In it, he says he has completed talks with the Reichsbank, Economics Ministry and Plenipotentiary for Economic Affairs and they were all in agreement for the takeover of BUB and Deutsche Agrar- und Industrie Bank. Deutsche Bank took the 56 branches it acquired and condensed them down to 21. BUB's shares were devalued by 90%[241] and thus easily acquired by Deutsche and all industry clients were transferred to Deutsche Bank. BUB continued on as a mere shell of its former self. The British Overseas Bank, Prudential Insurance and the Societé Generale de Belgique were all major shareholders of BUB before the expropriation – they all refused to participate in the new institution, so Deutsche was left with 80% of the capital.[242] Societé Generale de Belgique fell under the control of Deutsche Bank in 1940, so that party became a non-issue.

The provisional Military Government report had this to say about Dresdner in the aftermath of World War II (again, italics mine, not the report's): *"The bank took the same leading part in formulating policies for organized fraud and robbery as it did in all other occupied countries.* By obtaining a monopolistic delegation of authority from Göring, by utilizing close relations with the Nazi Party, and by milking dry Czech industry in Jewish hands, the Bank was a foremost participant in the subjugation of the Czech economy."[243]

Not your standard dry government reading. The report does go on to back up these allegations, rather vividly. Dresdner Vorstand head Carl Goetz negotiated with the Foreign Office to take over Czech banks four days after the Munich Pact was signed by Hitler giving him control over the Sudetenland area of Czechoslovakia. Goetz was interested in the Böhmische Escompte Bank and the Zivno Bank, which subsequently were put under the Dresdner umbrella. Of course, the bank didn't stop there. With the full backing of the Reich, Dresdner went on a spree of pillaging, mainly at the behest of Hermann Göring Werke (HGW), of which Dresdner board member Karl Rasche also sat on the management board.[244] The coal and iron deposits in the Sudetenland were of special interest to the Göring Werke, and so also to

Dresdner. With the acquisition of Böhmische Escompte Bank (BEB) came that bank's industrial securities, which were then sold to HGW. Perhaps the most important of these was Skoda, an engineering firm specializing in locomotives and the Sudetenländische Treibstoffwerke, a maker of fuel products which had a share capital of RM100 million. Skoda Werke was the largest munitions factory in Europe, so HGW had great interest in adding it to its empire.

So complicit in the Third Reich, Dresdner was favored over the Nazi's own Bank der Deutschen Arbeit (NSLR) in purchases of the Czech sports organizations by the Nazi Sport Organization. Dresdner actively kept other banks, such as the NSLR and Deutsche Bank, from acquiring positions in the Czech sports groups, as well as 800 movie theaters, sports facilities and recreation halls. Dresdner took it upon itself to print admission tickets to boxing matches and to distribute them through their Berlin office and as with banks today, Dresdner was named as the sole bank selling tickets – in effect they were venue and event sponsors and thus, an important part of the Nazi propaganda machine.

Poland

There was one very helpful partner upon which all banks relied – the Deutsche Umsiedlungs-Treuhandgesellschaft (DUT) – the German Resettlement Trust, a very noble sounding organization which was under the jurisdiction of Heinrich Himmler. Its main thrust was to resettle ethnic Germans in areas which had been cleared of ethnic Slavs in Poland. The SS confiscated 75% of the commercial trade and small industrial concerns in Poland and evicted millions of people to make room for Germans. Most of the Polish citizens moved were forced into slave labor in Germany. The DUT made for some good business for Deutsche and Dresdner – both were members of a syndicate which extended a loan of RM100 million to the DUT for resettlement purposes.[245]

The DUT wasn't the only three-letter acronym Deutsche Bank liked to deal with – its BUB division in Prague had numerous dealings with the HTO – the Haupt-Treuhandstelle-Ost, or Chief Trustee Office, East. Once Deutsche Bank had acquired stocks in Polish companies from French banks, it forwarded them to the HTO which in turn traded these stocks for assets which had been "sequestered for political and racial reasons."[246] The HTO was established by Göring as a component of his Four Year Plan and it was responsible for the confiscation, administration and ultimately the liquidation of Polish property. Five of the most important of the acquisitions made by Deutsche for the HTO were Huta Bankowa, then a 100-year-old steel foundry; the Dombrow Coal Mines, the Galician Coal Mining Company, the Sosnowitz Tube and Iron Works and the Sosnowitz Mining and Smelting Company – though these last two the Germans were only able to acquire the capital the French had, not the entire company.

All of these transactions were funded by the French clearing account; so, like in Belgium, the French people paid for Deutsche Bank to pilfer French securities from the French. In return for these properties, Deutsche Bank acquired iron works in Drzynietz and smelters in the Katowice region, and these were incorporated into the Bergshütte-Konzern, a Deutsche interest. Bergshütte-Konzern started from the former BUB client Berg- und Hüttenwerke-Gesellschaft, which Walter Pohle purchased in 1941 from the holding company of Krupp's French archenemy Schneider-Le Creuzot.

Pohle was instrumental in the procurement of Böhmische Union Bank by Deutsche, actually showing up in Prague two days *before* the Wehrmacht on March 13. By the 17th, he was demanding BUB turn itself over to Deutsche Bank, as its branches in the Sudetenland were already in the bank's hands and the rest of the enterprise was Jewish and therefore should be aryanized as quickly as possible for its own good.[247] As for the purchase from Schneider-Le Creuzot, the French Ministry of Finance claimed it was funded by "francs of unknown origin." In other words, stolen money.

By 1942, Deutsche Bank was ready to divest itself of Bergshütte-Konzern. Deutsche Bank had RM75 million worth of stock and had acquired another RM83 million – 33 of which came from Schneider and also "a small parcel of shares which had come into the hands of the BUB from the Gestapo."[248] Since the Gestapo wasn't staffed by stockbrokers or investors, it's easy to ascertain its shares came through rather unsavory methods. Deutsche took the RM 83 million in stock and sold them on the open market for RM 113 million under the direction of the Ministry of Economics. It was not the bank's fault they were told to sell the stock for a 30-million Reichsmarks profit, though its Vorstand probably didn't complain too much – nor did it complain about the commission it would have made from the stock sales. Bergshütte-Konzern became a large combine, with divisions for coal mining, iron mills and foundries and machining plants making wire, ball bearings and chains, as well as other subsidiaries.

In Poland, Dresdner was just as vicious, engaging in the "financing of depolonization" of Poland. Again, from the report of the U.S. Military Government in Germany after the war, "it financed the redistribution of property from Pole to German; it participated in the cartelization and concentration of industry in typical Nazi style; it financed the war in the East. It was a full-fledged partner of a Nazi economy."[249] In brochures it printed for its "business friends" in Germany, Dresdner showcased its abilities to integrate and expand into Poland, much as it had in its informative pamphlets "Folk and Economy in the Sudetenland" and "Folk and Economy in the Reichsprotectorate Bohemia and Moravia and in Slovakia." ***Dresdner Bank – always serving your pillaging and plundering needs.*** From Berlin, Dresdner directed the branches it held in Poland previous to the occupation and the ones it acquired from Länderbank Wien of Austria and Ostbank AG in Posen.

Four days after the blitzkrieg, the Panzer engines were still warm and the Vorstand of Dresdner was already noting in its minutes its affiliates in Poland should be reopened as soon as the Wehrmacht issued permits. Four weeks later, Dr. Emil Meyer of the Vorstand already had discussions with the economic advisor to Reichsminister Hans Frank, the ruler of occupied Poland. Frank, by the way, was Hitler's personal lawyer, and after the brutality in which he ruled Poland during the war, he was tried, convicted and executed at Nuremburg. Meyer noted in the minutes from September 28, 1939 Dresdner would soon be opening branches in Cracow and Łódź under the Länderbank brand and under Bank für Handel und Gewerbe in West Prussia and Posen.

Dresdner acted as an exclusive Nazi government agent for acquisitions. One example is the Reich's own monopoly Ost Energie

AG. While it is obvious why the Nazis would set up an energy monopoly to control electricity consumption and disbursement, Dresdner was told to "coordinate all acquisitions so that they would be only to the benefit of Ost Energie AG."[250] This included seven Polish electrical companies which had been listed in the aforementioned brochure on business in Poland. These seven companies were targeted because they were of Polish holding and also the foreign shareholders would be easy to arm-twist into selling their holdings. Dr. Zimmerman, who was stationed in Cracow in the occupation government, sent a letter to the Reich Ministry of Economics stating it would be within the Reich's best interests if Dresdner or its affiliate Continentale Bank SAWV in Brussels were to open negotiations with the foreign shareholders in the interests of Ost Energie AG.

Electricity wasn't the only energy concern which Dresdner engaged in within Poland. The Reich monopoly Kontinentale Öl AG was involved in gathering up all loose ends in the oil industry and putting them under one Nazi umbrella. For this concern, Dresdner's newly acquired French holdings were drawn in. Dresdner had in its possession the equivalent of RM1.8 million in French francs to acquire an oil refinery in Upper Silesia, which was made readily available to Kontinentale Öl. Of course, the use of francs instead of Reichsmarks made it easier to obfuscate the purchase with readily convertible foreign currency.

Göring was heavily involved in the founding of Kontinentale Öl and proudly invited the heads of the existing oil companies, banks and prominent Nazis to its first meeting. There he made it clear Kontinentale was going to be built upon the Belgian shares of Concordia Oil and the French shares of Colombia Oil. Deutsche Bank followed up on this demand by acquiring majority interest in both companies, which were producing oil in Romania. According to Hermann Abs, nobody at Deutsche applied pressure to the Belgians to acquire their shares, though he wriggled around the answer in regards to the French. The banking syndicate purchased 600,000 shares of Colombia Oil, paying 300 million francs and almost 352,000 shares of Concordia, valued at 42 million francs.[251]

Kontinentale was divided up between a Reich holding company and the Deutsche Bank syndicate with each receiving 37.5% of the

RM80 million company and the German oil corporations splitting the remaining quarter. This reward was in part due to the support the banks gave the Reich in its acquisition. Walther Funk said: "The banks not only took over purely the business risk by supplying a considerable part of the capital of the Kontinentale Öl...but undertook a general political risk."[252] Deutsche and Dresdner took a 35% share of the syndicate and the Aufsichtsrat of Kontinentale was headed by Keppler Kreis members Heinrich Bütefisch of IG Farben; Dr. Hans Fischböck the Reich Economics Commissar in Holland and Karl Rasche of Dresdner. Hermann Abs, though not a Keppler Circle member, also served on the board.

And of course, what better pillager could Dresdner team up with than Hermann Göring? The Hermann Göring Werke was adept at, if nothing else, seeking out and seizing assets in occupied countries to add to its corporate holdings. On December 7, 1942, Dresdner head office in Berlin sent this letter to the Katowitz branch:

With respect to the Zementwerke Schakowa, the interest of Hermann Göring Werke is a foregone conclusion. At present the acquisition of the Schakowa shares from Swiss possession is impossible... Hermann Göring Werke have, with the consent of the Reich Ministry of Economics, solved the difficulty in an original manner by renting the Swiss shares for a yearly sum of SFR50,000. 25% of the Schakowa capital has been acquired by the Hermann Göring Werke by other means. We have mentioned your interest in establishing a continuing relationship with Schakowa...Also with respect to the RM 31 million shares of Hydrierwerke Blechhammer assigned to Hermann Göring Werke, we have been negotiating for giving to the Dresdner Bank for safekeeping. The fact that the nucleus of the Upper Silesian coal property of Hermann Göring Werke arises out of the consortium of the Dresdner Bank is a significant justification for this.[253]

Dresdner extended credit to many companies within Poland which had been administered by the occupation government. Records show at least 36 separate loans to companies under the control of the Commissarial Administrator.

It wasn't just companies profiting from Dresdner's loans and credit extensions. The settlement of individual ethnic Germans into Poland also figures highly in the bank's business in the country. Sixty separate loans were issued to "politically reliable" ethnic Germans who were moved into Poland by the German Resettlement Trustee Corporation, totalling RM 784,130. The resettlement trustee wasn't the only government agency interested in recolonizing and "depolonizing" Poland – SS Reichsführer Himmler, under the auspices of DUT secured a credit of six million zloty for this purpose. The DUT regulated all economic and financial questions regarding the confiscated property of millions of Polish people who were forced out of their homes and communities to make way for ethnic Germans. Kommerzialbank in Cracow, yet another division of Dresdner had over forty million zloty on its books in loans to German companies which had acquired Polish firms and another 65 million zloty to the Germany monopoly Landwirtschaftliche Zentralstelle – or Central Agricultural Office. Add into this another 93 million zloty to other government agencies including Ost Energie, the Plenipotentiary for the oil industry, the Nazi Labor Division, the Wehrmacht and the SS and the total of these loans of over 198 million zloty, or $618 million in 2013 were used to strip Poland clean of natural resources, goods and raw materials and Polish citizens.

Competition was fierce in the Nazi banking industry. Dresdner affiliate Ostbank AG noted in the minutes of its supervisory board in November 1940 the bank Deutschland-Kasse was attempting to gain control of the sugar potato starch industries in Poland. Deutschland-Kasse was supported in this by the Reich Food Office, but no matter – Ostbank had managed to acquire two-thirds of all sugar refineries in the region. It was so fierce, in fact, the Katowice branch actively and aggressively sought to have head office place pressure on the head offices of various German companies with Polish affiliates so they would do business solely with Dresdner. This worked extremely well, as credit increased at Dresdner Polish branches and partners 46% from June 1941 to June 1942 and profits in the same period increased 82%.[254]

After Deutsche Bank got its claws into Czechoslovakia and Austria, the next step was Lithuania. Germany excised the Memel area from the country in the last of the bloodless annexations. Deutsche Bank set up shop in 1939 shortly before the outbreak of war when they took over the business of the Landschaftsbank in Memel and Heidekrug. When war was declared, the next logical step for the bank was to expand into the new regions of Poland. Deutsche opened branches in eleven cities in Poland, though except for the branch in Cracow, this was actually organic growth, not one of conquest.

Latvia, Lithuania and Estonia were of high importance to the Third Reich as it was considered a buffer zone against Soviet aggression and Bolshevism. Therefore, much more control over political, social and economic development in the countries fell directly under the Nazi government. The Nazis, in turn, left the economic control of the region to experts – those at Dresdner. Dresdner was not a stranger to the area – before the Soviets invaded in 1940, Dresdner had branches in Latvia (the Libauer Bank) and Lithuania (the Litauische Kommerzbank). All countries were under strict control, with only five permitted business types: government monopolies, government agencies, central economic offices used for export, private concerns "in the service of the Reich,"[255] and companies under trusteeship. Dresdner sent a letter to the Ministry of Economics in August 1941 proposing the establishment of a bank in Riga. Karl Rasche had travelled to Riga to speak with Reichskommissar Lohse to discuss the situation and Lohse was enthusiastic about having Dresdner in the country. The letter noted due to "the express desire of your ministry we (Dresdner) acquired an interest in the Dorpater Bank…in spite of the great risks of which we were aware"[256] Two days later, permission was granted by the Ministry and two days after that, a corporate charter was signed and the branch opened in October.

Dresdner acted as an agent of both German companies operating in the Baltic States and Nazi Party organizations, including divisions of the SS. The companies used their position as clients to exert whatever pressure they could, including the use of Dresdner as an instrument of government intervention. An example: Dresdner's services were requested by a German concern requesting "natural restitution" – or theft as we like to call it nowadays – of an Estonian cotton factory. The factory owners had assessed the property at 54.4 million krona, the German Resettlement Trust had reduced that figure to 25 million and finally after the intervention of Dresdner, further downgraded to 16.8 million krona, or about 30% of the original value.

Having companies grossly undervalued by the Reich was a great way for firms to be picked up for a song but sometimes this didn't work. The other way companies would gain control of competitors was the use of trustees and custodians to navigate around the legalities of poaching assets. Mitteldeutsche Zementwerke proposed the appointment of custodians in the case of two Estonian cement companies, which were in the hands of their owners and capably managed. Trusteeship was a short term provision. Even in inter-office memos, Dresdner pointed out the company would become a trustee, but "It is anticipated that the trusteeship contract will soon be supplanted by a conveyance effecting transfer of the property to this company."[257] Dresdner acted as both the credit bank for these transactions and was also asked if it could place a man on the supervisory board of the new cement company, so as to be in constant contact.

In the Baltic States, Commerzbank opened Hansabank Riga in 1941 to supply financing for property seized from the Soviets...which had originally been seized when the Soviets nationalized companies in the 1920s and 1930s. This proved to be a somewhat lucrative – and very short-lived – enterprise for Commerzbank, as it extended loans of between two million and 12.5 million Reichsmarks to a variety of companies, including TreuhanDeutscheetrieb Zuckerzentrale (sugar refineries), Baltische Öl GmbH (oil refineries) and phosphorus and resettlement trustees. Since most credit was guaranteed by the Kommissariat, Commerzbank was quite liberal with its lending practices. Being good little Nazis, they were only too happy to indulge in this business in Riga. From a 1943 management report:

We considered it as our foremost duty to serve the war economy and private business which was to be reorganized. In this reconstruction and transformation of the economy, credits could not always be granted in a manner consistent with conventional Reich banking practices. We were able, however, to overcome most of the difficulties in a liberal fashion…We participated in all syndicates which supplied credits in the interest of the war effort.[258]

One of the strangest episodes in wartime finance came during the period from August 1939 to June 1941, when the German bank syndicate funded a loan to the USSR at the behest of the Nazi government. At the time, it was imperative to fund friendly relations with the Soviets, as the Nazis had just signed the Molotov-Ribbentrop Pact in late August 1939. When the Reich government let it be known it would float the RM350 million loan to finance exports to the Soviet Union, Deutsche Bank reacted by expressing its desire to lead a syndicate. Hermann Abs wrote to Emil Puhl at the Reichsbank, stating "You will understand our desire not to be eliminated from participating in the new credit agreement with the Soviet Union."[259] Later, when Operation Barbarossa progressed and the Germans invaded the USSR, Deutsche Bank was there to extend financing for the reconstruction of industries destroyed by the Soviets scorched earth policy. It is unclear, however, what happened to the loan made to the Soviets in the first place.

Mannesmann followed Deutsche Bank into the Soviet Union; much like a little dog follows its master. Under the guise of government requests, Mannesmann was to become trustee of manufacturing facilities in Taganrog, Dnepropetrovsk and Mariupol. The Red Army drove the Wehrmacht out of Russia before Mannesmann had a chance to implement its plans. Hansabank Riga was evacuated in November 1944 when the Red Army came knocking and moved first to Weimar then to Hamburg, where it was liquidated after the war.

Romania was the next stop on this joyless ride, with the acquisition of the Banca Commerciala Romana(COMRO) in Bucharest, the third largest bank in the country. COMRO was jointly held by Societé Generale and the Banque de l'Union Parisienne (now part of BNP Paribas). The Belgian shares were easily taken control of by Deutsche Bank – not so much the French ones. So much difficulty came of this that Deutsche Bank asked the Romanian government and the Reich Ministry of Economics to intervene and put pressure on Parisienne. Their efforts amounted to new Romanian laws stating corporate boards must be made up of two-thirds Romanians and that there only be seven members on a board. This excluded all the French managers. Now Deutsche just had to get its hands on the shares of COMRO, which they were able to do by exchanging French government bonds for the shares. The bonds were purchased in Holland with Reichsmarks by German agents and then sold back to the French. Hermann Abs denied putting any pressure on the French bank.

Why was Romania so valuable to the Third Reich and Deutsche Bank? Romania is predominantly agrarian, but is also rich in natural resources, particularly petroleum, natural gas, coal, iron ore, copper, bauxite, lead, and zinc, all of which were intensely important to the German war effort. Romania was also targeted as a long-term dependant on the Fatherland. While Germany would strip clean its natural resources, Romania would depend on Germany's industry to help it. For this, a syndicate led by Deutsche Bank and Dresdner Bank loaned the country over one billion Reichsmarks, of which Deutsche loaned RM215 million. Hermann Abs' assistant described the business as unusual because of its low margins, but tells the banks were willing to cooperate with the government.

Yugoslavia

Not so imperative, yet still valuable, were the assets Deutsche Bank purchased in Yugoslavia, particularly Allgemeiner Jugoslawischer Bankverein – the General Yugoslavian Bank Corporation. This bank was acquired easily through the shares owned by Creditanstalt-Bankverein, Societé Generale de Belgique and Böhmische Union Bank, who together owned 83% of the bank. While Societé Generale was adamant against both the share transfer and the appointment to the Aufsichtsrat of the German consul general in Belgrade – a known Nazi – Deutsche Bank won out after the Wehrmacht marched into Belgium. The 12.4 million Belgian francs worth of stock were transferred to Deutsche and the payment was made not to Societé Generale, but to the Belgian clearing account for occupation costs. The Yugoslav government protested the change in ownership, but to no avail, and its lifespan was short-lived. When Germany occupied the country in 1941 and split it into Serbia and Croatia, the complaints were nullified.

Deutsche Bank took the opportunity to split the bank in two, with the Serbian unit renamed Bankverein AG Belgrade and the Bankverein für Kroatien in Croatia, both majority held by Creditanstalt-Bankverein. Commerzbank had a minority interest in Jugoslawischer Bankverein, purchasing 6.25% of the Deutsche Bank-controlled institution.

What was very important in Yugoslavia was the Mines de Bor – the largest copper mining company in Europe. Mines de Bor was in French hands, and was causing a bad case of avarice in Berlin. So, Mines de Bor was purchased from its French owners using money taken from the occupation costs of France. It was then put under the umbrella of Südost Montan GmbH, a government company created explicitly for the plunder of the Balkan mineral resources. Along with Mines de Bor, Südost held Yugomontan, a molybdenum miner, and mining operations in Albania and Greece. Deutsche Bank funded all of these purchases and Hermann Abs sat on the board of Südost. When Mines de Bor needed to expand and required RM185 million in credit, again Deutsche headed a syndicate. This was in addition to credits loaned to Südost totaling 67.5 million Reichsmarks. Deutsche Bank made it clear the banks were in it for the long haul and could not pull out. According to a report by the representative of Berliner Handelsgesellschaft:

> *Mr. Abs and Dr. Schaeffer pointed out at the end, that under no circumstances it is possible to withdraw from this loan business as it is a political affair where a 100% Reichs-guarantee was given, but which is also the only justification for our participation.*[260]

In Yugoslavia, there was little action with Dresdner, as it was considered too volatile, even for Dresdner.

Greece

The situation was different as there was not a direct takeover of a banking institution by any German interests. Instead, after the occupation of the country by the German army, Deutsche Bank moved in to collaborate with Nationalbank of Greece. Nationalbank was the largest commercial bank in Greece, with 97 branches and assets of 12.5 billion drachmae. Its only interest was the economic reconstruction and industrialization of the country, of which a syndicate with Deutsche Bank would be a definite benefit. By the middle of June 1941, an agreement had been signed and a syndicate committee was formed. Members of the committee included the Governor of Nationalbank, the head of the Siemens telephone company in Athens and a professor of economics at the University of Athens on the Greek side, Hermann Abs and Helmuth Pollems from Deutsche. This was not for the benefit of the Greeks though – as the contract between the two companies stated: "The Banque National de Grece will submit to the Deutsche Bank Berlin memoranda on various projects especially concerning construction of hydroelectric plants, industrialization, production of bituminous coal and minerals."[261]

Why was Deutsche so interested in this type of investment, and not perhaps textiles or pharmaceuticals? As indicated many times in this book, Germany was resource poor and needed every possible source to exploit. Nationalbank would have inadvertently been acting as agents of the German government by supplying it with information on natural resource development. Opposite Deutsche, Dresdner had an agreement to take over the Banque d'Athens when the war was over, an agreement which did not come to fruition. In the meantime, it set up the Griechisch Deutsche Finanzierungs Gesellschaft in 1941 to handle commercial transactions between Greece and Germany. Plunder and pillage was not on the table in Greece, as the Greeks had managed to hold the Wehrmacht at bay through most of the war.

Holland

On the other side of the Reich occupied territories, Dresdner did not so much pilfer companies as it did exploit them. As in Czechoslovakia and Poland, Dresdner was a willing and enthusiastic participant in the acquisition of industry and assets. They started by creating the Handelstrust West NV in October 1939, just one month after the Germans had stormed Poland. Handelstrust was formed for the explicit reason of encouraging and financing Dutch exports to Germany. This was done through the purchase of and investment into Dutch firms, and of course, by the removal of "unreliable persons, particularly Jews."²⁶² The Reich Minister of Economics goes further in September 1940, when he reiterates the German position:

> *I consider it important that German capital should participate in economically important Dutch, Belgian and French firms. It is also desired that securities held in the Netherlands, Belgium and France of foreign undertakings, particularly in the Balkans, be transferred to German ownership. I therefore intend to give German banks the possibility of acquiring securities in the Netherlands, Belgium and occupied France, for their own account.*²⁶³

Dresdner, as well as 20-30 other German banks, was given carte blanche in the acquisition of companies, stocks and bonds in occupied Western Europe, especially those which the Reich wanted complete control over in Czechoslovakia and Poland. Particulars were sent not only to the banks, but the Reichkommissar for the Netherlands, the Commercial Banks Section of the Ministry of Economics, the Reichsbank and other interested parties, so nothing was left to chance or miscommunication. Dresdner subsidiary Handelstrust was most implicit in its position, stating in a memo from December 1940 after talking with Carl Goetz, Karl Rasche and Hans Pilder, they unanimously agreed to keep all Dutch banks out of competition for assets and Handelstrust's main task is the "far-reaching protection of all interests of the Dresdner Bank."²⁶⁴

Dresdner pre-emptively compiled lists of companies and shares which were of interest to German concerns. The lists were already sent on their way when the Minister of Economics published the memo above. Not only were the shares of these companies to be turned over right away, Dresdner also decided arbitrarily to block shares of eleven other companies which may be of interest in the future.

Differing from the position Dresdner took in Eastern Europe, the bank sought to block out Dutch competitors as opposed to outright purchase of them. Dresdner, as well as other banks, would approach the matter as Stützpunkte – spearheads – so the German banks would provide a unified front against the Dutch and slowly starve them out. Dresdner set up another bank in The Hague in December 1941, permission being given by the Reichkommissar in the Netherlands, on the basis it would "involve exclusively German clients who require banking assistance in connection with armament contracts."[265] Whereas in France, it could be said French banks helped the Nazi war effort, it would seem hardly possible for Dutch banks to engage in the same way, as they were being squeezed out of business by Dresdner and others.

The only time the Dutch were allowed to participate in credit services by the German banks was when it affected the state itself. In June 1941, Handelstrust Director H.F.R. Knobloch advised Karl Rasche about the floating of a Dutch State loan in cooperation with Dutch banks. The loan was to pay for Nazi occupation costs, so in effect Dresdner was double dipping – making money off business services provided to the Reich, which were in turn paid for by the Dutch government, which paid interest to Dresdner as well.

Jewish property acquired and liquidated by the Germans in Belgium and Holland was liquidated by the Jewish sounding bank Lippmann, Rosenthal & Co. The true Lippmann was a 100-year-old bank when the Nazis entered the country and set up a dummy company with the same name. The Jewish citizens of Amsterdam were first encouraged then later forced by decree to deposit cash, stocks and other valuables at the bank. These deposits were not only systematically stolen from their rightful owners, but now the Reich had lists of Jews ready for deportation. When the Jewish population was deported, many arrived at the transit camp Westerbork. At Westerbork, the Nazis had set up a satellite branch of Lippmann to complete their deed, by forcibly removing anything else the Jewish citizens attempted to hide, including fur coats and shoes. These valuables were then sold quickly to generate cash. By 1944, it is estimated the shell company absconded with over 326 million guilders of property for Holland's Jewwish population – about $1.6 billion in 2016. The last cruel irony of this program was the money was then used to pay for the German occupying forces and for the building of the Westerbork concentration camp.[266]

Lippmann then delivered securities to Dresdner's subsidiary Continentale to be sold on the Brussels exchange. Between January and August 1944, turnover in the accounts amounted to 30.6 million francs. When the executives in charge at Lippmann finally abandoned the branch in December 1944, they had in their possession "several hundred million Belgian Francs" worth of securities.

Belgium

Dresdner subsidiary Continentale Bank SA was the official agent of the Nazi Party, not just in name, but also in its actions. Continentale "contributed vast sums to the German military machine directly, to...the Organization Todt, the Four Year Plan Office, the Brussels Armament Office, etc., as well as indirectly via credits to German war industries."[267] Dresdner:

- financed Nazi purchases on the Belgian black market,
- disposed of Jewish property in cooperation with Lippmann Rosenthal,
- made "penetration purchases" of key Belgian securities and
- acted with the customs police to make sure all foreign exchange transactions were dutifully expropriated.

Acting as a clearing agent, Dresdner profited from the Belgians paying for the plunder of their own country through occupation costs. Continentale was set up by Dresdner in Brussels and Antwerp much as Handelstrust was set up in the Netherlands. The share capital of the company was set up with Dresdner owning 80% of the company and Handelstrust owning the other 20%.

Some of this move into occupied territories was pressure from government bodies – most was not. The pressure was mainly from Reichsmarschall Göring, who not only wanted "the Jewish question" answered, but also wanted in very strict terms, occupied economies to be penetrated and integrated by the German economy. Thus, the commissar of the Belgian national bank made sure the intentions of the Nazi regime were known. In the bank's annual report in 1941, he states:

...it is desired to transfer to German hands Belgian investments in foreign companies administered from Belgium...The first and main task of German banking in Belgium is the creation of business according to the interest and demands of the German economy.[268]

As with other occupied regions, the German banks were given free rein. Continentale was proud of its position in Belgium, financing the Wehrmacht, as well as war industries and procuring goods – illicit and otherwise – for the use of the Reich. October 23, 1944, two days *after* the German city of Aachen fell to the Allies and Belgium and the Continentale Bank were *behind* enemy lines, a letter was written by Continentale staff, saying unfortunately, they were stretched a bit thin by the lag between transfer payments from the Belgians and the requirements of the Wehrmacht. This did not stop the Wehrmacht though – Continentale kept paying Belgian companies, such as the garages used to repair Wehrmacht vehicles!

While this was going on, Dresdner continued forwarding letters of credit to Continentale to keep the war moving smoothly. This included a credit letter to Ford's Belgian division, which had fallen under the purview of Ford-Werke and was making vehicles for the Wehrmacht. The credit, for RM1 million, was secured by Ford's outstanding invoices and claims against the German army.[269]

Not always did Continentale – and Dresdner – come out ahead. By the time the bank was evacuated, it was shown that Organization Todt had owed the bank about 1.7 million Belgian francs as the lag outpaced the Allied armies. Todt was the group responsible for building the V-1 rocket launching ramps in Belgium. But Organization Todt was small potatoes compared to the monies changing hands between the Belgian clearing account and the Wehrmacht. By early September 1944, Continentale had loaned the Wehrmacht 79.7 million Belgian francs, of which only 36.7 million was secured by invoices. The importance of this was not lost on the Commissar of Belgium's National Bank or the Wehrmacht, as without Dresdner acting through Continentale as a clearing house for payments extorted from the Belgian government to the German armed forces, there would probably have been mutiny.

Belgium was also used as a source for luxury goods and services not available anywhere else which would help the war effort at home – what better way to tell the German people the war is going well than by supplying them with luxury goods from conquered lands? Pimetex, was a Nazi agency code name which made purchases on the black market of gold, silver, diamonds and precision tools and Pimetex had 16 million francs on deposit in September 1944. Continentale itself also engaged in purchases on the black market, though its purchases were solely for luxury items for German officials. Items such as cigars, cigarettes, cognac, coffee, soap and ham were all delivered by Continentale to notables such as Joachim Entzian and Karl Rasche, both of Dresdner and Count Felix Czernin of Ländermark Wien.

In Belgium, there was also the Verwaltung Jüdischen GrunDeutscheesitzes – the Administration of Jewish real estate – which held not just cash but securities at Continentale, under the guise they were left at Continentale as collateral for rent payments. The Reich government kept extensive amounts of money on deposit at Continentale, including over 129 million francs for the Armed Forces procurement agency and 53 million francs for the Enemy Property agency.[270] The Armed Forces procurement agency, though sounding very official, channeled money from Belgium into the purchase of black market materials – not just luxury goods but also munitions and raw materials which were not readily available through official channels. On August 31, 1944 there was 125 million francs in the procurement account received nine days earlier from the Banque d'Emission to continue the war effort, though by this time Cherbourg, Caen and Paris had been liberated and the Allies were less than 350 kilometres from Brussels. That didn't matter to the occupiers though, who continued pillaging the country and purchasing whatever they could on the black market.

One of the more important tasks assigned to Continentale and Dresdner was the "increase of German influence with foreign enterprises," demanded by Hermann Göring. Not only was the acquisition of securities important, but the wholesale acquisition of companies was imperative. This job fell mainly to Herman Prinsler, whose services were so invaluable to the bank Dresdner fired off a series of letters to the government asking for his deferment from army service. About Prinsler, the president of Continentale had this to say:

> *He also worked on capital penetration…with the aim to return former German enterprises into German hands, or to obtain influence in Belgian corporations for German concerns. It was not limited to transactions primarily benefiting private enterprise, but extended to transactions important to the Reich and the war economy.*

> There is, for instance, an inquiry from a German official about the possibility of acquiring French shares in Belgium. Such an inquiry can only be answered by a specialist...[271]

The letter goes on to itemize why Prinsler was a specialist in the area and invaluable to Continentale. It also shows how the bank worked tirelessly to the benefit of the Reich through these purchases. Continentale continuously purchased securities throughout the occupation, as noted by Dresdner's stock purchase department. In October 1943, a lot of ten million francs worth of stock owned by Dutch Jews became available and the bank pointed out how difficult this would be to carry out surreptitiously, as was their goal. The bank was not only purchasing from the Jewish population but also conducting bogus transactions in an effort to hide their task. The bank continued these purchases up to the end of the occupation and had a special account maintained for "penetration purchases" which still had a balance of over 19 million francs when the branches were abandoned by the Germans.

Other purchases by Continentale were guaranteed against losses by the Reich's Golddiskontbank. When sales were made on the Brussels stock exchange, proof of ownership had to be provided. This was somewhat difficult when the stocks were obtained illegally by the customs police. One such case involved shares acquired by De Neuflize & Co. in Paris and the Golddiskontbank. Continentale sold them on the Brussels exchange and then was guaranteed not to lose money when Golddiskontbank transferred its profit to Continentale. In fact, the Dresdner subsidiary made a 20% profit on the transaction, or about four million Belgian francs. In a different transaction, Continentale justified its actions by saying the confiscation of securities by the customs police was a lawful transaction for "the benefit of the military administration."[272]

Dresdner acted as an agent for Göring's plan to acquire enterprises in the Balkans which were controlled by Belgian interests. In one case in June 1944, Hermann Göring Werke was interested in a munitions company near the former Polish border which was owned by Belgians. Continentale negotiated with the Belgian owners and was told by Dresdner Head Office "whatever we propose to do has its (the Army

High Command's) approval."[273] Göring's Four Year Plan was executed in various countries, both occupied and neutral, with the help of Dresdner. In Spain, the company dealt with Rowag, which had been established by the Economics Ministry in 1936 to take care of the import-export business in Spain. Later, Rowag acquired interests in mining in both Spain and Portugal.[274] These interests included tungsten, which was badly needed to strengthen steel in armaments. Elsewhere, Dresdner handled top secret transactions such as:

- RM350,000 a month for Deutsche Benzin und Petroleum for oil development in Iran
- £30,000 to Mitsubishi Bank in London to purchase soybeans from the Imperial Japanese government in occupied Manchuria
- 700,000 schillings to Alpenländische Bergbau – a Krupp company – for importing ore into Germany
- RM50,000 a month to Becker & Haag to import of Russian asbestos through Hungary
- RM800,000 to an IG Farben subsidiary in Romania
- RM109,000 to Friedrich Krupp AG in Poland.

Commerzbank's subsidiary Hansabank NV in Belgium acted closely with occupation authorities, including the Brüsseler Treuhand GmbH, the clearing agency for gold and property collected from Jewish nationals. As the Dutch subsidiary had, Hansabank acted as a representative for Commerzbank clients looking to buy into Belgium. Most of the funding for this came from the Belgian clearing accounts – basically paid for by the Belgian people. From 1944: *"The Leinen-Export GmbH, Berlin, has been commissioned to buy up a considerable portion of the Belgian linen production and to import it into Germany. The merchandise has to be paid for at once. Immediate payment from Germany is impossible, as transfers via the clearing require a certain time. The Hansabank grants short-term advances up to RM500,000 which are later repaid when the clearing transfers come through."*[275]

It would be too obvious to just steal the linen – it was better to pay for it with money stolen from the Belgian people! Hansabank management evacuated the branch in 1944, but not before taking records and securities with them. Of these, one million francs worth of

Belgian treasury bonds had to be surrendered to the British Military Government in 1945.

Deutsche Bank fought for control of the Societé Generale de Belgique which was the largest bank in Western Europe. There were two reasons for this: pure avarice and the necessity to expand into regions which the Wehrmacht had conquered – the defeated needed banks too. This edict came down from Reichsbank president Walther Funk. Funk wanted Germany to economically dominate all European countries which it now occupied and the best way to accomplish this was to start with the banks and financial institutions and trickle down from there.

In September 1940, Funk left no doubt as to where he stood: **"Berlin will have to be the center of the European money and capital market…Germany must infiltrate the European banks as strongly as possible with capital and personnel**." And if that wasn't enough, in September Göring said it was necessary for German capital to invest in the occupied Western European countries, as well as the Balkans. To that point, he planned to "enable German banks to acquire these participations in the form of securities for their own account and registered in their name in Holland, Belgium and the occupied territories of France."[276] All of this came under the umbrella of Deutsche Bank's Foreign Department, which controlled 123 branches in ten European countries, Asia and Latin America. It was necessary to have an official department for foreign affairs at the bank due to the scope under which it operated.

Societé Generale de Belgique was the stepping stone Deutsche Bank needed to complete its subjugation of Balkan industry and trade. The Societé had assets of 6.8 billion francs in 1939 and 311 branches in Belgium. Some of these assets included interests in seven different banks in Luxembourg, Egypt, the Congo, London and Paris. As well, the bank controlled two banks in Yugoslavia and the Banca Commerciala Romana in Bucharest. Deutsche Bank and Dresdner fought bitterly for the Belgian banking crown jewel, and it is a testament to the persuasiveness of Hermann Abs that Deutsche finally secured Societé. Originally, Dresdner had won out but after Abs made an overture to the Reich Ministry, the decision was reversed. Carl Goetz of Dresdner was not impressed, writing to Walther Funk and voicing his displeasure, stating Dresdner had refrained from going into the Netherlands on the basis of a positive outcome in Belgium. Dresdner had also given up claims to banks in Alsace-Lorraine in favor of Deutsche.

That Dresdner was the bank of choice for the SS and various other Nazi Party organs was to no avail. Goetz was disappointed, but moved on. So did Deutsche Bank – right into the Balkans with its new capital acquired from Societé, as well as the majority of shares in the Banque Generale du Luxembourg. The Bank of Luxembourg was acquired through pure pilferage – 60% was held by Societé, the rest by Luxembourgers of German descent. These shares were acquired by paying off the citizens of Luxembourg with money from the Belgian Banque d'Emissions. This money came from occupation costs incurred by the Belgians and extracted by the Nazis. The Belgian people paid for Deutsche Bank to take over Banque Generale de Luxembourg. From there, Deutsche Bank reopened its Paris branch after France fell, and then on to Alsace-Lorraine, where Deutsche took over Credit Industriel d'Alsace et de Lorraine (CI), much to the displeasure of Goetz and Dresdner. Now it should be said that CI did not stay open long – the Reich ordered its 37 branches liquidated almost immediately, Deutsche Bank opened four in return and all accounts were transferred to Deutsche.

The war economy presented many problems for Germany, and one was a trade imbalance with countries which still would trade with them. As Germany imported items, it would have to pay for them in either the currency of the country or gold. The only way for Germany to get hard currency was to export items to that country, or with gold from the Reichsbank. Since the Reich was dominantly producing armaments, munitions, etc. it was exceedingly difficult to exchange oranges for tanks, for example, as most neutral countries had no need for Panzers.

Both Dresdner and Deutsche Bank acted as barter agents through a syndicate to finance exports to Romania. The syndicate raised RM200 million in credit and pledged to do more if necessary. To clear a trade deficit with Hungary, it was decided to steal Hungarian securities found in occupied countries and for this Dresdner was called on.

Dresdner already held on to many securities for "safekeeping," and used this as leverage to act as broker for these sales, thence profiting further. Barter is perhaps the wrong word, though it is the one used by the Germans. The barter involved the purchase and import of products, with the barter being nothing more than clearing balances credited to other nations. A more accurate term would be looting.[277]

Overseas

Always thinking of its clients, Dresdner sought to secure their assets overseas when the threat of seizure came. In October 1939, Dresdner hid as many assets it could in the Auslands-Incasso-Bank in Hamburg, a Dresdner-controlled company. Bank officials did this and suggested transferring assets to as many as three more corporations in order to hide them from seizure by British and North American banks. By November, most of the assets had been hidden and the only remaining was at the Mexican branch of Dresdner, which had an account with the private concern Royal Bank of Canada and lost US$160,000 to seizure by RBC

Dresdner employed the impossibly-named Herr A. de Chapeaurouge – Mr. Red Hat – to negotiate with all banks in New York to further make sure no assets were taken. As well, RBC released the money it had seized by December of 1939 thanks to Mr. Red Hat's efforts. Dresdner was anxious to continue having him in their employ, which was a bargain at US$500 a month plus expenses. Mr. Red Hat had served Dresdner at both their Mexican and Madrid branches and had acquired American citizenship after the First World War.[278] Deutsche-Südamerikanische Bank, the foreign subsidiary of Dresdner, was hopeful the parent company would split the costs of having this representative working for both banks' best interests, to which Goetz penciled in the margins of the letter "this seems to me very recommendable."

Allgemeine Waren Finanzierungs Gesellschaft (Allwafinag), again a non-descript sounding company (translated as the General Merchandise Finance Company) was formed by Dresdner in September 1939. Its purpose was to take over the foreign assets of companies which were in no position to own any foreign assets, though Dresdner was not as under-the-table with these transactions. Though it was supposed to be a shadow company, somebody at Dresdner circulated a pamphlet with the phone number of the main Dresdner switchboard for Alwafinag.

Far East

In Asia, Deutsche Bank had holdings in Shanghai, Peking, Canton, Tientsin, Tsing-Tao and Hangchow through its Deutsche-Asiatische Bank (DAB). Deutsche, Dresdner and Berliner Handelsgesellschaft were the main shareholders of DAB, with Deutsche Bank holding 60% of the share capital. In order to have complete control of DAB, other shareholders were pushed to the background when the bank issued 1,000 preferred shares with a 50-vote power attached to each. These shares were issued to the three banks with Deutsche holding 600 of them, Dresdner 200 and Berliner 100 with the rest distributed to smaller banks and private individuals. This was Deutsche's main outlet in China until the end of the war.

The need for a sound partner in the Axis led Nazi Germany to finance Japan – and Deutsche, Dresdner and Commerzbank went along for the ride. Deutsche Bank für Ostasien was founded in 1942 to handle banking transactions in connection with the German-Japanese trade agreement, with Hermann Abs as chair of the Aufsichtsrat. Japan was going to make Manchuria its arsenal, and Germany was going to help by financing the building of coal mines, power plants, automotive and aircraft industries in the formerly Chinese province. This time the syndicate provided Japan with RM155 million, with Deutsche contributing 73 million and Dresdner 23 million Reichsmarks. This was in 1937; by 1939, the Japanese were funding the importation of German weapons, precision instruments, chemicals and aircraft with money borrowed from the syndicate once again. By 1942, Japan had borrowed over RM600 million from the German banks to fund its war machine, and hence why the syndicate created the Deutsche Bank für Ostasien.

As Deutsche Bank was the *de facto* leader in import and export business finance, its involvement in Japan was the most logical step. It was not, perhaps, the most profitable, as quoted in the bank's 1934 annual report:

> *Although this part of our activities, which formerly prospered to a particular degree, is hardly profitable anymore, we regard it as a necessity and a duty not only toward our own interest, but also the interests of Germany in general, to devote our special attention continuously to Germany's foreign contacts even if incurring sacrifices.*[279]

Sounds like no bank I know. There was definitely money to be made in this arena, especially through the import of raw materials for rearmament. Also, both Deutsche Bank and Dresdner Bank's South American and Spanish affiliates bore fruit readily. Deutsche Bank subsidiary Deutsche Überseeische Bank (DUB) outdistanced Dresdner's Deutsche Südamerikanische Bank in all countries they competed in, with the Deutsche Bank subsidiary being the bank of choice of German companies operating outside the Reich such as IG Farben, Siemens, Mannesmann and Zeiss Ikon. The Deutsche Überseeische Bank was founded in 1886 and was the largest German bank in South America and Spain, though the branches in Brazil, Argentina, Chile and Peru were liquidated by their respective governments. One subsidiary which flew under the radar with Exportkreditbank AG; its only purpose was to conceal foreign credit balances and deposits to keep them from prying eyes and seizure abroad. DUB financed the export of machinery, chemicals and photographic tools and the import of rawhides, tungsten, cork, oranges and fruit pulp. So, while Deutsche Bank was griping about its involvement in overseas trade, in the same annual report it had this to say about DUB:

> *The Deutsche Überseeische Bank is able to report a gratifying stimulation of economy...the bank was able to extend valuable service to the cultivation and promotion of German foreign trade...and was increasingly active in the promotion of German export and particularly in providing Germany with raw materials...*[280]

So which is it, gratification or incurred sacrifices? South America was an important trade partner with Germany in the years leading up to the Second World War, with Brazil, Argentina, Uruguay and Chile leading the way. From these countries came raw materials and agricultural products and from Germany – or mainly Krupp – came arms and munitions exports. The trade agreements were mainly barter systems, which conserved Germany vital foreign currency reserves.[281] The most important part of this agreement was not trade however – it was the position Germany wanted and so desperately needed in the Western Hemisphere. Relations with the South American countries had soured after World War I, giving the United States and Great Britain a foothold. After the trade agreement, Great Britain was relegated to third spot in trade with Mexico, Ecuador, Paraguay, Colombia, Uruguay and Central America behind the United States and Germany. Deutsche Bank in particular was instrumental in the betterment of relations with South American governments since it was well established in the region.

This also helped with Deutsche Bank's effectiveness in hiding its foreign holdings in the years before the war. The clouds of conflict were gathering over Europe, and Deutsche Bank was incredibly prophetic in realizing this. In 1936, it was already hiding customer deposits in the United States. By the time war broke out, Deutsche Bank was using its connections in the Netherlands to hide German assets in the country and had started using a number of dummy corporations to camouflage German holdings in foreign countries. One of the shadow companies was AG für Vermögensverwertung (the company for asset recovery) which was founded in 1911 as a finance company. Deutsche transferred all of its stock and other securities in 23 separate countries to the AG in an effort to camouflage them.

Deutsche Bank then directed its branches in the U.S., Holland, Switzerland, Belgium, Sweden, Norway, Denmark and Finland to put at their clients' disposal all free foreign exchange. The money taken would be credited by the Reichsbank without mention of Deutsche and the bank's own accounts were transferred to the National Banks and the Federal Reserve of each country, under the Reichsbank's accounts. As the war closed in, the AG was used to cloak the purchase of Kronprinz by Mannesmann, as well as the protection of assets in neutral countries in South America and Europe.

Espionage and Propaganda, a side business for Dresdner

Dresdner put its leading foreign branch personnel at the disposal of the Foreign Office when the war broke out. When diplomatic relations between Turkey and Germany were starting to break down, Dresdner instructed its manager in Turkey to remain in the country to not only look after German assets but to also lay the groundwork for future German activities in Turkey. Dresdner was also the conduit for money between the Reich and spy-turned-diplomat Franz von Papen in Turkey. Hidden behind dummy transactions to the German School in Istanbul, Dresdner contributed RM13,000, to be used by von Papen for espionage and propaganda activities.

In Egypt, Dresdner employees embarked on a campaign of espionage and pro-Nazi propaganda in the years leading up to the war. Practically all employees of Dresdner in Egypt engaged in these events on behalf of the Nazi Party, the Foreign Office and German Intelligence. There was no financial reason for the two branches in Egypt to be open, only for the dissemination of Nazi information. Willy Lohmann and Hans Sieber, both Dresdner Egypt employees, were closely associated with the party in Egypt and acted as a liaison with the German Consulate in Alexandria. They were not the most rabid followers in Egypt – that title goes to Baron von Richter who was the director of the Cairo operations and was a constant companion of the German Ambassador. Then we have Ernst Otto, who worked for both Dresdner and IG Farben. He was one of the longest serving members of the Nazi Party and was specially trained in propaganda and spying.

It wasn't just limited to espionage either – Dresdner actively engaged in pro-Nazi propaganda in foreign branches. The Reich Foreign Department asked all banks with branches outside Germany to enlighten these non-German clients as to the benefits of the Nazi regime in Germany. Carl Goetz replied with a list covering Holland, Switzerland, Romania, Luxembourg, Denmark, Belgium, Sweden and the United States, then expanded the reach of the program to Dresdner branches in Argentina, Brazil, Chile, Mexico and Paraguay and to Bolivia, Ecuador, Peru and Venezuela through the subsidiary Deutsche-Südamerikanische Bank. And let us not forget the Aryanization requests from Berlin. Even in Buenos Aires, a Jewish manager was not safe. At Dresdner's branch in the Brazilian city, a Mr. Haase was dismissed even though he was "undeniably extremely valuable to the bank in difficult times."

7
Aryanization and the Banks

Persecuting Jews was not new to Nazi Germany – as history shows, Jews have been persecuted, robbed and murdered just for being Jewish for over 2,000 years. Catholic Spain was particularly nasty, especially during the Inquisition. A law issued in 1412 at the behest of the Dominican friar Vincent Ferrer was to force the Jews of Castile into ghettos and live in poverty to further humiliate them. The Grand Inquisitor Tomas de Torquemada took up the cause, forcing the conversion of thousands of Jews and Muslims.

Aryanization was the latest form of persecution and was a truly Nazi concept. It was used to describe the expulsion of mainly Jews from industry and commerce, which cost them their homes in the Third Reich or their lives. It is well known the Nazis believed they were the chosen ones, descendants of a great Aryan race – the irony of which is Aryans would not have been the blond-haired and blue-eyed ideal, but more Indian and Middle Eastern in nature. This minor detail didn't stop the Nazis from stealing the concept – as they did with the swastika – of a super race from which they all came.

But now to the twentieth century.

November 1938: Dresdner, Deutsche Bank and Commerzbank attended a meeting on the invitation of Göring. There, the Reichsmarschall voiced his desire to "transfer the entirety of Jewish property and material assets from Jewish hands to state and later, perhaps, private ownership."[282] The banks were all behind this request, but they foresaw a problem. Banks were no longer issuing credit to Jews, as they were clearly now a bad risk investment. This, in turn, caused the Jewish clients to sell off their assets, including stocks, bonds and jewelry to finance either their businesses or their escapes from the country. If this happened, the flood of securities on to the open market could cause an economic crash. What would the banks do?

Luckily, the very intelligent bankers had a solution: they would freeze the securities and sell them gradually to avoid a crash. This was great for the economy, but not for the Reich – it was broke and needed the money now. Again, the banks to the rescue. The group agreed to extend credit to the government, secured by the very Jewish securities they were holding on to. Not only would they profit from the sales of stocks and bonds they invariably picked up for a song, they would also receive interest payments from the Nazis. To top it all off, Deutsche Bank charged its Jewish customers an additional commission and an administration fee to dispose of the securities.[283]

Dresdner was the most aggressive in the use of Third Reich Aryanization laws to add to its holdings within Germany first, then the occupied nations. When Ignatz Nacher, the owner of Engelhardt Brauerei AG realized his brewing concerns was a target, he contacted the Eidenschink banking house to arrange for a purchaser. An agreement was reached, but Dresdner caught wind of it:

in a very short time, due to the fact the bank was interested in acquiring the business, Dresdner had seen to it that Nacher was arrested under some pretext. Before I (one of Eidenschink's partners) was in a position to find Nacher in jail, he was put under such pressure he had to give his lawyer an unlimited power of attorney for the disposal of his possessions. He was informed he would not be set free if he did not sign this power of attorney. When I visited him in jail, this power of attorney was already signed. After signing this, Nacher was released from jail.[284]

Nacher lost control of his brewery to Dresdner, who appointed Karl Rasche and Baron du Four von Farenco to the board with Rasche as chairman. From this, it is obvious someone at Dresdner greased a palm or two to expedite a "proper" transfer of assets to the bank. But it didn't stop there; when Eidenschink launched a lawsuit against Dresdner for breach of contract and damages, Eidenschink partners were summoned to Berlin and told if they did not drop the lawsuit, the Gestapo would have them arrested. Ironically, this small gesture on the part of the Gestapo would turn around on them. Georg Eidenschink, a member of the banking house, was a member of the Nazi Party and a suspected member of the Abwehr, or German Intelligence. When he was arrested and interrogated by the Allies in late August 1945, the Catholic Eidenschink informed them he had managed his own bank in Munich and was a member of the Deutsche Arbeitsfront – the Nazi

Trade Union. But it seems after the events in Berlin, Eidenschink became just a paying member of the Nazi Party and submitted few reports to the Abwehr, becoming active in anti-Nazi activities, including helping the Freiheitsaktion Bayern (Bavarian Freedom Movement).[285]

The Eidenschink banking house wasn't the only one pressured by Dresdner. Gebrüder Arnhold in Dresden, S. Bleichröder & Company in Berlin, Bank für Brauindustrie in Berlin and B. Simons & Co. in Düsseldorf were all targets. Dresdner used the Aryanization policies to acquire these extremely profitable and important banks, particularly Arnhold and Bleichröder. Arnhold was considered one of the soundest and best known of the small banks in Germany and the Arnhold family was worth RM15 million and their existence was made unbearable:

> *The Gauleiter persecuted them in the meanest way and made their life miserable. The Dresdner Bank approached and offered to buy the Dresden branch. The Dresdner Bank did not want to lose this opportunity for prestige reasons. One point which the Dresdner Bank refused to discuss was the question of how the Arnholds shall transfer their now tangible property. The purchase took care of the pensions excepts those of the Jewish employees.*[286]

Besides the banks, there were others. I. & C. A. Schneider, Frankfurt was a leather and shoe manufacturer, with annual sales over RM20 million. One of the owners, a naturalized American by the name of Fred Adler, recalled:

> *My brother and I were put under strongest economic and political pressure by the Nazis. This pressure was practiced on us with increasing force, and culminated in repeated threats on life and imprisonment if we did not yield. Particularly after the well known pogrom of November 9, 1938 (Kristallnacht), this pressure practiced upon us became unbearable, and we gave up our efforts towards either not selling or getting anything remotely equalling the true value of the enterprise. On November 9, 1938, I was arrested and put into the notorious Buchenwald camp. There I received official word from a representative of the Commercial Department of the Frankfurt section of the NSDAP that I could not count on being ever released from*

Buchenwald unless my brother and I accepted the proposition embodied in the enclosed contract. I accepted and I was released on November 23.[287]

The contract paid the brothers less 3% of the value of Schneider. Historical military records mention this case, as well as Dresdner making loans to Aryan members of society to claim their Jewish booty, such as:

- RM1.6 million to Karl Liedermann of the Dresdner board to Aryanize the Goetze company in Silesia
- RM100,000 to Graf Donnersmark to Aryanize the Wemag Eisen Giesserei
- RM1,048,000 to Grohag to Aryanize the shops it had purchased
- 300,000 Reichsmarks to Robert Koch Stiftung to Aryanize Holz Industrie Witkowitz
- RM 2 million to Alfred Bonneke to Aryanize Anselm-Kahn, Heilbronn.[288]

"Aryanize" has a very antiseptic sound about it, but there was nothing surgical about the cuts the Jewish business community was taking at the hands of the Reich and Dresdner. As of 1945, no German bank held accounts of Jews on their books – all assets were confiscated under the Aryanization policies of the Third Reich. This expropriation fell under the auspices of the Gauwirtschaftsberater (District Economic Advisor) and not surprisingly, three directors of Dresdner – Walter Schieber, Wilhelm Avieny and Karl Heinrich Heuser – were all appointed to the position of Gauwirtschaftsberater. They also served on Martin Bormann's Banking Committee and this gave Dresdner a unique and superior position among banks when it came to stealing Jewish businesses. Besides Lindemann, the directors of Dresdner personally benefited from the Aryanization process. Heinrich Koppenberg, who was also the general manager of Junkers aircraft, "acquired" from a Mr. Strauss the Argus Motor Company. Strauss was Jewish and interred in a concentration camp. Dresdner extended a RM2 million loan to Koppenberg for the purchase.

Dresdner actively purchased or help Aryan Germans purchase Jewish firms; it also cleansed itself and its affiliates and the firms it controlled of Jewish and non-Aryan employees. An example of this is the Mimosa Company in Dresden. A Mr. Busch, who was a director of Mimosa and a manager at Dresdner had this letter in his personal files: "In this company and its affiliated companies, all non-Aryans must immediately disappear."[289]

The Böhmische Escompte Bank (BEB) served as the banker of choice for all of the acquisitions of Herman Göring Werke (HGW) in Czechoslovakia, including lignite mines taken from the Jewish Petschek family. Lignite, also called brown coal, was to be used to distill synthetic gasoline, a needed commodity for the oil-starved Nazi regime. The Petschek holdings in Germany, which were even vaster, were taken by Friedrich Flick and the acquisition of these was administered by Deutsche Bank. HGW assets in Czechoslovakia included steel mills, coal mines, locomotive and machinery manufacture and small weapons and explosives manufacturers with a total value of half a billion Reichsmarks. Most often with these transactions, a little arm twisting was necessary on the side of Dresdner. Under the guise of legality, Dresdner used blackmail, fraud, force and pressure on the occupation government of Czechoslovakia to get what it wanted.

An example of this comes from the Georg Stenzel & Co. machine tool company. Stenzel was a Dresdner Bank customer that had its eyes on the tool division of BATA. Baron von Richter put his wheels in motion:

Stenzel does considerable business with BATA's machine tool division in Zlin, and is anxious to affect a close relationship. In case BATA should desire to separate itself from machine tool production, Stenzel would be an interested party. The purpose of Stenzel's visit was:

1. *to request us to ascertain, in the most discreet manner possible,* **whether BATA is considering cessation of machine tool production**
2. *if not,* **whether such cessation could be suggested to BATA by the Protectorate authorities**
3. *to ask us if we are prepared to consider a combination with Stenzel & Co.*

> With respect to #2, Stenzel would appreciate a most discreet approach...²⁹⁰

Imagine, your bank calling on the government to ask them to "suggest" your competitor closes up shop! Aryanization such as this was the most common way for Dresdner to plunder Czechoslovakia. When the Gestapo wanted to dispose of shares in Königshofer Cement held by Jews, they approached Dresdner. The Gestapo held 7,500 Jewish shares in a frozen account, and 1,000 more were held by foreign Jewish nationals. Dresdner negotiated for the purchase of these, though it is most likely the Czechoslovak Jews who held these shares were not likely involved in the purchase. As well, the purchase of 7,874 Jewish shares of Westböhmische Bergbauverin by a German company was facilitated by Dresdner.

Sometimes it was not as surreptitious as Stenzel – there was no discretion in the purchase of the Schick coal mines in Slovakia. LIHAG was a German competitor in the same town and found the best way to be competitive was to have the Schick firm closed down. LIHAG wrote to its Austrian banker – a division of Dresdner:

> Since Schick has never operated in a clean business way and disregards price controls...would it not be possible in line with the confiscation of Jewish interests in Hungary, to assume the Slovakian interests of the Ungarische Allgemeine Kohlen AG and to confiscate the Jewish firm Schick?²⁹¹

If you can't beat them, steal them? Dresdner was so busy at this, they had four people employed in its "Arisierungsgruppe" or Aryanization Group, which dealt exclusively with all matters requiring the purchase, acquisition, theft or plunder of non-Germanic businesses and industry. The Aryanization Group had high administrative expenses – BEB's reporting to Dresdner Head Office stated they were ten times the amount paid for wages. BEB apologized in its reports for this anomaly, stating: "the various divisions have been occupied with special tasks, such as the organic inclusion of the economy of the Protectorate into Greater Germany and the exclusion of Jews from the economy."²⁹²

So well-known was Dresdner and BEB's attention to this subject, companies would call on them on a regular basis. The Gildemann Cigar factory in Hamburg was looking for "an aryanizable object," which from letters the director of Gildemann sent to Karl Rasche, it was obvious they were just looking for plunder. When Gildemann director Helmut Ritter corresponded with Rasche, he stated BEB director Leonhard Stitz-Ulrici had, through a friend of the Göring family, "offered us the firm Waldes & Co." in Prague. Though Gildemann was interested and was heading to Prague, the company was off the market. Below is a 1942 letter from BEB to Karl Rasche:

We inform you we had a discussion with Ritter (from Gildemann) yesterday. Ritter has had previous occasion to discuss with Dr. Hölzer of our board of directors possibilities of acquiring firms in the Protectorate (Czechoslovakia) through Aryanization. As you know, we have given Ritter very detailed written suggestions in this matter...discussion of bank's further aid to Ritter. At any rate we have done everything we can to support his efforts. We will continue to make suggestions to the gentlemen with the scope of our activity.[293]

It can't be said BEB employees were sweet on Helmut Ritter or Gildemann – this was endemic of the entire "dejewification" of the Czech and Slovak people. The acquisition of Herman Pollack Söhne – a Bohemian textile factory by another German company is an example. A letter dated late February 1942 from Reichsprotektor Reinhard Heydrich to BEB itemized the factories owned by the Pollack concern, some of which had already fallen into Aryan hands and the rest to be sold through Dresdner affiliates. Heydrich made clear the purchase price would be applied:

- First against the bank's claims against the company – real or imagined
- 10% to back taxes
- 1½% goes again to the bank for services rendered to Pollack, including negotiations with Swiss banks and other interests.
- Of the remaining, 60% goes to Heydrich as an "adjustment fee"
- 40% goes to Polysamplex GmbH in Prague.

None of the sale price actually goes to the Pollacks!²⁹⁴ SS-Obergruppenführer Reinhard Heydrich was not only the most hated man in Czechoslovakia, but chaired the conference which formalized the Final Solution; was the main organizer of Kristallnacht; was the man Hitler himself called "the man with the iron heart,"²⁹⁵ and was finally killed by an assault team of Czech and Slovak soldiers in June 1942. The town of Lidice was falsely linked to the assassins and was razed; its men over 16 summarily executed and its women and children sent to the Chełmno extermination camp to be gassed.

BEB had prepared a catalogue of 34 other companies which were both "aryanizable" and would be of interest to prospective buyers, including textile mills, cement mills, paper mills, machine shops and chocolatiers. Unfortunately, with atypical inefficiency, BEB apologetically informed the prospective buyer that "21 of the firms are textile firms, which are not interesting objects as most have been shut down or nationalized." But on a cheerful and optimistic note, "perhaps other firms available for confiscation, out the realm of Aryanization, will be discovered in further discussions."²⁹⁶

In Czechoslovakia, as in other jurisdictions, the Reich used "Dejewification" Commissioners to handle such purchase negotiations. Dresdner would act as an agent prospecting out potential buyers for Jewish properties, then the government-appointed – and much more offensively named – Dejewification Commissioner would handle the final terms of purchase from the Nazi authorities, not the rightful owners of the companies.

Dresdner used Aryanization to increase its coffers in ways other than straightforward pillaging of industries; it also used the accounts of Jewish and non-Aryan depositors as a sort of constant cash flow. In 1940, the BEB noted it had moved 125 million Czechoslovakian koruna from blocked accounts to "the benefit of our current accounts."²⁹⁷ This "benefit" was through so-called Evidenzgebühr – Jewish Bookkeeping Fees and totalled just over 2.1 million koruna from 1939 to 1941, or about $1.2 million today. BEB was the greatest profit center for Dresdner during the Second World War. Dresdner noted in its 1942 annual statement BEB profits grew 25%, while profits at the mother institute grew by only 5%. By the end of 1942, this profitability would slow, as the Jewish properties in the Protectorate had been stripped clean as bleached desert bones

In the Netherlands, again Dresdner was a willing participant in Aryanization, engaging in fraud and duress upon Jewish citizens. Not only did it purchase, pillage and otherwise acquire Jewish assets, Dresdner "went far beyond the broad authorizations of Nazi law and attempted to collect ransom or extort funds"[298] from Jewish clients. Dresdner prepared for the Aryanization laws by carefully noting not just Jewish account holders, but also businesses which it did not deal with which were in Jewish hands. These businesses were to be doled out to interested parties at a "fair" price derived by the custodian of Jewish assets. The more businesses Dresdner was aware of, the more commission and fees it could make through the "dejewification" of Holland.

Dresdner's Dutch affiliate Handelstrust West NV was active in the theft and disbursement of Jewish property and like BEB, it set up an Aryanization division with high priority office space adjoining the Vorstand meeting room. Director Knobloch was adamant about having an experienced "Aryanizer" come in from head office, stating it was for the successful protection of their German clientele and it was said in Amsterdam banking circles the filling of the position was urgent.[299] The Aryanization business was brisk for Handelstrust in 1941, and Dresdner wrote in its annual report: "In connection with the Aryanization of Dutch industry, inland clients made use of the Handelstrust West to a significant extent. Countless visitors from Germany, averaging 150 monthly, found advice and support."[300]

Dresdner was gushing with praise at Handeltrust's results. The head of securities at Dresdner wrote in September 1941 about "large packets of Dutch bank securities" being made available, which were formerly in Jewish hands, and this acquisition would allow Dresdner to take significant minority interests. By January of the following year, Jewish-held shares were becoming even more readily available, of which Dresdner availed itself. The largest company Aryanized was Bijonkorf Kaufhaus, a very respectable department store chain with three locations in The Hague, Amsterdam and Rotterdam. It was valued at the equivalent of $90 million (2016) when it was aryanized from the Goudsmit family.

In the Netherlands, Dresdner acted as an extortion racket *par excellence*. Dresdner accepted ransom payments from Dutch Jews imprisoned in concentration camps outside Holland and who held assets abroad. These Jewish clients were of paramount importance to Dresdner – at least until the bank got its hands on their assets held outside the country. Benjamin Soot was a Dutch Jew being held in the Mauthausen camp. Soot had deposited 20,000 Swiss francs at the Schweizerische Bank Gesellschaft (now UBS). The agreement was for Soot to be released to the Swiss Consulate in Amsterdam and his money would be paid to Dresdner. Dresdner would then send the much-needed Swiss currency to the Reich; the Reich would in turn pay Dresdner out in Dutch guilder. Unfortunately for Soot, permission was not obtained from the Nazis and the money was not transferred. Mr. Soot's fate is unknown, though not hard to extrapolate. Unfortunately for Handelstrust, the "appropriate fee for its services" was also not forthcoming.[301]

Dresdner was also an agent for the Gestapo when it extorted assets from Dutch Jews. One prominent case was that of Isaäc Keesing Jr. and his crossword publishing company. Keesing was held by the Gestapo until he handed over control of his publishing house to the Aryanization authorities. In exchange, the Gestapo would release him and furnish a passport to America. Keesing complied and fled to America, returning after the war to reclaim his company, which still exists today as a division of the Telegraaf Media Groep. Isaäc's brother Jacob, Jacob's wife and two half-sisters were not so lucky. Fearing the worst after the Germans invaded in May 1940, the four committed suicide rather than fall into the Nazis' hands.

The forced Aryanization and extortion negotiated by Dresdner was not an isolated incident. Dutch director Knobloch issued a memo stating policy and how the Nazi governors of Holland would facilitate such matters by supplying passports to Jewish citizens. The cost: one valuable business enterprise. In December 1940, the managing director of Handelstrust was replaced by Karl Rasche and all current business fell to Berlin. It is not clear whether the current management was doing a subpar job or if, as the U.S. Military Government report states, Rasche and Joachim Entzian wanted to add to their laurels. It is also conceivable the Netherlands was an important part of Dresdner's business and Rasche wanted to be on top of everything happening there.

Aryanization was not just profitable for Dresdner. Deutsche Bank gained politically from doing its master's bidding and Aryanizing as it was told to do; it also increased profits in the process. Singular to the banking industry, the money held by Jewish clients stayed at the bank if the bank aryanized it. If Deutsche Bank (or Dresdner, or Commerzbank for that matter) waited for the government, the money would be lost.

Deutsche Bank realized this very early on in the process – in 1935 a manager over at Dresdner mentioned to his associates that Deutsche Bank had already set aside five million Reichsmarks to fund the transfer of properties into Aryan hands – at bargain rates.[302] By the time of Kristallnacht, Deutsche already had the dubious title of industry leader in Aryanization. This from Ehrhardt Schmidt, a manager in Berlin:

I recall that letters regarding aryanizations were sent by the Vorstand of the Deutsche Bank to the individual main branches around the end of 1938...they stated first of all that aryanizations were now quite common and then pointed out that the Dresdner Bank was deriving appreciable profits from such transactions. For the same reason, the Deutsche Bank in its own interest would have to take advantage of all opportunities along these lines.[303]

Very rarely in recent history have banks engaged in such flagrant theft to their own ends. Deutsche would go on to own the banks of Simon Hirschland in Essen and Mendelssohn & Co. in Berlin, the largest private bank in Germany up to that time. The Jewish partners at Mendelssohn resigned, the firm was liquidated and Deutsche picked up all client accounts without paying one pfennig in compensation. An easy way to make profit, though by no means the only one; the extension of loans to individuals and companies wishing to Aryanize firms was especially profitable, even if they were at better-than-normal terms. It helped that these companies were severely undervalued, so the loans were never crushing. In Breslau, where there was a heavy concentration of Jewish garment businesses, Deutsche Bank was given the upper hand by Gauwirtschaftsberater Jacob in the city, who later went on to work on the advisory committee of the bank.

As a rule, these enterprises were taken over by managers or buyers who did not have large funds at their disposal and who initially obtained a short-term loan against the cheaply acquired stock on hand. Through the sale of the stock at increased prices, they were in a position to repay or substantially reduce such loans in a relatively short period.[304] Buy low and sell high was the order of the day. It was bad enough some companies were acquired at bargain rates to be added to larger firms; it was even worse some were just speculators, making money from Jewish citizens who had their livelihoods and, more often than not, their lives shattered.

Those who weren't speculating were buying up everything in their path – companies like Mannesmann and Siemens. Mannesmann acquired the Coppel tubing factory through funding obtained from Deutsche Bank to the tune of 1.5 million Reichsmarks. M. Stern AG was acquired by Mannesmann, Hoesch and Rheinmetall equally – this was of particular interest to Deutsche, as it was an existing client of the bank, and it did not want to lose such a prominent customer. Karl Kimmich of the Deutsche Vorstand – as well as the Aufsichtsrat of Hoesch – engineered the deal and helped in funding the RM3.1 million takeover. When Mannesmann wanted to acquire the rest of its subsidiary Kronprinz AG, Deutsche Bank consulted the Prüssische Staatsbank, which had on hand Kronprinz shares which had been confiscated from Jewish citizens. And when Mannesmann wanted to take over the Jewish Hahnsche Werke AG, Deutsche Bank took lengths to acquire non-Aryan shares of Mannesmann to exchange.

Siemens meanwhile exercised its position of strength. When Manfred Aron's company, which made electric meters and radio receivers, became a target, Siemens and Deutsche trained their sights on it. Aron had been arrested by the Gestapo many times and had been pressured to sell. Finally he did in August 1935 at an extreme discount and managed to make it to New York where he lived out the rest of his life. The factory did not fare as well, being destroyed in 1943 during Allied bombing. Extreme discounts were the order of the day during the Aryanization process – when Deutsche acted as buying agent for the shoemaker Bernhard Schulenklopper, it made sure the buyer received a good deal. When the company was originally evaluated, the machinery alone was worth RM90,000 – this amount was then reduced to RM30,000 to make the purchase more feasible since Schulenklopper was not a Deutsche client, and was in a concentration camp at the time. The company had annual sales of over RM700,000, but was sold for under RM94,000.

The term "fraud" comes to mind with many of these transactions – and this is the term used by the lawyers of Franz Müller & Kramer. When Kramer was asked to leave the country, his share of the company was valued at RM1.5 million, of which he received one third. But Kramer was Jewish, and he was targeted by the president of the Gauwirtschaftskammer (District Economic Chamber) in Eastern Thuringia, Alfred Schütz. Schütz received RM550,000 in loans to purchase the shares and a duplicate amount to pay a Commerzbank loan the company had taken out previously.

Larger transactions such as these came under the purview of Gauwirtschaftskammer and Gauwirtschaftsberater (District Economics Advisor of the Nazi Party). The Gauwirtschaftsberater of Berlin was Deutsche Bank board member Heinrich Huncke and this gave him unlimited scope in the area for acquisitions, some of which were to his favor. Before he joined Deutsche, he acquired the formerly Jewish Erste Berliner Rosshaarfabrik – the First Berlin Horsehair Factory through his connections at Deutsche. Though Deutsche's Vorstand first refused to extend him the RM100,000 loan he required, they changed their mind when told of Huncke's "important political connections" and they could not afford to decline his request.[305]

It is doubtful the owners of Erste Berliner received much of the Rm100,000, as Deutsche Bank was also the main collector of fines against Jews instituted by the Reich government after Kristallnacht. The levy was deposited into the Compensation Account for the damages to Berlin and after two weeks swelled to over RM5 million in cash and securities. The securities were then disposed of at leisure by Deutsche. Other banks, including the Reichsbank, forwarded payments into this account, which not only could Deutsche Bank use as a loaning facility, but also took a commission for its work. This was in addition to supplying loans to prospective buyers of aryanized properties and acting as a broker between buyer and seller, incurring more fees.

Of Aryanization, it seems Commerzbank was the least aggressive of the three big banks in pursuing this avenue – except in Holland. While the bank did not actively engage in the program, it did extend loans to those who purchased aryanized enterprises. Deputy chair Hans Harney personally profited from aryanizations, acquiring the lady's coat manufacturer Lachmann & Meyer in Berlin as well as Deutschland & Jassinger in Vienna. In Czechoslovakia, Commerzbank took over shares of Böhmische Industrialbank which had been confiscated from Jewish citizens and other "black-listed Czechs."[306] This acquisition totalled 13% of the bank totalling RM2.2 million. This turned out to be a poor investment however, when Böhmische Industrialbank was merged with Gewerbebank in Prague and Commerzbank was forced to dispose of its shares.

In the Netherlands, its subsidiary Rhijnsche Handelsbank NV acted as intermediary between German Aryanization agencies and Commerzbank clients who were interested in taking possession of Jewish firms. One letter sent from Rhijnsche head office in Amsterdam to Berlin stated

"We should like to inform you that our customer, the Columbia Schönfabriek NV...may be considered for Aryanization...in case customers of yours should be interested to take over the firm we would be pleased to take further steps if necessary also the registration with the Reichkommisariat."[307]

The Aryanization and purchase of NV Magazijn de Bijenkorf (Bijenkorf Warehouse Co.) by Köster-Konzern was financed by Rhijnsche, with the shares acquired from Lippmann, Rosenthal & Co. Köster-Konzern also acquired Maison de Bonneterie (The Hosiery House), bicycle manufacturer Gruno NV, clothing maker Plonka Confectie Bedrijven NV, Kalker NV and Impex NV, all with financing from Commerzbank's Rhijnsche division.[308]

Other Aryanized firms in Holland of which Rhijnsche took advantage were the Jewish firms of Ernst Herz and the clothier Gerzon

Modemagazijn NV, the latter purchased by Dr. Walter Spiecker of Berlin and from which Rhijnsche received a commission of 12,500 guilders. Rhijnsche funded some of the larger Aryanization loans, between 100,000 and 500,000 guilder (over $4.5 million in 2016). Rhijnsche had a sycophantic relationship to military authorities in Holland, to the extent this report was sent to Commerzbank's head office in 1943:

> *As you know we have very close relations with the Headquarters in charge of fortifications. From this Headquarters we receive regular payments for the numerous Dutch and German construction firms working on fortifications. We have augmented our ties to the extent that our bank is favored almost exclusively.*[309]

From Dresdner's 1936 Annual Report: we have given special one-year courses for selected members…by whom the participants received a thorough education in banking and political points of view

Aryanization of the banks themselves

With Hitler's rise to power, industries were pressured to Aryanise, and Deutsche Bank was not exempt from this. Jewish Deutsche management board members Georg Solmssen, Theodor Frank and Oscar Wassermann were all forced to resign by 1934. Wassermann came from a proud banking family, his ancestor Amschel Elkan Wassermann having founded a bank in 1785. The Wassermanns were the bankers of the Kings of Bavaria, financed Turkish and Balkan government interests and Oscar's father August Wassermann was knighted in 1909 when he became the banker to the court of Kaiser Wilhelm. Oscar headed the Berlin branch and later joined Deutsche Bank becoming CEO in 1933. The fall of the Wassermanns was completed when Oscar was forced out later that year and died the next.[310] The Jewish Georg Solmssen replaced Wassermann briefly, was replaced and immigrated to Switzerland, where he died in 1957

Solmssen "in a prophetic letter to the chairman of the bank's supervisory board, wrote: 'I fear we are embarking on an explicit, well-planned path toward the annihilation of all Jews in Germany.' Mr. Solmssen lambasted the 'passivity' and 'complete lack of solidarity' of the country's elite, most of who had not yet become members of the Nazi Party."[311]

These moves were minor compared to what Deutsche did afterwards, but the changes were not seen by the outside world as a criminal purge. In 1939, a naïve economist at Cambridge told "early in 1938 there had been an enormous increase in the sale of pictures, old furniture, objet d'art, etc. in Berlin and this was a sure sign of great prosperity in the business community."[312] Much of this property had been expropriated from the Jewish community, which was being ransacked wholesale.

It didn't stop at removing Jews from German life in general – over at Dresdner, the edict came down the bank had to be fully Nazified. Employees who did not submit were purged from the bank. Those who remained were indoctrinated into the ways of the party. From Dresdner's 1936 Annual Report: we have given special one year courses for selected members…by whom the participants received a thorough education in banking and political points of view.[313]

Between 1933 and 1937, 219 employees were dismissed for political reasons. Robert Stuck, the manager of the Bremen branch confirmed this by saying "we would have come into difficulties with our chief office in Berlin in case we refused (to join the Nazi Party)."[314] Even board members were not exempt. Mssrs. Kopher-Aschoff, Bachem, Meindl and Löser were all dropped since they were "an old line Democrat (Kopher-Aschoff); a manager of a socialist bank (Bachem); had to make room for a Party appointee (Meindl); and because of Party troubles in Essen (Löser).

Those that remained were high up in the SS, which is not extraordinary as Dresdner was the SS bank. On the supervisory and management boards, there were three SS Brigadeführers (brigadier general), one SS Standartenführer (colonel), one SS Obersturmbannführer (lieutenant colonel), two SS Sturmbannführers (major) and one SS Hauptsturmführer (captain). In 1939 Dresdner extended a loan of RM2 million to the Society for the Promotion and

Care of German Cultural Monuments and another of RM5 million to the German Earth and Stone Works Ltd.[315] Both ventures sound legitimate, but they both were under the auspices of the SS Obergruppenführer Oswald Pohl, you realize they are a sham. Perhaps Dresdner management didn't realize this; perhaps they didn't care.

Seven members of the Dresdner boards were also members of Himmler's inner circle of industrialists and bankers, the Keppler Kreis. They included Karl Rasche, Emil Meyer, Fritz Kranefuss, Karl Lindemann, Friedrich Flick and Hans Walz. Walz, though a member of the Keppler Kreis and thoroughly lambasted in the U.S. Military Government report after the war, used his position at Robert Bosch to help Jews emigrate and hide from the Nazis.

As an example of Dresdner's implicit knowledge about the murder of Germany's Jewish population after their deportation to camps in Nazi occupied Eastern Europe, the bank was unwilling to pay pension payments for retired Jewish Dresdner employees directly to the Reich. The Nazis claimed the government should get the pensions to pay for the deportees' living expenses, but Dresdner officials wanted proof the Jews in the camps and ghettos were actually still alive. The issue ended there.

Looted Jewish gold

Deutsche Bank and Dresdner Bank engaged in the purchase of gold bars from the Reichsbank, the origins of which was looted Jewish property. This may not have been completely evident at the time, but recent studies – one by Jonathan Steinberg on Deutsche Bank and one by Johannes Bähr on Dresdner Bank – show the banks actively engaged in the trade of bullion. The gold contributed very little to the bottom line – 0.15% at Deutsche – but it was very important to the German government, who needed the hard currency to pay for commodities abroad, such as tungsten from Portugal and Spain and chromium from Turkey.[316] Towards the end of the Great Depression, Germany's gold reserves were around US$109 million; Belgium's were almost four times that and France had over $3 billion in reserves. Without adequate gold reserves, the Reich's war machine would have sputtered to a halt:

> *Should supplies from Turkey be cut off, the stockpile of chromium is sufficient for only 5-6 months. The manufacture of planes, tanks, motor vehicles, tank shells, U-boats, almost the entire gamut of artillery would have to cease from one to three months after* – Albert Speer to Adolf Hitler in November 1943[317]

This was due to the Reichsmark being virtually worthless outside German and the occupied territories and by mid-1941, the U.S. dollar was also off limits to the Germans. Besides the Swiss franc, the only non-traceable, easily-convertible form of payment was gold. Many times the Reichsbank would convert the gold into Swiss francs, pay the Portuguese government which would accumulate the francs and eventually sell them back to the Swiss National Bank for gold. Deutsche was a minor player in this arena – accounting for less than one percent of the gold laundered through the Reichsbank; the Swiss commercial banks took in ten times as much. The question remains then: why did Deutsche and Dresdner get such a small piece of the pie?

The answer is twofold: firstly it would be easier to launder the gold through a neutral state, such as Switzerland, so as to avoid suspicion. Secondly, Hitler and his cronies didn't like the commercial banks. The Nazis felt the banks, as well as department stores and jewelers, were the bastions of the Jews, making money off the Aryans. As an example of this, Himmler banned Karl Rasche, who sat on the board of Dresdner Bank, from taking a board position at the department store Kaufhof, believing a department store was an "ideologically unsound enterprise."[318]

In conjunction with the Swiss, Deutsche Bank's international presence was very much needed by Hitler, as it could facilitate the U.S. dollar transactions necessary for the Germans to buy hard goods in neutral countries. Through the 1930s and early 1940s, Deutsche Überseeische-Bank (DUB) in Lima and Buenos Aires worked as an agency of the German government. DUB worked with Credit Suisse to exchange gold for U.S. dollars at the set rate of $35 per ounce after Chase National expressed "a rather unfriendly attitude in respect to carrying out its transactions."[319] The Reichsbank approached DUB to act as its agent considering the unfriendliness on the part of the New York banks. In June 1941, a similar agreement was set up between

DUB and Swiss Bank Corp. (now UBS). This arrangement lasted less than a week before Franklin Roosevelt signed the Trading with the Enemy Act into law which made it next to impossible for the German banks to operate in the American sphere of influence. Deutsche never really had a physical presence in the U.S., so this move served only as an irritation.

It did have a presence in Turkey, and this served the Reich well. Turkey remained neutral until February of 1945, but before then would deal only in goods for goods. While the United States and Great Britain pressured Turkey to not take gold from the Nazis, Turkey stated simply the Germans were supplying goods – gold, as well as Panzers and FW-190 fighters – and the Turks were responding with chromite for use in armor, shells, etc. The Allies attempted to preclude Germany and buy up all the available chromite from Turkey in exchange for upgrading Turkey's aged armed forces. Turkey doggedly stayed neutral throughout the war, taking delivery of gold from the Reichsbank via the Turkish offices of Dresdner Bank and Deutsche Bank.

Dresdner and Deutsche Banks also took advantage of higher rates on the Turkish free market for gold, exchanging plundered coins, ingots and bars for Swiss francs. Some of the gold bars came from gold stolen and melted down from concentration camp inmates including jewelry, coins and gold fillings. The man in Istanbul who coordinated the efforts of the banks with the German government was Franz von Papen.

Papen has figured highly in many parts of this book as a spymaster in the United States in World War I, as the chancellor of Germany and vice-chancellor to Hitler and now as the German ambassador to and spymaster for Turkey. Papen was an aristocrat, wealthy, charming and handsome, with slicked back greying hair, trim moustache and pinstripe suit, he cut the figure of the debonair spy about town, a German version of Cesar Romero. Perhaps his years of spying gave him the feeling he could control any situation – he agreed to German President Paul von Hindenburg's request to form a government with Hitler as chancellor and von Papen would serve as vice chancellor. Papen naïvely agreed, believing he would be able to restrain Hitler – and we all know how that went. Hitler kept von Papen around, perhaps realizing his value as a diplomat/spy. He sent von Papen to variously postings, including ambassador to Austria in the years leading up to the Anschluss, the ambassadorship to Turkey and to Rome to negotiate a Concordat with the Vatican. Of the latter, von Papen claimed in his memoirs Pope Pius XII "welcomed my wife and myself most graciously, and remarked how pleased he was that the German Government now had at its head a man uncompromisingly opposed to Communism and Russian nihilism."[320]

Papen lobbied hard for Catholics to support the new regime, based on the shared anti-Marxist principles. As von Papen and his wife were devout Catholics, this served his own interests well, though did not go over well with the anti-Church group which included Göbbels and Himmler. Papen's belief was the Concordat signed with the Vatican would not only give the Nazis the power of the Church behind them, but would make the joining of the very-Catholic Austria with Germany easier. Of course this was not the intent of Pius XII and by 1938, the Nazis had started persecuting Catholics as well.

Again, von Papen believed he could control the situation, as he had with his spy rings. After the Anschluss, he was shipped off to Turkey to act as a conduit for information, documents and espionage on the Allies, which he compiled with the kind donations of the Reichsbank gold filtered through Deutsche Bank and Dresdner. Papen must have done an adequate job – when he was expelled from Turkey in August 1944, he was the "brains of the most complex sinister espionage propaganda ring of our times" though true to his ego, von Papen claimed he could transmit military and diplomatic information to Germany within 24 hours and he spends $1 million a month."[321] Maybe it's just me, but I don't think spies of the highest caliber go bragging to the newspapers about their achievements.

As the conduit for German gold to Turkey, the banks and von Papen bloated the belly of the Turkish central bank, which claimed the increase in its reserves was through trade only. That increase was from 27 metric tons in 1939 to 216 tons by war's end. Turkey's argument was its trade surplus was almost equivalent to the amount of gold received. However, Deutsche Bank alone shipped five metric tons of gold to Turkey, which would not have been a trade transaction but rather a diplomatic one. Dresdner Bank, as it was on the same footing as

Deutsche Bank, would have probably shipped around the same amount. The source of the gold is what is troubling.

Germany only had minimal gold reserves heading into the war. Since you can't conjure gold out of thin air, you have to acquire it by other means. There are no gold mines in Germany and the only active areas were in the Carpathian Mountains in Romania. Of course, there were other means of acquiring gold available to the Nazis.

By the end of 1940, the gold reserves of Belgium, the Netherlands and France were readily available to the Germans as the spoils of war. This can sometimes present issues at the international level, which Germany tried to avoid. Internal civilian gold reserves are another matter. The confiscation of goods from the Jews allowed Germany to build its gold reserves surreptitiously, starting with businesses confiscated or sold to Aryan Germans at ridiculously low prices, some of which would have been paid with gold, some with hard currencies not readily available to the Reich. Then the looting of personal items would have added more to the gold accumulated by the Reichsbank. Many of these personal items, such as watches, eyeglasses, jewelry and dental fillings would have been taken by force and most by the death of their owners.

One such incident was the gruesome massacre of at least 8,000 Jewish men, women and children at Stanislau in the Ukraine on October 12, 1941. The security police (SiPo) as well as the Ordnungspolizei (police) and the Bahnpolizei (railway police) herded the group up, marched them out of town to a Jewish cemetery where mass graves had already been dug, and started shooting. The machine guns fired from morning until dusk and the mass graves were filled. A single entry from the Prussian mint with the notation "Reichskreditkasse Stanislau" is the only clue to the origin of this gold.[322] Dresdner Bank used these and other gold reserves to finance the Reich. According to a memorandum from the U.S. Military Government at the time, Dresdner managed to hide 380kg of bullion and 10,000 gold Napoleons in Vienna, 1.5 million Turkish gold pounds in Istanbul and 150,000 gold mark in Sofia, Bulgaria. The bullion in Vienna alone would have been worth the equivalent of around $18 million today.

Gold wasn't the only item of interest to the Turkish government – in 1942 Germany exported RM100 million in arms to the country in exchange for chromium ore. Tanks, airplanes and ammunition all made their way to Turkey from Germany. To pay for the arms in advance, Turkey sent the equivalent amount of Turkish government bonds to the Nazis, which were held by Deutsche Bank. These bonds were, in turn, used as collateral for loans taken out by arms manufacturers to supply weapons to Turkey. Deutsche Bank extended loans of RM12 million and after diplomatic relations were severed between the two countries, there was still RM90 million worth of Turkish bonds sitting in a vault somewhere at Deutsche.[323]

8
Insuring the Reich

Insurance is an essential business and has been in the modern world since Edward Lloyd set up business in his coffee house in London in 1688 and began underwriting ships in the 1700s. Besides a cemetery plot, it is the one item everyone buys but nobody wants to use. It is perhaps the least wanted commodity on the planet, with apologies to the industry. Another person who apologizes, but this apology is not to the insurance industry but for it, is Henning Schulte-Noelle, former CEO of Allianz AG:

> *Allianz recognizes its moral responsibility and stands up to its history. Our goal has always been to ensure that the best interests of Holocaust survivors, their families and heirs remain at the center of our efforts. This is why we have at all times remained committed to the expeditious and fair settlement of all valid claims.*[324]

Allianz is a company which has been lionized in recent years over its involvement in Nazi Germany. Its beginnings were much more auspicious – in 1890 Carl Thieme and Wilhelm Finck created Allianz as the daughter company of Munich Re. Allianz listed on the Berlin Stock Exchange in 1895, underwritten by Deutsche Bank. By World War I, the company had operations in the United States and Europe and was collecting 50 million marks in premiums a year, though this was only just over 2% of the German insurance business.

The war made for a different environment for insurance and insurance companies. In Great Britain, it became necessary for many companies in London to take out zeppelin insurance in case of an air raid. In the U.S., the American government issued war risk insurance to its soldiers, paying $4,500 to the soldier's family in case of death or disability. The government also sold low cost insurance to soldiers, which ended up generating $40 billion in life insurance in force by the end of the war.

In Germany, drafting of able-bodied men meant women started working at Allianz (as a sign of the prudish times, they left work ten minutes earlier than the men so they don't meet up on the way home). Sales decreased both domestically and internationally – internationally of course due to either trade restrictions with enemy entities or declining public opinion. On the other hand, payouts increased in Germany, mainly burglary and theft, though property claims are also an obvious choice as the war continued to take its toll. Allianz countered this by entering new fields during the war years, including flight insurance, and with Munich Re, automobile insurance. A double-edged sword was civil commotion insurance after the 1918 overthrow of the Kaiser – by 1920 it provided excellent premiums, but payouts were also high due to continued unrest. The next year Kurt Schmitt became general director of the company and one of his first orders of business was to increase premiums on civil commotion insurance and exit the cartel with other providers, believing their premiums were too low.

Kurt Schmitt figures prominently in Nazi Germany. As a member of the Keppler Circle, he was privy to many of the inner machinations of Nazism. Schmitt also attended the infamous industrialist meeting in February 1933, where he pledged 10,000RM on behalf of Allianz to the Nazi election campaign. That same year, he became Nazi Party member number 2,651,252 and at the end of June he was appointed Reich Minister of Economics, a position he held for only a year. Schmitt then went on to become chairman of the board at AEG and Deutsche Continental Gasgesellschaft and in 1937 became chair of Munich Re, a position he held until 1945. He still maintained a presence on the Aufsichtsrat of Allianz until the end of the war.

Kristallnacht and the Insurance Industry

Kristallnacht – the Night of the Broken Glass – was truly the beginning of the Jewish pogrom in Germany. Leading up to Kristallnacht there was sporadic violence and property destruction against Jewish citizens, mainly in the breaking of plate-glass store windows. The Association of German Glass Insurance Companies had started urging its clients to use either emergency glass or board up the windows with wood until the violence had passed. This was on June 17, 1938 – a day on which Josef Göbbels had also given an inflammatory speech to the Berlin Police: "…police officials (should) consider on their way to work how they can best employ chicaneries against the Jews that day."[325] Don't think about serving and protecting, think about how to cheat or swindle a Jew today! The police took this to heart and arrested around 2,000 Jews in the next four days, some for as ridiculous a crime as jaywalking. While the Jewish citizens were incarcerated, their shops again were broken into, windows destroyed, inventories stolen and the police turned a blind eye.

It was at this point Hitler himself put an end to the actions, but not for humanitarian reasons. Economics Minister Funk complained to Göring this was devaluing the Jewish businesses the Reich wanted to buy up, Göring intervened and Hitler issued the directive. The destruction of the Jewish businesses, especially those in the middle of Aryanization negotiations was not in the best interests of the Reich economy. As well, German insurers were taking the brunt of the fallout as they had to pay out claims to Jewish policyholders. This last part was set to change very shortly.

The actions which precipitated Kristallnacht are well documented, so here is a very concise version. Herschel Grynszpan was of Polish Jewish descent and was sent to Paris to live with his aunt and uncle until he could immigrate to Palestine as he wished. This was in 1938 – at the same time his father Zindel's Hannover grocery store was losing business rapidly from anti-Semitic sentiment. This culminated in a Reich decree that all foreign-born Jews would be forced to leave the country. The Polish government did not want back its ex-citizens either and issued an order stating it would not accept Jews of Polish origin after October 31. To beat the deadline, the Gestapo herded up as many Polish Jews as it could on October 27 and sent them on trains to the Polish border – Zindel Grynszpan and his family were among this group. Zindel, who survived the war, testified at the trial of Adolf Eichmann in 1960:

> On the 27th of October, 1938, it was a Thursday night, at eight o'clock, a policeman came and told us to come to Region [police station] Eleven. He said: 'You are going to come back immediately; don't take anything with you, only your passports.'...there were people from all over town, about six hundred people. There we stayed until Friday night...then they took us in police trucks, in prisoners' lorries,

about twenty men in each truck, and they took us to the railroad station. The streets were black with people shouting: 'Juden raus to Palestine!'(Jews go back to Palestine)...They took us by train to Neubenschen, on the German-Polish border...There came trains from all sorts of places, from Leipzig, Cologne, Düsseldorf, Essen, Biederfeld, Bremen. Together were about 12,000 people...

When we reached the border we were searched to see if anybody had any money, and anybody who had more than ten marks – the balance was taken away. This was the German law, no more than ten marks could be taken out of Germany. The Germans said, 'You didn't bring any more with you when you came, you can't take out any more.'...The SS men were whipping us, those who lingered they hit, and blood was flowing on the road. They tore away our suitcases from us, they treated us in a most brutal way...When we got to the open border...the Poles knew nothing. They called a Polish general and some officers who examined our papers...it was decided to let us enter...The rain was driving hard, people were fainting...There was no food, we had not eaten since Thursday...[326]

It was under these conditions Herschel Grynszpan received a postcard in Paris from his sister on the third of November. Herschel brooded on the postcard for three days until he left his aunt and uncle behind and went to a Paris gun shop where he bought a revolver. From there he took the Metro to the German Embassy, where he inquired to see an embassy official. The unlucky man to meet with Grynszpan was Ernst vom Rath, who ironically was under investigation by the Gestapo for his anti-Nazi and pro-Jewish sentiments. Grynszpan followed vom Rath into his office, where he took out his gun and shot him five times. Rath died in hospital six days later – Grynszpan surrendered to French police and was extradited to Germany, where he disappeared.

Hitler was informed of vom Rath's death at a dinner commemorating the Bierkeller Putsch. Hitler decided to let slip the Nazi dogs and said the "spontaneous actions in response to the vom Rath assassination were not to encounter interference"[327] and so started the violent purge known as Kristallnacht. Over 7,000 Jewish businesses and hundreds of synagogues were destroyed and 91 Jewish citizens were brutally murdered. Thirty thousand Jews were taken away by the

Gestapo for internment – usually brief yet still terrifying – in concentration camps.

This was exactly what Hitler and Göbbels wanted. In his diary, Göbbels noted: "The Führer wants to take very sharp measures against the Jews. They must themselves put their businesses in order again. The insurance companies will not pay them a thing. Then the Führer wants a gradual expropriation of Jewish businesses and to give the owners paper payment for them that we can void any time."[328] The German insurers then received a directive from the Reich Association of the Insurance Industry – headed by the vice chair of Allianz's Vorstand Eduard Hilgard – to have a uniform policy when dealing with the destruction. This uniform policy was set out *if* the policyholders would be compensated; Kristallnacht could be considered a civil disturbance and then all claims could be denied.

Eduard Hilgard directed all members of the association to acknowledge all reports of damage, yet not to pay any monies out yet until the Reich had determined the appropriate steps. These steps would be considered at a hurriedly called meeting at the Reich Air Ministry on November 12, 1938, where Göring had assembled 100 top civil servants, party officials, businessmen and Hilgard to address the next steps. Before going into the meeting room, Hilgard was approached by a few of Göring's adjutants, some of whom intimated that Göbbels was on the ropes after the purge and Hilgard had the ability to finish him off and rid Göring of one of his archenemies. Hilgard sat at the head of the horseshoe-shaped table, flanked by Göring and Göbbels.

Right away Hilgard was in a difficult position – the man on his right wanted the man on his left dead, yet both were extremely powerful in Nazi Germany and both had the Führer's ear. Göring claimed at the meeting he had enough of the civil disturbances. Göbbels said there was no such thing as a civil disturbance in Nazi Germany, an irony which shot holes in the insurance companies' hopes of not paying out the exorbitant damage claims. Göring stated the demonstrations didn't hurt the Jews, but it did hurt the insurance companies, which would have to pay out the claims and this would cause great harm to the economy, since most goods stolen would have to be bought with foreign currency. Göring wanted Göbbels to put a full propaganda feast together, in which he would state it was the insurance companies, and not the Jews, who were hurt in the latest round of rioting.

But there was a way in Göring's mind the insurance companies could pay and he could get his hands on foreign exchange – what if the companies could use the reinsurance companies in other countries? These reinsurers could cover the losses and pay them out in American dollars, French francs or pounds sterling. The Reichsmarschall continued, but Hilgard explained to him the lapse in logic this idea presented. However, there were foreign insurance policies that could pay out and this was an avenue worth pursuing.

The Allianz board member explained to the group there were three major kinds of insurance which came into play after the riots: theft, fire and glass. The fire insurance would be mostly claimed by Jewish citizens according to Hilgard's reports; the glass insurance would be overwhelmingly claimed by Aryan citizens, as they owned the properties – the Jewish shop owners usually just rented; the theft insurance would be divided fairly evenly between the two groups. At this point Göbbels said the Jews must be made to pay for the damages. Göring flew into a rage, saying there were no raw materials to make the repairs, the glass itself was imported, which would cost foreign exchange. Hilgard told the group the glass mainly came from Belgium and would cost at least RM3 million to replace and take probably six months for the Belgians to manufacture that much glass.

Göring's anger boiled over when Hilgard insisted the policies should be paid out, if for no other reason than for the insurers to save face in the international fields in which most of them exercised. If not, confidence in Germany would fall and many of the companies' international customers could cancel their policies as many would assume a German company wouldn't pay out if required. It was at this point Reinhard Heydrich spoke up and suggested the insurance companies pay out the claims, but then the Reich would confiscate the money and return it to the companies. Hilgard had already considered this as the proper course of action, though Göring's take on it was a little different; yes the money would be confiscated, but the Finance Minister would receive the money and what he does with it is his business.

Two major decisions were made at the meeting:

1. *Under the pretext of atonement for the murder of Ernst vom Rath, the entire Jewish community was obliged to make a so-called "expiatory payment" - a payment of 1 billion Reichsmarks - to the state.*
2. *By means of the "Ordinance for the Restoration of the Appearance of Streets," the Reich confiscated any property insurance claims to which German Jews may have been entitled. All shop owners were then obliged to repair any damage to their businesses. The compulsory "Aryanization" of all business enterprises was to be pursued as quickly as possible.*[329]

All claims from non-Jewish citizens and foreign Jewish policyholders were to be settled and all claims from Jewish Germans were abolished by ministerial order. Walther Funk argued the insurance companies should not pay and the Jews should. The plan to levy a fine of RM1 billion on the Jewish population – equivalent to $6.8 billion today – was to absorb the costs of the riots, though Göring wanted every pfennig. Göring is quoted in the meeting as saying the insurance companies should have the money to cover the losses and if they don't, they shouldn't be in business at all: "Such an insurance company would absolutely be a fraud against the people…The insurance companies have to accept the full legal liability for them and to pay."[330] At this point, the issue came up of goods on consignment from American and British companies which had also been destroyed. Göring stated these goods would be paid by the offshore insurers these companies obviously would have used. Göring felt Hilgard should be happy, since it meant there was less for the German insurers to pay. Hilgard still stuck to the view the companies should be recompensed by the Reich for its losses, at which point the Reichsmarschall stated:

Excuse me! If you are legally liable to pay 5 million, and suddenly an angel in my somewhat corpulent form comes and tells you: you can keep 1 million, then damn it, is that not a profit? I only have to look at you; your whole body exudes satisfaction. You are getting a big rake-off.[331]

An angel in my somewhat corpulent form? Who knew Göring was a self-effacing comedian? In any event, Hilgard made one last plea to Göring, saying the German community as a whole would suffer, as this would lead to higher insurance premiums. The Reichsmarschall responded by saying: "Then please be good enough to take care that not so many window panes are broken." The meeting ended, and the Reich issued new anti-Semitic decrees. One of these was the remittance of 20% of their assets as part of the damages levy. This would include all insurance payments, which were to be made directly to the Reich. If the insurance payments exceeded the 20%, too bad, the Reich was taking them anyway.

Hilgard returned to his office after the meeting and received a call from an official at the Finance Ministry, who told him Göring would be happy with a RM20 million payment to let the matter slide. Hilgard was not in the palm-greasing mood though, and decided to consult his friends at the Reich Economics Ministry, stating such a payment would be catastrophic for the German insurance industry. Hilgard worked with Hans Goudefroy, an Allianz lawyer who became CEO of the company after the war. They narrowed down the scope of the damages, sticking to the letter of the law by paying out policies only when it affected the appearance of the streets and how businesses and houses looked from the outside. Any damages inside businesses, loss of product, and so forth, as well as damages done to synagogues and Jewish schools, were not to be covered. Further, the companies would not pay out liability claims, since the Reich courts declared there was no liability, citing it was a civil disturbance – although Göbbels still claimed such a thing never happened in the Fatherland!

Goudefroy and Hilgard went on to say there was no liability because the event was akin to an earthquake, an "eruptive outburst of anger of the population" in response to Grynszpan's assassination of vom Rath, an argument backed up by Göbbels publishing an article on November 12, 1938.[332] The two patted themselves on the back for their skillful maneuvering, and said the Aryan claims of restitution were the result of the Jewish population – if the Jewish shopkeepers hadn't rented from them in the first place, their buildings would never have been damaged, so it was the Jews' fault.

Through the decrees of November 12, 1938, the entire Jewry has been pronounced guilty of the Paris murder and thereby of a provocation against the German people. When the provocateur brings about the event provoked, then he must accept being treated like the perpetrator himself. It will not do to treat the politically condemned Jews as being legally guiltless with respect to insurance. As a consequence, it is justifiable to raise the objection that the German and stateless Jews were responsible for being intentionally, or at the very least being grossly negligent in bringing about the insurance case. Thereby, however, all insurance claims are rendered inapplicable.[333]

For the two Allianz men to state it was the Jews fault just because they were Jewish is incomprehensible today. Goudefroy and Hilgard continued backing up their argument by saying a payment of Jewish claims would have been "a violation of good morals," since all Jews were criminals. This defence goes part and parcel with the companies' determination not to pay out outrageous sums which they knew would be deposited in government coffers. Of the almost 44 million Reichsmarks in damages, only 3.3 million was for Aryan citizens and foreign Jews, the rest being claimed under "Jewish liability."

The Nazi government became involved further when it was realized the scope of the destruction. On December 8 1938, another meeting of various ministries was held to decide who was and was not getting paid. Of particular interest were foreigners and those who had recently Aryanized businesses which were now in ruins. Also discussed was the real possibility of foreign insurers suing the government because of the unrest and therefore claiming zero liability, a stance which the German insurers were prepared to take as well. Hilgard attended the meeting as well and once again, the idea of the insurance companies paying monies to the Jews, who would then have it confiscated by the government, then returned to the insurance companies was put forward. The Finance Ministry and the Four Year Plan boys opposed this idea – they felt the insurance companies weren't so bad off and that they were shirking their responsibility in the matter. Again, the Reich government wanted every pfennig they could get their hands on.

Hilgard reiterated Kristallnacht was a civil disturbance and the companies weren't liable to pay in such circumstances. He backed up his arguments with international newspaper articles, specifically from the British paper *News Chronicle*, citing the disturbance would cause undue hardship and ultimately the bankruptcy of many of the German insurers. Also, the British reinsurers would not back up their commitments because it was a civil disturbance and therefore they were not liable to pay. A civil disturbance, in the eyes of both the Germans and the British, was an act which should be paid for by the state – or in this case the state after they had fined the Jews for being Jewish.

On behalf of Allianz, Eduard Hilgard again suggested the company would be recompensed for their damages payments by the Jewish fine, but would administer the reparations to get these businesses and homes back together again. A kindly gesture, surely, and he backed this up with the comment that paying out the Jewish policies would "weaken the profitability of German insurers in favor of the Jews and contradict the healthy feeling of justice among all national comrades to the highest degree."[334] And God knows they couldn't weaken their profitability by paying out monies owed to the Jewish population.

By May of 1939, Hilgard made clear his position once again – paying out the Jewish insurance claims would be the same as the insurance industry paying a special tax. Under German law at the time, there was no legal obligation to pay Jewish claimants, since the Jews were *persona non grata*. The question the insurers now had to ask themselves *was there a moral obligation to pay the damages?* On this, Johannes Tiedke of the Alte Leipziger Insurance Group felt only the legal position should be upheld, otherwise moral and technical issues would get in the way of the industry.

Moral objections aside, Hilgard now went back to the Nazi government after hearing a figure of RM1.5 million from Allianz's Alois Alzheimer – no relation to the famous neuropathologist of the same name. This was substantially less than the RM44 million figure floated about and much more palatable to the insurers. Hilgard went into a meeting with Reich Finance Ministry official Johannes Schwandt claiming the statute of limitations for break-ins and theft had passed, so again the insurers had no legal obligation. By the time everything was settled and synagogues, Jewish schools and broken glass was removed from all insurance calculations, the industry forwarded a payment of RM1.3 million to the finance ministry.

The smoke and mirrors did not stop there for the insurance companies – the industry group instructed its members in August of

1939 to make fictional payments to Jewish claimholders, who would then receive a nicely worded letter letting them know their payment had been made, then taken away:

The payment is made on the basis of...the Decree on the Restoration of the Appearance of the Streets at Jewish businesses...and the Implementation Decree for the Atonement Tax of the Jews...due to the events of November 1938 on the basis of an understanding with the Reich Finance Ministry, Economics Ministry, Justice Ministry and the Reich Interior Ministry without recognizing a legal obligation in view of the doubtfulness of the case.

You are entitled to deduct the above mentioned sum from the last partial payment due on the Atonement Payment of Jews of German Citizenship...No further claims against us exist on the basis of the existing insurance policies...[335]

The money Jewish citizens were counting on, many of them just to flee the country, was now in the hands of the Nazi government. I don't imagine most Jewish citizens kept up their insurance after that letter – assuming they hadn't already been deported to concentration camps.

As we speak of policies, let us delve into the issue of life insurance policies. Today, there are two major types: term and whole life. Term policies have a set time for which they are in force – for example, you would negotiate a 20-year policy paying maybe $500 a year for $50,000 in insurance. At the end of the 20 years, there is no value to the policy and you renegotiate. A whole life policy has a cash value, which builds over the term of the policy – you would have a policy for your entire life, paying perhaps $600 a year for $50,000 in insurance, but you can cash in the policy at any time and receive a portion of your premiums in return. An excellent way to save money especially if you run into financial difficulties you can use the cash value as a last resort to pay down debts or escape the Nazis.

This is precisely what Jewish policyholders contemplated in 1938 and 1939 after the pogrom; let's get our money and run and this is precisely what the Isar Life Insurance Company – acquired by Allianz in the mid-1990s – had to deal with. Isar had a very large part of its portfolio – up to one quarter – in Jewish and non-Aryan policyholders. Many had already cancelled their policies before Kristallnacht, but now many were trying to cash in their life insurance policies in order to either pay the atonement tax or get out of the country. Isar's directors wanted to switch the policies into paid-up versions – the Jewish holders would no longer have to pay premiums, but they would not be entitled to cashing out the policies either. When Isar approached the Reich government with the proposal however, they were turned down.

Isar ended up paying out RM6.4 million to policyholders, though much of this money went to the Reich in the form of the atonement tax.[336] One of the interesting things to note was the insurance business ran counter to Nazi ideology, specifically towards the Jews. A good insurance client is a live one, continuing to pay into their policies. When a client decides to cash in their policy, that is money the insurance company no longer has and is no longer profiting from. Also, when a client is exterminated in a concentration camp, their policy is payable; in other words, the Final Solution was bad for business.

One point is clear: the insurance companies were not going to profit from National Socialism. According to Gerald Feldman in his book *Allianz and the German Insurance Business 1933-1945*:

the National Socialists were highly successful in achieving their purpose of relentlessly collecting the cash value of most Jewish life insurance policies in one form or another...the National Socialist government, not the insurance company, benefitted from the confiscation of such insurance assets, and that it was the government, not the insurance company, that cheated the customer of the fruits of his policy.[337]

The insurers in Germany were doing what was in their best interest, and having live clients is always in an insurance company's best interest. Allianz has been implicated as a ready participant in Nazi Germany, and it is true that Kurt Schmitt, the head of Allianz up until 1933 and again in 1938, was a member of the Keppler Kreis, Himmler's inner circle. Schmitt had this to say about his membership in the Keppler Kreis:

During my term as Minister I received numerous invitations written by Fritz Kranefuss (of Dresdner Bank) in the name of Heinrich Himmler to attend as a guest of honor a variety of political ceremonies...and...to attend meetings of the Circle of Friends of the Reichsführer SS. I attended one of the meetings of the Circle soon after and that was the manner in which I became identified with it. Sometime during in 1935, I sought Kranefuss' support in stopping the repeated attacks on Allianz which were launched by the "Schwarze Korps," the publication of the SS. Kranefuss put an end to the attacks and thereupon mentioned to me that since he had been helpful in my interest it would not be out of order for the companies in which I played a leading role to make a contribution to the Circle of Friends. I understood that the contribution was to be for a single time and hence only recommended to the companies in which I held leading positions...[338]

These companies included Allianz and Munich Re, which combined gave around RM21,000 and AEG which contributed RM15,000 in 1935. In 1936, Kurt von Schröder approached Schmitt with a similar request. Surprised, since he claimed he felt it was a one-time deal, Schmitt went forward with the donations yearly until 1942. Schmitt continued to go to meetings of the Keppler Kreis, by his estimates five or six times and only "for the express purpose of promoting or protecting the interests of the various companies in which I assumed a leading role."[339]

When Schmitt became Economics Minister in 1933, he was replaced at Allianz by Hans Heß (pronounced Hess), who was definitely not the poster child for Hitler's Germany. Heß never joined the Nazi Party, preferring to concentrate more on business than politics. He never used the Nazi salute at the office, would not sign documents with the standard "Heil Hitler!" and did not let his children join the Hitler Youth.[340] Heß was, by all accounts, a company man, setting up the company newspaper in 1921 and "Papa Heß," as he became known, was much respected in the company both for his talents and his integrity.[341] A stately corporate type, Heß was integral to the company's values during the period. After the war, Hess claimed to be a member of the plotters against Hitler in the July 1944 assassination attempt, though this has never been proven. It would, however, be in line with his persona.

Schmitt was somewhat identified with the July conspirators, having housed former economics minister Eduard Hamm, diplomats Franz Sperr and Ulrich von Hassell at the offices of Munich Re; Sperr and von Hassel were executed for their parts in the conspiracy, Hamm committed suicide before his hanging. Schmitt himself was under surveillance by the Gestapo though managed to survive through the war.

Allianz and the other insurance companies looked after their interests, as any good business would do, but there were times when they were unable to do what was best for their clients and the fault for this lies solely with the Reich government. Under the *Seizure of Assets of Enemies of the People and the State* law of 1933, the government had the right to take assets of those they deemed enemies – and Jews fell into this category. The cash value of insurance policies was an asset the government was only too happy to get its hands on and the insurers had no choice but to follow this directive. Feldman tells this story: In April 1939, the Gestapo informed Allianz of the revocation of the citizenship of a Munich lawyer, his wife, and his four children – all of whom had emigrated to Australia – and announced that their property was confiscated. Allianz was asked to pay the repurchase value of the policy (RM3,611) to the revenue office, from whom the company subsequently received a receipt.[342]

One thing Feldman points out in his book is the lawyer had still been paying his premiums, under the assurances from Allianz he would be able to collect when the policy came due in 1952. The insurers would receive lists of "Enemies of the People and the State" regularly and would be required to submit the cash values, though Feldman points out the Reich Group of insurers stopped publishing the names in September 1939 with the flimsy excuse it was to save paper.

The companies didn't have much of a choice after a new decree was issued in January 1941. The Nazis were clear: if the money wasn't handed over, whether through negligence or deliberate act, those in possession of any assets – whether banks, insurance companies or the like – would be subject to prison or fines. The insurers and banks came back to the Reich, stating it was difficult to tell who was Jewish and who was not, especially if they were no longer in the country. And since many of the banks and insurance companies had international subsidiaries, it would not only damage their reputation abroad, but could also prove to be legally fatal as these subsidiaries could come under attack from foreign governments and the same people who have had their assets confiscated.

A customer's religion was irrelevant to the insurance company when issuing a policy. Consequently Allianz had no category or special designation for Jewish policyholders. Allianz itself knew that Jewish citizens were more likely to take out insurance policies and therefore were a good customer base. After Kristallnacht, both the state and the Nazi party began the radical plundering of the Jews. Many Jewish customers now instructed their insurers to pay the surrender value of their cancelled policies directly to the tax authorities. In this way they attempted to pay the compulsory state levies and astronomical taxes that were imposed on emigrants. At this point, almost all Jews who had not already emigrated were deported to concentration camps in Eastern Europe. According to Nazi logic they had therefore left Germany and forfeited their German citizenship. All their assets were then seized by the state and banks and insurance companies had to notify the authorities of any assets these "foreigners" had on deposit. These assets then had to be paid over to the tax authorities.[343]

Still, the insurers did not move quickly on identifying Jewish policyholders who had left the country. In 1941, there were over 29,000,000 life insurance policies in force, spread over 85 companies. If each company had twenty people working on weeding out these policies to see if the holder was Jewish or had left the country, and each person looked at fifty policies daily, it would still take almost a year to look through every single policy in the country. That doesn't even include group insurance, the Swiss-owned subsidiaries in Germany and pension funds, and all at a time when employees were being drafted into military service, or being killed in air raids.

Though life insurance policies, specifically Jewish-held ones, were not a profit centre for Allianz, Munich Re and others at the time, the possibilities being opened up by the Reich government and the Wehrmacht were to become an important part of the insurance business. Allianz and Munich Re went about looking for opportunities, starting after the Anschluss. As Munich Re already owned part of the struggling Austrian insurer Elementar-Phönix, it was a great point to start. Munich negotiated with its Italian partner in the venture, Assicurazioni Generali, and offered to buy out its share, leaving Munich Re and Deutsche Bank's Vienna subsidiary Creditanstalt-Bankverein in control of the company. At first reticent, Generali decided to sell its shares in the

Austrian insurer less than three weeks later, though it would seem there was not any arm-twisting involved and the two companies continued a long relationship afterwards. Creditanstalt was not so lucky, having been forced to sell its shares to Allianz and Munich Re by October 1938 and Elementar-Phönix was renamed Wiener Allianz. The former Phönix held many Jewish policies and employed many Jews and it seems Allianz treated some respectfully as they booted them out the door.

Two stories of interest: a Jewish female employee was given her full severance pay when fired and Georg Schlesinger, former director general of the company was given a full year's consultancy fee and allowed to emigrate to South America. These were the good stories; the bad stories were much more prevalent though Allianz itself seemed to be fair. In 1934 James Freudenberg had to step down from his post as Chairman of the Board at a Frankfurt subsidiary of Allianz. He was pensioned off in 1936 at the age of 61 and Allianz paid him a full year's salary in order for him to receive his full pension. Freudenberg was deported and murdered in Auschwitz in 1944. Another case is that of Martin Lachmann, a Jewish agent for Allianz in Berlin. The company did not renew his license in 1938 due to new anti-Semitic laws in Germany. Lachmann's family emigrated to Sweden in the mid-1930s; Lachmann stayed in Berlin – a fatal error as he was deported to Minsk and murdered in 1941.[344]

Though profitability for insurers was hard to come by – with bombs dropping on your customers – Allianz did find opportunities as the Wehrmacht marched into the Sudetenland. Allianz picked up the portfolio of the Slavia Insurance Company in Prague though this was the only success the company had in Eastern Europe. Its ambitions were thwarted throughout the war by the Reich government as well as the Hungarian, Romanian and Czech governments and by the conditions in each country. The company tried to set up operations all across the region, but for the most part the Reich refused to allow it to set up shop. In Poland, Allianz and the Italian company Generali were made trustees of the Polish insurers and in return, the companies along with Munich Re would be given a portion of the portfolios as compensation.

Allianz took over the greater part of the trusteeship of the policies and used this as a base for expansion in the region. Part of this expansion included work for the Head Trusteeship Office East, which was tasked with the Germanization of the Polish economy. This included administering formerly Jewish companies confiscated by the Reich as well as the liquidation of the last Polish-owned insurance company, Vesta. The policies involved only paid to ethnic Germans – Jews and Poles being excluded from their own life insurance policies. Allianz was the insurer of choice for the Head Trusteeship Office and issued policies for liability, automobile, break-in and theft insurance – on this point Gerald Feldman inserted an exclamation point in his book, the irony of an organization whose principal motivation was theft would need theft insurance is not lost on the Berkeley professor. Allianz also engaged in transport insurance for securities confiscated from Polish nationals and sent back to the Reichsbank, much as it did in the Netherlands with Lippmann, Rosenthal & Co.

It is at this point we come to what must be the darkest chapter in insurance and Allianz's history – the insuring of the Łódź ghetto, the Cracow labor camp and of the concentration camps Sachsenhausen, Ravensbrück, Dachau, Buchenwald and Auschwitz. On the subject of Łódź, there was some vagueness on the particulars, since the companies were not allowed to inspect the grounds. On this case, you would think an insurer would be somewhat suspicious, especially by 1941 when Allianz was issuing a combined policy for RM11 million – the equivalent of $72 million today (as a frame of reference, the insurance on the Titanic was $114 million). The company received assurances though that safety standards were adequate, the Łódź fire department could deal with any fire and the warehouses were guarded at all times at the behest of Chaim Rumkowski, head of the Jewish council of elders. Cracow was the labor site for Oskar Schindler and though Schindler worked hard to keep Jews safe, Allianz insured a particularly brutal forced labor camp. And yet, that was not the worst.

The deputy director of Allianz's Berlin office was an insurance salesman of epic proportions. Max Beier had sold insurance in 1937 which garnered over RM1 million in premiums and this made him an excellent candidate to go after even bigger fish. In 1940 he decided government business would be much more lucrative and called on the SS at the Dachau concentration camp. Allianz sold fire and marine insurance policies to *SS-Wirtschaftsbetriebe* (set up at concentration camps to make a profit from slave labor) to cover buildings and goods starting with Dachau. In most cases Allianz transacted this business as a member of a consortium made up of a number of insurance companies.

Representatives of the insurance company were granted access to concentration camps in singular cases. For example, in 1940 Deutsche Ausrüstungswerke (German Equipment Works, an SS defense contractor) granted Max Beier access to the Dachau concentration camp in order to inspect the camp's manufacturing facilities prior to drawing up the terms and conditions of a fire-insurance policy.[345]

Beier joined the SS like some men would join the Rotary Club or the Masons. He used his contacts to penetrate deeper into the business enterprise Himmler was building around himself. When informed of a new factory complex being set up at Auschwitz, Beier contacted the Katowice office to arrange an inspection. Premiums in 1941 on Auschwitz were set at RM1,360. It was a good investment for Allianz, since "The SS territory and the concentration camp is constantly guarded by SS men." In addition, there was a separate camp fire department.[346]

Allianz headed a consortium of insurers to later increase the amounts at Auschwitz, taking 25% of the RM3.2 million RM policy in 1943 and earning the same percentage on the premium. This continued throughout almost the entire the lifespan of the concentration camp, though the insurers did take a hit when there was a fire in one of the barracks in December 1944. Beier was an incredible salesman, actually convincing the SS of the need for Nazi camp employees to have either a pension plan or group insurance. Contract negotiations continued into 1945 at which time the camps were either overrun or the Reich had collapsed.

The only real problem Beier ran into was in February 1945 when he was informed his contracts at the concentration camps were to be terminated. Since the war was in its final stages and Germany would surrender in less than three months, you would think that was the reason. No, the reason was far more bizarre; a different consortium of insurers wanted the business. Why a group of men would get together in the bomb-cratered Reich and want to insure something which was obviously going to be lost in a matter of weeks is ridiculous; either they were zealous believers in the thousand-year Reich or in the power of their salesman.

By the time the war switched to Western Europe, Allianz and Munich Re saw more potential and made more gains. The companies took the portfolios of various British insurers in France, which were the reinsurers of choice in the country. British Victory Insurance Co., for example, had its portfolio transferred to a new company which was formed from the merger of *La Minerve*, *Cité-Accidents* and *Préservatrice*, all of which had used the reinsurance facilities of Munich Re in the past. In 1942, the portfolios of the Hartford Insurance Company in France were added in a surreptitious way – the clients were offered three months of free insurance if they converted over to the new company.

Finally in the Netherlands, Allianz was able to engage in the plunder every other company was, although on a much smaller scale. When Lippmann, Rosenthal & Co., the Nazi front for the collection of Jewish assets, came into possession of shares of Dutch insurer Assur. Mij. de Nederlanden van 1845, Allianz was more than interested. Eduard Hilgard sent this note to Alois Alzheimer in March 1942 regarding the impending purchase:

it can be expected that very shortly the Jewish securities, under which shares of the aforementioned company can be found, will be up for sale. In view of the desired amalgamation between the German and Dutch economies, the relevant German agencies naturally have an interest in seeing that the delivery of the blocks of shares gathered among the Jewish goods...be directed over to the German hands most appropriate for such amalgamation.[347]

In the instance of Assur. Mij de Nederlanden, the German hands most appropriate were those belonging to Allianz. The company purchased large blocks of shares formerly in Jewish hands, totalling 416,000 guilders over the course of five months. Most of these came from Lippmann, Rosenthal, though a large consignment came from Dresdner Bank as well.

As could be expected after the death, destruction and mayhem of the war, Allianz was essentially bankrupt by the time the tanks rolled over the remains of the Wehrmacht and Admiral Dönitz surrendered the country, which then-Vorstand member Herbert Hansmeyer reiterated at the Washington Conference on Holocaust-Era Assets on December 1, 1998.

Did the companies keep the money, as was the case with the dormant (Swiss Bank) accounts? The answer is no they did not. After the war all German life insurance companies were technically bankrupt and kept alive through government subsidies which exactly matched their liabilities. The German Insurance Department conducted audits for a period of 18 years on these subsidies. If the liability did not materialize, then the subsidy had to be paid back to the government. Therefore the companies could not enrich themselves with funds due under unsettled policies. In other words, there are no dormant assets from unclaimed policies. Despite this fact, it is our firm belief that policies that remained truly unsettled should be paid regardless of statutes of limitations and bureaucratic red tape. This has always been our policy, and it remains our policy as part of our voluntary participation in the International Commission. [348]

Allianz, along with four other insurers joined the International Commission on Holocaust Era Insurance Claims and since then up to 2014, more than 48,000 insurance claims with a total value of more than $300 million were compensated.

9
The Electricians

Fewer companies are more diversified and powerful than General Electric. GE's history goes back to the dawn of the light bulb, when Thomas Edison secured the financial backing of J. P. Morgan and the Vanderbilt family to create the incandescent light in 1879. Ten years later, Drexel, Morgan financed Thomas Edison's research and helped his company incorporate. In 1892, the firm helped create General Electric through the consolidation of the Edison General Electric Company.

In Germany, Emil Rathenau purchased the rights to some of Edison's light patents and Allgemeine Elektricitäts-Gesellschaft (AEG) was founded in 1883, with financial backing from Siemens & Halske, among others. AEG was largely responsible for installing Germany's first electric power system and strung transmission lines and built electric trolley systems across Germany before 1900.[349] In 1900, AEG invented the hairdryer and three years later, AEG and Siemens & Halske merged their radio divisions to form Telefunken.

As World War I began, AEG head and Emil's son Walter Rathenau offered his services to form a new central management for the distribution of crucial war supplies. Prussian War Minister Erich Falkenhayn agreed with the concept and Rathenau started the task right away. Rathenau's tenure was brief and less than a year later he was forced to resign – the businessmen under Rathenau's control resented operating under a Jew. Rathenau returned to AEG and became chairman after his father died two months later.

While GE focused on power generation and large scale projects such as the Panama Canal locks and harnessing Niagara Falls, AEG was getting into the aircraft business. AEG put into service in 1916 the first of over 300 twin-engine biplane bombers, powered by Mercedes. All aircraft were confiscated at the end of the war – one survives at the Canadian Air & Space Museum – and AEG was forced back into the electricity business.

It is at this point the story usually intertwines; I choose to take a different route. Many websites and books have made mention of

General Electric's ownership of AEG. There is no evidence of control of AEG by GE, there is only hearsay spread by Antony Sutton is his book *Wall Street and the Rise of Hitler*. In it, he repeats the line "The A.E.G. of Germany was largely controlled by the American company, General Electric," which is a line from James Stewart Martin's book *All Honorable Men*, though Martin makes mention of it once, does not back the claim up and does not footnote his source for his accusation. General Electric *did* purchase 25% of AEG shares between 1923 and 1929, but did not exercise any control over the company. In a memo to then-chairman of the board Charles Coffin, Owen Young recommended GE's participation in a proposed new issue of AEG shares on a scale sufficient to assure a voice in AEG affairs but only that.[350] GE took advantage of the postwar situation and purchased up a good chunk of a competitor. That being said, GE put four American directors on the board: GE President Gerard Swope, GE Chair Owen Young, International GE President Clark Minor and Vice President Arthur Baldwin and had a vetoing minority on AEG strategic decisions. In exchange, AEG received RM78 million and was guaranteed exclusivity in certain markets by International General Electric in 1929.[351]

So we now know four American GE executives sat on the board of AEG, but what pull did they have? GE's acquisitions were historically known for the freedom they provided to subject companies "This basic line of GE's strategy, which was also stressed in negotiations with other companies," historian Harm Schröter argued, "was designed to sustain the feeling of independence in the respective firm."[352] GE's ownership stake was more sharply criticized than any other American industrial investment, both in direct attacks by Siemens, the other electrical giant, and in nationalistic arguments appearing in the German press. A public debate on foreign infiltration occurred, and the Nazi Party demanded a boycott.[353] The year after GE's stock acquisition, Gerard Swope urged Siemens and AEG towards a common policy or even a merger, which would have given GE a share of a much larger combined company but ultimately failed. In the late 1930s, GE mainly aimed to protect its own investments in AEG and Osram, which was a joint venture between GE and Siemens.

One of the biggest theories postulated by Sutton in his book *Wall Street and the Rise of Hitler* is that GE funded Hitler:

> The significance of this General Electric ownership is that AEG and Osram were prominent suppliers of funds for Hitler in his rise to power in Germany in 1933. A bank transfer slip dated March 2, 1933 from AEG to Delbruck Schickler & Co. in Berlin requests that 60,000 Reichsmark be deposited in the National Trusteeship account for Hitler's use.[354]

Yes, there is incontrovertible proof AEG paid Hitler's campaign fund RM60,000. Let us put this into perspective: on February 27, the Reichstag (Germany's parliament) was set on fire and the government blamed Dutch Communist Marinus van der Lubbe. President von Hindenburg agreed to Hitler's request to emergency powers to combat the "Communist threat." Under this guise, AEG made a donation to Hitler, who was facing election on March 5. GE funded Hitler, througha campaign donation during a time of national distress in Germany, well before the Jewish purges and rearmament had started. This does not make the company or the American board members evil – it makes them a group who were trying to protect their investment from what was at the time seen as a Communist threat to their existence.

In 1938, Swope and Young resigned their positions as members of AEG's supervisory board, officially as part of their age-related withdrawal from active service. This move also has to be seen in connection with the anti-Semitic policy in Nazi Germany: in the same year when the Polish-Jewish Swope left his position, the Nazis issued a new law which prohibited the membership of Jews in supervisory boards. Since 1933, AEG had been attacked as "Jewish AEG." Due to pressure from the Nazi party, by 1938 most of AEG's Jewish employees – hundreds of men and women – had left the company. Only a single Jewish member remained on the supervisory board, and only until 1939. When the United States entered World War II, all International General Electric stakes in German companies were treated as alien property in Nazi Germany. During the war, patent and trade agreements with AEG were suspended[355] and all of International General Electric's foreign investments in Axis and enemy-occupied countries – just over $1 billion in 2013 dollars – were written off.

General Electric is one of the largest conglomerates in the world. As the largest electrical manufacturing company, GE actively participated in the war effort by producing an unequaled range of military equipment for all branches of the American Armed Forces. Among the wide variety of war materiel produced in these factories were turbine generators and motors for the Navy's battleships, components for torpedoes, and instruments and engines for airplanes. Scientists from the General Electric Research Laboratory contributed to the development of the atomic bomb.[356]

All well and good. General Electric contributed to the Allied war effort, but also made sure it made a handsome profit from it. In April of 1941, the United States government filed the *United States v. General Electric et al.* as an antitrust suit. The et al. in this case is GE's subsidiary Carboloy and Fried. Krupp AG, the German concern controlled by Gustav Krupp. Krupp's involvement in the Nazi war machine is well documented and will be delved into later. The agreement Carboloy and General Electric made with Krupp predated the war, going back to 1928. "Because of a patent agreement between General Electric Company and the Krupp Works of Germany, the price of tungsten carbide in the United States became more expensive than gold. It rose from approximately $50 per pound to $453 per pound while the price in Europe remained in the $45 to $50 per pound bracket. In April 1942 after an indictment, under the antitrust laws, the price in the United States dropped to a range of $27 and $45 per pound."[357]

The effect of this patent agreement was a virtual monopoly by GE and Carboloy in the United States and Krupp elsewhere. Competitors were excluded by purchase or by boycott, prices were fixed and world markets were divided between the two. General Electric and Krupp executed a 15-year agreement on November 5, 1928 to fix high and unreasonable prices for hard metal compositions and products in interstate trade. By its terms, General Electric fixed exhorbitant minimum prices for the hard metal compositions in the United States and agreed to compel its patent licensees to observe them. Krupp agreed to be bound by the prices and not to sell below those levels in the United States. In consideration, a fund was created to pay royalties to Krupp.[358]

Tungsten carbide was a very valuable composite in World War II, used for high speed machining of metal, tools, etc. as well as armor-piercing antitank shells. Germany had bought up almost the entire world's supply of off-grade tungsten ore prior to the war, including stocks from China, Peru, Mexico and the United States. Germany's use of tungsten carbide shells was a contributing factor to Rommel's early successes in North Africa when they would shred the hapless British tanks.

The Krupp laboratories had found a way in 1927 to make tungsten carbide more usable by mixing it with a cementing agent. This is the patent agreement GE entered into with Krupp the following year.[359] In its case, the U.S. government proved from 1928 to 1940, GE and Krupp had excluded numerous competitors and by pooling patents they threatened competitors' legal right to make tungsten carbide.[360] General Electric was fined $50,000 by the United States as a result of the trial, though they made around $650,000 a year in profits from overcharging the government for tungsten carbide products. The royalties GE collected for Krupp on the cartel agreement, which in 1936 was amended to 10% of all sales in the United States continued until Germany declared war in December 1941. Not only did General Electric profit handsomely from their sales to the American war effort, Krupp also profited from their agreement, and this money was no doubt ploughed back into the German war effort.

The cartel first came to the attention of the Americans in late 1940, when the Firth-Sterling Steel Company tried to sell the U.S. military shells at a price under the cartel minimum. The cartel's hindrance of war materiel production – though the U.S. was still technically neutral – outraged the Senate Committee on Military Affairs. American executives including Carboloy chairman Zay Jeffries, GE trade manager Walter M. Stearns and Carboloy President W. G. Robbins stood trial. GE was found guilty of five counts of criminal conspiracy. Though the Department of Justice requested heavy sentences, Judge John Knox fined Jeffries and Stearns $2,500 and Robbins $1,000.

That's General Electric – more profiteer than slave driver. The same can't be said for AEG. In 1957, five Jewish Germans approached the head of the Central Association of Jewish Congregations in Germany asking for help to get compensation for labor performed at a concentration camp. Secretary General Dr. Henry van Dam pursued the matter in a letter to AEG. AEG's legal department responded with an unequivocal *Nein!* and denied all knowledge and responsibility. Three more people contacted van Dam, who sent another letter, this time asking for the pitiful combined amount of $10,000. Again, a swift "no" from AEG; a third letter was sent before the end of 1957 and a third "no" was sent back. Dr. van Dam turned the matter over to a Frankfurt lawyer.[361]

Were the AEG lawyers correct; was AEG not responsible?

The plaintiff Rivka told a fairly typical story. She had been deported from Bavaria in November 1941 to a Vernichtungslager, or extermination camp, at Jungfernhof in German-occupied Latvia. She avoided being put to death, and in July of 1942 she was sent into the ghetto of Riga as a forced laborer. In November 1943 she was moved to a nearby concentration camp in an area known as Kaiserwald. There, together with some 1,500 other concentration camp inmates, she was sent to work in one of AEG's factories. There was no freedom for Rivka. She was told if she did not lacquer the allotted quota of electrical wiring, she would be shot. According to her testimony, the Jewish girls were beaten by SS and Latvian supervisors and if there was some food left over by Latvian workers, the Germans would through it away with the remark "Better to give it to the pigs than the Jews."[362]

The classic legal tricks of obfuscation and denial were clearly in use. Rivka's story continued when she was moved in October 1944 to another camp as the Red Army advanced. Again, she worked for AEG; this time, the Jewish girls had to march 90 minutes to the plant in Thorn. There, the barracks were unheated; the food inedible. As the Soviets approached, the women were herded towards the concentration camp at Bromberg and abandoned to the fate the Red Army had planned.[363]

AEG's Telefunken division also engaged in such legal wrangling. When approached in 1957 to either settle or give an extension to proceedings, Telefunken's lawyers agreed to an extension, fully believing the case would die. It did not. *Ellfers and 115 others v. Telefunken* was launched and quickly quashed by the Berlin District Court, claiming the plaintiff's lawyer, Dr. Alfred Werner, had failed to itemize the particular individual damages each plaintiff had suffered in great detail. Telefunken's response was:

During the war government agencies assigned workers to us – in addition to your clients – with whom we were not authorized to conclude any employment agreements and with whom no agreements were made. No payment was due from us to these workers who were assigned to us. On the contrary we were obliged to pay the government agency which supplied such labor to us. If your clients believe they are entitled to submit a claim may we suggest that they make such claims to the authorities competent to deal with it.[364]

Telefunken was a supplier of vacuum tubes, transmitters and radio relay systems, and developed radar facilities and directional finders, adding extensively to the German air defence against British-American aerial bombing. Therefore, it was critical to the war effort – but as with many companies operating in Germany at the time, its use of slave labor was appalling. The claim the Nazi government forced workers on Telefunken, AEG and other companies rings hollow. SS Lieutenant-General Oswald Pohl administered the concentration camps during World War II. Before he was executed in 1951, he had this to say: "This is how it worked. The enterprises would either apply to the camp commandant directly or to the office – it depended on their connections and on their situation."[365]

Plaintiffs did not give up against Telefunken with Werner's case. Two days after the verdict, Dr. Karl-Heinz Schildbach launched another case, this time with two co-plaintiffs who had ended up at Auschwitz, then at the Reichenbach camp. Rebecca was 13, her co-plaintiff Magda was 17. In August 1944, after Rebecca's parents had been gassed at Auschwitz, she arrived at the Reichenbach camp, was stripped naked and had all possessions taken away, was issued prison-style pyjamas and wooden sandals and worked for Telefunken twelve hours a day, seven days a week. They lived in overcrowded, lice-infested barracks, were beaten, malnourished, denied access to air raid shelters, all well known to the company's directors. The management would curse the teenagers: "You damned Jews will finally understand what a Hitler-Germany means. Our Führer knows what he is doing and we are proud of him that he will finally drive you Jews to your death."[366]

AEG, which had previously made benign electrical components, converted its factories to armaments. It manufactured tank and aircraft parts and used laborers from the Sachsenhausen camp. The Hennigsdorf plant near Berlin housed nearly 4,000 inmates in a camp near the Hohenzollern canal and included the Jewish, *Ostarbeiter* (Eastern Europeans) and French and Soviet PoWs. In 1942, Hennigsdorf management consulted with Pohl's administration and agreed to take 200 people from the Łódź ghetto to work on separating glimmer, which was a mineral composition using in electrical insulation. According to the AEG representative at Łódź, "As this work is a very simple process needing neither technical skills nor strength, children and youths can be used."[367]

This was not the only camp AEG used for forced labor. At the AEG-Kabelwerk Oberspee in Berlin, about 680 Polish women were used in forced labor in the latter stages of 1944. At both factories, the women were guarded by SS female guards who, like their male counterparts, were known for their brutality. The civilian workers who taught the women their tasks were not. Janina Krafczyk was an inmate at Hennigsdorf and tells she "was drilling deep holes into the metal plates...At one moment I lowered my head too low. The foreman jumped over to me, grabbed my head and pulled me up from behind. Apparently my hair had come very close to the drilling machine. When he saw that...he seized my head...he was very attentive. He did not talk a great deal; indeed, I never heard him talk. I never saw him talk to the wardresses. But now he scolded the wardress! Why did we not have scarves! The next day we all had scarves."[368]

The AEG camps were dissolved shortly after air raids in March of 1945. Most of the remaining inmates were marched to the Ravensbrück concentration camp. Many died en route of either exhaustion or gunshot wounds from the SS guards marching with them. Following the end of the war, AEG lost many assets in the former East Germany including the bombed-out corporate headquarters. Head office was eventually rebuilt in Frankfurt in 1950 and AEG and Telefunken officially merged in 1967. The company started falling apart during the recession in the early 1980s and was sold off to Technicolor SA and Daimler-Benz by 1985.

General Electric's largest competitor in the world at the time was the German conglomerate Siemens & Halske AG. Siemens and Halske's history goes back to October of 1847, when Werner Siemens and Johann Georg Halske started the Telegraphen-Bauanstalt von Siemens & Halske, based on their pointer telegraph invention. In 1834 Siemens finished grammar school and with the blessing of his father, joined the Prussian army. With incredible forethought, Werner's father said to him: "The present condition of things in Germany cannot possible last. A time will come when everything will be turned topsy turvy. The only fixed point in Germany is however the state of Frederick the Great and the Prussian Army, and in such times it is always better to be hammer than anvil."[369]

While serving in the Prussian army, Werner became involved indirectly in a duel between an infantry and an artillery officer. As Werner knew the artillery officer, he served as his second in the duel. Usually such occurrences were dealt with by a wrist slap; this time the antagonists – and their seconds – were put through a court-martial. Werner was sentenced to five years in prison for his part and showed up at the Magdeburg fortress to begin his term. On the way, he befriended a young chemist who would later smuggle in ingredients for Werner's experiments. One of the experiments Werner conducted was into electroplating or the process of applying a thin metal coating to another using an electric charge. Werner's first commercial success was selling the process to a company making silver spoons, which could now be gold-plated – all while he was still incarcerated.

This was Siemens first great success and by 1870, Siemens & Halske had built telegraph networks in Russia, Finland, Crimea and from London to Calcutta. Werner's brother Karl Wilhelm – later Sir William Siemens – headed the company's growth and expansion in Great Britain. Sir William was a great inventor in his own right, studying mathematics, physics and chemistry at the University of Göttingen. He interned at an engineering factory in Hamburg, where he sold his brother Werner's electroplating process. With this success, he headed to London with next to no money and sold the process to a British competitor for £1,600. William returned to Germany to finish his studies, then back to Great Britain where he sold Werner's water meter design and was able to live off the royalties. This allowed

William and his brother Friedrich to pursue scientific interests and in 1861, William invented the open hearth steel furnace.

This is perhaps where one of the great misconceptions surrounding Siemens comes – that Siemens manufactured the crematoria at the concentration camps. The ovens were built by the Erfurt firm J.A. Topf und Söhne, not Siemens. Topf was situated near the Buchenwald concentration camp and was chosen in 1939 to dispose of victims of a typhus epidemic running through the camp at the time. Similar ovens were built for Dachau, Malthausen and Belzec and then larger industrial ovens for Auschwitz. At no time was Siemens involved in the construction or installation of the ovens – the only part of the process the company was involved with was supply of electricity and related items, which bearing in mind the size of the camps would have been considerable.

The company grew into a behemoth in the electrical industry in the early part of the twentieth century, which was the prime reason it received the lions' share of business in the Reich. Of note was the business it garnered before the war for the rebuilding of the German armed forces, something which was in direct violation of the Treaty of Versailles. This was discussed in detail in a meeting held on April 6, 1933. With Fritz Thyssen chairing the meeting, Albert Vögler from steel manufacturer Vestag, magnate Friedrich Flick, aircraft man Ernst Heinkel, Reich Air Ministry head Erhard Milch and Siemens was represented by Heinrich von Buol, Wolf-Dietrich von Witzleben and Carl Friedrich von Siemens. The discussion was about the need for rebuilding the Luftwaffe and on this, Milch was very precise – because of Germany's geographical and military weakness, there was a need to build a strong air force for defensive and aggressive purposes.[370]

A further meeting was held on September 22, with representatives of Siemens, BMW, Argus and Junkers meeting with Admiral Rudolf Lahs, president of the *Reichsverbandes der Deutschen Luftfahrt-Industrie* – the Reich Aviation Industry Association. Lahs laid down the law at the beginning of the meeting, by saying it was strictly confidential and anyone passing information on from it would be sent directly to a concentration camp. At the meeting, the attendees were told about attempts to procure aircraft engines from foreign suppliers to rearm the country, which was in blatant disregard of Versailles. Lahs expressed his frustration at attempting to buy Armstrong Panther engines from Armstrong Siddeley of Coventry.

We know of at least one interoffice memo at Siemens, from Chief Engineer Ludwig Rellstab to Vorstand member Georg Grabe. Rellstab informed Grabe in 1933 of the need to keep in mind the possible use of aircraft being designed by Siemens for military purposes:

It is, therefore, of importance that our engineers also should become well acquainted with the facilities for possibly equipping planes with machine guns, ballistic directors, aiming devices, in order to facilitate the changing of a civilian aircraft into a military aircraft. This applies especially to the bomb and torpedo release apparatus.[371]

Siemens was a large enough concern to not be worried about petty politics, and was able to somewhat dictate terms under which it would do business. Two major indications of this independence come from Siemens and from OSS documents from the end of the war. The OSS reported the company had a Nazi director on the board, but was forced to resign because of the anti-Nazi sentiment expressed in the boardroom. This is truly unthinkable, considering how virulently the Nazis spread through the Vorstands and Aufsichtsrats of the interwar period. This is a testament to the size and power of Siemens. The other story comes from a letter Carl Friedrich von Siemens sent to Erhard Milch in 1936, regarding funding for a new aircraft engine plant. Carl Friedrich told Milch aircraft engines were a field foreign to the company which had caused it to invest more than RM40 million in research, development and building a plant:

I pointed out that we were making every effort to support the development of aviation. We are aware, however, that the great new investments we have made constitute a great risk and a considerable future burden because they must be regarded as excess investments and are not justifiable from a business point of view. We feel that we have already made a very considerable contribution by authorizing an additional expenditure of 6 millions for the construction of airplane engines.

You told me that the expansion of our old factory would have to be supplemented with an auxiliary plant because it is now necessary to work in two shifts to fill orders...and present peacetime production will have to be more than doubled in case of a war.[372]

The irony of this is Siemens did manufacture aircraft in World War I for the Germany Air Force, so some of this knowledge, ability and infrastructure would still be there. Carl Friedrich goes on to "make a suggestion" as to how this obvious oversight could be rectified: Siemens would merge all of its aircraft engine production into a single company, "Corporation X," assuming Siemens would be exempt from foundation and merger taxes, and the RM15 million investment Carl Friedrich believed would be required will be funded half by the Reich and half by a credit, which the Reich will pay interest on. A truly generous offer, finished off with the requisite "Heil Hitler," signed C. F. von Siemens!

There were many who worked for Siemens who were Nazis, but ironically, most of the company heads were not or at least not particularly active. Carl Friedrich von Siemens, the youngest son of company founder Werner, was chairman of the supervisory board of both Siemens-Schuckertwerke and Siemens & Halske AG from 1919 until his death in 1941. Carl Friedrich opposed the persecution of the Jews by the Nazis (as did other leading industrialists such as Carl and Robert Bosch).[373] This is indicated in a letter he wrote to Flora Meyer, the widow of one of Siemens managers who died during World War I. The letter, written March 17, 1933, is contradictory in that Carl Friedrich says he is upset with the anti-Jewish rioting which had taken place in the weeks before his writing, but also blames the rising anti-Semitism in Germany on a "massive influx of foreign Jews after the (first world) war" and by "excesses in the press and in the arts, where the Jewish element plays an important role."[374]

An interesting dichotomy. He helped Flora Meyer's son get an internship at Siemens in 1933 and Carl Friedrich personally contacted the dean of the Technical University to protest her son's expulsion from the German student body. Siemens also stood by Flora's daughter, helping her get a job after she had been dismissed from Berlin-Anhaltische Maschinenbau AG in the summer of 1933 because of her Jewish background.[375] One thing is notable though: Carl Friedrich was not a Nazi – this is true, as he resigned all government posts when they came to power – but he did use certain facets of their ideology to the positive use of the company. Slave labor was being used before von Siemens' death and as the head of the House of Siemens, he would have been at least culpable, if not knowledgeable, of foreign forced labor.

Though Carl Friedrich signed his letters with a "Heil Hitler," he was not a Nazi, just an opportunist and pragmatist. As with many of the men within this book, it was practical business sense to go with the Nazi flow, no matter what you privately believed. Sadly, almost the entire German industrial community behaved this way, and parallels can be drawn between 1930s Germany and the southern United States in the 1950s. As the Jews were excluded from everyday life in Germany, so were the Blacks in South Carolina, Mississippi and Alabama, all under the auspices of segregationist governors. It wasn't just about segregation in Germany though – it was the full removal and elimination of the Jewish people from within the country's borders.

Dr. Wolf-Dietrich von Witzleben ran Carl Friedrich's office as well as being personnel director and Aufsichtsrat member for Siemens & Halske. Along with Ludwig von Winterfeld, von Witzleben represented Siemens – and specifically, Carl Friedrich's office – at the secret meeting in 1933 held to finance the Nazi election campaign before Hitler's rise to power. On behalf of Siemens, von Witzleben pledged RM100,000 to the cause. As the head of personnel, he was particularly active in finding replacement workers for those drafted by the armed forces. Under von Witzleben, thousands of concentration camp inmates worked for Siemens in Berlin under appalling conditions, a fact which was well known to the head of personnel.[376] From 1941, von Witzleben and the other Aufsichtsrat members knew the fate of the deported Jews and Georg Siemens alleged to have personally tried to delay the deportations. In February 1943 the 2,000 remaining Jewish Germans were deported.[377]

One man who is rarely mentioned in the history of Siemens is Karl August Nerger. Kapitän Nerger was the commander of the *SMS Wolf*, one of the most illustrious German cruisers in World War I. *SMS Wolf* was instrumental in sinking thirty different ships, usually through its minelaying. After the war, Nerger started working at Siemens-Schuckert Werke running factory security at a subsidiary. An ignominious end to a brilliant naval career, but not strange in the annals of history. When the Nazis came to power, the need for heroes was great and Nerger was at the levels of Hermann Göring when it came to war idols. When the Nazis wanted to celebrate past triumphs, they called on Nerger. When they commemorated the Battle of Tannenberg, the Nazis brought in Nerger and promoted him to the honorary rank of rear admiral – retired. Nerger took advantage of his newly found celebrity and in 1936 bought a villa in Potsdam at a "formerly Jewish-owned" discount.

In 1938, Admiral Nerger was promoted to head of security for both Siemens-Schuckert Werke and Siemens & Halske and in this capacity knew of the plight of the forced laborers and concentration camp inmates being used in the company. It is not certain to what degree Karl Nerger was involved, as he was picked up by the Soviets after the war and interred at Sachsenhausen, the Soviets believing the former sea captain was military intelligence. Nerger died in 1947 at the camp after he was beaten to death by Wilhelm Wagner with an iron rod. Wagner, for his part, was brought to trial in 1967 and was acquitted of the murder of Nerger, though he was jailed for five years for the abuse of other inmates.[378]

After Carl Friedrich von Siemens' death in September 1941, he was succeeded by his nephew Hermann von Siemens. By the winter of 1941-42, the German economy had become entirely dependent on forced labor and Siemens was not immune to this. It could be said Siemens and others had no choice – Hitler was going to get the goods he needed to win the war at any cost; Siemens and other companies would comply or else. "In late 1944, at the height of World War II, Siemens' total workforce of 244,000 included some 50,000 people who had been put to work against their will. The overall number of men and women who served as forced labor at Siemens during the war years was, however, higher."[379]

At Buchenwald, Siemens-Schuckert Werke (SSW) set up facilities at the sub-camp Neustadt bei Coburg. The company's reasoning was purely economic – it was short on labor and to be competitive with other arms manufacturers, it needed a cheap supply of it. Siemens was looking for increased production, but its methods were a little suspect. Under the guidance of the Gestapo – not known for its HR finesse – the company would punish prisoners and threaten to withhold rations. Siemens employed its forced laborers on 12-hour shifts – 6:30 to 6:30, half starting in the morning, half in the evening, and they were allowed a 40-minute break during their shift. The camp was considered somewhat better than Auschwitz only because investigations could prove no deaths at Neustadt.[380] To say this was a positive is misleading though – prisoners who were deemed unfit for work due to their health were transferred to the Bergen-Belsen camp, which was a known extermination camp.

Siemens moved production to a subcamp at Ravensbrück, a women-only concentration camp, in 1942. By March of 1943 Siemens had 290 female prisoners from the camp working for the company producing bearing assemblies. One of these prisoners was Anna Vavak, a saleswoman working in Vienna who was a member of the communist resistance in the city. She was taken and sent to a prison in Prague, then to Leipzig and Berlin before ending up at Ravensbrück. Described as pretty, intelligent, extremely gracious and charming, she was selected to work for the new Siemens & Halske operation.

Anna thought she could enlighten the German civilians who surrounded her to the plight of the concentration camps. The Germans employed by Siemens at the camp were well-picked – they had neither the intelligence nor the inkling to care about the plight of the women at the camp. Anna worked as a typist at the Siemens subsidiary *Wernerwerk für Fernsprechgeräte* which made telephone equipment. That work was acceptable, life at the camp was not: food was horrid and clothing was worse – footwear consisted of wooden clogs, which as they were often soaked, would cause blisters and extreme pain. Medical conditions at the camp included boils and vitamin deficiency, scabies, malnutrition and tuberculosis. Tuberculosis seemed prevalent in the young French and Soviet girls and the camp treated it with aspirin. Another worker at the Siemens camp had this to say:

(It was) a bright, well-furnished and well heated, spotlessly clean factory floor...adjustable work chairs with back and armrests. Of course, the comfort was not created for the sake of the prisoners. Without these job aids the performances of bobbin winders would be lower and the rejection rates would have been much higher[381]

The Siemens management were well involved with the workers at the plant – they would continuously send letters to the camp commandant detailing workers who did not show up for work or their work was considered subpar. For this, SS-Oberscharführer Pflaum und SS-Scharführer Heckendorf would mete out punishments as they saw fit: beatings, slamming the heads of the female prisoners against the walls, withholding of food, and they were made to stand for hours on end or sent to detention blocks.

Hermann von Siemens said he knew about the use of forced labor, but denied knowledge of any prisoner abuse. He said the prisoners welcomed the opportunity to work, and he said he was not aware of any undernourishment or ill-treatment.[382] Hermann was never charged with war crimes and went about rebuilding Siemens after over 80% of the company assets were destroyed by Allied bombings. Of Hermann, this is what the OSS – the precursor to the CIA – had to say about him: "He is described as a rather timid, modest person, who though not a Nazi cooperated completely with the Nazi Party because of the lucrative business which resulted."[383] He died in 1986 at the age of 101. The OSS hay have been fooled into thinking von Siemens was a timid, modest man, but he couldn't have been too timid as he was also a member of the Aufsichtsrat of two other major Nazi concerns: Fried. Krupp AG and Deutsche Bank.

Siemens had 20 different workshops built on the outskirts of the camp, which by the end of the war saw over 130,000 men, women and children go through its gates. Many thousands did not leave back through them and many of their ashes are spread around picturesque Lake Schwedtsee. One of the workshops set up by Siemens was used to make the electrical components for the V-1 and V-2 rockets. During Carl Friedrich and Hermann's tenures, Siemens became the Third Reich's largest producer of electronics and was essential to weapons production, including the V-series rockets. Factories were spread across the country, though after Allied bombing started, they had to be relocated. According to company records, Siemens was operating almost 400 alternative or relocated manufacturing plants at the end of 1944 and in early 1945.[384]

These factories were relocated for two reasons: they were out of reach of Allied bombers; and, it could be argued it was the main reason, was their proximity to the Russian front and to cheap labor. The other major facility which Siemens ran with the help of concentration camp labor besides Ravensbrück was the Auschwitz subcamp of Bobrek.

Auschwitz sends a particular shiver down one's back, if for no other reason the name signifies gruesome death, torture and the height of Nazi atrocities. It was also the home camp of Josef Mengele, the doctor with the quaint nickname "The Angel of Death."

Kurt Bundzus was the manager for building the new plant at Auschwitz when the Berlin factory was destroyed by air raids. "When I arrived in Auschwitz, I gave 100 preselected inmates a competency exam. Fifty met the technical demands. I asked the commandant's office that these inmates be given additional food and preferential treatment."[385] Unfortunately for these inmates, frat boy mentality took hold and they were treated especially poorly by inmates employed as kapos, envious of their better treatment. Bundzus asked for the labor force to be increased two months later in January 1944 to 1,000 prisoners. Ironically, the prisoners were transferred to the punishment block to recover and get better food.

The plant was to be huge – over one million square feet – to replace the bombed out Siemens-Schuckertwerke in Berlin. Siemens was exceptionally interested in the camp because of the 100,000-strong unused labor force.[386] At the same time Siemens wanted to start building the factory, SSW had also negotiated with the SS to build a facility to disinfect the prisoners' clothes using short-wave radiation. In January, there were 251 prisoners detached to building the subcamp, including 24 children between 11 and 18 years old. Male prisoners were tasked with making machine tools, the women with parts for electrical switches and for work in the kitchen and cleaning.

Treatment at the subcamp, like Ravensbrück, was somewhat better than at the main Auschwitz camp, though there were still five men to a straw bunk and they were given a spoon and hand towel, "which was terrific as up to now we had had to eat with our hands from a communal, unbelievably filthy trough." Also, the standard 12-hour day was not standard for Siemens – here prisoners worked ten hours a day, the youths eight hours. Nikolaus Rosenberg was transferred to the Siemens detachment in May of 1944. He states "the Siemens-Schuckert officials were…relatively human and treated the Jewish prisoners with good intentions, sometimes closing their eyes when an exhausted prisoner could no longer work."[387]

This relative comfort ended on January 18, 1945 when the remaining prisoners of both Bobrek and Auschwitz were forced to march 70 kilometres when the camps were abandoned. The march killed many; the SS guards en route killed many more. Ten thousand prisoners left the camps, which included the Siemens subcamp and the Buna Monowitz camp IG Farben ran. Wearing nothing save for the thin prisoner uniform and wooden clogs, the prisoners were forced to march through deep snow, sometimes even carrying the possessions of the SS men who guarded them. When they arrived at Gleiwitz two days later, they were given a loaf of bread and then loaded on to open cattle cars and taken by rail to all parts of the crumbling Reich.

Georg Siemens, in his *History of the House of Siemens* published after the war, obscured the truth with his account of the use of forced labor:

On the whole about 2,000 Jews were employed during the first years of the war and the firm as well as the Jews themselves believed that it would remain so until the end of the war. But at the end of January 1943 the Secret State Police started to remove all the Jews from the Berlin factories and to transport them elsewhere. The members of the Board of Siemens were horrified at these measures for they knew what it meant for the victims. A member of the Board of Directors went into the lion's den, in this case the Office of a first squad leader of the SS, and succeeded by urgently remonstrating with him and painting a picture of the collapse of vital war production, in obtaining authorization for the firm to keep the Jews for the time being. They could breathe again, but not for long, as four weeks later, just as work had started for the morning, a column of lorries appeared in front of the factories, police brought the Jews out and loaded them on the lorries and before anyone had time to do anything to stop them, the lorries and the victims were gone.[388]

Somebody at Siemens *did* know where they were going – not just *elsewhere* – as it was just months after this the company started setting up branch factories at the very concentration camps the Jewish Germans were taken to. The other sleight of hand von Siemens employs in his writing is that "2,000 Jews were employed during the first years of the war." Possibly in 1939 and 1940, only 2,000 Jewish Germans were employed by Siemens, but the company itself admits by 1944

"Siemens' total workforce of 244,000 included some 50,000 people who had been put to work against their will. The overall number of men and women who served as forced labor at Siemens during the war years was, however, higher."[389] It is extremely doubtful only 2,000 of that number was Jewish.

While the SS was responsible for running the concentration camps, they were also responsible for running and supplying the factories with labor. Some of this labor came from Siemens plants in Berlin, which had their Jewish employees excised at the behest of the government. The Siemens family, while implicitly guilty in the use of slavery at their factories, were not the worst offenders at the company. Dr. Rudolf Bingel was the CEO of Siemens-Schuckert and a member of the Keppler Kreis. Bingel was an ardent supporter of the cause, contributing to the Kreis on behalf of Siemens. In September of 1943, Bingel donated RM100,000 to the Keppler Kreis according to Nazi banker Kurt von Schröder. Siemens website does not mention this, only saying Bingel was "highly innovative and successful in the areas of drives and marine equipment. He was particularly involved in promoting the development of diesel and turboelectric drives."[390]

When he wasn't busy with developing diesel power, Bingel was negotiating for the use of prisoners with SS-Gruppenführer (Major Genernal) Richard Glücks, inspector of the concentration camps. It could be said he was trying to help these prisoners avoid extermination, but it is more probable he was trying to secure a stable work force for the war effort and Siemens bottom line. Bingel died September 22, 1945 while interred by the Soviets at their camp in Landsberg where he reportedly died of exhaustion, not unlike many of his former "employees," so this question will never be answered.

We have noted the use of forced laborers and concentration camp inmates adding to Siemens bottom line – but did the company use Aryanization to cheaply acquire competitors? Rarely, since besides AEG, Siemens had no real competitors. In most of the occupied countries, it was already the leading supplier of electrical components and telegraphy and had factories set up in most of these countries. One notable Aryanization from which Siemens-Schuckert profited – as did Deutsche Bank with its RM188,000 commission – was that of the Aron Works Electricity Company in Berlin, which Siemens purchased when its owner agreed to sell after spending some time nursing his decision in a concentration camp.[391]

That relationship between Deutsche Bank and Siemens stretches back to the beginnings of the bank itself. When Deutsche Bank opened for business in April of 1870, Werner von Siemens nephew Georg sat on its managing board. Georg was a well-known lawyer before that, consulting on the formation of Siemens, Halske & Co. Georg set up the Indo-European Telegraph Company in London at the request of Werner and he seemed the obvious choice for not only launching Deutsche Bank, but also helping the bank establish a branch in London to open up foreign money markets. Under Georg von Siemens, Deutsche extended credit to Friedrich Krupp and BASF. In 1887 Georg joined the Aufsichtsrat of the future competitor to Siemens, AEG. AEG's reorganization at the time was funded by Deutsche Bank.

That's a little prehistory on Siemens and Deutsche Bank; fast forward from the Second Reich to the Third Reich. Siemens and Deutsche intertwined substantially by this point. Carl Friedrich von Siemens was close friends of Deutsche's Aufsichtsrat chair Georg Emil von Stauß (*pronounced Shtawss*). This friendship developed when von Stauß was personal secretary to Carl's cousin Georg von Siemens and continued as Carl sat on the Aufsichtsrat of Deutsche with von Stauß. Carl vacated the Siemen's seat on the board in 1938 and was replaced by Hermann von Siemens. From the very start of Deutsche Bank's life, the institution was considered Siemen's banking outlet of choice and this continued until the end of World War II. Deutsche Bank representatives had sat on the board of Siemens and there was always a Siemens seat on the Aufsichtsrat at Deutsche.

Siemens Aufsichtsrat Members 1939	
Hermann von Siemens	
Carl Friedrich von Siemens	
Friedrich Carl von Siemens	
Oskar Caminneci	Siemens cousin
Emil Georg von Stauß	Deutsche Bank
Albert Vögler	Vestag (steel manufacturer)
Oskar Henschel	Henschel & Sohn (railways)

The two companies intertwined their interests so well, it is sometimes hard to see where the board of one ended and the other began.

Deutsche Bank men sitting on Siemens or SSW's boards in 1945	
Oskar Sempell	Deutsches Überseeische Bank
Ernst Kraus	Creditanstalt-Bankverein Vienna
Fritz Jessen	Deutsche's Advisory Council for Berlin-Brandenburg
Herman Münchmayer	Deutsche Bank Aufsichtsrat
Hermann Reyes	Deutsches Überseeische Bank
Hans Rummel	Deutsche Bank's Vorstand
Albert Pietzsch	Deutsche Bank Aufsichtsrat[392]

It was not just in Germany the two companies were woven together – overseas interests as well as European concerns mixed just as easily. In Czechoslovakia, the manager of Elektrizitäts AG was also on the managing council of Deutsche's Prague subsidiary. The Vorstand chair of Siemens Elektrizitäts AG in Prague was also on the Vorstand of Böhmische Union Bank. Siemens' Argentinian affiliate Compañia Platense de Electricidad Siemens-Schuckert had the manager of the DUB location in Buenos Aires on its Vorstand and in Vienna, the chair of Wiener Kabel & Metallwerke AG was also on the board of Creditanstalt Bankverein.

There is an even clearer picture of how the two concerns mixed besides sharing personnel. The stock each company controlled of the other is also telling. At Siemens' annual meetings, Deutsche Bank voted considerable chunks of Siemens stock; in 1933, Deutsche voted RM13 million of stock – by 1943 that had risen considerably to RM42 million. In the same period, Siemens purchased RM5 million worth of Deutsche Bank stock.

After the war, Siemens was not singular in its efforts to distance itself from its Nazi past. The Aufsichtsrat tried to convince the military governors it was anti-Nazi and opposed National Socialism in all its forms. How can anyone say this truthfully all the while profiting from the very regime it says to oppose? The standard answer on this question was the pressure exerted by the Reich government, the Gestapo and the

SS and failure to comply would mean possible deportation to a death camp, torture or death. Fritz Thyssen would be an excellent example of this. On the other hand, men like Robert Bosch and Oskar Schindler did what they could under extraordinary pressure. There is very little sign Siemens did. Siemens was of course not the only company to use slave labor, but they were probably the most prolific.

10

The Thyssens and the Krupps

This story begins with two of the oldest and wealthiest families in Germany. One fell out of favor with Hitler when conscience finally kicked in; the other had its Judgement at Nuremberg.

The Krupp dynasty started in 1587 when the merchant Arndt Kruipe arrived in Essen. He started to amass his wealth by purchasing the homes and estates of those who had fled or died during an outbreak of bubonic plague. Arndt's son Anton took over the family business and began gunsmithing for both sides in the Thirty Years War until 1648. By the mid-18th-century, Friedrich Jodocus Krupp, Arndt's great-great-grandson, headed the Krupp family. In 1751, he married Helene Amalie Ascherfeld. Friedrich died six years later, leaving his widow to run the business – a family first and something very rare in 18th-century Europe. Helene, however, was up to the task and greatly expanded the family's holdings, acquiring shares in four coal mines, and in 1800 the iron forge Sterkrade Works located near Essen.

Sterkrade was owned by Eberhard Pfandhofer who, though an excellent smith was a poor businessman. After loaning Pfandhofer substantial amounts, Sterkrade still went bankrupt and Helene purchased the assets for 12,000 thalers.[393] After her son Peter died in 1795, Helene taught her grandson Friedrich the inner workings of the business. Helene died when Friedrich was 23 and left the young man the family fortune. Friedrich was enamored with a new process for casting steel, which was a closely guarded secret in England. With Gottlob Jacobs, Krupp made his first experiments at the Sterkrade Works. In 1810 he founded a small forging plant near Essen, and five years later started production of cast steel, excellent for dies for minting coins and stamps for buttons. There was not enough demand for buttons and by 1820 Krupp had to sell his house and move into a small laborer's cottage near his plant.[394] Friedrich died in 1826 at the age of 39 and left the company to his son Alfred.

Alfred continued his father's work, making sales calls and working to improve the works. Alfred's brother invented – and Alfred subsequently patented – a roller for making silver-plated spoons. This allowed Alfred to enlarge the factory and he got back into the gunsmithing business his ancestor Anton started 200 years earlier. Alfred introduced his first cast-steel cannon at the *Great Exhibition of the Works of Industry of all Nations* in London and in 1851, he exhibited a cannon made entirely from cast steel which would fire a six-pound shell, and a solid flawless ingot of steel weighing one ton, more than twice as much as any previously cast. He surpassed this with a 5-ton ingot for the Paris Exposition in 1855 which was so large, it snapped the truck carrying it down a Paris street. The publicity from that and from the ingot crashing through the floor of the exhibition hall caused a sensation in the engineering world, and the Essen works became famous.

The largest boost to Krupp was the invention of seamless railway tires, which gave Krupp an immense market in the burgeoning United States. Cannons were a secondary, though large, part of the business and Alfred revelled in his moniker "The Cannon King." Clients included the Prussian War Ministry and the governments of Holland, Belgium and Egypt and his breach-loaded steel cannons helped seal the fate of the French during the Franco-Prussian War in 1870. Alfred's credo of "Krupp steel must be above suspicion" meant Krupp armaments were the darling of the munitions world. A Krupp-manufactured cannon shot farther and more accurate than its competitors. In fact, the precursor to today's large corporate shows was the Völkerschiessen, which were firing demonstrations of cannon for international buyers. These shows allowed Krupp cannons to be showcased to the nations of the world and through them, Krupp's reputation and munitions spread to 46 countries. And, Alfred's responsibility to his employees became the blueprint for Bismarck's social systems, including good wages, company housing, and widow, orphan and death benefits.[395]

Alfred believed in vertical integration and not only owned steel mills but also invested in coal mines and iron ore beds necessary for steel production as well as shipping concerns. When Alfred died in 1887, Krupp Werke employed 75,000 people, half of whom worked on munitions. It was the largest industrial concern on the planet at the time. Alfred understood sole ownership was the key to the strength of the business, so he left the entire enterprise to his son Friedrich Alfred, or

Fritz. Alfred was a hard man, keeping Fritz on an allowance until he was 28 and when they were finally permitted to marry, Fritz and his bride Magda were required to move into quarters next to the 200-room monolith the children called "the tomb of our youth."[396]

Fritz was a skilled businessman, though of a different sort from his father. Fritz was a master of the subtle sell, and cultivated a close rapport with Kaiser Wilhelm II. Alfred was the door-to-door type; Fritz let the customers come to him and be wined and dined on his terms. Fritz was no social butterfly though – in fact he hated social engagements. He tended to keep to himself, as his high blood pressure and asthma made him very self-conscious.[397] Under Fritz's management, the firm spread across the globe and he focused on arms manufacturing now, as the U.S. railroad market purchased from its own growing steel industry. Thyssen chose to stay mainly in Germany, but also manufactured and distributed railway rolling stock, tubing, tin-plating, boilers and furnaces

In 1892, Krupp bought his main competitor Gruson in a hostile takeover. Gruson became Krupp-Panzer and manufactured armor plate and ships' turrets and a year later Rudolf Diesel brought his new engine to Krupp to construct. German tariffs, while a haven for inefficiency for many companies, was a boon for both Krupp and Thyssen & Co., stopping the flow of Belgian and British steel into Germany and allowing companies like Thyssen to develop internally. Thyssen acquired all shares of the *Gewerkschaft Deutscher Kaiser* coal mine in 1891. Vertical integration, just like with Alfred Krupp, was an advantage to Thyssen, though even this did not help the company during a recession at the beginning of the twentieth century.

The expansion into other fields stretched the company's finances, and company head August Thyssen loaned from one division to another, which built up credit between the divisions, but earned August a negative reputation in the banking industry. In one particular instance, the coal mine's bills had to be covered by Thyssen & Co., which in turn had taken out large loans with German banks. At one point, August's younger brother Josef had to press upon his wife to dip into her personal funds to pay wages. By 1904, when Thyssen finally joined the steel cartel, the company was the fifth largest producer of coal in the country, had the largest untapped coal reserves of any company, and had the largest quota of steel production, surpassing Krupp.[398] But Krupp was no slacker. Fritz Krupp managed to triple profits at Krupp, thanks to the contracts Fritz developed which led Krupp to build almost the entire World War I German Navy.

Fritz and his wife Magda had two daughters: Bertha, born in 1886 and Barbara a year later. After Fritz died, Bertha inherited the family empire and though Helene was able to build and grow the enterprise a century before, the Fatherland decided a woman couldn't now. No less than Kaiser Wilhelm handpicked Bertha's husband, the virtually unknown diplomat Gustav von Bohlen und Halbach. Gustav took Bertha's name and became Gustav Krupp von Bohlen und Halbach. The emperor himself became godfather to their first born, Alfried Felix Alwyn, the first of eight children. Gustav was starched around the edges, "walking ramrod straight in a body corset, timing his phone calls so as to not get cheated out of a penny and allotting one hour a week to play with the kids."[399]

Interestingly, Gustav was of American descent. His grandfather was the Civil War hero General Henry Bohlen, who died in the First Battle of Rappahannock Station. Gustav's father, Gustav Halbach, married Bohlen's daughter and honoring his late father-in-law, hyphenated his name. The younger Gustav Bohlen-Halbach was born in 1870. Gustav moved back to Germany, from whence both the Bohlens and Halbachs originally came and settled at the court of the Grand Duke of Baden. The Grand Duke ennobled him and Gustav added the "von" to his name.[400] Bertha and Gustav had a marriage of convenience, by most accounts – they both did their duty to the Fatherland. This duty was sometimes not to the German Fatherland – more to the Krupp Fatherland.

While the Kaiser was marrying off Bertha Krupp, Thyssen had become Germany's largest iron and steel manufacturer and was also a major coal producer. Josef Thyssen died in 1915 in an industrial accident when he fell between two railcars and left August in complete control. August put the company into the names of his children, though he retained control over it. Fritz, August Jr., Heinrich and Hedwig Thyssen became the legal owners of Thyssen & Co., though through August's trusteeship, they had no say in the running of the business

Thyssen's children remained attached to his ex-wife Hedwig, preferring her warmth and approachability to their father's cold, business-like demeanor. August Jr. would not work with Fritz, and Fritz and Hedwig had fundamentally different ideas about how the business should be run; however, Fritz did work closely with his father. Though they worked together, August Sr. did not have a very high opinion of his son, writing to his close friend Carl Klönne at Deutsche Bank: "Fritz's character is unpredictable; he is too easily swayed by outside influences."[401] This would be Fritz's undoing some twenty years later.

The bickering between father and children continued for years, with the children taking out loans which they agreed to mutually back each other up with, but this agreement fell apart quickly when Fritz and Heinrich refused to support the lavish lifestyles of Hedwig and August Jr. August Sr.'s divorce from the children's mother and their ownership led to many misunderstandings and hard feelings between August and his children over the years. In 1907, most of the situation was finalized with the mother Hedwig getting a sizable payout to pay off her debt and an allowance of 60,000 marks a year (Approximately US$369,000 a year – 2013) and the children getting one million marks when they turned 25.[402]

August Jr. was not satisfied with the million and purchased the noble land of Rittergut Rüdersdorf in 1907, planning to run it as a business. This appealed to the father, hoping it would make an honest businessman out of the son. August Jr. had other plans. He eyed up his father's newest venture, Stahlwerke Thyssen AG in Alsace-Lorraine, andn demanded to be put in charge of the concern, saying: "I am once more giving you the opportunity to provide me with an employment that is suited to me."[403]

Wisely, August Sr. chose not to employ his son, who declared bankruptcy the same year. August Jr. had over eleven million marks in liabilities (equivalent to US$67 million – 2013) and two million in assets. August Sr. offered to clear up his debts in return for giving up his inheritance and the junior sued him for access to the money. The next year, August Jr. and his sister joined forces again to get more money out of their father. The situation worsened the following year when Josef died and his two sons Julius and Hans became part owners, but as with their cousins they were excluded from executive decisions.

By the end of World War I, August Jr.'s bankruptcy threatened Thyssen & Company's very existence, so at the father's behest, the partnership was dissolved and a new stockholder company, Thyssen AG, was formed. The upside to this was all creditors' claims to the private assets of the family were null and void, including the divorce agreement. August Sr. paid out August Jr. and the daughter Hedwig and left the company to Fritz and Heinrich. August Jr. became an international playboy, dying under mysterious circumstances in 1943; though when the coroner was to begin the autopsy, he realized it was a young soldier, not August – who was never seen again.

The Stahlwerke Thyssen AG was the largest steel operation on the continent by the beginning of the First World War, with a blast furnace which could turn out 550,000 tons of steel a year, operated by only eight men. Unfortunately, the iron ore field in Alsace was of low quality, and Thyssen ended up having to buy high grade Swedish ore. This led to the beginning of the Thyssen shipping enterprise, which started with five steamers plying the Rhine bringing raw materials and finished product back and forth.[404]

When Count Ferdinand von Zeppelin began manufacturing and selling a lighter-than-airship known by the name of its inventor, Gustav Krupp saw the need and began selling "anti-zeppelin guns" to Germany's enemies – France, Russia and Great Britain. During World War I, Gustav wholeheartedly supported the Kaiser's war machine, making artillery, shells, and other armaments; a policy that nearly drove the company into bankruptcy after the war was lost, according to Theodor Grütter, curator of Essen's Ruhr Museum.[405] Krupp made many contributions to Germany's arsenal. Always the romantic, Gustav named Krupp's 43-ton howitzer Big Bertha after his wife. Big Bertha could fire armor-piercing shells nine miles and had to be cemented into the ground to fire properly.

Others included the 98-ton howitzer that shelled Liège and Verdun and a cannon that bombarded Paris from a range of about 75 miles. As well, Krupp built Germany's submarines, which were constructed at the family's Kiel shipyards. One of these submarines, the U-20, was the submarine which sank the Lusitania in 1915, an act which almost brought the United States into the war.[406] What did bring the United States into the war was the 148 other Krupp-built U-boats patrolling the Atlantic, sinking merchant marine vessels at will. By November 1917, the Germans thought the Allies would have to surrender from lack of supplies;[407] what the Germans didn't count on was the Russian Revolution. The Germans feared the spread of Bolshevik revolution so much they moved most of their forces to the Russian front. This allowed the Allies to take the upper hand and with revolution starting to boil over in Germany, the war soon ended.

Before the start of the war, August Sr. realized the need for decentralization and once companies within Thyssen were large enough and disparate enough, he spun them off into their own concerns, still running under the Thyssen umbrella. For example, a coal mining operation has a different management requirement than a high-tech steel milling operation, so it was logical to August to have them run by different boards, albeit lean ones, which were controlled by the family.

The group executive in 1912 consisted of August Sr., Josef, Fritz, Heinrich and Josef's son Julius. They were in turn advised by five managers. The group was then subdivided into four sub-groups, of which the family held supervisory positions and various others held management positions.[408] I was always taught it is easier to surround myself with people smarter than me than to try to learn everything myself – this is true of the Thyssen concerns. While I would never say the Thyssen's weren't smart, many a family business have failed when family members attempt to manage enterprises which are outside of their sphere of knowledge.

World War I was very profitable for Thyssen, being the preeminent steel producer in Germany. Employment at the machinery shop went from 3,000 before the war to over 22,000 by 1917 and the need to change the financial structure of the Thyssen companies caused the group to reform in 1915 as an Interessen Gemeinschaft or IG – much like IG Farben – after the war. The end of the war sliced a large chunk out of Thyssen's empire, with the loss of the Alsace-Lorraine territory, and therefore Thyssen's modern mill and Stahlwerke Thyssen AG. Thyssen's crown jewel was divided up among Peugeot, Renault and other smaller industrial concerns, with no recompense to Thyssen and a loss of some 246 million marks – a staggering $827 million today. Thyssen also lost all overseas interests, including Normandy, Russia, North Africa and India amounting to another 88 million marks. Though

Thyssen AG was large, this was a loss which would cripple or bankrupt most concerns. As well, the tariff barriers set up at the turn of the century were gone, and Belgian and British steel poured into the country at deflated prices. With the depreciation of the mark, Thyssen started to become uncompetitive, but was able to retrench.[409]

Bolshevism, which had taken Russia by storm in 1917, overshadowed Thyssen's coal mines, so August Thyssen separated them from the main company and renamed it August Thyssen-Hütte. Also, peacetime conversion of Thyssen's works cost substantial amounts, as did renovations to the plants which had been neglected during wartime. By 1923, Fritz started taking a more active role in the company, as the hyperinflation engulfing Germany at the time disoriented the 81-year-old patriarch of the family, with financial discussions becoming hard to follow. What would cost a billion marks one day could cost a trillion a week later. Once the mark stabilized in 1924, Thyssen turned to Dillon Read & Co, the American investment banking house to float a loan, based on the company's reputation only.[410]

It was also at this time the division between the brothers became more pronounced. While Fritz controlled the hard assets of steel, coal and iron, Heinrich had maintained control of the more liquid assets, mostly in foreign currencies and mostly from his new home in Rotterdam. Heinrich threatened to freeze credit to his brother, which the elderly August derided as the moves of a banker, not an industrialist. Heinrich violently resisted the movement of Thyssen to join a new super cartel, claiming the Thyssen name was strong enough without the need for others. At the end, Heinrich withdrew his financial support of the merger and the assets he held in his banking concerns forever became separate from the Thyssen steel concerns. By May 1926 – Thyssen and five other major steel producers formed Vereinigte Stahlwerke AG (shortened to Vestag or in English, United Steelworks). Conspicuously absent were Krupp and Hoesch.

It was initially chaired by Fritz Thyssen and Albert Vögler was the management chair. In its first year, it produced 50% of Germany's pig iron and crude steel. Vestag attracted more loans from Dillon Read and enlisted Price Waterhouse as its accounting consultant. Antitrust agreements had to be signed though, and the Thyssen Machinery Works were sold to DEMAG, a competitor which immediately dissolved it and sold the electric dynamo production to Siemens.

Vestag proved to be unwieldy, almost going bankrupt during the Depression. Its ridiculously large bureaucracy was never pared down with the mergers and Vögler conceived a radical decentralization patterned on DuPont and General Motors. Subsidiaries were farmed out to work on their own, yet contribute as profit centres to the whole. Profits continued to grow as Nazi Germany rearmed, yet so did tensions with the Nazi regime.

Heinrich Thyssen had taken his inheritance and with the wealth his stocks provided, he obtained a PhD in philosophy after going to university in both Heidelberg and London. He settled in Hungary in 1905, marrying the Baroness Margit Bornemisza de Kászon et Impérfalva. Margit's father, the Austrian Emperor's chamberlain, adopted Heinrich and the Emperor made the title hereditary to Heinrich. Heinrich and Margit left Hungary in 1919 for the Netherlands with their children Henrik, Margit and Gabriella, and their substantial holdings. Heinrich founded Bank voor Handel en Scheepvaart in 1924, three years after the birth of his last son Hans Heinrich.

Margit and Hans Heinrich became interesting in their own right. Heini, as he was known, became an art collector of some repute. Margit, on the other hand, took quite a darker path. Heini always claimed his older sister was "shy and retiring," a claim his Hungarian lawyer Josh Groh disputed, saying she had "a voracious sexual appetite."[411] Big deal, you say. Well, when the appetite is fed by the SS officers who used the Thyssen castle as a rest retreat, it gets a little more interesting.

The father Heinrich left the castle in her name and fled to Switzerland when war clouds loomed. Margit remained at the castle and Joachim Oldenburg, a Thyssen employee and Nazi Party member, assisted her managing the estate. Locals said the "young, dashing and virile" Oldenburg accompanied Margit on hunting trips – and was soon sharing her bed. The problem was Margit was already married to Count Ivan Batthyany, whose family had originally owned the town as well as a chunk of the Hungarian countryside. The countess shared the castle with her SS guests and her bed with Joachim Oldenburg, while her husband continued to enjoy his wife's money and bred horses on one of the his other estates.

Six hundred Jews were assigned to strengthen the defence of the town and were kept in the castle's cellar. Many were arbitrarily beaten and shot by Franz Podezin, the local Gestapo man who also shared Margit's bed. According to David Litchfield who was researching a book on the elder baron, the countess derived obvious sadistic pleasure from observing these barbaric acts: "She always stood right at the front when anything like that was going on," said one witness.

The countess hosted a party at the castle on March 24, 1945, inviting local Nazi, SS, Gestapo and Hitler Youth leaders. At around midnight 200 half-starved Jews, pronounced unfit for further work, were taken to a barn within walking distance of the castle. Podezin then ushered Margit and 15 of the more senior guests to a store room, gave them weapons and ammunition and invited them to "kill some Jews." The prisoners were then forced to strip naked before being shot by drunken guests, who returned to the castle to continue to drink and dance. The bodies of the victims were buried by 15 of the prisoners saved for the purpose. The burial party were kept in the local abattoir before being shot the following evening by Oldenburg and Podezin. Podezin fled to Pretoria after the war; Oldenburg to Argentina; Margit lived until 1989.[412]

Back to the elder Heinrich; Bank voor Handel en Scheepvaart figures prominently in many conspiracy theories, as the bank owned the Union Banking Corporation. Union Banking Corporation made many purchases of gold from 1931-1933, amounting to $8 million or 228,000 ounces. Five million dollars' worth was sent abroad, with three million being deposited in the Federal Reserve Bank of New York. This gave rise to the theory Fritz Thyssen had large gold deposits hoarded in the United States, even though Fritz and Heinrich ran their businesses as separate enterprises and as an investigator at the time pointed out: "in my examination of the books and ledgers of the Union Banking Corporation all of the purchases have been satisfactorily accounted for."[413]

Gustav Krupp was branded a war criminal after World War I, a moniker he held in the Second World War as well. Because Germany was defeated the war was, on the whole, bad business for Krupp but not a total loss. Twelve years before the war, the British Vickers company, a manufacturer of artillery shells, had leased a Krupp fuse patent. After the war, Vickers paid off in a settlement based on German artillery casualties, which placed Krupp in the awkward position of having profited from Germany's war dead.[414] Correction: the war was good business for Krupp. The company employed 82,000 people in 1914 – that ballooned to 150,000 by the end of the war. Krupp was selling nine million artillery shells and 3,000 cannons per month by 1917 as well as armored steel for the Imperial Navy's battleships.[415] In an odd twist of fate, during the Battle of the Jutland both sides were using Krupp shells and Krupp armor plating on their ships. Krupp knew war could be profitable, especially if you are selling to both sides, a lesson Anton Krupp had learned almost three hundred years earlier.

Experience was definitely on the side of Krupp in World War II – not only was it the prominent arms manufacturer in both wars, it also used forced labor in both wars. In the First World War, the company used Belgian workers who were conscripted against their will. This came after a meeting between Bayer's Carl Duisberg, Gustav Krupp and General Erich Ludendorff. When both magnates complained about a lack of labor, Ludendorff solved it with a flick of his magic wand – use the Belgians! Krupp did treat the forced laborers substantially better in World War I than it did twenty years later.

With the money from the Vickers settlement and with subsidies from the government of the Weimar Republic, Gustav began the secret rearming of Germany within a year of the Armistice. In his words, he was determined Krupp should be ready "again to work for the German armed forces at the appointed hour without loss of time or experience."[416] Submarine pens were furtively built in Holland; new cannons were covertly perfected in Sweden. This rearmament was a direct violation of the Treaty of Versailles, but to Gustav, the treaty was humiliating and a disgrace to Germany. But Krupp also took a pragmatic approach; the treaty was bad for business. A company which mainly built armaments would suffer without its biggest customer – and the 56 other nations who originally bought artillery from it. Hence Krupp's covert actions with the blessings of the government.

Gustav did his duty for king and country. In 1921, Krupp sold patents and licenses to *Aktiebolaget Bofors*, a three hundred-year-old arms manufacturer in Sweden. In return, Krupp received enough shares in the company to have control over the company's production. The production started with a 75mm mountain gun and since it was produced in neutral Sweden, Krupp could continue arms productions at arm's length. Another move the company made at "arm's length" was the government-sanctioned sale of submarine blueprints to foreign powers. In exchange for this, the company supervised construction of U-boats in Finland, Spain, Turkey and Holland and made a tidy profit as well.

Krupp was an avowed monarchist and there was a permanent suite of rooms kept for the Kaiser at the Krupp's family estate even after the revolution which deposed Wilhelm. With the rise of Nazism, Krupp found himself on the opposite side of Hitler – national socialism sounded bad for business and he viewed the party as a destabilising element within a nation that needed stability. When it became clear the Nazi Party was becoming the most popular party in the Reichstag, Krupp actively used his friendship with President von Hindenburg to advise against the appointment of Hitler as Chancellor. Unfortunately, von Hindenburg followed Franz von Papen's advice and Hitler was appointed. Always the practical man, within three weeks Krupp offered Hitler his full support and others who knew him referred to Krupp as a "super Nazi." He later claimed this was because Hitler stated to industrialists on February 20, 1933 he would reject disarmament as a way ahead. Krupp Works would clearly benefit from this.

Fritz Thyssen, as his father had presciently stated years earlier, was unpredictable and too easily swayed by outside influences. In the years after World War I, Fritz feared the rise of Bolshevism as an enemy to industry generally and Thyssen AG in particular. As he had seen in Russia, the nationalisation of industries could very easily destroy everything his family had built over the last 60 years. And, he had seen his brother Heinrich narrowly avert the same fate in Hungary in 1919. Communism was on the rise in Germany, as many people looked for a better way than the Kaiser's autocracy and his failed war, which cast ruin upon the country. Days before the Armistice was signed ending World War I, the Bavarian Soviet Republic was declared and there were many signs other parts of Germany, mainly rural, might follow this communist revolution.

Within two months, a general strike in Berlin threatened to spread, with workers demanding the end to the postwar government and a move to communism. The Sparticist Uprising, as it was called, started when left wing Chancellor Friedrich Ebert's policies were too generous to the right wing and conservative elements of German society. A number of things led to this dissatisfaction turning from relatively peaceful, pacifist rumblings about the government, into a bloody uprising. The trigger was the dismissal of Berlin's police chief, Emil Eichhorn. The following day shop stewards, communist leaders as well as the leaders of the centrist USPD party met and agreed to work together to oust the Ebert Government. They quickly mobilised their supporters and took control of communication centres and important locations within Berlin. The government briefly negotiated but neither side were willing to make significant concessions and as the negotiations faltered, the protests became violent. Ebert moved his government to the safety in Weimar and called in a combination of German soldiers and members of the Freikorps, who were mainly right wing and conservative veterans. Armed and obviously experienced soldiers, they recaptured most of the buildings the Spartacists had taken within a week. Communist Party leaders Karl Liebnecht and Rosa Luxemburg, were arrested and summarily executed upon their capture.[417]

This led to anti-communist sentiment and fear in the country. One man who feared Bolshevism was Fritz Thyssen, but he also feared and despised the results of the Treaty of Versailles. The turning point for Thyssen came in 1923 when Germany was unable to make her war reparation payment. As a consequence of a German default on timber deliveries in December 1922, the Reparations Commission declared Germany in default, which led to the Franco-Belgian occupation of the Ruhr in January 1923. The Allies believed the government of Chancellor Wilhelm Cuno had defaulted on the timber deliveries deliberately as a way of testing the will of the Allies to enforce the treaty. The situation worsened when the Germans defaulted on coal deliveries in early January 1923 – though this should not have been a surprise, as the Germans had only twice delivered to quota in the past three years.

French Premier Raymond Poincaré was reluctant to order the Ruhr occupation and took this step only after the British had rejected his proposals for non-military sanctions against Germany. Poincaré often argued letting Germany defy the treaty's reparations' clauses would create a precedent that would lead to the Germans dismantling the rest of the Versailles treaty, and with amazing forethought he maintained once Germany had started ignoring the treaty terms, it was inevitable that Germany would plunge the world into another world war.[418]

Wilhelm Cuno was a short-lived German chancellor, who like most, believed the economic terms of the Treaty of Versailles were untenable:

We should stress Germany's readiness to pay an indemnity, but we should also make our position clear that if we are expected to pay, we must be allowed to work.[419]

As chancellor, Cuno also tried to renegotiate the settlement of reparations as well as stabilize the mark, but the Allies would have none of it. On January 11, 1923 France and Belgium entered to Ruhr as occupiers. The industrial heartland of Germany would have none of it, and neither would Fritz Thyssen. As a captain of industry, he was ordered by the occupiers to resume production at the Thyssen facilities in the area, but according to Thyssen, "the Ruhr population made passive resistance under my leadership." Thyssen was arrested by the French authorities and placed on trial before a military tribunal, accused of having dismantled the whole economic structure of the Ruhr and the Rhineland by inducing organized labor to resist and to sabotage. He also faced charges of failing to heed French military authority during martial law in the Ruhr. Thyssen's response was: "I am a German, and I refuse to follow French orders on German soil."[420]

Gustav Krupp behaved in much the same manner. Thyssen was acquitted and angered by the events. Krupp was convicted and sentenced to 15 years in prison, though this was reduced substantially. Gustav went back to the workshop and started secretly making arms and munitions. Fritz Thyssen saw a bigger picture when he was approached by World War I hero and retired General Erich Ludendorff, who spoke to him about a new direction for the country. Thyssen decided to sit in on a political rally led by a furious 5'8" Austrian war veteran. Hitler hit a note with Thyssen when he chastised the government for selling out the country to the Treaty of Versailles, a view Thyssen held as well as his virulent anti-Bolshevism. It is doubtful Thyssen shared Hitler's view on Jews, given his later actions. Thyssen immediately began donating to the Nazi Party, based on his assumption Hitler was the only man to keep the communists at bay. His initial donation of 100,000 gold marks was only the beginning and was the main part of the funding for Hitler's failed Bierkeller Putsch in 1923. Thyssen would go on to contribute 650,000 Reichsmarks to the Nazi Party over the years, though Thyssen himself did not join until 1933. He vehemently denied the report in the New York Times which stated Thyssen contributed RM3 million to Hitler in 1932.[421] Most likely, the three million figure came from the amount raised by Vögler, Schacht and others for the Nazi Party in 1933.

Some of these claims have been refuted by historian Henry Ashby Turner. Truly, Thyssen did fund the Nazi Party at the outset. In declassified intelligence reports, Thyssen clearly states "I gave Ludendorff altogether 200,000 – 250,000 Marks. He gave it to Hitler. This was after the Ruhr invasion, when Ludendorff intended to form a bloc together with Bavaria, the Hitler part and independent commanders of partisans, with the object to stop further aggression on German soil."[422] Fritz Thyssen's supposed autobiography *I Paid Hitler* was ghostwritten by Emery Reves and is generally accepted as a hoax. Thyssen claimed he did not write it and the denazification bureau at the end of the war believed him, as do most academics today. Turner believes the Thyssen claims he did not make the payment to Hitler himself but to General Ludendorff "to use it as best he could." Whether Ludendorff would have favored the Nazis more than any of the other groups operating in Bavaria at that time remains doubtful.[423] This is especially evident in Thyssen's statements after the war, when captured by the Allies. In these, he unequivocally states "After the finish of the Ruhr invasion, which ended without success for France, I called on General Ludendorff, who introduced me to Hitler and asked me to help him. I did so, but not directly, only through Ludendorff. When Ludendorff separated himself from Hitler, I did the same."[424]

Thyssen would see Hitler again in 1928 at the advent of the Young Plan to reorganize reparations. At the time, the economy was in tatters still, unemployment was high, and according to Thyssen, anyone who didn't follow communism followed Hitler. Thyssen was asked by the Führer to invite leading industrialists to a meeting, so he could answer their questions. At this meeting, says Thyssen, Hitler declared he favored two things: restoration of the Hohenzollern monarchy based on the constitutional monarchy of Great Britain; and alliances with Great Britain and Poland. It is no secret Hitler always held a fascination and a deep respect for the British, so this is no surprise.

Hitler was a great presenter – he had the industrialists, who distrusted him and his socialist platform, eating out of the palm of his hands by the end. As a rule, socialism and capitalism do not make great bed mates, but Hitler smoothed this over with promises to restore social order, his treaties with Poland and Great Britain and his concordat with Pope Leo XII. It is claimed Thyssen, along with Hjalmar Schacht, wrote to President von Hindenburg, stating they felt Hitler would be the best choice as next chancellor, to move Germany forward. Thyssen denied this in his testimony after the war, saying he was never consulted by von Hindenburg about Hitler becoming chancellor.[425]

In 1930, Thyssen was approached by industrialist Emil Kirdorf, who had in turn been approached by Rudolf Hess. Hess had purchased the Brown House in Munich, yet lacked the funds to do so, and came to Kirdorf, hand outstretched. Kirdorf refused, but suggested his neighbor Thyssen might help. Thyssen also refused, yet did arrange for credit for Hess with Rotterdam's Bank für Handel und Schiff, or known by its Dutch name, Bank voor Handel en Scheepvaart N.V. – his brother's bank. Thyssen claimed it was better dealing with a Dutch bank because he did not want to get mixed up with German banks in his position. While this sounds good at the time, it seems much more likely that though the brothers were not on the best of terms, Fritz could easily have requested a favor of Heinrich.

Thyssen fully admits that in 1926 he was the Nazi Party's principal supporter. Later, Ernst Tengelmann, the CEO of Gelsenkirchener Bergwerks-AG, Emil Kirdorf, Vestag chair Albert Vögler and Gelsenkirchen Mining-AG CEO Gustav Knepper also funded the Nazis, though Thyssen was considered the first major benefactor. Thyssen was rewarded for this with a seat in the Reichstag and appointed to the Council of State of Prussia. It was only when he was appointed to the Reichstag the finally joined the Nazi Party. Thyssen was adamant saying he "did not pay one farthing when the Party came to power." Though he does not dispute claims Thyssen AG or Vestag contributed to the Nazis, he did say he did not arrange them – they were the purview of Gustav Krupp. In the early 1930s, these were given "on the impression that there was a big struggle going on between the community and Nazi parties. Each party had its own private army, which was going through maneuvers, and the Nazis always pretended they were the enemies of the communists. My father and myself and several other gentlemen of our acquaintance always helped whoever was against the communists, and the men well remember in 1918 when the communists were in power and had arrested nine industrialists whom they intended to shoot – my father, myself, Hugo Stinnes"[426] and others.

Thyssen welcomed the suppression of the Communist Party, the Social Democrats and the trade unions, as all of these were bad for business. Fritz, though initially enamored with the concepts espoused by Hitler and Nazism, began to take a dim view. As Thyssen put it, Hitler acted against the constitution, outlawed all opposition, broke the concordat and started religious repression against Catholics and Jews. In 1934 he was one of the business leaders who persuaded Hitler to suppress the bullying, violent and virtually uncontrollable SA. The SA had become very powerful, with more men than the German Army and the possibility existed of the army being absorbed into this paramilitary group, with Ernst Röhm as its head. While Röhm and Hitler had been close since the early 1920s, Hitler had started to fear the power Röhm now wielded. For industrialists like Thyssen, the socialist leanings of the SA leader were again bad for business. There were still others who disapproved of Röhm's overt homosexuality. Hitler's fears, fed by Göring and Himmler with information on Röhm's purported coup, heightened. Their masterstroke was to claim Gregor Strasser, whom Hitler hated, was part of the planned conspiracy against him. With this news Hitler ordered all the SA leaders to attend a meeting in the Hanselbauer Hotel in Wiesse.

Göring and Himmler drew up a list of people outside the SA they wanted killed, which could also happen very surreptitiously during the purge. The list included Strasser, former chancellor Kurt von Schleicher and Gustav von Kahr, who crushed the Bierkeller Putsch. On June 29, 1934, Hitler, accompanied by the SS, arrived at Wiesse, where he personally arrested Ernst Röhm. During the next 24 hours, 200 other senior SA officers were arrested on the way to Wiesse. Many were shot as soon as they were captured, but Hitler decided to pardon Röhm because of his past services to the movement. After pressure from Göring and Himmler, Hitler agreed Röhm should die and insisted Röhm should be allowed to commit suicide but when he refused, Röhm was shot by two SS men.[427]

Though initially enamored with the concept of Nazism and its outlook for a better Germany, Fritz became disillusioned with the depravity. He wrote a 1937 letter to Hitler, asking for moderation with anti-Catholic policies. At the same time though, he instituted Jewish purges of his own companies. But still, he kept on – until Kristallnacht. After the November 1938 purge of everything Jewish in Germany, Thyssen resigned from the Reichstag and the Prussian Council. Along with Schacht, Thyssen vocally believed the rearmament of Germany was hurting the economy, diverting production away from essential consumer goods.

When war finally broke out in 1939, Thyssen left the country, sending a telegram to Göring telling him of his shame. Thyssen told Göring he was not only entitled to his opinion, but obliged to speak it, especially when he believed Germany was heading towards disaster. In a note which would have meant certain punishment in the country, Thyssen said "Mr. Hitler has no right to threaten me when I say what I think."[428] The message was not delivered to the Reichsmarschall as requested, and a response was sent by Gauleiter Josef Terboven of Essen. In it, Terboven states Göring had not read the letter, though if the industrialist returns to Germany, Göring guaranteed nothing would happen to Thyssen. Thyssen saw the contradiction and sent off another telegram. In it, he said it was impossible Göring hadn't received the first telegram for two reasons: first, how could Terboven state Göring's response, if Göring had nothing to respond to; and second, "it is to be hoped in Germany that a telegram addressed to the field marshal will always arrive." In other words, neither rain nor snow nor Nazi storm trooper will stop the Western Union.

Thyssen continued: "I have never asked you to protect me against personal or economic consequences resulting from my political actions. I do not understand how such a thought could have ever entered your mind." At this point, Thyssen decided returning to Germany was not within his best interests, and so he might as well say what he had to say:

> *I protested to you when the police chief of Düsseldorf distributed a more than vulgar pamphlet against the Catholic Church. I was always a good Catholic and I shall always keep allegiance to my faith and now even more so than ever before. My protest against that outrage had no effect.*
>
> *I protested to you, when on Nov. 9, 1938, the Jews were robbed and tortured in the most cowardly and brutal manner, and when the Government Chief of Düsseldorf, whom you had installed yourself, was almost killed and driven away. There again was no response! As a sign of my protest, at the time I resigned at that time my position as State Councillor. I asked the Prussian Minister of Finance to stop my State Councillor salary. There was no answer from you! The payments, however, which were made in disregard to my request, are deposited in a blocked account with the Thyssen bank, awaiting your pleasure.*
>
> *I protested to you when the greatest misfortune happened and once more Germany was plunged into war without the consent of Parliament or the State Council. I declare as firmly and clearly as possible that I am against this policy, and I shall always be against it, even at the risk of being branded a traitor. I can but address this urgent appeal to you and to the Führer to cease pursuing a policy which at best will drive Germany into the arms of communism or otherwise mean the end of Germany.*[429]

Thyssen saw the writing on the wall for Germany, well before even the invasion of France. With perhaps a hint of an ironic chuckle, Thyssen responded to the last point in Terboven's initial message, saying it would be "pure idiocy" for him to return to Germany, considering those who were unlucky enough to be caught up in the Night of the Long Knives. Thyssen even takes a little extra kick at the Reich, when he points out foreign minister von Ribbentrop had moved into Thyssen's dead nephew's house, who had mysteriously died at Dachau after being taken prisoner during the Anschluss. His nephew was a political activist, and as Thyssen points out, in 1934 political opponents were taken care of with guns, truncheons and knives, and "these methods have not changed."

Well before the Night of the Long Knives, rearmament was again on the table, and Gustav Krupp hid weapons designers in a nondescript building in Berlin, away from the prying eyes of arms inspectors and the press. Gustav hoodwinked them all – *The Manchester Guardian* reported at the time: "Peace is taking its revenge at Krupp's…one can have no hesitation in affirming, after a visit at Krupp's, that everything connected with war industry has been scrapped away."[430] A fine job indeed, as General Telford Taylor, the chief prosecutor at the Nuremberg trials said after the war: "In 1938 a stupefied world was to gape in frightened amazement at the nation which had suddenly achieved such terrifying strength. How? Much of the story was in the Krupp files in Essen."[431] But hiding weapons designers wasn't the only way Krupp rearmed Germany.

By 1934, Krupp was in full war production. Hitler ordered 100 new tanks by March of that year and 650 more a year later. He wasn't just violating the Treaty of Versailles; he was wiping his backside with it. In Holland, the shipyard Krupp was using was given the go-ahead to start laying the keel for six new submarines and told to prepare to build one a month. In Kiel, the naval yards started building the ships which would be the bane of the British navy: *Tirpitz, Graf Spee* and *Bismarck*. The armor plating and guns were supplied by Krupp. Word that Germany was rearming was good for business in Germany; it was better outside the country. Turkey, Greece, the Soviet Union and Bulgaria all wanted Krupp guns on their side. Not to say Krupp's interests weren't protected in Germany – Göring told all industry in 1937 "Our whole nation is at stake…the battle we are approaching demands a colossal measure of productive ability. No limit on rearmament can be visualized…If we win, business will be sufficiently compensated."[432]

Gustav himself plunged headlong into Nazism, and as with most of the men in this book, because of economic rather than ideological reasons. He didn't hate the Jews, as long as they purchased Krupp steel. But if Krupp's largest customer – the Reich government –

told him to hate them, then by all means, the customer is always right. Bertha's husband found it his duty – and good for business – to sit as chair of the Adolf Hitler Spende, the "election fund" of the Führer. In 1936, he sent this fawning letter to his good friend:

> *2 January 1936.*
>
> *Mein Führer,*
> *With reference to my letter of last November 1, I declare my willingness to continue to head the Board of the Adolf Hitler Spende of German Industry again in its fourth year, to conform with the wish expressed in your letter of last October 31.*
> *May I be permitted to take this opportunity, my Führer, to express my most sincere wishes to you for the year 1936, for the continued preparation of your far-reaching plans and the confidence that this fourth year of its development will bring this first part of your program much nearer to fulfillment than could have been hoped or expected three years ago. It remains a deep satisfaction to me to have been able to serve you in a modest way during this time.*
>
> *Your obedient servant,*
>
> *Dr. Krupp von Bohlen und Halbach.*[433]

Gustav was a true fan of the man and anyone who said differently risked a lot. When Carl Bosch of IG Farben voiced his concerns over corruption in the Reich, Gustav flipped his lid, told Bosch he was insulting the Führer and refused to ever meet with him again. When Gustav's brother-in-law Baron Tilo von Wilmosky made a comment about the men Hitler surrounded himself with, he was chastised with a "not in my house" from Gustav. The only one safe was the woman who actually owned the house. Bertha Krupp despised Hitler – she would not even let him stay at the villa while visiting the works. Hitler would never be as good as her beloved Kaiser – Hitler was…a socialist. In the mind of an industrialist the only thing worse than a socialist is a communist. When Hitler did visit, he would leave and spend his time at the Kaiserhof, the only hotel in Essen not owned by the Krupps.

Gustav Krupp fawned over Hitler, since any warmonger would be good for an arms manufacturer's business. The same could not be said for Fritz Thyssen. Disillusioned, Thyssen, fled to Switzerland. He was out of contact with his company, and at the receipt of his latest message, the Reich made sure it is known it is not his company anymore. In a letter sent to banks – though not to be made public – "the total property of Fritz Thyssen is confiscated by the State Police according to Section I of the Law concerning the Secret State Police. It is Mr. Terboven who is exclusively authorized to dispose of the property."[434] Albert Vögler personally delivered the declaration to Thyssen in Switzerland, and added he should destroy all copies of his tirade. Thyssen's response was he would have to sacrifice his political creed for financial or personal benefit, which he could not do. Quite a cost for someone worth in excess of the equivalent of $650 million!

Thyssen's last words to Hitler, were printed in *Life Magazine* in April 1940. This could not be seen as hedging his bets on the defeat of Germany, as by this point the U.S. had not entered the war and all was looking well for the Nazis.

My conscience is clear. I feel free of any guilt. My sole error was that I believed in you, Adolf Hitler, the Führer, and the movement you led. I believed with all the ardor of one passionately German. Since 1923 I have made the heaviest sacrifices for the National Socialist movement. I solicited membership for the Party and fought for it, without ever wishing or asking anything for myself. I was always inspired by the hope that our endeavours would rescue our unfortunate German people...I felt it necessary to voice by protest against the persecution of Christianity, against the brutalization of its priests, against the desecration of its churches. When on Nov. 9, 1938, the Jews were robbed and tortured in the most cowardly and most brutal manner, I protested once more. All my protests obtained no reply and no remedy...I refuse to cover your crimes with my name...I refuse to condone this war into which the German nation has plunged so frivolously, and for the horrors of which you and your advisers will be held responsible...Your present policy amounts to suicide...Your new

policy, Mr. Hitler, is driving Germany into an abyss and the German nation into perdition.
Heil Germany!
FRITZ THYSSEN.[435]

With that, Fritz Thyssen decided the next best step was escape to Argentina from Switzerland, but first he had to make it there. Germany issued a warrant for his arrest February 4 1940. In its April 29, 1940 issue, Life Magazine published Thyssen's accounts and also stated he was now in Paris, "on his way to join his daughter in the Argentine." Thyssen made the fatal error of visiting his mother Hedwig, who was near death in Brussels. He stayed at the Palace Hotel there and Hedwig died on the 21st of April. Fritz and his wife Amelie were headed for Spain, and then on to Argentina, but they had to stop in Paris when Amelie became ill. After three days, they headed out again, this time going to Monte Carlo. They stayed there for six weeks while Amelie recovered, but by this point, Hitler had invaded the Netherlands, Belgium and France. The two were detained in Cannes, where the First Prefect of Cannes and the Bishop of Nice assured them they would not be turned over to the Gestapo. The Thyssens were turned over to the Gestapo anyway on December 21, 1940.

The American Ambassador in France, Drexel Biddle, attempted to get the pair out of France, but the French authorities would have none of it. Thyssen was back in Germany, and spent the next 28 months in a lunatic asylum at Neu Babelsberg, near Berlin.[436] The Gestapo believed Thyssen must be mad, as he was the only one in the Reichstag to vote against war. The industrialist was in good company though – one of his fellow inmates was purportedly the Archduke of Austria, also sent there by the Gestapo. In 1943, he and Amelie were transferred to Sachsenhausen and the two were held in relative comfort – or as comfortable as a concentration camp can get. In February 1945, they were transferred to Buchenwald, separate from the other inmates. Two months later, they were transferred again, this time to Schönberg, where the two met up with the family of Claus Schenk Graf von Stauffenberg, the Nazi colonel who had planted the bomb-laden briefcase next to Hitler in the June 1944 assassination attempt. Ten days later, the group ended up at the Dachau concentration camp. Fritz Thyssen was liberated after the war by the Americans and charged with being a member of the Nazi party. While being interrogated, Thyssen stated very bluntly "I made the biggest mistake of my life when I trusted Hitler in the beginning."

In 1939 Gustav Krupp suffered a stroke. He remained until 1943, no more than a figurehead. His son Alfried took over the company in 1943, the same year Hitler ordered Krupp Works to become a private company after forty years of being a public one. All the profits made by the company went to the family as opposed to former shareholders.

After the end of World War Two, both Krupps were arrested. Gustav was to stand trial before an American tribunal in 1948 but was declared unfit after a diagnosis of senility. It was accepted Krupp would not be able to understand the legal proceedings and as such would not or could not receive a fair trial. Provisions were made however to try Krupp if he showed any signs of recovery after his case was dismissed but this never happened.

At Nuremberg, Alfried was put on trial with eleven others on four counts:

COUNT I: Crimes Against Peace and
COUNT IV: Conspiracy

The Krupp firm had contributed substantially to the ability of Germany to wage war not only during the First World War but also during the Second. Krupp was the principal German manufacturer of large calibre artillery, armor plate and other high quality armament, the largest private builder of U-boats and warships and the second largest producer of iron and coal in Germany.

The evidence further showed as early as 1919 and onwards the restrictions which the Versailles Treaty placed upon the armament of Germany in general and on the Krupp firm in particular had been "systematically circumvented and violated by the firm and persistent attempts made to deceive the Allied Control Commissioners."[437]

It was well known during the trial Gustav Krupp despised the crushing terms of Versailles and the prosecution introduced an article purportedly written by Krupp in 1941 for the company newsletter – remember, Gustav had a stroke two years earlier and was only a figurehead by 1941, so it is dubious he actually wrote the article:

At the time (1919) the situation appeared almost hopeless. At first, it appeared even more desperate if one was not firmly convinced that "Versailles" did not mean a final conclusion. Everything within me – as with many other Germans – revolted against the idea that the German people would remain enslaved forever. I knew German history only too well, and just out of my experiences in the rest of the world, I believed to know the German kind; therefore, I never doubted one day a change would come. How, I did not know, and also did not ask, but I believed in it. With this knowledge however – and today I may speak about these things and for the first time I am doing this extensively and publicly. Consequences of the greatest importance had to be taken. If Germany should ever be reborn, if it should shake off the chains of "Versailles" one day, the Krupp concern had to be prepared again. The machines were destroyed, the tools were smashed, but the men remained; the men in the construction offices and the workshops who in happy co-operation had brought the construction of guns to its last perfection. Their skill had to be maintained by all means, also their vast funds of knowledge and experience. The decisions I had to make at that time were perhaps the most difficult ones in my life. I wanted and had to maintain Krupp, in spite of all opposition, as an armament plant – although for the distant future.[438]

So, was Gustav waxing philosophic in his final years? The humiliation of the Treaty of Versailles was felt by most Germans, as he said. Not only did Germany lose World War I, they lost almost everything of value to them and when they were unable to make reparation payments in 1923, the French moved in and occupied the Ruhr valley industrial heartland, a heartland where both Krupp and Fritz Thyssen had extensive holdings. Thyssen was told to mine coal for the French and he told his men to put down their equipment and passively resist. For this, Thyssen was arrested and briefly imprisoned. For Gustav Krupp, it was a time for obfuscation. Krupp's resistance to disarmament was great and always encouraged by the German government. The company anticipated it would eventually restart the production of arms and many special tools, jigs and gauges which gave the best results in the war, although ordered by the Commission for destruction, were saved under various pretexts.[439]

The Krupp newsletter became an excellent source for incriminating information. The War Crimes Trial prosecutors introduced an article written in 1940 by the head of accounting:

Without government order, and merely out of the conviction that one day Germany must again fight to rise, the Krupp firm has, from 1918 to 1933, maintained employees and workshops and preserved their experience in the manufacture of war materials at their own cost, although great damage was done to their workshops through the Versailles Treaty. The conversion of the workshops to peace-time production involved losses, but only this procedure made it possible at the beginning of the rearmament period to produce straight away heavy artillery, armor plates, tanks and such like in large quantities.[440]

"Merely out of conviction that one day Germany would rise again," and "at their own cost" and talking about losses taken by poor Krupp AG. On the counts of *Crimes Against Peace* and *Conspiracy*, the tribunal concluded the prosecution did not, within a reasonable doubt, prove Alfried Krupp et al. had initiated a war of aggression.

COUNT II – War Crimes – Plunder & Spoliation

Again, from the Krupp trial:
The attitude of Alfried Krupp during Germany's aggression was indicated by evidence from the 18th May, 1940, when Krupp and three others were gathered around a table intently studying a map while listening to a broadcast of German war news over the radio. The four men learned of the great advance of the German Wehrmacht through Belgium. At the conclusion of the broadcast the four men talked excitedly and with great intensity. One, according to Rümann, said: "This one is yours – that one is yours – that one we will have arrested – he has two factories." They resembled, as the witness put it, "vultures gathered around their booty."[441]

This is a generalisation about Krupp's attitude toward plunder. There are a few specifics, such as the Austin plant at Liancourt. The factory was owned by Robert Rothschild, who as a Jewish businessman felt it wise to high tail it out of the occupied areas and headed towards Lyon. Rothschild sent his brother-in-law Milos Colap to take charge of the plant, but the factory was taken over by the Wehrmacht in June, 1940. The German commander refused to turn the plant over to Colap because it was Jewish owned, but upon the German commander's advice Rothschild assigned his stock to the non-Jewish Colap, and the property was released in October 1940. Colap remained in charge at the plant for only two months, when he was dismissed under the provisions of the anti-Jewish Decree issued by the Chief of German Military Government for France.

In June, 1942, Krupp AG approached the administrator of the Austin plant, Maurice Erhard, with an offer of five million francs. A month after the offer, Erhard was still delaying. Krupp called in the military authorities, who gave Erhard an ultimatum: give the Krupp AG a three-year lease if he could not make up his mind, or find a new job. Erhard caved and Krupp AG purchased all but thirty of the machines in the plant at a ridiculously low price. After the company took possession of the Austin factory they manufactured parts for other Krupp arms factories in France and Germany. Less than one quarter of the production was devoted to spare parts for tractors.

Krupp also used their arm-bending techniques to secure a corporate office in Paris at 141 Boulevard Haussmann, which today would rent for around €25,000 a month – in 1943 the company leased it for about US$5,000. This stellar deal was possible only because the property had been owned by the Jewish firm Societé Bacri Frères and had been sequestered by the commissioner for Jewish affairs. Krupp's representative in Paris, Walter Stein, leased the property with the right to purchase – not from the rightful owners but from the provisional administrator.

Then there is the example of S.A.C.M., a 125-year-old French company which owned eight plants, four in Alsace and four scattered around France. Before Germany invaded, the company mainly built textile machinery. When the Germans occupied Alsace in June of 1940, a German administrator was appointed to take charge of the S.A.C.M.

properties which they re-abbreviated as ELMAG. ELMAG still used produced textile machinery but this rapidly declined in favor of direct and indirect production for the German Armed Forces.

Air raids on Krupp's Gusstahlfabrik-Essen plant in March 1943 forced production to the ELMAG plant. On the 27th, a meeting was held in the Reich Armament Ministry, with Krupp officials, representatives of the Armament Ministry, the German Civil Administration for Alsace, and of ELMAG. Opposition was raised by the administrators for Alsace and the ELMAG representatives to the taking over of the plants by Krupp, but transfer of the automotive factory from Essen to the ELMAG plant had been decided and nothing could be done to alter the decision. The Krupp representatives obtained a statement by the Armament Ministry stating "the entire (ELMAG) plants at Mulhouse, Masmünster and Jungholz will be for Krupp...."[442]

As it began to look grim for the Germans, Armament Minister Speer ordered the plant in Alsace evacuated, which Krupp did – and took all the machinery – whether it belonged to it or not – along with it. In September 1944, an ELMAG/Krupp employee made his way to the Peugeot plant in Sochaux to itemize machines to be harvested by Krupp. This was done the following month. Sales manager Karl Eberhardt supervised the removal of machinery from both plants while keeping Alfried Krupp, directors Eduard Houdremont, Erich Müller and CFO Fritz Janssen apprised.[443]

In the early part of 1941, the German High Command instituted a new submarine building programme, which Krupp Stahlbau AG headed. One of the managers of the plant was sent to France with a Kriegsmarine officer in order to find bending roll machines of greater dimensions than were available at the Krupp plants. They proceeded to the Alsthom plant where they located two and immediately placed "seized" signs on them. The director of the Alsthom plant objected to the confiscation to no avail and the machines were dismantled by Krupp workmen and carried off to Germany. They were installed in the Krupp Stahlbau plant and used in the submarine building programme until the end of the war when they were found and finally brought back to the Alsthom plant.[444]

Krupp AG not only took over French industrial enterprises, it also considered occupied France as a hunting ground for additional equipment which was either shipped to the French enterprises operated by the Krupp firm or directly sent to Krupp establishments in Germany. Krupp obtained this machinery partly through their own efforts and partly through those of various government offices. Some French machines were obtained from so-called booty depots. Some were directly requisitioned from French firms with payment offered to the owners *after* the confiscation. Some were purchased by Krupp through its representatives in Paris, and some could only be obtained after negotiations conducted by Krupp officials had been backed up by the intervention of German authorities. The booty goods were not paid for and the only cost from the Raw Materials Trading Co. was the cost of transportation from the occupied territories to Germany.

Raw Materials Trading Co. (ROGES) was founded at the request of the German Army High Command, the Economic and Armaments Office and the Reich Ministry of Economics to utilise the raw materials in the occupied countries of Western Europe and to accelerate their use in German war economy. Both black market items and "requisitioned" equipment were confiscated by the German military agencies and turned over to the branch offices of ROGES for shipment to Germany. The black market goods were procured by buyers, acting under orders of the German Economic Ministry and the Armaments Ministry. All purchases had to be approved by the competent military commander in the occupied area. Prices were fixed by the buyers and the owners were paid by ROGES in the currency of the occupied country, which was furnished by the Reich, but came out of occupation costs.

A large portion of these booty and black market goods was distributed at the request of the Reich Iron Association (RVE) to its member firms. Alfried Krupp was vice-chairman of the RVE, and many times the goods were shipped by ROGES direct from the occupied country to the firms in Germany when those firms had placed their orders in advance. In other cases the booty goods were sent by ROGES to a special booty centre where they were then allocated by the Reich agencies and sent to the respective businesses. During the war, Krupp received pilfered goods from ROGES worth over RM14 million. Krupp, former CFO Ewald Löser, former head of sales Karl Pfirsch, Eberhardt and the deputy head of plants Heinrich Korschan were aware of the circumstances under which these war booty and black market goods were acquired.[445]

By the fall of 1944 the Ruhr district had suffered heavy damage from air raids, especially the Krupp Gustahlfabrik in Essen. Reichsminister Speer went to Essen to inspect the damage and during a meeting with the Krupp Vorstand and other officials, Speer proposed German firms should now seize machines and materials from the Dutch to fix the factories of the Ruhr. Through the local German government offices, four Krupp employees obtained the names of enterprises in Holland, including *Metaalbedrijf Rademakers N.V.* in Rotterdam; *de Vries-Robbe & Co., N.V.* in Gorinchem, *Lipps Brandkaster-Dlotenfabrieken N.V.* in Dordrecht and Hilversum and *Nederlandsche Seintossellen Fabrik* in Hilversum, which was a subsidiary of Phillips. Practically all the machinery, goods and equipment from these factories was confiscated and shipped to Krupp on government orders and with the participation of the company.

Of Count II: *War Crimes – Plunder and Spoliation*, the Tribunal found Krupp, Löser, Houdremont, Müller, Janssen and Eberhardt guilty.

Count III: War Crimes and Crimes against Humanity – employment of Prisoners of War, Foreign Civilians and Concentration Camp Inmates in Armament Production under inhuman conditions.

Crimes against Humanity is perhaps the most horrible of all charges, and puts Alfried Krupp up there with Moammar Gadhafi, Slobodan Milošević, Pol Pot and Saddam Hussein. Krupp had 81 separate plants within greater Germany during the war and employed a total of 23,076 prisoners of war, 4,978 concentration camp inmates and 69,898 foreign civilian workers; the overwhelming majority were forcibly brought to Germany and detained. German industry in general and Krupp in particular used PoWs in armament production in violation of the laws and customs of war. In many instances, including employment in the Krupp coal mines, PoWs were assigned to tasks without regard to their previous training, in work for which they were physically unfit and which was dangerous and unhealthy. By the time of the D-Day invasion in 1944, Krupp still had 22,000 prisoners of war working for it.

At the Nuremberg trials, it was shown Krupp and its managers knew it was in violation of international law by using PoWs in the production of arms. The Nazi government had decided when it invaded the Soviet Union, Soviet prisoners of war would not be protected, since the Nazis believed the Slavs were *Untermenschen* or sub-human. This does not explain how Western European PoWs could be used – but an internal memorandum does:

According to international agreement Prisoners of War may not be employed in the manufacture and transportation of arms and war material. But if any material cannot be clearly recognised as being part of a weapon, it is permissible to get them to work on it. Responsibility for this decision is not the Intelligence branch but the Commandant of the Prisoner-of-War Camp.[446]

This is akin to the ostrich sticking its head in the sand; I can't see it, so it's not a weapon's factory. The Krupp management decided to turn a blind eye towards using PoWs, but when it is brought to their attention, they use smoke and mirrors to explain themselves. Again at Nuremberg, the manager of the Krupp shipyards at Kiel had reservations about using PoWs. He went to Essen in order to discuss the matter with Löser and Krupp. Instead of giving him a direct answer to his question, Alfried Krupp had a plant manager show the man around the factories in Essen to demonstrate how the matter was handled there. The shipyard manager stated Krupp and Löser had told him "the legitimacy of employing foreign workers on war work was not to be discussed" and "we'll show how to do it and then you can draw your own conclusions of how to arrange matters in Kiel where conditions are different."[26] The defence introduced this statement by Stalag VI-F Commander Hans Jauch, who was in charge of the use of prisoners of war in the Essen area: "At Krupp's the assignment of workers was governed by principles of expediency – that is they were put wherever they were needed. A clear separation of production for war purposes and peace purposes in a firm like Krupp's was presumably impossible under the sign of total war."[27]

Krupp held the *Untermenschen* view of Soviet and, later in the war, Italian PoWs. The Soviets were given little food, usually a watery cabbage soup once a day. This left them weak, unable to do all but the lightest work and on occasion, they died of malnutrition or tuberculosis. Werner Lehmann, who was in charge of labor procurement at Krupp, was made aware of this by the Labor Allocation department, which in a report stated it was obvious to everyone who had an opportunity to observe the conditions in the facilities. Even the Wehrmacht doctors commented they had never seen PoWs in such poor condition, and the Army High Command issued a complaint to Krupp based on this. Krupp's defence lawyers conceded the conditions were unsafe, dangerous, prone to air raids, unsanitary and overall deplorable. By the end of the war, the conditions worsened for all PoWs as well as all forced laborers.

The forced laborers overtook the free civilian laborers gradually, as "free" did not necessarily mean that. The free western labor was compelled to sign contracts and when they didn't, they were sent to re-education camps run by the Gestapo. As well, free men from the east were rounded up in organized manhunts and labeled as convicts, even though there was no charge, no trial and no evidence. In 1943 it became apparent slave laborers reported to the Gestapo for punishment were not always sent back to Krupp. In October of that year the head of plant police Friedrich von Bülow made plans for a Krupp-operated penal camp at the Gusstahlfabrik. Construction of the Dechenschule camp started in January 1944 and von Bülow took it upon himself to make sure iron bars were on the windows, locks on the doors and an air raid shelter was built – for the guards. About 90 per cent of the inmates were Belgians and the rest were French, Italian, Polish, Yugoslavian, Bulgarian, Chinese and Algerian. Upon their arrival they were told they were prisoners, their heads were shaved and they were issued convict clothing.

The inmates were deliberately assigned to heavy and dirty work. They were fed once a day, if it can be called food, as it consisted of liquid and little else. Improper nourishment caused at least 15 to die from illness and malnutrition. Mistreatment and beatings were a daily occurrence in the camp and the beaten and sick were denied medical assistance. They were also denied religious consolation. As an air raid shelter, they were allowed to use only a trench; when the trench was hit in an air raid, 61 of them lost their lives. After the destruction of

Dechenschule, the penal camp was transferred to Nerrfeldschule, where the conditions were even worse. According to a witness, the inmates actually had to fight for a dry spot to sleep at night. Those who lost were forced to stand all night.

Both the Dechenschule and the Nerrfeldschule camps belonged to and were managed by Krupp. The inadequate facilities were provided by the company's officials; the food was provided for by the company; the guards were members of the Krupp Werkschutz; medical treatment was also the responsibility of Krupp. When Krupp employees protested on behalf of the Soviet civilians, one of von Bülow's underlings said "one was dealing with Bolsheviks and they ought to have beatings substituted for food."[447] These workers included old men, children and pregnant women. In 1943 some of the Soviet children employed were between 12 and 17 years old; in 1944, the age dropped to as low as six. Eastern workers were beaten as part of their daily routine both in the Krupp plants as well as in the camps. Several Soviets were beaten to death on various occasions and no action was taken against the culprits even though it was a matter of common knowledge.

Concentration camp labor was of a different, even lower standard. The SS oversaw their use in the beginning, and restricted it to within the camps themselves. Erich Müller made a proposal to Hitler for a plant to produce automatic anti-aircraft guns in a concentration camp. The Krupp Auschwitz project was a part of this programme. Krupp wanted to obtain skilled labor through the concentration camps. Müller discussed the employment of concentration camp inmates with Hitler and Krupp executives. When the artillery fuse plant in Essen was heavily damaged, Krupp met with Nazi officials hoping to move production to Auschwitz. The plan was approved and within three months, production started. It stopped almost as quickly when the Red Army offensive made the factory untenable.

Again, many companies used concentration camp labor as a means of replacing the able-bodied men who had been drafted into the war effort. But unlike most other companies, Krupp also saw it as a way of expanding production. This was seen at the Berthawerke plant. The factory was expanded in 1943, solely using Jewish forced labor from concentration camps and numbered around 4,000 men, women and children. They were interred in nearby camps, forced marched to work every day, received minimal clothing, wooden shoes and one bowl of soup at night to eat. The conditions were so bad, most inmates begged for scraps of food. They were beaten regularly, usually for nonsensical reasons such as not working the machines properly – which was ridiculous since they had never been shown how to work them in the first place. The beatings were provided by supervisors using whips made with iron and rubber.

The Krupp camp at Humboldstraße in Essen had 520 female concentration camp inmates. The housing, sanitary and medical facilities were extremely bad, the protection against air raids also consisted only of open trenches. After the barracks had been burned down in an air raid in October, 1944, all the inmates were crowded into the patched kitchen building. During another air raid in December, 1944, this building was also hit and thereafter the entire population lived in the cellar of this bombed-out building. The food was disgusting and only one meal was served each day. The mistreatment of these girls was a matter of common knowledge. Although these conditions were known to all responsible parties, no efforts were made to improve things.

In February, 1945, Lehmann learned the SS did not plan to let the concentration camp inmates live and be liberated by the advancing American troops. CFO Janssen advised the head of personnel Max Ihn and Lehmann of the SS' decision. On March 17th 1945, the women were marched to Bochum, a distance of about 10 miles. There a train waited for them together with 1,500 male inmates. They were shipped eastwards under SS guards. With the exception of a few girls who had escaped shortly before, they were never seen again.

The fate of those accused

Ewald Oskar Ludwig Löser, head of finance for Krupp, was sentenced to seven years in jail. Löser was not a member of the Nazi Party. His sentence was commuted to time served in 1949 due to an illness and he lived until 1970. Löser has the unique distinction of facing a death penalty not just from the Allies but also from the Nazis. Löser served as deputy mayor and city treasurer under Mayor Carl Gördeler in Leipzig from 1930 to 1934. Following Gördeler's recommendation, he joined the executive board of Krupp AG in 1934. In 1943, Gördeler succeeded in convincing Löser a coup against Hitler was necessary to save Germany. The conspirators intended for Löser to become the future minister of finance. After the unsuccessful assassination attempt of July 20, 1944, Löser was arrested. During his trial, Löser feigned partial amnesia and was committed to the sanatorium in Wittenau near Berlin for observation. Gördeler was not so lucky. Upon his arrest, eight members of his family were sent to a concentration camp, he was hanged in February 1945 and his brother Fritz a month later.

Dr. Eduard Houdremont was director and head of the steel works and Nazi Party member 8,301,922, joining in 1940. Houdremont was sentenced to ten years and was released by John McCloy in 1951. He then served on the board of the German Metallurgical Society and died in 1958.

Dr. Erich Müller the head of the artillery designing and machine construction departments; armaments advisor to Hitler; advisor to the War Ministry; head of the Armament Committee in the office of the Reich Minister for Armament and Munitions; chairman of the Weapons Development Committee of the Ministry for Armament and War Production and Nazi Party member, was sentenced to twelve years. Müller was also integral in the building and design of the largest gun ever built. The "Gustav" gun weighed 1,344 tons, stood four stories tall and could hurl a 16,000-pound shell 23 miles, which would penetrate a concrete bunker 260 feet thick. To compare, the main guns on the battleship USS Missouri weighed 108 tons and fired 2,700 pound shells. Müller was released by McCloy in 1951 and died in 1963.

Dr. Friedrich Wilhelm Janssen succeeded Ewald Löser as head of finance in 1943. He was the head of the Berlin office previous to that, a member of the Nazi Party and sponsoring member of the SS. Janssen was sentenced to ten years in prison and was paroled by McCloy in early 1952. He returned to Krupp and worked for Berthold Beitz until 1955 when he retired. Janssen died a year later.

Max Otto Ihn was the deputy to Ewald Löser and Friedrich Janssen, head of personnel and intelligence; deputy plant leader at the Gusstahlfabrik, Essen; and Nazi Party member number 3,421,752, joining in 1933. Ihn was sentenced to nine years and was paroled by McCloy in 1951. Subsequently he worked for Krupp in 1953 and then was General Manager for the German Federal Association of Employers from 1954 to 1957. Ihn died in 1983 at the ripe old age of 93.

Karl Adolf Ferdinand Eberhardt succeeded Karl Pfirsch as head of the war material and machine sales departments and was Nazi Party member number 4,038,202, joining in 1937. He was sentenced to nine years which was commuted in 1951, after which he disappeared from public.

Dr. Heinrich Leo Korschan was the head of the department of steel plants and deputy head of the metallurgical department; trustee and administrator of Krupp in eastern and southeastern Europe; managing director of Krupp Berthawerke in Breslau and Nazi Party member number 3,419,293, joining May 1, 1933. Korschan was sentenced to six years, again commuted in 1951. He lived out the rest of his life in anonymity in Essen until 1973.

Friedrich von Bülow looked after intelligence and public relations, was the head of the Berlin office from 1932-36, military and political chief of counterintelligence at Krupp, Essen, and direct representative of Krupp with Nazi officials, the Gestapo, and SS; and chief of police at Gusstahlfabrik in Essen. Though a particularly cruel and brutally efficient man, von Bülow was not a member of the Nazi Party. He was sentenced to twelve years and was released in 1951. He died in 1984 at the age of 95.

Werner Wilhelm Heinrich Lehmann was deputy to Max Ihn and in charge of Arbeitseinsatz A or labor procurement; and Nazi Party member 8,303,913, joining in 1941. Lehmann was sentenced to six years and was released in 1951 by McCloy, after which he also disappeared from public life.

Hans Albert Gustav Kupke was head of experimental firing ranges at Essen; head of the foreign workers' camps and Nazi Party member 1,988,328, joining in 1933. Kupke was sentenced to two years, ten months and nineteen days – in other words, time served. He disappeared into obscurity after the trial.

And finally, **Dr. Alfried Felix Alwyn Krupp von Bohlen und Halbach**, who must have had trouble fitting that on his driver's license. Krupp was the sole owner, proprietor, and director of Friedrich Krupp works, Essen; Wehrwirtschaftsführer; deputy chairman of the Reichsvereinigung Eisen (Reich Iron Association) and member of the Präsidium of the Reichsvereinigung Kohle (Reich Coal Association); member of the Verwaltungsrat of the Berg- und Hüttenwerksgesellschaft Ost GmbH (East Mining and Foundry Association, Ltd.); member of the Rüstungsrat (Armament Commission) in the office of the Reich Minister for Armament and War Production; supporting member of the SS; member of the National Socialist Flyers Corps, where he reached the rank of Standartenführer (colonel) and from 1938 he was a member of the Nazi Party.

Krupp was convicted and sentenced to twelve years in prison and was ordered to forfeit all of his property, both real and personal. Krupp always denied his guilt, saying Krupp AG never engaged in politics. His sentenced was commuted in 1951 by John McCloy and his property was restored. By the early 1960s, Alfried Krupp was worth over $1 billion (about $7.6 billion in 2013). Alfried Krupp's only child, Arndt, renounced his succession rights and his Krupp name. When Alfried died in 1967, the company went public, and the Krupp industrial family came to an end. Arndt was not allowed to use the Krupp name, as this was saved for the sole inheritor of the fortune and went by the name Arndt von Bohlen und Halbach. Arndt married Princess Henriette von Aürsperg in 1969, though he was homosexual. Thus ended the Krupp dynasty in 1986 when Arndt died of jaw cancer at the age of 48.

The non-profit Alfried Krupp von Bohlen and Halbach Foundation was founded on January 1, 1968, with all of Krupp's assets contributed. Its first chair was Berthold Beitz, who had convinced Krupp of the good acts which could be taken with the foundation. Beitz served as chairman until his death in 2013 at the age of 99. In 2013, the foundation was the largest single shareholder of ThyssenKrupp AG, with a 23% holding worth about €2.9 billion.

Fritz Thyssen was held by the Allies after the war and interrogated thoroughly. He was arrested again in 1948 and by the Obertaunus Denazification Tribunal for being a supporter of the Nazi Party. This he did not deny – before 1938 – and he accepted responsibility for the company's mistreatment of Jewish Germans under his leadership. He paid DM500,000 in restitution and he and his wife emigrated to Argentina in 1950. He died there on February 8, 1951. Eight years later his widow Amelie and daughter Anita established the Frtiz Thyssen Foundation with DM100 million worth of Thyssen stock – almost $200 million today.

Fritz Thyssen was in part responsible for the rise of Hitler; but he did not profit from Nazi Germany's war machine – at least after 1938. Before that as chair of Vestag, Thyssen directed the company, which certainly made contributions to Hitler's rearmament. Afterwards, the company was run by Albert Vögler, who became chairman in 1939. Vögler was integral to the founding of Vestag and was a mining executive long before its existence. Vögler, unlike Thyssen, was not taken with Hitler. At the speech the Führer delivered in the Düsseldorf Industrie Club, Vögler and his Number Two Ernst Pönsgen were unimpressed by the National Socialist experiment. That was in January of 1932; however, by the end of the year Vögler was a member of Himmler's inner circle. It was not Thyssen and Schacht who petitioned von Hindenburg to make Hitler chancellor – it was Vögler and banker Kurt von Schröder. It is possible the rumor of Thyssen's involvement comes from an invitation to sign the petition sent by Vögler, which Thyssen refused.

In 1934, Vögler was appointed Reich Plenipotentiary for the nationalization of the Rhenish-Westphalian coal mines and in 1940 he became the president of the Kaiser Wilhelm Society. His two predecessors at the Kaiser Wilhelm Society were Max Planck and Carl Bosch, both men of character. Vögler, however, willingly placed himself at the disposal of the Nazi regime. He was a true dichotomy, because at the same time, he campaigned for freedom of scientific research and opposed the state's attempts at dictation. As a close adviser to Fritz Todt and then Albert Speer, he organised the coordination of the armaments industry and made sure the research capacities of the Kaiser Wilhelm institutes were optimally used for war aims. Vögler resigned as chair of Vestag in 1943 to become Plenipotentiary for the Rhine-Ruhr area, which authorized him to make all decisions in armaments and war production. He was succeeded by Walther Rohland. With capture by the Allies imminent, Vögler committed suicide in April 1945.

Vestag was perhaps too cautious of an enterprise for the Nazis – in the mid-1930s, RLM attempted to sell the Junkers aircraft company to Vestag, but the finance department deemed the transaction too risky. Also too risky was the development of the low grade iron ore in the Ruhr valley, an opinion not shared with Reichsmarschall Göring. Göring believed it was imperative to develop raw materials in Germany and not import the higher grade Swedish ore. Göring was adamant to have Vestag develop its ore fields and when they wouldn't, they were basically blacklisted by the Nazis. In June of 1937, Göring berated the executive of Vestag. When they didn't respond, a month later he had Reichswerke Hermann Göring incorporated to compete with Vestag and develop the area. Göring's outrage boiled over at an after-dinner address at the Air Ministry. He delivered a blistering attack criticizing the industrialists on hand for their foot dragging and how they had wasted the time allocated in Hitler's Four Year Plan. In short, Göring's job was to "throw down the saboteurs of rearmament and the Four Year Plan and send them where they belonged."[448] The industrialists were then handed a list of the mines and ore fields which were going to be expropriated from them. Reichswerke Hermann Göring went on to expropriate Fritz Thyssen's coal fields after he fled the country, as well as many holdings in Austria and Czechoslovakia which were either taken from Jewish owners or purchased in the interests of the Reich.

11
Hitler's Tailor?

Compare 50,000 slave and forced laborers at Siemens with the 200 which Hugo Boss used – as well as how he treated them – then compare the shellacking Boss has received in the media. Hugo Boss may not have been an angel, but he didn't have a workforce the size of a large town forced to work for him. The other thing to note about Boss was he did not use laborers from concentration camps. Siemens did extensively, including Buchenwald, Ravensbrück and Auschwitz.

The legend of Himmler and Hugo Boss

Heinrich Himmler was born into a middle-class, conservative Catholic family in Munich, Germany. He studied agriculture at the Technical University in Munich, where he took a special interest in breeding and genetics. The university is also where he, like many university students, joined a fraternity. The fraternity was virulently racist and by the time he graduated from university in August 1922 he was already a fanatical racist and nationalist. After university, Himmler embarked on his first career, that of a fertilizer salesman. A bland, milque-toast fellow with a pince-nez and rather small voice, his days in sales were numbered before they even started.

Himmler went on to work for the Nazis, first during the Bierkeller Putsch, later as a propaganda leader for the party. He met his wife in a hotel lobby in 1926 while dodging a thunderstorm. He removed his hat to introduce himself and promptly soaked her with the water from its brim. Margarete was a blond-haired, blue-eyed daughter of a wealthy Prussian landowner. She had worked as a nurse in World War I and now owned a clinic in Munich, a clinic she sold when the couple married when Heinrich convinced her chicken farming was the wave of the future. The couple purchased land near Munich, built a small house and some chicken coops. The farm failed and Himmler spent most of the next decade in Berlin alone.

How does a bankrupt chicken farmer and failed manure salesman become the second most powerful man in Germany – and arguably the evilest – within 16 years? The ability to kill off all opposition and...an uncanny fashion sense. How else could you explain SS-Reichsführer Himmler's decision to have the dreaded SS' uniforms designed by Hugo Boss? Himmler was not what you would call a traditional Hugo Boss model. He was not the definition of Aryan supremacy, and looked almost comical when surrounded by his tall, muscular, blond-haired and blue-eyed SS bodyguards in their nattily-attired Hugo Boss suits. Designs for high ranking military officers, party members and officials were the work of Hugo Boss[449] as were many of the uniforms for the SS, the Wehrmacht and the Hitler Youth. That's the legend; the truth is far less spectacular.

The initial design was by SS-Oberführer Karl Diebitsch. Research has shown no hard evidence of Boss designing the uniforms. As a clothier, Boss would have had to implement designs based on practicality, but anything else was most likely suggested by SS lackeys, not the minor tailor from Metzingen.

Hugo himself was a card-carrying Nazi for business appearances – very hard to sell your wares to the government if you don't support it – and because he wanted to: "It is clear that Hugo F Boss did not only join the party because it led to contracts for uniform production, but also because he was a follower of National Socialism."[450]

So a little history on Mr. Boss: Hugo was born in 1885. attended school until he was 14 and then started a 3-year apprenticeship in a stamping shop. Boss married Anna Freysinger in 1908. The same year he took over his father Heinrich's trousseau business when the father passed on. The company had been a family business since 1870, when Heinrich opened shop at Hindenburgstraße 10. In 1914 he entered the Kaiser's army and saw action as a corporal, a rank he held throughout the war. After the war he went back to work in the trousseau shop, but during the hyperinflation of 1923, he moved from sales to production and started making a variety of items including jackets, raincoats, men's shirts, work clothes, underwear, sporting goods and uniforms – though not the work of a master haberdasher you would expect today. Most of the designs were very utilitarian, especially the uniforms the company made for the postal service.

He started his eponymous company in 1924 with the help of Metzinger brewery owners Albert and Theodor Bräuchle who both held one third of the new company. When the Depression hit, it took its toll on Boss as well – before, the company had 33 employees and was one of the eight largest textile concerns in Metzingen. By 1931, the creditors pushed Boss to the brink of bankruptcy and he shrank his workforce to 22 and had only six sewing machines to his name.

Also in 1931, he became a Nazi party member and a supporting member of the SS, as well as joining the German Labour Front in 1936, the Reich Air Protection Association in 1939, and the National Socialist People's Welfare in 1941. But why would Boss join any of these groups? Economics is a clear indicator – the Depression hit Germany hard and the Nazis were an alternative to Bolshevism and one that appealed to most businessmen, Boss included. Small craftsmen, shopkeepers and farmers would normally lean to the right of the political spectrum. The country was in disarray and it became apparent another political party had to step forward, and unfortunately for history, that was the Nazis.

When Hugo Boss opened his company, it was the beginning of his ascent into the middle class, a middle class which was ripe for Hitler's pro-economic gibberish and Boss was in the "economic and social situation of which a typical Nazi party supporter is characterized."[451] Hitler promised to eliminate unemployment, an obvious selling feature to anyone who has gone through the terrible hardships in Germany after World War I. Hugo Boss himself declared he had joined the National Socialist Party because it had promised to do something about the rampant unemployment afflicting the country. He expanded on this, stating he would never have received the orders that rescued his company had he not been a member.[452]

This networking in the pre-LinkedIn era allowed him greater access to contracts. Dr. Roman Köster of the Bundeswehr University in Munich has been studying Boss' past. He says "The fact that he was a party member in 1931 certainly didn't hurt him, but if you look at the rest of Boss' career, then it's clear that he did not join the party just out of economic calculation. Instead, one can clearly see that he was a convinced Nazi."[453] This is something Boss himself disputed at his denazification hearings: "I never warmed up to the National Socialist doctrine. Membership was strongly encouraged and the withdrawal of the orders was the menacing specter for refusing to join."[454] Dr.

Elisabeth Timm is the Chair of Cultural Anthropology at the University of Münster. In her study of Hugo Boss in the late 1990s, she stated this was often a motive for small entrepreneurs to join the Nazi Party, though she could find no evidence of the possibility of orders for uniforms being rescinded if Boss did not join.

Though this may have been acceptable in the defense industry, as clothing was not vital to the war effort, any advantage would have helped a company greatly. As today, many companies would receive orders from standing governments because of their aligned ideologies. One thing is certain: Hugo F. Boss did not personally participate in anti-Semitic incitement – at least not publicly. He did however distance himself from his old hunting buddy Adolf Herold, who had financially helped Boss in the past. Herold, who owned a small textile concern in Metzingen, had financed Boss when his bankruptcy loomed and also leased two hunting grounds which Boss patronized with his friend. Adolf Herold and his wife Jenny were eventually deported to Riga in 1941 and exterminated at the Jungfernhof concentration camp.[455]

If it can be argued Hugo Boss joined the Nazi Party for purely economic reasons, what were his reasons for joining the SS, the German Labour Front, the Reich Federation for Physical Education or the Reich Air Protection Association? The Reich Air Protection Association is a fairly easy and innocuous one: he was responsible for the enforcement of air protection arrangements at the local level and provided training and campaigns to motivate the civilian population, much like the Civil Defense leaders would do in the 1950s in the United States. The German Labour Front was a necessity due to Boss' management position at the time – it was only later the position became truly Nazified. The Reich Federation for Physical Education sounds innocent enough, though its mandate soon was to become the pursuance of the Aryan master race through exercise. When Boss joined, it was still a Weimar Republic-era sports body, and when all sports were put under the umbrella of the Federation, he naturally went along with it.

On his denazification paperwork, Hugo Boss admitted to being a supporting member of the SS. Again this is troubling, though when you take into account the large volume of orders he would have been receiving from the SS for uniforms and also the minimum annual contribution of a *Fördernde Mitglieder* (supporting member) was one

Reichsmark, it is not like you had to give greatly to the cause. In fact, in 1934, there were more than 340,000 "Supporting Members" who gave a total of RM581,000 RM to the SS, or 1.71 RM each, possibly enough to buy a loaf of bread and a coffee.[456]

By 1934, he was an official supplier to the SS, SA and Hitler Youth in an industry which was hit particularly hard by the Depression. This does not mean Boss solely made uniforms for the Nazis – they were just a good customer. Boss did sell other items, especially at trade shows though this was a minor segment of the business. In 1938 the company's luck changed when it received a major order for army uniforms. As the former seamstress Edith Poller recalled: "When the large orders began coming in, they were dizzy with relief. They had the feeling: 'We've finally made it.'"[457]

Again something to be noted is Hugo Boss never received the title *Wirtschaftsführer* or business leader, a leading designation given to men like Krupp, or the heads of Deutsche Bank or IG Farben. Much of what Hugo Boss did during the prewar years was out of business interest and not much else. A study of the economics at the time shows the textile industry was beat down by the Reich government, mainly by indirect means. These means included, but were not limited to: import prohibitions on cotton in favor of synthetics (which would have been manufactured mainly by companies like IG Farben), export bans and quotas on raw materials and labor all in favor of the defense plants, which were gearing up to a war economy. Since underwear and sporting goods aren't really essential for a war, Boss would have had his enterprise put to the back burner if he did not openly solicit government orders for uniforms.

Sales went from RM38,000 RM in 1932 to just over RM3 million by 1943[458] – small, considering the size of the other enterprises mentioned in this book though still a huge increase. To meet demand in 1940, he employed homeworkers as well as prisoners of war and slave laborers in his plant to a grand total of 324 employees.[459] The factory in Metzingen made uniforms for the Wehrmacht and the Waffen-SS with 40 French PoWs and 140 slave laborers imported from the Baltic States, Belgium, France, Italy, Austria, Poland, Czechoslovakia and the Soviet Union.[460] The first forced laborers started work at the company in April 1940 when company representative Martin Eberhard traveled to

Poland's former textile district to "recruit" workers with the help of the Gestapo. At this first visit, Eberhard had four men and sixteen women rounded up and put on a train for Metzingen. One of these women was Elzbieta Kubala-Bem, who was 19 when she was whisked off the street and forced onto the train:

In Metzingen I worked from May 26, 1940 for Hugo Boss as a seamstress, and in the kitchen of the Baumann Inn. As a reward for our work, we got six, seven marks a week. The first year I was staying in the camp for easterners but in 1942 I could live at the inn. When I was at Boss, working time was 12 hours, then I had another four hours in the kitchen at the inn. We were not allowed to have any contact with German workers and vice versa. The bosses at Boss were always diplomatic but unfriendly. Special treatment for children or pregnant women did not exist. Also, there was no way to visit a doctor. We helped ourselves when we were sick. From my time in Metzingen I developed rheumatism. Shelters during air raids were only available for the Germans.[461]

And from Maria Klima, who was 14 when she was forced to work for the company:

First, I want to ask you some questions:
- *Have you ever slept in a dirty bed where it snowed?*
- *Were you ever beaten in the face because you have picked an apple from the ground?*
- *Have you ever bathed together with 20 people aged from 14 to 40?*
- *Have you ever spent Christmas Eve in a warehouse?*

I could ask many more questions. On May 1, 1943 I was brought alone to Metzingen at the age of 14 and had to work in the factory Uniform Hugo Boss. Initially I was put up in a private home, then later in the camp for Easterners, where the supply of food was poor. I had to wear the letter "P" on my clothes all the time. At Hugo Boss we sewed uniforms for the army; we had to work 12 hours a day. Among the managers there were some Nazis – you could recognize it from their behavior; they called us "Poland pigs." Herr Boss was supposed to be a Nazi, but to us young people he was friendly. With the people of Metzingen we had little contact – I think the Germans were afraid of us.[462]

The *Ostarbeitern* received lower wages, poorer nutrition, poorer medical care and accommodation according to the racial ideology the Nazis followed. They also paid taxes, a so-called 15 percent "social compensation levy," health and social security contributions and expenses for room and board. The Western Europeans were allowed to move freely around Metzingen, the *Ostarbeitern* were strictly regulated and had to wear a "P" or "Ost" on their clothes. They were not allowed to attend church, use public transit or talk to Germans, under punishment of death.

Boss didn't use slave labor to the extent of IG Farben and Siemens. In fact, he tried to improve conditions in 1944, by asking to house his workers himself and attempting to improve their food situation. Specifically, Boss tried to have the female workers excluded from the terrible food at the Eastern workers' camp and have them fed at the company canteen. Hugo Boss also had the canteen provide lunch for the workers as much as they could – possibly from humanitarian reasons, possibly because Boss realized a starving employee doesn't produce as well. From affidavits filed after the war French and Polish forced laborers reported "that the food was very good; that the treatment was significantly better than any other company in Metzingen; that Mr. Boss fed me in his canteen and they had been very well fed."[463] Hugo Boss' response to this at his denazification proceedings was simple: the camp food was inhumane under which no man can work.

Hugo Boss himself did not get involved in punishment of workers; that seems to have been left in the hands of managers and supervisors, some of whom were particularly harsh. The case of Josefa Gisterek is a valid one. Josefa's younger sister Anna was brought to the camp by Martin Eberhard in the first wave in April of 1940 and Josefa joined her in October of the next year. Two months later Anna and Josefa's father contacted the girls, asking for help – their mother had an accident and their father needed help looking after their other eight children. Josefa asked for a leave of absence, which was declined since she had only started working two months previous. She fled anyway and returned to their hometown of Oswiecim in Poland.

In January, Anna was allowed to leave on holiday and returned to Oswiecim; her sister never made it, having been picked up by the Gestapo en route. Josefa was interred in a number of concentration camps including Auschwitz and Buchenwald before being returned to work at the Boss factory in March of 1943 after the personal intervention of Hugo Boss. During her time at the concentration camps, the guards batted Josefa around continuously, causing her terrible head injuries. When she returned to Boss, she had a difficult time working from the constant headaches, though her supervisor would not allow her any leave time or a visit to a doctor, wanting to make an example out of her. After she suffered a breakdown, she was finally allowed to take three months off. When it was time for her to return, Josefa Gisterek committed suicide. Hugo Boss arranged for the company to pay for the funeral and covered the travel expenses of the family members who attended it.[464]

One thing that is important to realize is Hugo Boss' company was never a major player in the Third Reich, employing about 320 people at its height – compare this to Allianz with 16,000 workers. In fact, it was never even a major player in the clothing industry at the time, again something which leads one to believe a little shop in Metzingen would not be tasked with designing the uniforms for the SS. Boss' son Siegfried defended him in 1997 to the Austrian magazine *Profil*: "Of course my father belonged to the Nazi Party, but who didn't belong back then? The whole industry worked for the Nazi Army."[465] It is easy to point out without a (Nazi ID) card, you don't play. But most of Hugo Boss' management were card-carrying members of the Nazi Party and ardent supporters. At the time, Hugo Boss was producing uniforms for the Wehrmacht, the SS and the Hitler Youth, but so were many other companies and Hugo Boss was not the main producer. Also, the rumor that Hugo Boss himself was Hitler's personal tailor is completely false.

Because of his early Nazi party membership, his financial support of the SS and the uniforms delivered to the Nazi party, Boss was considered both an "activist" and a "supporter and beneficiary of National Socialism." In a 1946 judgement he was stripped of his voting rights, his capacity to run a business, and fined the very large sum of 100,000 Deutschmarks. He died in March 1948 during an appeal of the penalty, from complications of a tooth abscess. As a result of the ban on Boss being in business, Boss's son-in-law Eugen Holy took over ownership and running of the company.

ADIDAS and PUMA

Hugo Boss was not the only member of the clothing industry involved in the German war effort, though as a name he was the most prominent. Brothers Adolf and Rudolf Dassler were also involved, though at times more directly than Boss' company. Adolf (who went by Adi) and his older brother Rudolf were born into a shoemaking tradition, their father Christoph having worked in a shoe factory. Adi was the cobbler and Rudolf was the loud, extroverted salesman.[466] Adolf apprenticed as a baker, and when his apprenticeship was done, so was the baking – he was drafted and sent to the Belgian front with Rudolf and his other brother Fritz. They all returned in 1918 unharmed, but now with no prospects in the postwar Weimar Republic. Adi decided baking was not for him and started making shoes in his mother's home laundry business, which was sitting idle as sending your clothes to the laundry was now a luxury. He scoured the countryside for tools, bits of leather and shoe soles to make his shoes. He started making running shoes, with his friend and the son of the local blacksmith supplying the spikes for the shoes.[467]

In 1924 Adolf and Rudolf formed *Gebrüder Dassler Schuhfabrik* (the Dassler Brothers Shoe Company). In the 1920s, unemployment in Herzogenaurach was around 70% and the only out for most people was sports. Adi became a member of the local soccer club, FC Herzogenaurach, and played centre forward, an excellent opportunity for him to start showcasing his new shoes. Gebrüder Dassler's first big order came when they offered their new soccer shoes to FC Herzogenaurach at reduced prices. This led to their first marketing breakthrough: give all of Germany's burgeoning soccer clubs samples and brochures. The Dassler's quality sold their product and this brought about their first big break. Josef Waitzer, the head trainer for the German track and field federation, stopped by the Dassler plant to talk shoes. Waitzer ended up becoming an adviser to the brothers, running together and talking shoes. For the 1928 Olympics, Waitzer and Adolf worked together to design shoes for the German athletes. The results: one gold, one silver and two bronze for Dassler shoes.

Their biggest coup before World War II came at the 1936 Summer Olympics in Berlin. As history will tell, this was supposed to be Hitler's greatest showcase for Aryan supremacy. He assembled 433 athletes (by comparison, Germany fielded 392 athletes at the 2012 Summer Olympics in London), and pulled in 89 medals, far ahead of the second place United States at 56. The German Olympic Committee barred Jews and the Roma from competing for Germany, but that didn't stop other countries from competing with non-Aryans. One of these was the **not** blond-haired and **not** blue-eyed Jesse Owens. Owens had already, as a high school student, tied the world record in the 100-yard dash. Just before the competitions, Owens was visited in the Olympic village by Adi Dassler. He persuaded Owens to use Dassler spikes.[468] Jesse Owens won four gold medals, sales exploded and Hitler was undeniably irritated that a black man would beat his Aryan supermen.

As with the overwhelming majority of businessmen in the Third Reich, Adolf and Rudolf both joined the Nazi party in the 1930s. Adolf was ordered to the front in August 1940, though he was exempted from service in February 1941. Rudolf volunteered for the Wehrmacht in 1941. By 1945, his unit had been integrated into the SS, and this was enough for him. He deserted shortly thereafter, claiming later "My disapproval of Himmler's police rule, the proximity of the front and the fact that the war had long been lost, prompted me to refuse any further military duties."[469] His unit in Poland had disbanded, a result of the Red Army rolling through the area, and his SS overlords told him to report to the *Sicherheitsdienst* branch of the SS, which was its intelligence service. Rudolf was imprisoned in 1945 for his ties to the SS by the Allies.

As most of their competitors were closed by Berlin, Dassler Bros. had no problem continuing in World War II Germany. Due to staff shortages, they did employ prisoners of war in their plant, but only a middling five Russian PoWs.[470] Since the production of the company was mainly leather boots for the Wehrmacht, they were able to continue for some time, but in December 1943 this changed, when production in the plant had to change to war materials. Specifically, the sewing machines were moved out and spot welding equipment was moved in. Seamstresses were given a crash course in welding and then in early 1944, production moved completely to the manufacture of bazookas.

Military contractor Schricker & Co. was supposed to be the lead manufacturer of the new *Panzerschreck* (Tank Terror) bazooka, but since the area Schricker was operating out of was increasingly being hit by Allied air raids, the decision was to move production to the small town of Herzogenaurach, and the best factory to manufacture the bazookas was the Dassler Bros. Seamstresses welded sights and blast shields on the "stovepipes" which were the basis of the weapon. Along with the seamstresses and the Soviet prisoners of war, the company also used French forced laborers on the production line. As with the American bazooka which the Panzerschreck was designed after, the weapon was the first time a single infantry soldier could go toe-to-toe with a tank and win. The Panzerschreck had the ability to fire a rocket which would penetrate eight inches of armored steel. According to Christian Hartmann, a military historian at the Munich-based Institute of Contemporary History, "If large numbers of Panzerschrecks could have been deployed during the Russian campaign in 1941, Moscow would have probably fallen."[471]

But back to Adi and Rudolf Dassler; tensions increased between the brothers over the years, mainly because their wives hated each other and they all lived in the same villa. Two major incidents cemented their feud. One occurred in 1943: Rudi and his wife were escaping Allied bombing raids and went into a bomb shelter already occupied with Adi and his wife. Adi said "The dirty bastards are back again," apparently referring to the Allied warplanes. Rudolf was convinced his brother meant him and his family. The damage was never repaired.[472] The second item is somewhat hearsay, though it is corroborated by an American GI's testimony after the fact. Rudolf ended up near the Russian front during the war, which he claims was Adi's doing. He was imprisoned for desertion by the Nazis, then imprisoned by the Allies for allegedly being a member of the Gestapo. Rudi claimed Adi gave him up to the authorities, a claim backed up by the American officer investigating the case at the time.[473]

The company only survived the Allied invasion because of the good graces of Adi's wife Käthe, when she charmed the Americans as they contemplated blowing up the factory, saying the company and its employees were only interested in manufacturing sports shoes. The U.S. Air Force set up its own operations at the former military air base in Herzogenaurach. When the Americans found out the Dasslers made the shoes Jesse Owens won his gold medals with, they started placing large orders for basketball and baseball shoes. This did nothing to mend the fences between Adolf and Rudolf. The split between the two brothers was finalized after the war. Adi remained at Gebrüder Dassler, renaming it Adidas in 1948 (Adi for his first name, Das for his last). Rudolf went to the other side of the river in Herzogenaurach and started his own company Ruda, which he renamed Puma shortly after.

The feud continued up until this century in Herzogenaurach and worldwide, as Adidas and Puma staff never peacefully co-existed. In the town, you either worked for one or the other. There were Adidas butchers and Puma butchers. You did not date Adidas employees if you worked for Puma and intermarriage was absolutely forbidden! The town became known as the town of bent necks, because people looked at the brand of shoes you wore before they spoke to you.[474]

12
The IG

There are few companies in the history of mankind which are so reviled, so hated and considered so evil as IG Farben. You may not have heard of *Interessen Gemeinschaft Farbenindustrie AG*, but you have probably heard of a few of its component companies. In 1926, six of the largest chemical concerns in Germany joined forces to become Farben, only to be broken up into their constituent parts in 1951 by the Western Allies. These companies were BASF, Bayer, Agfa, Hoechst, Chemische Fabrik Griesheim-Elektron and Chemische Fabrik vorm. Weiler Ter Meer. The three smaller ones were gobbled up by the others, and Hoechst split up and sold its chemical business to Celanese and merged its life sciences business with Rhône-Poulenc to form Aventis. Originally, a grandiose plan – after World War I, with the German economy completely obliterated by the Treaty of Versailles, the six chemical companies merged together into a "community of interests" or *Interessen Gemeinschaft*.

A brief history on the constituent parts

All these companies were proud old businesses in Germany. Agfa-Gevaert N.V. began life in 1867 as Aktien-Gesellschaft für Anilin-Fabrikation, a dye manufacturing business. It merged with Gevaert Photo-Producten N.V. of Belgium in 1964, with Gevaert and Bayer both owning 50% of the company. Bayer divested in 1999 and Agfa continues as an imaging and IT company, mainly in the healthcare field.

BASF was originally founded in 1865 as Badische Anilin- und Soda-Fabrik by Friedrich Engelhorn. A monolith of a chemical company today, it employs over 110,000 people with sales in excess of €73 billion. Again, starting life as a dye manufacturer, its first big success was in 1869 when it successfully synthesized Alizarin, the first natural red dye. In 1880, Adolf Baeyer, a chemist in Strasbourg, successfully synthesized indigo, the most important natural dye at that time. BASF, together with the Hoechst dyeworks, acquired the rights to exploit the indigo patent and produced indigo on an industrial scale.[475]

For his work he was not only elevated to Germany's nobility – becoming Adolf von Baeyer – but also received the 1905 Nobel Prize in Chemistry. BASF's biggest success, however, occurred in 1913.

Haber, Bosch and BASF

Fritz Haber was born in 1868, the son of Siegfried Haber, a Jewish merchant. In 1908 he came to the attention of BASF for his work in nitrogen fixation, an essential ingredient in fertilizer. At the time, it was believed there was only a finite amount of nitrogen in the world and it only came from decomposition and from animal manure. There are tales of English gangs roaming Europe, digging up corpses for fertilizer in the 18th century.[476] The threat of a finite amount of fertilizer and therefore a finite sustainable population loomed over late 19^{th-} and early 20th-century Europe. In 1911 Haber was appointed Director of the Institute for Physical and Electrochemistry at Berlin-Dahlem. In this prestigious role, he was instrumental in inventing a process for removing nitrogen from ammonia. He received research money from BASF to continue after receiving visits from BASF chemist Carl Bosch and technical manager Heinrich Brunck. BASF, along with Hoechst, purchased the rights to the Haber process.

Unfortunately, Haber's process was pricey – it required expensive osmium as a catalyst. It was Carl Bosch's job to make the process more economically viable. He did this by moving the process from Haber's lab to BASF's Oppau plant in 1913 and using a less expensive iron-based catalyst, which is still in use today. It was the basis for one of the greatest food-based technologies of the twentieth century – nitrogen-based fertilizer. It was also the basis for one of the greatest munitions-based technologies of the twentieth century – synthetic saltpeter. On the upside, nitrogen-based fertilizer has helped increase the world's population from 1.7 billion people in 1900 to over 7.4 billion today. Over 130 million tons of synthetic nitrogen was being produced by 1999, 80% of that as fertilizer.[477] On the downside is the military applications and Fritz Haber and Carl Bosch were also responsible for this. Haber was an passionate German nationalist and was not going to see the Fatherland go down in flames in World War I. The stalemate in the trenches meant it had become a war of attrition and there was no way Germany could win such a war. The British Royal Navy was blockading Germany, as well as their major source of saltpeter; Chile. After some initial victories, the German Imperial Navy was no match for the Royal Navy.

Dr. Carl Bosch came from a prodigious family (his uncle Robert invented the spark plug). He started working for BASF in 1899 as an entry level chemist. He was viewed as a miracle worker for his work with the Haber process (in 1931 he won the Nobel Prize in chemistry for his work)[478] and was tapped for solving this crisis for the German Army as well. He was supportive of the war effort in World War I, so much so he made his famous "saltpeter promise."[479] In a meeting with the War Ministry, he promised to keep up with nitric acid production, which was essential to production of saltpeter and therefore munitions. As second in command at BASF, he tasked a plant at Oppau to convert to nitric acid production. Production continued to fall short of requirements and this worried Haber.

Haber was 46 when World War I started He was considered too old to fight and the army considered him too Jewish to have a reserve commission, so he did what he could – he thought of different ways for Germany to win the war. His brainchild was to use the excess stores of chlorine at BASF against the Allied powers. The gas was used in April 1915 at Ypres, killing between 800 and 1,400 people:

Following a heavy bombardment, the enemy attacked the French Division at about 5 p.m., using asphyxiating gases for the first time…What follows defies description. The effect of these poisonous gases was so virulent as to render the whole of the line held by the French Division mentioned above practically incapable of any action at all…Hundreds of men were thrown into a comatose or dying condition.[480]

The Allies were incensed, but so were many Germans. Many saw it as un-gentlemanly, whereas lobbing an artillery shell at a trench and horrifically dismembering 200 men was much better! Throughout the war, at least 65,000 were killed by poison gas attacks and perhaps over half a million wounded. The original chlorine gas was released from tanks and blown by fans at the enemy, which was not particularly effective (or safe) as a stiff wind could (and did) blow it back to the Germans. This happened to the British in September 1915. The night before the attack, the winds died. The following morning the British commander, General Sir Douglas Haig, made a controversial decision to proceed with the attack despite not knowing if the gas had dispersed on the German lines. It did on his right flank, but on the left the gas wafted back into the British trenches, engulfing the troops waiting to attack.[481]

Because of the inherent dangers, Carl Duisberg, the head of Bayer at the time, directed company chemists to develop other, more effective, poison gases, including phosgene and mustard gas. BASF also manufactured phosgene and contributed to mustard gas production as well. Exposure to phosgene can cause coughing, burning in the throat and eyes, difficulty breathing, vomiting, skin lesions and fluid in the lungs within two to six hours. After 48 hours it can cause pulmonary edema, low blood pressure and heart failure.[482] Mustard gas, while seldom lethal right away, causes blindness, skin burns and respiratory cancers. It is estimated the work of both Bosch and Haber during World War I probably kept Germany in the war for an extra year, and though both wanted a quick end to the fighting – with Germany as the victor – the extra year would bring the United States into the war and continue to escalate the casualty rates.

Fritz Haber won the Nobel Prize in chemistry in 1918 for his work on nitrogen fixation. This outraged many in Britain and France, who deemed him a war criminal. Haber went on to continue his work until 1933, when Hitler's rise caused waves of anti-Semitism. According to his daughter Eva: "in early 1933 he went to his institute. There was the porter, who said: 'The Jew Haber is not allowed in here,'"[483] He left Germany shortly thereafter and died in exile in Switzerland the next year, turned away by the country he dearly wanted to protect.

Carl Bosch also had his problems and successes. In 1919 he was made managing director of BASF and in 1925 was appointed chairman of IG Farben. An open critic of Hitler's anti-Jewish policies, he used his position as head of the Kaiser Wilhelm Institute (he was Haber's successor) as well as IG Farben to plead with Hitler to allow Jewish scientists to continue work in Germany. His pleas fell on deaf ears and he was silenced for his views. However, he did profit from IG Farben's relationship with the Nazis. As Farben was the largest chemical conglomerate in Germany, and by 1938 almost completely "Nazified", Farben had virtual monopolies on the production of the Reich's requirements for synthetic rubber and synthetic gasoline (both at a set price). Bosch, however, was stymied by his pro-Jewish views and was considered *persona non grata* by the Nazis. He spiralled into alcohol abuse and depression and died in 1940.

Bayer AG is a €40 billion company, with its fingers in healthcare, crop science and plastics. As with BASF, its beginnings were not so auspicious. It was formed in 1863 by Friedrich Bayer and Johann Friedrich Weskott, again as a dye manufacturer. Their first foray into pharmaceuticals was in 1884 when Carl Duisberg, who had been recently hired to increase Bayer's outreach into other fields, was cajoled into drug manufacture. One of Bayer's dye-manufacturing competitors (Kalle and Company) had recently introduced a trademark drug – Antifebrine – for use as a pain reliever. This was the first time a drug had been trademarked, and the possibilities for profit were high. At the time, pharmacists in Germany would fill prescriptions generically, using the lowest possible pricing. Now, if a doctor prescribed Antifebrine, pharmacists were obligated to supply exactly what was prescribed. And the only place they could purchase it was from Kalle.

Duisberg also saw this as an opportunity. He tasked Oskar Hinsberg with using a by-product of dye manufacture, paranitrophenol, to come up with a similar product. Hinsberg came back with a pain reliever which was slightly easier on the system than Antifebrine and called it Phenacetin. This was Bayer's first trademarked drug and received a big boost in 1888 during a flu epidemic. Bayer's biggest coup, however, was still eleven years away.

Both Phenacetin and Antifebrine were hard on the stomach, so the idea was to come up with a drug which could be taken as a pain reliever and which wouldn't cause other pain. Felix Hoffmann was a chemist at Bayer who worked for Arthur Eichengrun. Under orders from Eichengrun, sent down from Duisberg, Hoffmann and others were to find ways to make salicylic acid more palatable to the stomach as a pain reliever. By 1897, Hoffmann had a formula for removing the hydrogen from salicylic acid and replacing it with an acetyl compound, giving us acetylsalicylic acid, or ASA. The chief pharmacologist at Bayer was unconvinced of the drug's safety and was keen on developing an opium derivative called diacetylmorphine, which was originally marketed as a children's cough medicine. The employees who tested it felt it made them feel heroic, giving Bayer the name of the new drug: heroin. In 1899, ASA was released in sample form to doctors under the trade name Aspirin.[484] Yes, the company that gave the world the granddaddy of all pain relievers also gave the world the other granddaddy of all pain relievers!

The first years of the twentieth century were extremely lucrative for Bayer, until the First World War. Granted, Bayer was able to retool and manufactured munitions for the German Army, but many of their lucrative overseas ventures were not open to them. In Russia, Bayer's assets were confiscated by the interim government after the Russian Revolution; in the United States, all of Bayer's assets were expropriated and sold to competitors. With most able-bodied men at the front, there were labor shortages in manufacturing facilities as well. Carl Duisberg proposed the use of forced labor to General Erich Ludendorff. This was taken up by the Ministry of the Interior and 60,000 Belgians were imported to alleviate the problem. Fortunately for them, the German government at the time was much more lenient. When the Belgians refused to work, they were actually allowed to go home!

After the war, one of the stipulations of the Treaty of Versailles was the expropriation of German property abroad and access to industrial patents. Industrial plants engaged in the production of poison gas were to be shut down. Carl Bosch negotiated with the French to keep the plants in Oppau and Leuna open, in exchange for industrial secrets such as dye production and the Haber-Bosch process. BASF, whose munitions output in 1917-18 amounted to 78% of their sales, had to retool again and refocus as did the other component companies of IG Farben. Spiralling inflation in Germany made the prices of products cheaper for export, increasing profits for companies like BASF. The German people were not so lucky, though. As their prices skyrocketed, basics such as bread became unaffordable. *Der Spiegel* tells the story of a man who bought two cups of coffee, figuring it would cost 5,000 marks. His bill was 14,000 by the time he had finished the second cup.[485] In 1914, a mark purchased $4.20US. By 1923, a US dollar bought 4,200,000,000,000 marks (that's trillion with a "T").[486]

This was the economic climate which allowed Hitler to come to power. His promises of a better Germany, a need for the return of a great empire and his blame of the Jews, their businesses and banking were what the German people looked for; in short, a savior. The mood in Germany was tense – political assassinations were a common occurrence, as were mob riots, street fighting and tense political meetings. It was at this point the IG's exports were exceedingly profitable, so it was in the company's best interests foreign relations remained at a high. Bosch chose to strengthen the company inwardly; perhaps he realized it would be a good idea to tie the company's fortunes to a man who talked of a brighter future, with low unemployment, high incomes and good times for industrialists (and bad times for the Jewish population). Political support is as old as the Roman republic and continues today in the form of companies and special interest groups lobbying for what they deem are their rights. Nazi Germany was no different. Though Bosch never particularly agreed with the precepts of National Socialism, he did believe a stronger, united Germany was good for Germans and the IG.

The Aufsichtsrat always had the problem in the interwar years of what political party to support. Social Democrats were always the friend of the trade unions – and therefore the enemy of the industrialist. Communists were even worse – there was no such thing as an industrialist to a communist, so that option was non-existent. There was the *Deutschnationale Volkspartei*, the German National People's Party, which was conservative in nature, but Alfred Hugenberg was a loudmouth and loose cannon, which didn't sit well with the Aufsichtsrat. Then there was *Die Deutsche Volkspartei* or the German People's Party, which was similar in both name and doctrine to the German National People's Party. Its leader was thoughtful, conservative, was good towards big business – his famous quote was "Without IG and coal I have no foreign policy."[487] Unfortunately for Bosch et al, the Volkspartei could never get enough support to form a government, much like the middle-of-the-road Democratic Party and the German Center Party. Only one man could organize his troops, his funding and his party better than all others. Too bad it was Hitler.

The IG funded many of the parties simultaneously, as it was easier to gain support in government circles if you were a member of all of them. The company also funded newspapers throughout the country, in an effort to have its agenda at the front and fore. This was a complete and utter failure, as public opinion continued to grow towards Hitler and the Nazis. Germany had been hit hard, not just by the terms of the Versailles Treaty, not just by the hyperinflation of 1923, but now in October 1929, the New York stock crash and subsequent Depression. The effect was staggering – three years later over a third of workers in Germany were unemployed, farmers lost their land, civil servants lost their jobs, even doctors had a hard time making ends meet. Again, the time was ripe for someone who made claims of a better tomorrow.

At the IG, the crisis was felt more deeply than in the general German economy. Where 33% of workers were unemployed in the country, 46% of Farben workers were cut. This affected not just the workers who now had to scrounge for food, but the local butcher, baker and candlestick maker. By 1932, most of the company cash reserves were gone and sales were down a ridiculous 85%.[488] The IG could not rely on its exports as much as before – many countries were in the throes of protectionism, trying to bolster their own economies without having cheap exports flood their markets and kill their own industries. Germany would have to go it alone, as would the IG. Carl Bosch believed synthetic fuel was the future, but he was pretty much alone. Even his onetime ally Carl Duisberg was against the project. Duisberg commissioned a probe of the subject and the assessment was the project would fail unless massive government subsidies were forthcoming. This would hit hard at the company's independence. IG Farben CEO Hermann Schmitz also commissioned a probe, but his was much more amenable to continuing the project. Since neither side was in agreement, the synthetic fuel kept dripping out of the Leuna plant slowly.

Bosch approached the government in 1931, looking for tariffs on imported petroleum. Knowing other countries were acting on protectionist agendas, he knew he had a shot. The new government of Heinrich Brüning agreed and raised duties on imported oil by a whopping 70%. To add to this, the government banned all imports of nitrogen-based fertilizers, which gave the IG an extra boost, as the Haber-Bosch process was a pure money-maker. Duisberg backed off and Carl Bosch continued.

The IG was very much involved in the Reich government – so much so that many of its employees served in government positions from the time of the merger until the end of the war. The most important of these was Dr. Carl Krauch. Krauch founded the Office for the Expansion of Trade and Industries (chemical division) to expand production of Buna rubber, synthetic oil and nitrogen, among other items. This was in 1939; also that year, he was appointed head of chemicals for Göring's Four Year Plan. According to Günther Frank-Fahle, one of the IG's directors: "the fact that Dr. Krauch has this leading position in the working of the Four-Year Plan was perhaps the greatest contribution IG paid to the party, because not only the men whom Dr. Krauch took into his office were at his disposal, but in his capacity as member of the Vorstand and even more when he became chairman of the board, he could use the whole IG."[489]

This close interlinking of the IG and the Nazi government went over very well with the company, contrary to its long-standing belief working with the government would mean a loss of identity and freedom for the company. From the point of view of the chemists, research scientists and technical directors, it was great news; working with the government meant government money coming into the company, which would mean more money for research and development.

Krauch was not alone serving the Reich government. Other IG luminaries, including Otto Ambros, Heinrich Bütefisch and Carl Wurster all served in the Ministry of Armament by chairing committees. Ambros, who headed two chemical factories for the IG, as well as developing some of the most lethal nerve agents known to man, headed Buna rubber production and poison gasses. Bütefisch headed the synthetic fuel committee and Wurster the production of sulphuric acid.

All along, the IG would contribute to every party in the spectrum, including that of Brüning. By 1931, they threw their lot in with the Nazis as well. Hitler was a master public speaker and the IG came under his spell at the many-times mentioned meeting at Göring's home in February 1933. Twenty of the country's leading industrialists were invited; at the head of the group was Gustav Krupp von Bohlen und Halbach. Directly behind him were representatives of the IG, Georg von Schnitzler and the non-descript Gustav Stein. Conspicuous in their absence were Carl Duisberg and Carl Bosch. Duisberg had a very good reason – he had to throw the switch on the world's largest Aspirin sign. Carl Bosch just didn't like this kind of thing – he liked science over theater. You don't win Nobel Prizes by attending political meetings.[490]

Hitler stated at the meeting he had formed an alliance with the *Deutsch-Nationale Volkspartei* and at the end of the meeting, Dr. Hjalmar Schacht asked everyone to pony up – to the tune of three million Reichsmarks, to be distributed between the two groups. The alliance had been arranged by Franz von Papen, under the guise of his misguided theory he could control Hitler. The payment was made, after von Schnitzler met with Bosch, who supposedly shrugged his shoulders[491] and five days later, RM400,000 was donated into the Nazi Party's account. Bosch wasn't political; he was pragmatic – better to have a stable government in Berlin than another twenty years of coalitions and garbage in the Reichstag. What Bosch didn't realize was the Nazi agenda. The night the IG deposited the money, the Reichstag burned – supposedly set by a communist sympathizer. Many theories abound, one of which is the arsonists used a tunnel which existed between the house of the President of the Reichstag and the building itself. The president was conveniently Hermann Göring. The end result was the same – it was a call to order by Hitler, who was immediately given emergency powers equivalent to martial law by President von Hindenburg.

Later in 1933, tensions increased with the SA, who continued to go on witch-hunts for communists, Jews, academics – basically anyone they didn't like. By June, Carl Duisberg attended a meeting of the Hitler-Spende fund, in which it was stated another RM3 million was needed to "meet the urgent social distress which existed among 500,000 SA-troops."[492] Duisberg told the meeting the IG was prepared to pay its share right away, recognizing the necessity of the money to stabilize the country. The company also contributed to a housing project for SA members in Munich, as well as for winter clothes in 1933 – a total payment of between two and three hundred thousand Reichsmarks.

Contributions to the Nazi Party and affiliates continued on until the end of the war, many of them clearly indicated on the books of the IG. Some, however, were disguised by Hermann Schmitz. Schmitz hid these payments in subsidiary companies where they couldn't easily be found. From 1932 to 1944, Schmitz secretly gave over RM4 million to the party and affiliates, virtually unknown to other members of the Aufsichtsrat. These payments were made under the codename "Cassella" which was one of the minor companies which merged to form IG Farben. Some of this money went to Kurt von Schröder at the Stein banking house for the Keppler Kreis funds – usually RM100,000 a year. Himmler would then make withdrawals from the account and deposit it into his personal account at Dresdner Bank (account number 30/6440/41 if you want to look it up).

IG Farben was formed in December of 1925 with Carl Duisberg at the helm. As the German economy ramped up military production in the 1930s, so did IG Farben. In 1932, Heinrich Bütefisch, the technical director of Leuna, (and later plant manager at IG Auschwitz) and Heinrich Gattineau, the head of the economic policy division, obtained pricing agreements from Hitler on synthetic fuel and rubber. "Hitler agrees that he will grant our gasoline production the necessary protection."[493] The Nazi government also had Farben increase production of other raw materials, such as synthetic rubber, for which they also provided price guarantees. The integration of IG Farben and the government was so complete that by the summer of 1938, company officials were dealing directly with the government officials who themselves worked for IG Farben (but were on sabbatical). The Office for Economic Expansion was made a full government agency by December 1939, with IG Farben director Carl Krauch as head.

The company knew the value of political capital and lobbied the Second Reich during the First World War, the Weimar Republic in the intermediary and the Third Reich during World War II. Besides IG Farben managers and directors actively becoming Nazi Party members, the company also contributed political funds. In one infamous meeting,

Hitler, Göring and Hjalmar Schacht, the incoming president of the Reichsbank, met with leading industrialists on February 20, 1933, and came away with pledges of 3 million RM to fund the National Socialist campaign for the March 5 Reichstag elections. The representatives of the chemicals and nitrates industries promised a total of 500,000 RM. I.G. Farben paid the entire sum, wiring 400,000 RM to the NSDAP leadership and 100,000 to Franz von Papen. This was only the beginning of a checkbook offensive worth a total of 4.5 million RM already in 1933 and systematically beefed up in the following years. According to card-index files kept by the I.G. Central Committee through 1945, the largest amounts were paid under the cover of industrial coordination measures to two funds: 12.7 million RM to the "Adolf Hitler-Fund for the German Economy" and 16 million RM to the "Winter Charity Campaign" (Winterhilfswerk). At the same time, substantial payments went to the leadership groups of the NSDAP, SS, and SA, and to most of the Nazi movement's mass and professional organizations. Just the centrally tabulated tributes and bribes totaled 39.6 million RM by the end of the war.[494]

This is the equivalent of over $126 million today. IG Farben supplied Germany production, research and economic prestige and power unparalleled in any other part of the world. Dr. Georg von Schnitzler to the Spanish ambassador in February 1943: "Only during the war could German chemistry prove itself worthy of the task. It is no exaggeration to say that without the service of German chemistry performed under the Four Year Plan, the prosecution of modern war would have been unthinkable"[495]

Since IG Farben was not only the largest chemical company in Germany but also the world at the time, von Schnitzler implied without the IG specifically, German could not have pursued the war as it did. This is true in many respects – advances made in chemistry by the company made it possible for Germany to pursue the war as long as it did. Non-aggressive advances such as the Haber-Bosch process allowed Germany to supply more food to its people and soldiers than would have been possible just 30 years earlier. Discoveries such as the poison gasses saran and mustard gas, though not used widely, allowed Germany to consider more extreme measures to win. The discovery of synthetic fuels through the processing of brown coal, as well as the processing of jet fuel, allowed companies such as Messerschmitt to keep their BF-109 piston fighters in the air and the invention of the Me-262 jet fighter to slow down bombing runs by RAF Lancaster bombers and USAAF B-17 Flying Fortresses and B-24 Liberators. Willy Messerschmitt's jet was the first jet fighter to go into production, and though the war was practically over, the Me-262s performed extremely well. In their first few weeks in action, the small number of jets managed to shoot down 22 enemy airplanes, with over half of those being the heavy bombers.[496] All of this would not be possible without the work of the IG in production of synthetic jet fuel. The two problems the jet fighter encountered were shortages – of experienced flyers and of fuel. The latter problem was brought on by the constant bombing of the fuel production facilities, though in a classic Catch-22 situation, the bombing could have been significantly slowed if there was enough fuel for the fighters.

Besides poison gas and synthetic fuel, the IG was responsible for making synthetic rubber, lubricants, fibres, plastics and other synthetics, mainly derived from the hydrogenation of brown coal, of which there was a large amount in both the Ruhr valley and Upper Silesia. Though Germany was poor in other raw materials, the coal production of the country far outstripped its requirements. It was in the synthesis of other materials the country fell behind. Dr. Carl Krauch, chair of the Aufsichtsrat was also in charge of the chemical industry for Göring's Four Year Plan, so the IG was integral to all parts of chemical production. The Wehrmacht was totally dependent on IG Farben for its requirement of synthetic rubber – by 1943, the company was making 144,000 tons of synthetic rubber for the German armed forces in a year, mainly used for fan belts and tires for tanks, aircraft, self-propelled artillery and trucks.

Methanol was another important and exclusive product to the IG – by 1943 the company produced 100 percent of all methanol in Germany, which was necessary for explosives and certain plastics and rubber. In other words, without IG Farben, Germany would have stalled in Austria in 1938 and probably never would have been able to start a full scale war. [497]

The Wehrmacht was but one organization dependent on the IG for materials – almost the entirety of German chemical concerns as well as many other industries relied heavily on raw materials and partially finished products which came from IG Farben. The German soap industry relied almost exclusively on the IG for raw materials for detergents; tanneries obtained half of the artificial tanning agents from the company; paint and coating manufacturers needed two-thirds of resins, pigments, solvents and polymers – the most important of these was Röhm and Haas, which used IG Farben almost exclusively.[498]

And raw materials were not the only items obtained from IG Farben – patents and other technical assistance were supplied for a fee. Synthetic gasoline production – a process devised by Dr. Friedrich Bergius in 1913 and for which the patent was bought by the IG in 1927 – was done under the auspices of the company, though IG Farben only produced 23% of Germany's total production. When plants which had licensed the technology – though not owned by IG Farben – are included in this figure, it rises to 90%. These patents were a seemingly endless supply of revenue for the company, both in Germany and out, with Standard Oil in the United States salivating over the Bergius patent. Standard paid $30 million before the declaration of war between Germany and the United States just for the American rights to the hydrogenation process.[499]

But the company could not just wait for independent chemists and researchers to come up with the next great thing – it needed to invest in research and development. This research totalled just a little under one billion Reichsmarks from 1932-1943, or about four percent of its sales volume.[500] IG Farben dealt not just in the pharmaceuticals and dyestuffs it had built its business on in the prewar years, but reached out into non-chemical related industries, such as the mining of coal, iron, gypsum, salt and light metals like magnesium. Compared to other giant companies in Nazi Germany such as Vestag and Hermann Göring Werke, IG Farben may have employed less people – still 250,000 by 1943 – but its reach in the country was far and above that of any other company.

The specialty metals were of particular interest to the Air Ministry and the Luftwaffe. Metal cowlings for jet engines which had to be heat resistant, as well as lightweight aluminum and alloys necessary to make superior aircraft, were essential to winning the air war. As such, the Air Ministry helped the expansion of this industry by investing "contributions" in IG, growing the assets in this area from RM8.6 million to RM135 million within nine years.

War materiel was especially profitable for the IG – in 1943 alone its subsidiary Dynamit AG rang in revenues in excess of half a billion Reichsmarks. No other company came close to the firm in revenues – its next closest competitor Henkel & Cie, which though its sales were 200 million Reichsmarks, was dwarfed by the RM3.1 billion

IG Farben brought in. Before the outbreak of war, the company's sales were around one billion, and the three-fold increase was, according to von Schnitzler, "a 100 percent result of the rearmament and was policy of the government."⁵⁰¹

It was not, however, without problem. Astronomical growth of that kind meant administrative nightmares, which began when Carl Krauch took his position as chief of chemicals in the Four Year Plan. The Wehrmacht almost immediately started giving purchase orders directly to the technical departments and not management, meaning groups could be working on the exact same project for different areas of the armed forces.

The Aufsichtsrat had complete of the company, both in day-to-day operations and at shareholder meetings. Though there were almost four million common shares outstanding, German banks proxy voted 93% of all shares, the largest voting bank being *Deutsche Länderbank*. Länderbank did not figure into the chapters on banks for one very good reason – it was IG Farben's own banking institution. The preferred shares, of which there was only 40,000, voted in similar fashion. Thirty-eight thousand of the shares were registered to a wholly-owned subsidiary of the IG, *Ammoniawerke Marseberg GmbH* and the other 2,000 were in the possession of Deutsche Länderbank. Shares of IG Farben that probably were not voted were in the possession of DuPont and Imperial Chemical Industries (ICI). DuPont owned upwards of thirty million Reichsmarks in stock and ICI another seven million. By the sound of the annual meetings, neither company would have had a voice anyway:

*In the last twelve years, the general assembly (stockholders' meetings) of IG had become a pure formality; all the decisions were agreed upon unanimously on the proposal of the chairman and no discussion has ever taken place. I think, in all those years, perhaps a total of half a dozen questions have been asked, mostly on sidelines of no decisive importance. The chairman, formerly Mr. Bosch and later on Mr. Schmitz, gave a short report about the general situation of the firm and then the legal formalities were fulfilled. With all the formalities, the counting of the votes, all lasted about one-half to three-quarters of an hour*⁵⁰²

Aryanization

When you hear the term corporate raider, you think of Michael Douglas in *Wall Street* – ruthless, unethical, an overall mean bastard with good hair. The term took on a whole new meaning at Farben. As the Wehrmacht rolled through countries in the 1930s, IG Farben "acquired" certain holdings. *Skoda Werke Wetzler AG, Dynamit Nobel Bratislava, Aussiger Verein*, and *Boruta S.A.* were some of the companies which were purchased by Farben (many through the Nazi government trust fund or in joint ventures with the Luftwaffe or the Wehrmacht). Companies they weren't interested in – such as a Jewish-owned dye manufacturer in Wola, Poland, were shut down and liquidated, proceeds of which were bought up at fire sale prices by IG Farben. Companies that were purchased had their Jewish employees and managers summarily tossed out on the streets – literally. Skoda executives Isidor Pollak and Franz Rottenberg, who were already under arrest by the SA, were fired and Pollak savagely murdered by an SA agent.

Pulverfabrik Skoda Werke Wetzler in Austria was of particular interest to Farben, as it was a large explosives and gunpowder manufacturer. The company had been unavailable, mainly due to the heavy ownership of Creditanstalt-Bankverein. Creditanstalt, owned primarily by the Rothschilds, decided policy for Skoda Werke, but once Deutsche Bank gained control of the bank after the Anschluss, "by virtue of this Nazi plundering and in the full knowledge of what had happened, IG was able to obtain the long sought-after Skoda Werke Wetzler. Dr. von Schnitzler, a leading figure of IG has said himself: 'IG acquired the Skoda Wetzler works from the Deutsche Bank which had acquired it by participating with the Nazi government in a theft of the property.'"[503] Skoda Werke was merged with the IG-controlled Carbidwerke Deutsche-Matrei AG to form Donau Chemie and the Jewish Rothschilds received nothing.

Negotiations for Skoda Werke had been conducted for years, yet the IG was no further ahead until March 13, 1938 when Nazi troops entered Vienna. At that point, IG board member Max Ilgner reported to the Vorstand that the management of Creditanstalt and the Skoda Werke had changed and the IG was "facing a new situation." This new situation was that Ilgner managed to get on to the board of Creditanstalt, which not surprisingly made it very easy for the IG to take control of Skoda Werke. Ten days after the fall of Vienna, Ilgner was already reporting that:

No obstacle now stands in the way of the fusion planned before. IG can go ahead and acquire the majority of the Skoda Wetzler Works shares at once...neither the party and the administration in the old Reich and German Austria have anything against the plan which IG has had for a long time for unifying the Austrian chemical industry (Dynamit AG, Deutsch-Matrei and Skoda Wetzler Works) and recognize that it is a logical development for us to take over the management.[504]

In early June the Nazi State Commissioner approved the takeover of the three companies and the liquidation of *Anilin Chemie AG* by the IG. While Skoda Werke was large, the size of *Carbidwerke Deutsch-Matrei* was larger. The company had two manufacturing plants, as well as a majority interest in *Continentale Gesellschaft für angewandte Elektrizität* which made calcium chloride and ferro-silicon and had its own hydroelectric power plant capable of 55,000MW. The State Commissioner agreed to all this thanks to a carefully worded letter from the IG quoting the needs of the Four Year Plan and how amalgamation under the IG umbrella would make the companies better able to contribute to the coming war effort.

After this acquisition, the IG went on a land buying spree, purchasing large tracts along the Donau River for about thirty kilometres outside of Vienna. This land was to be used for future industrial development, and in conjunction with this, the company planned new plant investments in Austria. The company spent RM192 million, though the Luftwaffe loaned the IG RM65 million of this and granted a subsidy of an additional RM30 million. The IG built plants to produce aviation fuel, lubricating oil, sulphuric acid, chlorine and processed magnesium. As well, the company built railways and two power stations to support this enterprise.

The executives of the IG knew their company was integral to the German war effort. From Max Ilgner:

In regard to the chemical and related industries of the conquered countries, IG played an important role in adapting the industries of those countries to the purpose of the Nazi war machine. Of all German chemical firms, IG's part in adapting the chemical industries to the purposes of the Nazi war machine was by far the most important.[505]

Strangely, Ilgner points out the seizures in the occupied countries by Hermann Göring Werke and the SS as examples of looting, but he claimed the acquisitions conducted by the IG were purely business of an ethical nature. Ilgner claimed "IG did not participate in this whole domain (the looting of private interests) and remained solely on its 50 percent participations in Chemische Werke Aussig-Falkenau." In what sounds more like sour grapes, Ilgner said Göring took everything for himself and there was no opportunity for the IG to develop anything in Czechoslovakia.[506]

According to representatives of the IG, it attempted to acquire companies by legal means. In the minds of the IG's executives, legal was somewhat a vague concept, as in the case of the French shareholders of Norsk Hydro. Norsk was Norway's only nitrogen producer, a large producer of aluminum and also its largest company. The Luftfahrt Bank acquired control of the company, which was held mainly by proxy at the Banque de Paris des Pays-Bas. The French bank was forced to reduce the 64% holding the shareholders had down to 35%. According to Ilgner, the IG was forced to participate by the Nazis in the acquisition, though this does not hold true according to the Nuremburg trial of the company.

According to evidence introduced, Norsk was immediately targeted as a source of aluminum, important to the Luftwaffe's aircraft needs. As soon as it was known to the IG, the company carried out high-powered talks aimed at acquiring the largest possible participation in the company. A new company was formed – Nordisk Lettmetall – with one third held by the Reich, one third by the IG and one third still being held by the Norsk Hydro shareholders. The annual meeting of the new company was a farce – the French shareholders were barred from attending and the share capital was increased so they held only a minority interest.

Ilgner may have claimed the IG was forced into this endeavor, but they were not forced to participate in other acquisitions though, which contrary to the protestations of Ilgner, would be considered plunder and looting. In Czechoslovakia, a fight developed over the purchase of *Verein für Chemische und Metallurgische Produktion* in Aussig (Aussig-Falkenau). The IG was already looking at obtaining the company in April of 1938, almost six months before the German army moved into the Sudetenland. The Reich Economics Ministry moved in and mediated a settlement and the IG acquired 50% of the company and the other half was acquired by *Chemische Werke von Heyden*. The bargain basement price: just under one quarter of the RM120 million value of the company.

Aussig-Falkenau was controlled by *Zivnostenka Banka*, which was the only Czech bank to survive annexation by the German banks. As such, it had to contribute heavily to the German war effort by buying Reich treasury bills, but it did so to survive and help the remaining Czech industries to survive. Dresdner Bank forced Zivnostenka to sell the company to the IG and von Heyden. Refusal would have meant the company would have forcibly been taken from the bank, so to protect itself, Zivnostenka had no choice. The IG took the dyestuffs business from Aussig-Falkenau and divested it into a new company, *Teerfarbenwerke Aussig*, which gave the IG complete control of the Sudetenland's dye industry. Even before the Sudetenland was annexed, von Schnitzler petitioned to have his assistant appointed Commissioner for the Aussig-Falkenau plants – a request which was granted by the Nazis.[507]

The company was already planning other plunder in Czechoslovakia two months before Neville Chamberlain flew to Munich to sign the Appeasement Pact with Hitler. Meetings between the company and Reich officials were held through the summer of 1938, concluding with the Nazis agreeing to appoint Carl Wurster and von Schnitzler's assistant Kugler as commissars of the Aussig-Falkenau plants on September 23, 1938 – six days before the Munich Pact was signed. The Munich Pact was just a formality, since Hitler had already apprised Neville Chamberlain, French Premier Daladier and Italy's Mussolini of his intention to invade the Sudetenland and return it to the German fold. However, plans to cede business authority in the region were well-placed by the IG – and other companies – before the Wehrmacht went across the border.

On September 29, 1938, the day of the meeting in Munich, von Schnitzler sent a letter to fellow members of the Vorstand. He explained how he spoke with the Reich Economics Ministry and Secretary of State Wilhelm Keppler and "all parties acknowledged that after the German annexation of the German Sudeten-area all the works situated in this zone and belonging to the Aussiger Verein (Aussig-Falkenau) must be managed by trustees."[508] Of course, von Schnitzler had already managed to get Wurster and Kugler appointed as such, but he continued to tell the Vorstand how he believed the companies should be run by the IG and should have all future claims on the assets. The only person who did not agree with the IG's proposal was the director of the German Economic Board in the Sudetenland. Schnitzler had to drop Carl Wurster from the commissariat and accept a man the director believed would be better suited, as he was German, lived in the area and worked at the Aussig plants.

By October 9, the plants were under the control of Kugler, though they had to share their conquest with Chemische Fabrik von Heyden AG. The plants were still owned by Aussiger Verein, who protested bitterly the appointment of Kugler, stating he had no legal right to affect any contracts. One month later, the IG and von Heyden pushed through negotiations to purchase the Sudeten assets of Aussig. Schnitzler proudly commented the agreement was put together in one day and all clauses and subsections filled in over the next thirty. Pressure was placed on Aussiger Verein by Karl Rasche of Dresdner Bank to surrender the properties. The two plants employed 2,800 men and produced a wide variety of chemicals and dyes. The Aussig plant was the largest chemical plant in Czechoslovakia. Even with this, the IG invested RM15 million Reichsmarks in construction of new facilities at the plants. Much of this investment was to change production from dyestuffs to war materials, including additives for rubber, electrical insulation chemicals and synthetic tanning agents needed for soldiers' boots.

In Poland, the pillaging was more pronounced. The IG, as with other companies, launched its own blitzkrieg after the German armed forces marched through and subdued the country. This time, their sights were set on Boruta, formally known as *Przemysl Chemiczny Boruta*. On September 7 1939, Georg von Schnitzler telegraphed to director

Krueger of Farben's Directorate in Berlin, requesting the Reich Ministry of Economics be informed of the ownership and other facts concerning four important Polish dyestuffs factories which, it was assumed, would fall into the hands of the Germans within a few days. One of these was Boruta; the others were *S. A. Zigiers* – a Boruta subsidiary, *Chemiczna Fabryka Wola Krzystoporska* and *Zaklady Chemiczne Winnica*. Wola was owned by the Polish Jewish Szpilogel family; Winnica was half owned by French shareholders and subsequent to the fall of France, fell into Farben hands. Boruta was owned by the Polish state and according to von Schnitzler: "Although not wanting to take a position on further operation, we consider it of primary importance that the above-mentioned stocks be used by experts in the interests of German national economy. Only I.G. is in a position to make experts available."[509]

Schnitzler and Krueger met with Ministry officials a week later to discuss the disposition of the companies. At the meeting, von Schnitzler proposed the IG be named trustee for all four companies and do with them as it pleased, including amalgamation, liquidation or the sale of assets. The Ministry of Economics agreed with the proposal and put the four companies under the IG's control. By June the next year, the company was allowed to purchase the assets outright, as opposed to the twenty-year lease proposed by von Schnitzler, though it took almost a year for Reichsführer Himmler to agree to a purchase – as competition for the assets was fierce. After this, the Boruta plants stayed open, while the machinery and equipment from the Wola and Winnica plants were dismantled and sent back to IG Farben plants in Germany.

The IG exectuives knew the Polish owners of these companies would receive nothing for them. The IG camouflaged its 50% interest in Winnica years before the war, using Joseph Frossard, the man who would later help them secure the French dye industries. Once Poland fell, there was no need to hide its half ownership, and the IG acquired the other half through plunder. The Wola works were Jewish and therefore undesirable to the company. The machinery was desirable, and it was sent back to Germany to be installed at IG factories. Schnitzler made sure this was known to Reich authorities, addressing a letter to the Ministry of Economics in mid-September 1939. In it, he stated the Wola company was non-Aryan and a family property, and so von Schnitzler felt it should be shuttered. It was, and the IG acquired the raw material stock as well as the machinery. Four other minor dye concerns were shut down at the behest of the IG and the owners of these companies as well as Wola received nothing but a kick to the curb. The only one to survive was under Swiss ownership, though von Schnitzler did make moves against it as well. Under the guise of "safeguarding of Polish dyestuff factories," von Schnitzler wanted to know what were the Swiss' wishes regarding the Pabjanice plant. The Swiss owners of the plant were clear: it was a Swiss undertaking and they expected no measures of any kind would be taken against the company. They also pointed out they had contacted their federal government.[510] That was the end of the conversation and also the attempt by von Schnitzler to take over the last vestige of independent dye production in Poland.

The Winnica ownership was well hidden from everyone involved. In 1931 the French firm Kuhlmann and the IG were anxious to set up shop in Poland, but there was a problem – Polish law prohibited German ownership. So, through its Swiss subsidiary IG Chemie, the IG held 50% ownership of the new company and Kuhlmann held the other half. The new Polish company acquired a soap factory and built a dyestuff plant on the site. Once the Wehrmacht marched in, there was no need to hide ownership anymore and once Kuhlmann had been merged into IG's Aryanized company Francolor, the rest of the shares fell into the IG's hands. The ownership was short-lived – in May of 1942 when fuel shortages became acute, the IG was in an untenable position and liquidated the company, selling the machinery to Boruta.

But the IG wasn't really interested in Boruta – they just wanted to take out another competitor. Schnitzler even said the works were not very important, but they were able to make it the main plant in the later years of the war since the Leverkusen plant was constantly under attack by Allied bombers. He also felt the IG couldn't let a new competitor into the Polish realm as it was "IG's oldest and strongest domain." He did not move as fast in Poland as he did in Austria and the Sudetenland, taking a full six days after the start of the invasion of Poland to contact the IG's Berlin office to start negotiations. The factories did have substantial inventory of raw materials and semi-finished dye goods, which the IG felt should be used by Germans in their own economy – in other words, they should be stolen.

The IG was put off by the Reich government in its request to have its own technical and commercial experts placed in the companies. The government said there was no risk of the raw materials falling into the wrong hands and production was moving along nicely, thank you very much. The Nazis were moving very cautiously with industry in Poland at the outset of the war, as they did not want neutral shareholders to get their backs up if the Reich moved in and confiscated property. The only caveat placed by the government was that if the neutral stakeholders had no objections to the IG placing their own men in the companies, that would be fine.

Seven days into the occupation of Poland the IG played their hand, petitioning the Ministry of Economics to have IG appointed trustee of the companies. IG Farben was not going to take "no" for an answer. They *did* have to wait a full year though for their request to be realized, but not for trying. Schnitzler pleaded with the Ministry of Economics, stating the company was the largest manufacturer of dyestuffs in Poland, controlling almost half of the market. His rationale was the dye production at Ludwigshafen could easily be transferred to Boruta so the Farben plant could be retooled for war production. Even so, for some reason the Ministry as well as the administrative section for Poland was unwilling to sell Boruta to the IG. The Reich government did agree to lease the property to the IG in November of 1939.

While the lease negotiations were still carrying on, the government announced it would consider selling the company to the IG, and it would seem Himmler himself became involved at this point, for reasons unknown. What is known is Himmler's detestation of anything not Aryan, and the Slavic Poles were a thorn in his side. It is quite possible Himmler decided the *Untermenschen* Polish owners of Boruta deserved nothing, and the most logical beneficiary of this would be the IG. The IG had full knowledge the Polish owners were receiving nothing for their stake – a statement backed up by Kugler, who claimed the IG was "forced by the circumstances" to buy the property.

France was next on the plunder list for the IG. In Alsace, the Mulhausen plant of the *Societé des Produits Chimiques et Matières Colorantes* (Society of Chemical Products and Colorant Materials) was leased by the German Chief of Civil Administration to the IG in May of 1941. If the IG leased it, this is not considered looting; but it is when the German government confiscated the property and sold it to the IG in June of 1943. The same happened to the oxygen and acetylene plants owned by Strassbourg-Schiltigheim. It could be argued the company acquired the assets from the German government under the guise of accelerating war production, but members of the Aufsichtsrat and Vorstand knew the companies were seized from their rightful owners.

Compagnie Nationale de Matieres Colorantes et Manufactures de Produits Chimique du Nord Reunies Établissements Kuhlmann, (Kuhlmann National Company of Coloring Materials and Chemicals Manufacturing), Paris; *Société Anonyme des Materières Colorantes et Produits Chimique de Saint-Denis* (Saint-Denis Dyestuffs and Chemicals Company), Paris; and *Compagnie Française de Produits Chimiques et Materières Colorantes de Saint-Clair-du-Rhône* (French Colorant Raw Materials and Chemicals Company of St. Clair du Rhône), Paris were three French companies which had cartel agreements with IG Farben. After the Vichy government was set up in 1940, the IG pressured French authorities not to reissue licenses for the manufacture of dyestuffs and to stop the import of raw materials the companies needed. Once the thumbscrews were turned, von Schnitzler, Vorstand member Fritz ter Meer and Hans Kugler sauntered in to a meeting in Weisbaden hastily called by the French companies. Once their plight was heard, von Schnitzler read a prepared statement demanding the IG be given control of the French dye industry. The basis of this request was simple: the IG controlled half of the world's dye market and set the world prices for dyes, but that wasn't enough. The IG threw the Treaty of Versailles back at the French, claiming the irreparable damages done to the company by the treaty.

Negotiations continued, but the IG menbknew they had the three companies by the throat, and the IG wanted a 51% share of the entire French dye market. The three companies were to be merged together under the name Francolor. The companies resisted and even the Vichy government protested. The main sticking point was the majority ownership. In a meeting of the Vichy Ministry of Production, members refused to propose to Marshal Petain he give permission to the merger, as it would adversely affect public opinion, though they were not at all adverse to "Franco-German collaboration."[511] Joseph Frossard, who headed Kuhlmann, was anxious for negotiations to go through and pressured ministry officials to allow it. One of the officials, according to Frossard, "regrets very much to have made the remark 'that he would rather have his hand cut off' than grant IG a 51% participation"[512] The new company was formed in November 1941 and the IG retained majority ownership, though this was a joke. All of the assets of the three French companies were absorbed into Francolor; the IG put no money up. In return, the shareholders of the three French companies received less than one percent of IG shares. The exact numbers were: for the capital of the French companies, valued at 800 hundred million francs, the companies received 12,750 shares of IG worth about 255 million francs. The companies were also not allowed to dispose of these shares of the IG. All other competition was eliminated by order of the IG.

All of this was not meant to produce the colors for the latest summer frocks coming off the Paris runways in 1940 – the IG knew these chemical companies had to contribute to the Nazi war effort. Before France fell to the Germans, the IG began negotiating with the Ministry of Economics, originally planning to force French industry to work for the war machine.[513] Sadly, this strong-arm tactic was not required – the industrialists in France were only too happy to collaborate with the Nazis. Frossard was well known to the IG – he had been the civil servant whom Carl Bosch had negotiated with at Versailles in a last-ditch effort to save the BASF, Bayer and Hoechst plants from destruction. Bosch saved the plants, and perhaps Frossard felt the company owed him a return favor. This was not to be – von Schnitzler was not the sentimental type, saying he would rather "let the French simmer in their own juice."[514]

Frossard was hoping to renew cartel agreements with the IG, but von Schnitzler was not interested. When the French delegation to Weisbaden claimed the cartel agreements had benefited all parties involved and von Schnitzler himself had earlier praised them, they were chided by von Schnitzler, who stated: "After all that has happened, the French standpoint regarding the validity of the cartel must be considered imputation and insult."[515] Frossard pressed on, putting out feelers in Paris as well as to the Swiss Geigy company in Basel, though von Schnitzler was in no hurry. He wanted more than just partnership with friendly competitors; he wanted no competitors at all. In October 1940, Frossard laid it all out for the Germans – he was willing to collaborate with the Germans, as he felt they would win the war. Kuhlmann was prepared to produce for the IG whatever they requested, as long as it was a confidential agreement – no use putting your neck in the guillotine, just in case Germany loses.

The U.S. Military Government report was succinct in its assessment of the maneuvers by Frossard and Kuhlmann: "This was the full meaning of collaboration. As head of…the leading chemical firm in France, Frossard was offering to join the Nazis in their war against the free nations of the world, and was actually willing to participate in the subversion of the French economy, and the enslavement of the French people by Nazi Germany."[516]

The subversion, collaborating and enslavement of France was not limited to dyes and chemicals. IG Farben's Bayer division was also antsy to get its fingers into pharmaceutical competitors. However, the company it pressured was just a little too strong – Rhône-Poulenc, which is now known as a part of Sanofi. The IG did manage to exact its pound of flesh from the pharmaceutical company though, by charging exorbitant licensing fees for the manufacture of its drugs. Rhône-Poulenc managed to stay out of reach of the IG only because its head office was in the region still under control of the Vichy regime. Ironically, Rhône-Poulenc merged in 1999 with Hoechst AG – a founding IG company – to form Aventis.

As in World War I, a large labor pool was difficult to secure. As in World War I, forced labor was considered. Unlike World War I, these forced laborers were not allowed to protest, stop work, or go home. Carl Krauch proposed the work week to increase to 56 hours and the use of foreign laborers to expand the labor pool in 1937, two years before the start of the war. IG Farben recruiters were sent into the Sudetenland, Austria, Bohemia and Moravia to extract the workforce. In 1938, even Germans were drafted as workers at IG Farben.

In many areas of the world, industrialization has led to an increase in the standard of living, going back to the beginnings of the Industrial Revolution. Not so in the occupied territories. Hermann Göring had the gall to say in a speech to the Austrian people: "Now it's over with the Gemütlichkeit (calm, leisurely pace). You must spit on your hands and go to work." The populations of Czechoslovakia, Poland, France and the Low Countries were working harder, and in some instances for more money, but had less to buy. The Aussig plant workers, for example, quickly realized their nominally higher income represented a step backward in buying power, and the hardship of daily life to the population very soon became apparent.[517] Any luxuries were withheld for the armed forces and were becoming very scarce for the everyday person. In Germany it wasn't great – in the occupied territories it was much worse. Butter, ham, coffee and chocolate were bought up quickly for the Wehrmacht and Luftwaffe and the shelves were bare for everyone else.

By 1940, prisoners of war were added to the forced labor pool. The broad recruitment methods led to enormous differences among the personnel, depending on labor law, social and "racial" policies, and country of origin. Distinctions affecting rights and conditions of labor among the German personnel were made between men and women, and regular employees as opposed to drafted workers or those on leave from the armed forces. Distinctions were also made between workers for German companies as opposed to foreign companies, and between German and foreign contract laborers. Prisoner-laborers were separated into judicial prisoners, military prisoners, and concentration camp inmates. The usual national characterization patterns of Nazi racial ideology were applied to prisoners of war and civilian foreign workers. Among the foreign workers, only the Poles were explicitly labeled as forced laborers. This was an arbitrary usage, since many plants made use of "Ostarbeiter" ("eastern workers"), most of whom were young people drafted by force in the occupied territories of the Soviet Union. While the Western European and Italian workers (acquired by way of temporary manpower services, recruitment by third-party firms, or individual recruitment) received better treatment, this was belied by the increasingly terrible and dangerous conditions of work they also faced – and if they attempted to leave or escape, they were subject to arrest and internment by the *Sicherheitspolizei* (the security police or "SiPo") in Germany, their home countries or the occupied territories. The technical workers and salesmen from the level of foreman and up still received individual work contracts, but the great mass of the personnel were simply unfree.[518]

With the opening of the IG Auschwitz plant in 1942, at least 51,000 prisoners were used as forced labor, most from Auschwitz itself. IG Auschwitz was to become the largest chemical plant in eastern Europe and was built by concentration camp inmates. Buna/Monowitz was an IG Farben *corporate* concentration camp. It opened in 1942 with mainly Jewish inmates forced to work for IG Farben. Survival rates at the camps were extremely low, with a conservative estimate of 30% dying from their labors. Why Auschwitz for a chemical plant? Originally, IG Farben wanted a plant built in Silesia, as it was out of range of airstrikes. They settled on Auschwitz for a number of reasons, including proximity to coal and lime, required for the production of synthetic fuel. As well, according to authors Peter Hayes and Bernd C. Wagner, IG Farben was unwilling to give up its monopoly on synthetic fuel production, and they agreed on Auschwitz to concede to the interests of the Reich Ministry of Economics. Former head of Bayer business services Professor Gottfried Plumpe and Farben scholar Florian Schmaltz both believe the site was picked due to proximity to a cheap workforce – that is, the Auschwitz concentration camp. Either way, IG Farben profited from the use of forced labor.

When the first detachment of workers left Auschwitz for the Farben plant, they were trucked in. That stopped very soon after, when there were too many employees and they were forced by the SS to march the six kilometres to the plant. Farben found this a waste of manpower, as the chronically malnourished inmates tended to die en route. As well, the march took valuable time from their workday, so the company arranged for trains to bring their employees in to work – in freight cars. However, even this was untenable for IG Farben, so a call was put in to the commandant at Auschwitz, and a separate camp – Monowitz – was set up just for workers of IG Farben. The managers in the area were taken care of – the homes of deported Jews in the Auschwitz area were made available to IG Farben managers after their former owners were sent to the death camps. Farben employed Polish, Ukrainian and even their allied Italians at IG Auschwitz, as well as British PoWs. The enemy was treated better than the allies, as the Wehrmacht made sure the Geneva Convention on the treatment of

PoWs was followed. The SS had to be admonished on more than one occasion for severe treatment of the British. They were also allowed Red Cross packages as well as mail, which allowed them more food rations than most inmates. Farben finally abandoned the plant in January 1945, though its fate did not end there – it was a Polish manufacturing concern until the 1980s.

The gas chambers and IG Farben

Probably the most insidious, the most heinous of all of IG Farben's crimes is their manufacture of Zyklon B, the gas used by the SS in their gas chambers. Zyklon B was originally developed as an insecticide and was used intensively during World War II as a delousing agent in barracks, ships and hospitals, mainly by the Wehrmacht. Farben held 42.5% of Degesch, the company which supplied the Zyklon B. IG Farben initially profited handsomely from this, but then the company expanded its reach. They started supplying Zyklon B to the SS for use at death camps at Auschwitz, Birkenau Mauthausen, Neuengamme, Stutthof, and Ravensbrück. The SS could exterminate upwards of 2,000 people at a time, thereby decreasing the Nazi timeframe for their Final Solution. Unbelievably, the managers involved at IG Farben, Heinrich Hörlein, Carl Wurster, and Wilhelm Rudolf Mann – who also sat on the Degesch board – were acquitted at Nuremburg as there was no conclusive evidence the defendants "had a decisive influence on the corporate policy of Degesch or any legally relevant knowledge of the intended purpose of their products."[519] Only Gerhard Peters, the general manager of Degesch, was found guilty of being an accessory to homicide and he was sentenced to five years in prison.

Peters was free after the war, serving as a defense witness at the IG Farben trials. This did not serve him well, as he ended up on trial himself in 1949. After his conviction, he petitioned his innocence and was acquitted in 1955. He worked as manager of the Lahn-Plastic GmbH and manager in a hydrocyanic acid facility for Degussa chemical factory[520] as well as being a member of the Federal Commission for the Control of Air Pollution in the Ruhr. Peters died a free man in 1974.

Zyklon B was distributed in Germany by the Tesch & Stabenow company. Dr. Bruno Tesch, along with Peters and Walter Heerdt invented the insecticide and Tesch formed the company with his partner Stabenow in 1924. Stabenow left three years later and the company was majority held by Degesch until 1942 when majority interest was sold to Tesch. Tesch was arrested after the war and in his trial, the prosecution brought witnesses who stated they were instructed by Tesch on how to kill humans effectively with cyanide. The prosecutor also brought forward former Tesch stenographer Anna Ünzelmann, who said Tesch told her Zyklon B was being used for gassing human beings.[521] Tesch continued to buy Zyklon from Degesh for three more years after this, knowing it was used to kill Jews at Auschwitz, Sachsenhausen and Neuengamme. For this, he was hanged by the British in 1946.

The men at IG Farben involved were not innocent by any stretch. Heinrich Hörlein joined the Nazi Party in 1934 and was declared a military economy leader. He was tasked by the Nazis to identify and develop lethal chemical agents. This led to the development under his leadership of tabun and sarin nerve gases (sarin was used against the Kurds and Iranians by Saddam Hussein in the Iran-Iraq war). Hörlein was acquitted by the war trials and subsequently went on to serve as chairman of the supervisory board of Farbenfabriken Bayer AG before dying a free man in 1954.

Vorstand member Carl Wurster joined Bayer in 1924 and worked as one of Carl Bosch's close associates. Like Hörlein, Wurster was also a Wehrwirtschaftsführer. He was arrested in 1947 and also acquitted in 1948. Wurster became chairman of the managing board of Farben and set about restarting BASF. Decorated by the postwar German government, he died a free man in 1974.

Wilhelm Mann started his career in sales at Hoechst in 1920. His father Rudolf was the former head of pharmaceuticals at Bayer and later IG Farben and Wilhelm started to be trained as his successor in 1926. He was made a Vorstand member in 1931, when he also joined the Nazi Party and also sat on the Aufsichtsrat of Degesch. He was arrested by the U.S. Army in 1945 and tried with other Farben board members. He was acquitted in 1948 and in 1949 he was back to his old job as head of sales at Bayer pharmaceuticals. Mann died a free man in 1992 at the ripe old age of 97.

Was the supply of pesticides for eradicating concentration camp inmates the most heinous act IG Farben ever allegedly engaged in? Some would argue this, pointing to the funding for research Farben provided to Dr. Josef Mengele.

IG Farben and the Angel of Death

Josef Mengele. The name epitomizes evil along with Hitler, Himmler, Göbbels and Göhring. Mengele is better known as "The Angel of Death" and was assigned as doctor for the *Zigeunerfamilienlager* (Gypsy family camp) at Auschwitz. His job title is perhaps a bit misleading. During his time at Auschwitz, he did not heal any patients; instead he inflicted pain, suffering and death on inmates.

Mengele was often the first person inmates saw as they disembarked the freight cars at Auschwitz, as he wanted first pick of those coming into the camp for his experiments. Whereas most doctors despised their role in selecting, Mengele seemed to enjoy it: "Some like Werner Rhöde who hated his work, and Hans König who was deeply disgusted by his job, had to get drunk before they appeared on the ramp. Only two doctors performed the selections without any stimulants of any kind: Dr. Josef Mengele and Dr. Fritz Klein. Dr. Mengele was particularly cold and cynical."[522]

Mengele considered himself a researcher and thought he was one of the greatest Nazi scientists in existence. He was however, mediocre at best. From his captive assistant Dr. Olga Lengyel: "His experiments and observations were carried out in an abnormal fashion. When he made transfusions, he purposely used incorrect blood types. Of course, complications followed. He would inject substances and ignore the results. But Mengele had no one to account to but himself. He did whatever pleased him. He conducted his experiments like a mad amateur. He was not a savant. He had the mania of a collector."[523]

But research and observe he did. From the time he arrived at Auschwitz in May 1943 until he left in 1945, he experimented on thousands of people for a variety of reasons. He attempted various types of sterilization on Jewish men and women, not just to eradicate the Jewish people, but to further the Aryan purity he held dear. He injected dye into the eyes of 36 children, in a painful attempt to change their eye color to blue. Most went blind, though it wouldn't matter anyway – Mengele sent them off to the gas chambers after he was done. Many times, he extracted the eyes and according to two different witnesses, he had them lain out on a table, numbered and lettered and, even more gruesome, he had them pinned to a wall like butterflies.[524]

Mengele's research on twins is just as horrific. He waited at the train platform, well-manicured, with his glistening black boots, white gloves and polished cane. He waited for the freight cars to unload so he could separate out twins for his experiments. These experiments included twins forcibly having sex with other twins to see if they would reproduce more twins. Sadistic, yes; worse still were the amputations, lumbar punctures, typhus injections and other wounds to see how each twin reacted.[525]

Mengele took a personal interest in all the medical goings-on at the camp. His selection of inmates for the gas chambers was far and above any other doctor at the camp. According to Simon Weisenthal, two million men, women and children were put to death at Auschwitz. Of the 23 doctors on selection duty, Mengele has the distinction of selecting 400,000 inmates.[526] When a typhus outbreak threatened one of the cell blocks, he had the 600 Jewish women living there taken to be gassed, then had the cell block cleaned, deloused and new inmates moved in. When an outbreak of bacterial noma occurred in 1943, Mengele decided to study the cause and develop a treatment. The inmates were isolated and several killed so their heads and organs could be studied at the SS Medical Academy.[527]

It is certain representatives from the company knew about and sanctioned experiments by Mengele and others. As for Mengele, he received payment from IG Farben for his work. Wilhelm Mann, factory manager for Farben, authorized checks payable to SS Hauptsturmführer Josef Mengele on behalf of Farben.[528] After the war, Mengele escaped custody. Interred by the Americans, he avoided identification, using a false name. He stayed in Germany until 1949, then fearing capture, fled to Argentina under the name Helmut Gregor. Afterwards, he worked as a carpenter and a salesman in Buenos Aires before fear of discovery made him leave for Paraguay in 1958 and becoming José Mengele in 1959. He died of a stroke while swimming in the ocean in 1979. His victims, however, were not so lucky.

The "others" mentioned above, are not as well known, but were just as criminal and homicidal in their research, and again, this was funded by IG Farben. They included:

Dr. Friedrich Entress. Entress' specialty was to inject typhus into patients to see how communicable the disease was, then make an intracardiac injection of phenol. When 10ccs of phenol were injected directly into the heart, death occurred usually within 15 seconds.[529] [530] Entress used these experiments to test the effectiveness of drugs the Bayer division of IG Farben had produced. Entress was hanged in 1948 in Landsberg prison, professing his innocence, stating he was only following orders

Dr. Helmuth Vetter conducted experiments on women at Auschwitz, with IG Farben paying RM170 to the camp for the "guinea pigs." Every woman died while Vetter tested the Bayer drug Rutenol on them. Colleagues remembered him as a travelling salesman for IG Farben before the war.[531] Vetter was hanged in 1949.

Otmar von Veschür was the director of the Kaiser Wilhelm Institute of Anthropology, Human Heredity, and Eugenics and was a self-labelled racial hygienist. Mengele would send samples of blood, eyes and brains to him for further research.[532] **Karin Magnussen** was the research assistant of von Veschür at the Kaiser-Wilhelm Institute and her specialty was inheritance of eye color, specifically heterochromic irises or irises of different colors. Magnussen found out about preponderance to heterochromic irises among the Sinti people in and around Mechau, Germany. Members of the Sinti were taken in 1943 to the Kaiser-Wilhelm Institute to be photographed. Later in 1943, they were taken to Auschwitz, where Mengele carried out the experiments – which Magnussen had done on rabbits – on people.

According to a statement by Magnussen, Mengele dealt, among other things, with the eyes of these Sinti family using hormonal substances. Often, these painful interventions resulted in the discharge of pus from the eyes and blindness in the victims. These experiments aimed at the investigation and eradication of the abnormality in people with heterochromic irises. In the event of death of the prisoners,

Mengele pledged to Magnussen to give her the eyes of the victims for further research and evaluation.[533] Dr. Miklos Nyiszli, who was Mengele's slave pathologist, noted after the autopsy of Sinti twins that they had been killed, not due to illness, but because of a chloroform injection to the heart. Magnussen lived on until 1997, denying to the end Mengele would kill children for her research.

Unfortunately, many of the company's documents were destroyed or disappeared. Farben's NW7 offices in Berlin were completely destroyed and no documents were to be found. Max Ilgner arranged for two railcars stuffed with documents to leave Berlin, destined for the Hoechst plant in Frankfurt, but these mysteriously disappeared as well. When the war ended, Supreme Allied Commander Dwight Eisenhower took over IG Farben's headquarters in Frankfurt and made it Supreme Headquarters of the Allied Expeditionary Forces (SHAEF).[534] In the interim, American GIs made room for General Eisenhower by tossing everything deemed to have no value out the window. The sea of documents was all encompassing, yet disappeared when investigators for the IG Farben trial at Nuremburg showed up.

Eisenhower's main plan for IG Farben was to have the company dismantled and plants which manufactured munitions blown up. As well, all research initiatives taken over and any plant not used for munitions to be handed over as reparations. With the advent of the Cold War, it was decided the Allies needed Germany on their side, and one of the ways to do this was to help them rise up from the ashes of World War II. To do this, they needed industry and the IG was integral to that. It was proposed the company be broken up, and so the contingent parts existed once more. But who was going to lead them? The obvious choices were old IG executives. However, the IG Farben trial at Nuremberg spoiled that – for a time. Those men came back, including:

Dr. Fritz ter Meer, son of chemical industrialist Edmund ter Meer. He joined his father's company *Chemische Fabriken vorm. Weiler–ter-Meer* after finishing his doctorate in chemistry. Ter Meer joined IG Farben when Weiler-ter-Meer was made part of the cartel in 1925 and was a member of the Vorstand. He helped choose the site and was charged with decision-making for IG Auschwitz. He was in charge of production of Buna, poison gas, dyestuffs, chemicals, metals, and

Pharmaceuticals; and Wehrwirtschaftsführer. He was convicted at Nuremberg of *"War crimes and crimes against humanity through the plundering and spoliation of occupied territories, and the seizure of plants in Poland, Norway, France, and Russia"* and also *"War crimes and crimes against humanity through participation in the enslavement and deportation to slave labor on a gigantic scale of concentration camp inmates and civilians in occupied countries, and of prisoners of war, and the mistreatment, terrorization, torture, and murder of enslaved persons."*[535]

Ter Meer was sentenced to seven years in prison, which was commuted in 1951. In 1956 Fritz ter Meer became chairman of Farbenfabriken Bayer's supervisory board, a position he held until 1964. He died in 1967, aged 83.

Otto Ambros was a member of the Vorstand; Chief of Chemical Warfare Committee of the Ministry of Armaments and War Production; production chief for Buna and poison gas; manager of Auschwitz, Schkopau, Ludwigshafen, Oppau, Gendorf, Dyhernfurth, and Falkenhagen plants; Wehrwirtschaftsführer.

He advised Hitler on chemical weapons – he was one of those responsible for the development of sarin nerve gas. For this, he received eight years in prison, but was released in 1951. He went on to chair the advisory committee of Chemie Grünenthal, later known for its drug thalidomide and the subsequent scandal.[536] After his death in 1990 at the age of 89, BASF paid tribute to him, calling him "an expressive entrepreneurial figure of great charisma."[537]

Dr. Carl Krauch started work for BASF in 1912 as a chemist. He was in charge of rebuilding the plant at Oppau in 1921 after a devastating explosion levelled it, killing over 500. After that, he rose through the ranks at IG Farben, becoming a member of the Vorstand in 1926. He succeeded Carl Bosch as chair of the Vorstand in 1940. In 1941, he had Himmler agree to supply a steady workforce at IG Auschwitz to build the chemical plant there. He was indicted at Nuremburg and was convicted on Count 3 – slavery and mass murder. He was sentenced to six years, but was released in 1950 on good behavior. Krauch went on to be a member of the board at Bunawerke Hüls GmbH and died in 1968.

Hermann Schmitz was a Nazi Reichstag member in 1933 and succeeded Carl Duisberg as chairman of the Aufsichtsrat. He was convicted on Count 2 – plunder – and sentenced to four years. He was also released in 1950 and went on to be a board member for Deutsche Bank in Berlin and honorary chairman of Rheinische Stahlwerke AG. Schmitz died in 1960, aged 79.

Friedrich Jähne was a member of the Vorstand; chief engineer in charge of construction and physical plant development; and Chairman of the Engineering Committee. He was sentenced to 18 months in jail for plunder and after his release became a member of the board at Hoechst in 1952. He became chairman of Hoechst in 1955 and lived until 1965.

SA Hauptsturmführer Georg von Schnitzler: Vorstand Central Committee member, developed a scheme for Farben to fund German newspapers in Czechoslovakia to drive a massive pro-Nazi propaganda campaign which helped in the annexation of the Sudetenland and the destruction of Czechoslovakia.[61] Schnitzler was sentenced to five years but was released after one. He went on to be president of the Deutsch-Ibero-Amerikanische Gesellschaft, and died in 1962.

Fritz Gajewski, Member of the Vorstand, joined the Nazi Party in 1933. He was acquitted of all charges at Nuremburg, though it did come to light he had denounced his Jewish co-workers. He went on to become chairman of Dynamit Nobel in 1952 and died in 1965.

August von Knieriem: Vorstand Central Committee member; Chief Counsel and Chairman, Legal and Patent Committees. Knieriem was acquitted of all charges and went on to serve as chairman of IG Farbenindustrie IL (in liquidation). He died in 1978.

Hans Kugler was a member of the Commercial Committee and Public Commissar for the Falkenau and Aussig plants in Czechoslovakia. He was convicted of plunder and spoliation in France and sentenced to 18 months. After, he served as a member of the managing boards of Cassella-Farbwerke Mainkur AG and Riedel de Haèn AG. Kugler died in 1968.

SA Sturmführer Wilhelm Mann, chief of Sales for pharmaceuticals, was responsible for, among other things, approving payment for research done by Josef Mengele; he may or may not have known of the use of Zyklon-B gas in the gas chambers at Auschwitz. He was acquitted of all charges and went back to serving as head of pharmaceuticals at Bayer. Mann died in 1992, aged 98.[538]

Finally, **Carl Wurster**, Vorstand member, plant manager at Oppau and Ludwigshafen. After the war, he was allowed to remain plant manager, but was arrested in 1947 by the Americans. He was acquitted at Nuremburg and went on to re-establish BASF. He served on the boards of Robert Bosch, Degussa, and Allianz. Carl Wurster died in 1974.[63]

If you thought the actions of the IG differed from other industries, such as the German banks or the German coal and iron industries, you would be wrong. The IG marched side by side with its corporate brethren behind the Wehrmacht into Poland, Czechoslovakia, France and the Low Countries. Side by side – sounds pretty embellished. Not quite. According to Georg von Schnitzler: "Side by side with Germany's tremendous utilization of the industries of the conquered countries for the German war machine, there came to be a great German penetration of the economy of the conquered countries."[539]

And in the words of Max Ilgner: "In regard to the chemical and related industries of the conquered countries, IG played an important role in adapting the industries of those countries to the purposes of the Nazi war machine. Of all German chemical firms, IG's part…was by far the most important."[540]

13
The Reach of IG Farben

As a barometer, IG Farben was a RM 6 billion company in 1945 and was the largest chemical company in the world at the time, bigger than Dow, DuPont and Imperial Chemical (ICI). The former component companies – BASF, Bayer and the former Hoechst now have a market capitalization of over $357 billion, larger than Dow, DuPont and the former ICI combined. To state IG Farben was Germany's most powerful company is not a stretch – no company in the Third Reich had the reach, the resources and the aggression to accomplish what the IG did. Of the company, German Chancellor Gustav Stresemann said in 1927: "What have I as a trump in my hands apart from IG and the coal people?"[541] as well as stating without the coal mining concerns and the IG he would have no foreign policy.

Foreign policy was conducted at the IG by a variety of means, though its most surreptitious was in camouflaging foreign assets. When first examined by American military authorities in 1945, the IG's books showed RM65 million in foreign assets. A subsequent audit brought that figure to RM100 million and during the course of the investigation, 500 separate shadow companies were found with assets in excess of one billion Reichsmarks.[542] According to IG accountant Paul Dencker, a minimum of RM 1.37 billion had been in hidden reserves and did not show on the books of the company. This figure does not even include the camouflaged assets of General Aniline & Film of New York, which may have been upwards of $70 million.[543]

The main conduit for this cloaking was its Swiss subsidiary, *Internationale Gesellschaft für Chemische Unternehmingen AG*, Basel – IG Chemie as it was known. IG Chemie was initially set up by Hermann Schmitz. Chemie officially severed ties with the parent company in 1940 when Schmitz retired and his brother-in-law Dr. Albert Gadow conducted business for Chemie. Its primary purpose was to camouflage foreign assets held by IG Farben and make the company look like an arms-length enterprise, though contact was still made up to 1942 through the German Consulate in Basel. The consular staff reported "my confidants urgently requested to treat the information given by them as confidential in order to avoid that it becomes known that IG Chemie, Basle, is in connection with German quarters."[544]

IG Chemie was an amazingly well-organized affiliate, almost totally obfuscated in ownership from the parent company. Assets included among other things: a 95% share of General Aniline and Film Corporation and an interest in Jasco, which was a joint venture formed with Standard Oil. IG Chemie had its strings pulled through options contracts, ancillary legal ties and a web of enterprises which directly or indirectly controlled the company at the behest of IG Farben. During interrogations of IG Farben executives, the company owned no shares of IG Chemie, "and in view of the tortuous corporate relations revealed in the Farben files...such assertions are probably substantially correct. Whether Farben owned controlling shares of IG Chemie indirectly is another matter."[545]

The Swiss Consulate in Basel knew what was going on – in a letter from January 30, 1942, it stated: "Originally IG Chemie was founded as a holding company to IG Farben, in order to administrate important capital participations of the last named enterprise especially such in USA."[546]

The preferred shares of IG Chemie were represented by two Swiss banks: Industrie Bank AG and Societé Auxiliaire de Participations et de Depots. The shares were held, however, by Greutert & Cie, the Swiss banking house of IG Farben. Greutert was owned by Farben and acted as its agent for many overseas transactions, including those involving General Aniline and Film. The web continues to unfurl when we find out Greutert held 64% of the stock in Deutsche Länderbank, a bank which was housed with the Berlin offices of the IG and accepted the IG's instructions as though it was a subsidiary.[547] Greutert also acted as the surety when Farben borrowed 500 tons of tetra ethyl lead from Standard Oil at the behest of the Reich Air Ministry. Tetra ethyl lead is an important additive in the manufacture of aviation fuel.

To further obscure and to consolidate its holdings, IG Farben took steps in 1940 to change the ownership view of IG Chemie. Firstly, Hermann Schmitz retired from the board of IG Chemie (though stayed on as president of IG Farben). Secondly, Farben issued its own shares in exchange for shares of IG Chemie held in German hands. The shares of

Chemie were then taken by Deutsche Länderbank and exchanged for shares in other German corporations held by Greutert (which by now had changed its name to Sturzengger & Cie.) Once this was completed, the next step in this smoke and mirrors campaign commenced.

General Aniline and Film was originally an American company, started by Caesar Grasselli as the Grasselli Chemical Company. In June 1924, the company entered into a joint venture with Bayer and each company held 50% of the new Grasselli Dyestuff Corporation. The company held all present and future patents in the United States and Canada. Grasselli Chemical was bought in 1928 for $64.8 million in stock by DuPont and the Grasselli Dyestuff was sold back to IG Farben and renamed General Aniline Works.[548] The company supplied many different and very profitable dyes to the American and Canadian markets. Shortly thereafter, General Aniline and other IG foreign interests, including Bayer, Agfa, Winthrop Chemical and Norsk Hydro were consolidated into IG Chemie. The following year the American firms merged to become the American IG Chemical Corporation of New York. Financial control was exercised through IG Chemie with a unique agreement. IG Farben guaranteed the dividends of IG Chemie in return for the option to purchase IG Chemie's foreign investments at book value.[549]

When, in 1940, it was decided to change ownership, it was General Aniline which came out on top. It purchased 950,000 shares of its own stock back from IG Chemie, in order to make the company look independent. That money was then sent to the IG to pay for the shares of IG Chemie in German hands, as well as used to assist the operations of the Reichsbank in Holland. In addition, IG Farben acquired shares in a German dynamite manufacturer, though it surrendered the voting rights to the company to the German High Command.

How close were the ties that bound General Aniline with IG Farben? How about eighty-five separate patent agreements? Technical information continued to flow from the IG to the American company, which was also dependant on the IG for materials required for manufacturing these patented processes. IG Farben was also still the guarantor on General Aniline's principal debt obligation; and, people who worked for General Aniline were long time former IG Farben employees, some of whom were still covered under the IG's pension fund.[550] Perhaps the most telling part of all this is a comment from Georg von Schnitzler, stating it would be unreasonable to think IG Farben had no interest in General Aniline and Film, considering the assistance it was giving to the company.

Besides General Aniline, IG Chemie held interest in a Dutch company – *NV Maatschappij voor Industrie en Handelsbelangen* (Society for Industry and Commerce Holdings). This is important since IG Farben transferred ownership of one of its British concerns to Maatschappij to cloak it from scrutiny by the British. The British company, IG Dyestuffs, would have the stigma of being a German company, which would be considered alien property and subject to confiscation by the authorities. Interestingly, the bookkeeping department at IG Farben chose to look at this as a loan to the Dutch company and accounting entries regarding the transfer would be "not according to legal but to economic principles."[551]

IG Chemie throughout had tried to completely disprove any indication of ownership interest from IG Farben. From a May 1941 letter to John Pehle, the assistant to the U.S. Secretary of the Treasury:

In consideration of certain entirely erroneous opinions regarding our firm we feel, however, that it is of the greatest importance to demonstrate anew to the U.S. Authorities that we are a genuine Swiss corporation and that we have always followed a strictly independent policy. The policy, which, as we beg to insist upon, has no other aim than the protection of the legitimate financial interests of a neutral corporation.[552]

This is all very convincing, yet at the same time Dr. Albert Gadow was "conducting the business of IG Chemie as its most responsible officer." Remember, Gadow was also Hermann Schmitz's brother-in-law. Gadow applied for Swiss citizenship in September 1940 to emphasize the Swiss flavor of the company. Throughout this time Gadow used the German Consulate in Basel as a conduit for information to and from IG Farben, and this was treated highly confidentially by the consulate. Other officials at IG Chemie also acted as conduits: Carl Rösch was said by the OMGUS report as "being completely under Schmitz' control;" and Hans Sturzenegger handled all secret correspondence between the Agfa division of General Aniline and Film and IG Farben.

So while IG Farben was making very public its severance of ties with IG Chemie, it was still acting on and exercising control over certain items. As well, IG Farben was making overtures to American companies which held General Aniline and Film shares to either sell them or barter for goods or services. When the U.S. Government seized General Aniline in February 1942, there were three large blocks of A Class shares:[553]

IG Chemie owned almost 389,000 of the 471,000 outstanding; IG Chemie subsidiary Osmon AG held 66,000 and Brown Brothers Harriman held 16,000. The Brown Brothers Harriman shares were held as collateral for a lien against IG Farben. Of the B Class shares, large blocks were held by Maatschappij, *Eidgenössische Bank AG* of Zurich and L. D. Pickering & Co. of New York. Eidgenössische, which eventually became part of UBS, was also the bank which acted as the transfer agent of Greutert's shares to IG Farben. L. D. Pickering was acting as an agent for Greutert, so to be honest, all of the B class shares and all of the A class shares save the 16,000 held by Brown Brothers were in the hands of IG Chemie, not at arm's length from IG Farben.[554]

Maatschappij was owned by Cassella before 1925. When the IG transferred ownership of Maatschappij to IG Chemie, it still continued to use its facilities to cloak and obscure ownership of its foreign assets, including IG Dyestuff in Great Britain, as well as real estate in Belgium and Portugal. The shares in IG Dyestuff were transferred to Maatschappij in 1935 without any payment being made. Though the shares resided with the Dutch company, 99% of the shares were held under option by IG Farben and the IG continued to direct the British company's operations.[555] After the Munich Pact was signed in 1938, IG Farben once again decided to obscure its ownership of IG Dyestuffs by transferring ownership to a different Dutch company, *NV Chemikalien-Handel Maatschappij* (Chehamij). To make it look very official, the IG funded a bank account at the Enskilda Bank in Stockholm, which then loaned the money to an affiliated company, which hen sent a loan off to Chehamij. Chehamij's majority shareholders, according to a letter written by the IG to the Reich Ministry of Economics would have the illusion of having no relation between Chehamij or its shareholding companies and the IG. On selecting the shareholders, the greatest importance had to be attached to the IG's influence on Chehamij being made fully secure. "We therefore suggested three companies as shareholders which are connected with IG Chemie and the Bank Ed. Greutert & Cie, belonging to our friends, and entirely safeguard the maintenance of the IG influence on Chehamij."[556]

The irony of this is it was all for nought after the Nazis occupied the Netherlands. According to an IG memo from January 1941, it had reacquired the shares of Chehamij since the cloaking of this asset was now useless to the company. The cloaking of assets in the United States was still very much of use to IG Farben, so much so it falsified documents, backdating certain financial records to give the impression control had moved out of Dutch hands before the Wehrmacht marched into the country.

IG Chemie filed an application with the U.S. Treasury Department on June 12, 1940 to transfer the blocks of shares from Maatschappij into its custody. General Aniline and Film filed a similar application on August 29, 1940. Both cited the shares had been sold by the Dutch company to Greutert & Cie in September of 1939, well before the German invasion of Holland. However, documents did not surface in the United States until they were received by the Bank of Manhattan Co. on June 7, 1940, almost four weeks after the German attack and Dutch assets were blocked by the United States. Because of the time elapsed between the alleged sale to Greutert and their arrival at the Bank of Manhattan, American officials became suspicious. This suspicion increased when General Aniline and Film filed its similar application almost three months later.[557]

When it was certain the American troops would invade Holland and quite possible they would find evidence of the subterfuge, Farben's attorney Dr. Gustav Kupper suggested the files must be destroyed – legally, of course. So, to legally do this, the company had to be dissolved – which was carried out by IG Chemie under the auspices of an attorney from IG Farben. The attorney, a Herr Gierlichs, claimed not to know the reason behind the dissolution and it did not proceed to completion, a claim corroborated by the existence of certain memoranda.

Throughout all this, IG Chemie subsidiaries were obviously being controlled by IG Farben. IG Chemie companies such as Agfa Photo AG and Teerfarben AG (both in Zurich) were sales agencies which relied completely on IG Farben for product. Durand & Hugeunin AG of Basel was a dye producer which had a cross-licensing agreement with IG Farben; Norsk Hydro was a member of an international nitrogen cartel with the IG, and fell into the IG's hands after the fall of France.

The reasoning for hiding assets in foreign countries was far less ominous initially – in Latin America, for example, the assets were camouflaged so IG Farben could pay lower corporate taxes. However, when World War II started, it became clear the cloaking would serve a much larger purpose to the company. Many at the IG remembered back to the end of the First World War, when an asset could be taken as a reparation payment. The IG's management was so good at hiding foreign assets, they reported this to the German government in 1940: "our measures for camouflage have proved to be very good during the war, and have even surpassed our expectations in many cases."[558]

One IG company in Brazil kept secret bank accounts and cash hoards to deal with companies who wanted to do business but wanted no recorded dealings with the blacklisted group. These secret accounts were also used to illicitly buy up assets and hide their true ownership. Items like office buildings, cattle ranches and homes for employees were all purchased using this secret cache of money and to avoid the money being sequestered by the respective Latin American governments.

The IG used other methods in South America, including employees who pretended not to be employees, to buy goods from the United States for use in IG enterprises in the south. Alfrede Moll from Buenos Aires first set up dummy companies, fake names and numerous addresses, and when the Americans caught on, he convinced the American Consulate in Buenos Aires of his good intentions and his lack of attachment to IG Farben. Again he was able to continue purchasing for the company. Italy was another conduit used by the IG to Latin America, but this was a little more expensive – IG agents had to use fraud and bribery to get products out of the country and to Latin America.

The IG at this point was led by Hermann Schmitz, known by many of his associates as the master of financial camouflage. Schmitz led the company when it used a variety of techniques to obscure the true ownership of over 1,000 companies which IG Farben controlled or owned, directly or indirectly. This is a staggering figure, and explains the far reach of the company to every corner of the globe.[559] IG Farben conducted this camouflage for many years, establishing shadow companies which hid assets for a variety of reasons. These reasons were handily itemized by Dr. Kupper of the legal department during a meeting in October 1940. The first was taxation – what better way to avoid taxes than by saying you are someone else. The second was the cloud of war – as stated earlier, the post-World War I era was particularly painful for many German businesses, with France, Great Britain and other countries taking assets wholesale as reparations for damages. The third reason was an interesting one – the weakness of Germany after the First World War, which "made it advisable to give our foreign organizations the national character of the respective countries."

Number four was discrimination – many people will buy something if it has a "Made in (insert your home country here)" label on it, so if the company is from your home country, it makes you want to buy from them. Number five was to stop a branch office from being forced to disclose details from the company's balance sheet or income statement. Number six was the avoidance of controls on foreign companies. The seventh reason was to avoid the anti-dumping stipulations of the U.S. Tariff acts. By using cloaked importers in Canada and Australia, they evaded this. The final reason was to avoid Spanish industry protection taxes.

Dr. Kupper did not tell the meeting the other very good reasons for this camouflage, which were conveniently itemized in the OMGUS report: to act as listening posts and collectors of economic intelligence for both the parent company and the German government; to act as propagandists and in some instances as headquarters for espionage activities against potential and actual enemies of the Reich; and to aid the Nazis in preparations for and prosecution of the war, as well as provide the means for Germany's emergence from a military defeat with an unimpaired economic foundation for future aggrandizement.[560]

It was assumed at the October 1940 meeting Germany would win the war, as by October 1940 Western Europe had capitulated, the Battle of Britain had begun and Germany had signed the Tripartite

Treaty with Italy and Japan. After the war ended and Germany had won, decloaking would be the order of the day in most countries subjugated, including Great Britain, though it would continue in many other countries again due to tax implications. The legal department conducted may seminars in cloaking of assets, some as early as June 1939, when the IG was apprised of Germany's intention to attack Poland. For the Nazi government to inform a company of its intention to start a war is unfathomable, yet there it is.

It is important to note the company and the government were at times inseparable, acting as one in many instances. This explains the foreknowledge of attack, as well as the requirement for the company to conduct espionage for the Reich. Foreknowledge was important to the IG, if for no other reason than to hide its assets abroad. In Latin America, the company cloaked assets so they appeared neither on the head office books nor on the books of the agencies abroad. The IG went so far as to write off the important assets held in Brazil, Argentina and Mexico in 1940 while the war raged in Europe so as to hide them further. In 1942, the IG's bookkeeping department reported assets in South America of around RM21 million, yet the South American department reported at the same time there were RM37 million of "total risk." When an audit was conducted by OMGUS, inventory alone was valued at over RM34 million at cost and it was assumed at that point the total assets were at least double that.[561]

In a side note, the IG stated in a March 1934 report:

Externally the shares in our sales organizations are not taken over by the IG but by other persons or firms for reason of taxation and those of a different nature. A safeguarding of the IG is necessary here...Should there be scruples with regard to the shares represented by banks, the shares must be transferred to other firms or persons. By the war...it might be better for tactical reasons with respect to the foreign authorities if it could be clearly proved in which hands the shares are. On selecting the shareholders representing the IG, special care must be taken...the people taking them over can pay the value from their own resources. This way is the most favorable one because the participation can be least attacked as a fictitious one.[562]

Such an interesting commentary to put to paper. *If banks have scruples, then we shouldn't deal with them?* People should have their own resources to pay for the shares that will still be under IG Farben control, *just so it doesn't look fictitious?* The IG director in charge of dyestuffs in *Lateinamerika* stated the shareholders the company seeks out in the area should be from the respective country, or at least not German. They should have names like Gonzales or Bedout, not Müller or Schulze.[563] What's more, these fictitious shareholders had to pre-emptively sign letters which sent ownership back to the IG in case of their death or other urgent matters – the IG representative only had to fill in the date. This also stopped the shareholders from getting cold feet or double crossing the company by selling the shares to another individual.

One of the major shareholders considered was a large American bank with branches in Buenos Aires as well as other major centres in South America. The institution was National City Bank – now Citibank. The bank was approached in April of 1935 in hopes the bank would serve as a shareholder for the IG. The rationale was there could be no German banks involved – it would elicit too much suspicion. An American bank would not though, so the National City Bank representative in Berlin was approached. National City was interested in collaborating with the IG and the Berlin representative was going to send word back to New York, yet nothing further happened, and it is unclear what made the deal fall through. Dr. Kupper from the legal department maybe shed some light on the negotiations with this statement:

The plan, however, never came into operation. The legal department's opinion that banks were no good dummies at all, the same applied to lawyers, who were only taken as shareholders when better dummies were not available...officers of the NCB could not be considered as suitable for shareholding-dummies since the officers who might have come into question all were U.S. citizens by birth.[564]

Since the National City Bank plan fell through, it was up to nepotism to step in. Hermann Schmitz appointed his brother Dietrich, who was a naturalized American citizen, a shareholder of all IG Farben interests in South America and Mexico except for *La Union Quimica SA* in Mexico City. This happened in 1935, six years before he was removed as president of General Aniline and Film when it was seized by the American government. Dietrich Schmitz acquired the shares as a loan – the IG gave Schmitz the shares and he signed an IOU for the amount. By November 1939 Dietrich Schmitz wanted to unload the shares and the IG was in agreement. The talks continued into 1940, when the IG realized if one of the Latin American countries entered the war, its assets would be in jeopardy. In February of that year, Walter Duisberg who was formerly a director, vice-president and treasurer of General Aniline, was to become the new trustee of the shares. If the last name sounds familiar, it is – Dr. Walter Duisberg was the son of Dr. Carl Duisberg, who with Carl Bosch was the founding leader of IG Farben.

Unfortunately, the American authorities also realized the last name was familiar and the IG became wise to this, as was stated in a report prepared on February 5, 1940: "The idea, to replace him (Schmitz) by Dr. Duisberg, can not be realized under consideration of the difficulties resulting from the name."[565] Therefore, it was decided local IG officials with non-German sounding names would be ideal as trustees, as well as lawyers whose palms could be greased. This did not stop the company from worrying about "conflicts of conscience." For example, if Argentina went to war with Germany, the Argentinian national who is acting as a trustee may not be so trustworthy after all. The next step in this convoluted scheme was a shareholder pool, whereby a group would act as trustees and no member of the group could act unilaterally.

So we have fake shareholders, purchases of cattle ranches and office buildings, people named Gonzalez (not Müller). What else did the IG do to hide its participation in Latin America? How about fake invoices. The IG would issue false invoices to the cattle ranches and mark them as paid, which would then allow the money to be secreted in the country of choice – such as Argentina – but look like it had already left in the form of a payment to the parent company. By 1941, the affiliates in South America had hidden almost RM 2,700,000.

Other ways the companies in South America hid assets included:

- sell goods on consignment without recording the sale on the books. An internal invoice was generated, but the items were sold for cash, then the money was hidden in assets purchased by management of the South American affiliates.

- give employees their year's salary plus bonus up front. Then the employees would return the money to the manager or a trustworthy third party. This way, the company could claim the monies were paid out and the employees would have appeared to have spent it all, making it impossible for the authorities to get it back.

The major problem the affiliates had was making too much money. The *Cia. General de Anilinas* in Santiago had this terrible problem (as itemized in a June 30, 1942 telegram): "We shall have at our disposal more than 20,000,000 peses as of the end of this year. Transfers of importance very likely not possible. So we propose, with respect to the progressing devaluation of money and impossibility of using funds at our disposition for purchase of goods for our branch, the purchase of a large modern centrally located building insured against earthquakes."[566]

Cia. Colombiana de Colorantes y Productos Quinico, Ltda in Bogota had the same type of problem, as seen in an October 15 1942 cable:

Because further import of goods of our branch impossible, Banco Republica will try freezing our liquid capital in hands of government with all the risks which such a measure brings, including devaluation. We will try to avoid blocking by following proposal: purchase of buildings for offices in Bogota and Medellin; enlargement of Inquico; purchase of houses for employees of Bogota and Medellin; participations in agricultural and cattle enterprises and enlargement of research concerning the use of fertilizers.[567]

The response from head office was to do what the affiliates thought was best. Most of the business in South America was through sales agencies which would import products from IG Farben and resell them. There were some manufacturing facilities in the area, but most revenue came from importers, so most assets in the region could be hidden much easier than if it were in "bricks and mortar" assets.

When war broke out in 1939, Great Britain and France attempted to squelch any exports of product form Germany. The IG circumvented this in two ways: the first was to arrange for imports from neutral countries in which it had operations, such as the United States. The second was a more direct approach – it ran the blockades set up by the British and French. Blockade running sounds exciting and dangerous, yet there was little danger on the part of the IG. For the first few months of the war, the company used neutral vessels sailing from Italy and Holland. From January 1940, when Holland became off limits, the IG used Italian ports camouflaging their shipments with a convenient *Made in Italy* sticker. Once Italy entered the war, they moved to using Soviet ports in Siberia. Then when Hitler attacked the Soviet Union, they took the direct route – using German government blockade runners to transport goods.

How successful was the blockade running? The company managed to get over RM 17.5 million in goods to Latin America by circumventing the British and the French. This allowed the affiliates in South America to continue to grow sales. From 1938 to the end of 1941, sales grew from RM 29.3 million to RM 39.8 million, and that isn't even the complete picture for 1941, as records are missing for some of the period.

The trips through Holland and Italy were a milk run, comparatively speaking. Dr. Julius Overhoff of the dyestuffs department told the Military Government investigators the goods left Amsterdam, Rotterdam and Genoa in plain boxes with non-descript bills of lading. From the beginning of the war until January 1940, a scant four months, IG Farben managed to ship over RM 5.4 million worth of dyes and pharmaceuticals to South America. Once the Netherlands were cut off, the company shipped through Italy for six more months. They moved through the Italian company *Aziende Colori Nazionali e Affini*, which IG Farben conveniently had a minority interest. The Italian company then sent the goods through a neutral country – usually Spain – then off to the subsidiaries in Latin America.

The Molotov-Ribbentrop Pact between Germany and the Soviet Union had a provision for sending goods to Asia, North and South America via Siberian ports. This lasted about nine months, until Germany failed to deliver machinery to the Soviets as a condition of the treaty and the Soviets terminated the export provision. This was not without effort on the part of the IG though – the Nazi government even required the company to fill orders from the USSR, even before filling orders for the Wehrmacht. By April 1941, the route was opened again and shipments began. Unfortunately for the IG, the Wehrmacht's invasion of the Soviet Union made Stalin much less receptive to trade talks. The ruse the company used for shipments out of Siberia was to camouflage them as Japanese. The IG went so far as to make sure insurance papers were made out for the shipments bearing Japanese title and not show any outward signs of "Germanness." The trans-Siberian route accounted for another seven million Reichsmarks of sales.

Finally, there was the brute force of a blockade run. In October 1940, IG Farben was informed of a plan by the Kriegsmarine and the Ministry of Economics to carry products from the IG and "other important German firms." Three ships, the *Lech*, the *Herman* and the *Natal* left Bordeaux in early 1941. All three arrived in South America, but on the return trip, the *Lech* and the *Herman* were sunk by the British. The *Natal* made the return trip to Nantes in France in August 1941 with its cargo of cotton, beryllium (used for alloys in aircraft manufacture) and quebracho extract, a leather tanning agent. British spies informed their countrymen of the vessels leaving port, leading to the demise of the *Herman* and the *Lech*. The dismal failure of the blockade runners caused the scheme to be abandoned in September 1941.[568] The company did manage, however, to send almost six million Reichsmarks of goods to South America on the voyage.

Into Argentina, most of these imports came thanks to the efforts of Alfredo Moll, one of the managers at *Anilinas Alemánda*. Moll – whose name is much less suspicious than Müller or Schmidt – acted as an undercover purchaser in New York until the end of 1941, then with substantially less success in Buenos Aires. Not that Alfredo Moll was their first choice – he was their only choice. According to Julius Overhoff: "Moll was authorized to do all the necessary to maintain the interests of the IG. The main task was to get dyestuffs by all means and ways, in order to keep contact with customer so long as ever possible."

Moll would not only purchase for the IG concerns in South America, he would be helped along by his own customers: "in future, purchase neutral goods only directly through reliable customers, who will retain part of the goods purchased in this manner for themselves. The larger part will, however, be resold to the agency. In the opinion of Mr. M(oll), there can be found in practically all the Latin American States customers to carry through these transactions."[569]

Of course these customers would receive preferential payment terms and pricing for the help they rendered to the IG. One customer who did this (and paid afterwards) was Fezandie & Sperrle of New York. Fezandie & Sperrle would purchase goods from General Aniline and General Dyestuffs (both IG companies), then export them to South America. Unfortunately for Fezandie & Sperrle, the IRS is not so dumb. It looked at the sales of the company in the United States, and became suspicious, especially since the bulk of its purchases were from a company owned by IG Farben. In a December 1945 ruling, Judge Clarence V. Opper commented on:

the almost fantastic quality of the gift of a ready-made export business, complete with customers, products, protection against competition, and the consequent inevitable profit. This was no mere instance of the withdrawal of competing foreign commerce and the resulting liberation of a previously closed market. Fezandie did not produce a new business, solicit new customers, or discover new sources of salable materials. It was selected to be the heir to all of this under circumstances which would have to be, and in fact were, the product of an unprecedented and unique external situation.[570]

Judge Opper was appointed by Franklin Roosevelt in 1938, before which he served as counsel in the Treasury Department, where he helped develop the new monetary, fiscal and foreign-exchange policies of President Roosevelt's first term. Particularly, he participated in the economic-warfare planning that preceded the country's entry into World War II and helped form the Government position in refusing to export helium to Nazi Germany.[571] He was an expert in Nazi business economics and some would say his opinion was negatively tinged by this; others would say it gave him a unique point of view and would be adept as prosecuting companies who aided and abetted the Nazi war machine.

Moll arrived in New York on March 9, 1940. By October, Moll told the IG that deliveries were going well, but that was all. The IG sent a man from Berlin to deliver a message: forward a report of your activities. In mid-December, while travelling in Mexico, Moll finally delivered his report:

I believe I can assure you that it was possible by means of patient and persistent work to arrive at a normal and lasting relationship between New York and all important centers in Latin America...it is very difficult for the gentlemen in New York to make up *their minds about conditions in Latin America, especially considering they are used to a stable market as in the USA...According to the official figures of New York, US $1,218,345 was exported from the beginning (of March 1940) till November...I assure you that it was possible despite many obstacles...these figures show us that Chile and Colombia received practically their whole sales volume, but Mexico, Brazil and Argentina lost a part of their sales...partly by the activity of competitors and partly by the refusal of customers (to cooperate in the scheme).*[572]

Moll's tone changed by August 1941 when the United States clamped down on export licenses and he was forced to return to Buenos Aires to continue his business dealings: "the methods applied by the Latin American firms to veil their purchases in the USA were known. This is quite comprehensible bearing in mind...the investigations made by the USA authorities by which the traces of all the systems thought of could be followed up with ease."[573]

For Moll, when the going was easy, he was very happy to say he was doing an excellent job. When the U.S. government made it hard for him, it was obvious to him why the systems used by IG Farben to cloak sales were failing – and of course, it was not his fault. Moll stopped working for Anilinas and took the opportunity to act as an independent agent, purchasing items for firms not on the blacklist, then once the materials arrived in Buenos Aires, they would be transferred to Anilinas Alemanas. To accomplish this, Moll severed his ties with Anilinas, including the sale of his block of shares. This did not stop him from working for IG Farben, which still owned the affiliate. The company cabled back to the managers of Anilinas on December 22, 1941, authorizing Moll "to represent, without any restrictions, the firm giving this power of attorney, in all commercial matters in which IG Farbenindustrie Aktien Gesellschaft is interested within the Argentine Republic. Mr. Alfredo Moll is authorized in particular to freely manage every property of our company, to dispose freely of our property and our rights."[574]

This carte blanche could be construed two ways: either Alfredo Moll was doing such a bang-up job, he was to continue doing great things for the IG. Or, the directors in Berlin were so desperate considering Germany had just declared war on the United States, they would do anything to save their business. The latter was confirmed by Julius Overhoff, who stated: "because the U.S. had entered the war, and the danger was imminent that some of the other American countries would follow, these powers of attorney should be the last help to save IG's property, if ever possible, should no other way remain."[575]

Moll severed relations with Anilinas Alemanas and the IG, citing the strain of the "political situation." According to Overhoff, this was not necessarily a bad move for Moll. As an independent dealer, he would safeguard himself if Germany either won or lost the war; distancing himself from IG Farben in the event of a loss and he could always continue business with the company after the war if Germany was victorious.

South America wasn't just an important area of business for the IG; it was also an important area for espionage carried on by the company for the Nazis. IG Farben subsidiaries in South America would send monthly reports back to Berlin on economic, political and military developments. The company was an ideal avenue for this venture for two reasons: IG's corporate structure in South America was already established, so it would be easy for managers and employees to ask casual questions of business contacts without arousing suspicion. Propaganda was spread by these employees in South America as well. Not only pro-Nazi information was put out, but also the company directly funded local Nazi Party groups in the countries and provided libraries of Nazi literature to them. Managers funded so-called press committees, which funded and supplied anti-American and anti-British newspaper articles throughout the region.

The IG in South America perfected the art of cloaking and concealment in Latin America, and proved its importance to both the company and the Reich. Neutral countries are always a hotbed of illicit knowledge on foreign powers as it is safe for men and women of various backgrounds to intermingle freely – and exchange information freely. This information was important to IG Farben from a financial standpoint – which competitor is moving into which country, whose palm needs to be greased, etc. It was also very important to the Nazis, not just for espionage on other countries, but to also shore up support in neutral South American countries, which if the propaganda is well placed, could either enter the war on Germany's side, or at least be belligerent to Germany's enemies in the forum of trade or diplomacy.

The IG constantly changed its methods of concealment in South America. Sometimes they would replace German officials with South American or neutral officials in their subsidiaries in order make the company's holdings more palatable to foreign trade. Many of these non-German officials were in fact naturalized citizens of the United States but their allegiance to the Fatherland was still strong. The company also used undercover agents working out of neutral countries, who exported materials to the subsidiaries from the IG.

The IG's work with the Army Supreme Command (OKW), while less financially intensive, was nonetheless as important. Beginning in 1933, the company supplied statistics as to factory output of competitors outside of Germany. The reason for this was simple – it was easier for the Luftwaffe to plan bombing raids on areas of interest if the Luftwaffe knew where these areas were beforehand. This type of espionage was very easy to conduct and provided very important information. The value of this did not escape Admiral Wilhelm Canaris, head of the Abwehr – German Military Intelligence. Canaris had a working arrangement with the IG before 1933 for gathering military intelligence in other countries. The company would put members of the Abwehr on its payroll so that they could undertake missions abroad and not call any undue attention to them. The IG set up a dummy corporation to handle this, and Georg von Schnitzler was the president:

I recently had occasion in Berlin to discuss with Major Bloch of the OKW another matter pertaining to this subject, i.e. whether and to what extent the OKW wants to use the services of the Gesellschaft für Verkaufsförderung (the dummy company aka the Association for Sales Promotion)...The company is particularly well suited for the intended camouflaging maneuvers, since the failure of one of its emissaries will never lead to a catastrophe; if worst comes to worst this company might have to cease operating in some particular country and would have to confine its activities to the other neutral countries.[576]

Max Ilgner was instrumental in another company, this one set up exclusively in South America. The *IG Verbindungmaenner* – loosely the IG Fraternity – employed men from all over the continent who had left Germany many years previous and were directly appointed by and reported to Max Ilgner. The company men made contact with local governments, chambers of commerce, banks and so forth and reported back to the IG, who in turn relayed the information to the Abwehr. These agents also were told by Ilgner to work closely with local Nazi organizations and to take an active role in propaganda.

The idea behind these dummy fronts was it would save the IG the embarrassment and financial woe of being exposed as a centre for Nazi espionage. By 1944, it seems the company did not care and used the Bayer company itself to act as its spy group. Bayer had one of the most extensive sales and marketing force in the world and the IG was only too happy to oblige the *Sicherheitsdienst*, which by this time had succeeded the Abwehr after Admiral Canaris had been removed and placed under house arrest. The admiral was later executed for his role in the plot to assassinate Hitler in July 1944.

The IG and foreign exchange

IG Farben was Germany's largest producer of foreign exchange that wasn't a bank. The company exported many of the products it made, and accounted for 10% of all exports from Germany. Most of this was in the form of pharmaceuticals, dyestuffs and photographic equipment. And coming back into the country, the IG accounted for 10% of foreign currency. This money came in very handy for the purchase of raw materials necessary for rearming the country, and for conducting espionage and propaganda in other countries. The importance of this was not lost on the Reich government – it pressured companies to acquire foreign currency and rewarded them when they did. One such program was a guarantee against losses. The Reich subsidy export plan would make up the difference between sale price and the cost of an item if the item was exported below cost. IG Farben sold some items at 60% below cost, but was assured of no net loss thanks to the subsidy.[577]

Foreign currency was strictly controlled by the government. When monies came into the country, companies such as the IG would send receipts to a government committee, which would then disburse the currency to party, government or private organizations. In turn, IG Farben would receive Reichsmarks, and Nazi officials would take a skim off the top. In the two years up to January 1942, the Bayer division in Brazil paid over RM3.6 million to the German Embassy and to Nazi Party officials in the country for "reasons unknown."[578] The company did its part without reservation. In a letter to Göring, von Schnitzler and Ilgner stated the company had to reduce prices in Central and South America by one million Reichsmarks a year in order to secure a free flow of foreign currency.

After the German invasion of Poland, the IG decided it was in its best interests to transfer its patent agreements in the United States to other "friendly" business associates. This was no small task, as the company held over 2,000 patents in the country. Some of these patents the IG felt were safe, especially those which were licensed to American companies. However, the top 1,000 patents the IG held were assigned to close business partners, including General Aniline and Film, Walter Duisberg and the Standard Oil Company. Most of these patents were outright sold to the companies and Duisberg, to avoid the possibility of a cloaking action being detected. The patent department resignedly said in meeting minutes: "The transfer should not be regarded from the aspect of whether it is a good deal, but mainly as a security measure for IG patents."[579]

It was a good deal for General Aniline and Film, which paid $925,000 for 780 patents. General Aniline was still controlled by IG Chemie, so the sale was really a wash, and for all intents and purposes was a cloaking of assets. IG Farben realized this and knew after the war the patents would fall again into its sphere of influence. The deals cut with Standard Oil and General Aniline called for a lump sum payment, plus a provision that 25% of the profits earned from the patents would go back to IG Farben – in perpetuity. The deal with Walter Duisberg for 200 of the patents called for him to pay $10,000 cash and if he were able to exploit the patents, the profits would be split 80:20, with the lion's share going back to the IG. The company also had a clause in the agreement that it could purchase back the patent at any time for the original purchase price. The other 1,000 patents were assigned en masse to Duisberg, General Aniline and IG Farben's patent lawyers in the United States, Hutz and Joslin. While the company didn't feel they were particularly valuable at that time, if the government moved to seize them, then one of the three entities could act on behalf of the IG.

The IG and Standard Oil

At the start of the Second World War, the Standard Oil Company of New Jersey was the largest petroleum company in the world and the third largest company in the world period. Standard started the 20th century controlling 91% of production and 85% of sales of oil in the United States. Its founder, John David Rockefeller was the richest man in the world when the company was broken up in 1911 for violating anti-trust laws. Rockefeller, whose name is synonymous with wealth, was worth $1 billion at the time or according to a 2007 Forbes article, the equivalent of $336 billion. The Standard Oil Company was broken into 41 separate companies, of which the largest were called: Exxon, Mobil, Chevron and Amoco, as well as Pennzoil and Chesebrough-Ponds. Now that the size and scope of Standard Oil is known, let's get back to its involvement with the IG.

In 1923, Mathias Pier, who worked for Carl Bosch, developed a way for extracting methanol from coal. Methanol had previously been derived from the destructive distillation of wood, hence its other name – wood alcohol. It had been known that methanol works as a crude motor vehicle fuel, but the use of wood is not profitable, so when Pier discovered a way for taking the methanol from one of Germany's most abundant resources, it was very interesting to the IG. The process could be done in a commercially viable way on machinery which was already used by the company for distilling nitrates. But what was more important – and this is the possibility Carl Bosch realized – was that it pointed the way to the Bergius process being feasible on an industrial scale. (The Bergius process was a way of making synthetic fuel from coal)

Bosch was a visionary – he could see the gasoline dripping from the coal fields of the Ruhr, but he knew the initial investment would be massive. This was a risk he was unwilling to take alone, and knowing the rest of the Aufsichtsrat would have to be convinced of the success just around the corner, he approached a partner. In 1925, Bosch sent Wilhelm Gaus, the head of production at Oppau, on a goodwill visit to the Standard Oil refinery facilities. Gaus was told to drop hints about the IG's acquisition of the Bergius patents and plans to develop them. He was also under the strictest of orders to look for ways to invite the Standard executives back to Germany for a reciprocal visit.

Of course, Standard was extremely interested. They had researched the Bergius process for years and wanted to find a way to extract more precious petroleum from their leftover sludge, but as with the IG, they found it cost prohibitive. The main concern for Standard though was IG Farben might be able to produce cheap synthetic gasoline, which would cut into Standard's profits severely. Hence, Frank Howard of Standard Oil Development made the trek to Ludwigshafen in March 1926. Howard was given a tour of the facilities, which in themselves were extraordinary in their scale. Then he was shown the hydrogenation process, at the time being conducted on a small scale, but it was enough. Howard returned to his hotel and cabled Walter Teagle, the president of Standard Oil: "This matter is the most important which has ever faced the company...(they) can make high-grade motor fuel from lignite and other low quality coals in amounts up to half the weight of the coal. This means absolutely the independence of Europe in the matter of gasoline supply. Straight price competition is all that is left."[580]

Teagle was in Paris at the time and hightailed it to Ludwigshafen. Taking the same tour as Frank Howard, Teagle knew Standard had to get in at the ground floor of this revolutionary new process. Buying it outright or becoming a partner were the company's only two results, or Standard would be left in the dust by Bosch's synthetic gasoline-powered Mercedes. Carl Bosch had landed his marlin.

Teagle and Howard knew the IG would be unwilling to just sell their process outright – indeed, why would anyone give up the goose that laid the golden eggs? Standard would have to be happy with a piece of the egg output at what it hoped would be a fair price. Standard offered to join the IG in a limited partnership to develop and market the new product. Bosch negotiated with Teagle and Howard, but nothing conclusive happened until August 1927, when the two companies reached an agreement: for the American rights to the process and a half share of the profits from selling the technology to other companies, Standard invested in an R&D program with IG Farben in Louisiana. By

1928, the IG was producing 28,000 tons of gasoline, a middling amount, yet again enough to make the process palatable.

It was a small step – too small for both companies, but it was a start. Standard knew this was where the future of petroleum lay – when the Americans used the Bergius process, they were able to double the amount of gasoline made from a barrel of crude. Standard needed the rights to the process in order to increase profits almost exponentially. On the other hand, the IG needed Standard's money to expand its own production. Both companies did not realize the gravity of each other's needs, but they did realize the gravity of each other's abilities.

In Germany, the process was becoming ridiculously expensive, contrary to what the IG's marketing department was telling the world. Losses had already amounted to RM85 million by 1929 (over $250 million inflation adjusted), a figure which alarmed the Aufsichtsrat. The more conservative members of the board grumbled perhaps it was time to abandon the project and move on to more profitable ventures, yet Bosch was not swayed. He knew if he could get the money out of Standard, he could make the venture commercially viable and secure the energy independence of the Reich.

Bosch had the marlin almost in the boat, but needed one more jerk on the line. So, in November 1929, Hermann Schmitz, Wilhelm Gaus, IG lawyer August von Knierem and Bosch travelled to the United States with an offer. The IG would sell the rights to the process for the world – save for Germany – for a fair price. Teagle and Howard could barely sit in their chairs – they couldn't believe their luck. Standard gave the IG two percent of its stock – about 564,000 shares – in return for acquiring the rights.[581] Standard-IG was formed from this accord, with 80% resting in New Jersey, the other 20% in Ludwigshafen and was to be the cornerstone of this new technology. This was when Bosch went in with another golden egg.

Did Standard know that not only could synthetic gasoline come from coal, but also synthetic rubber? While the IG had tried the process and found it very expensive, it could be very much less expensive, even less than natural rubber if it was made from oil. Bosch and Carl Krauch traveled back to the United States in early 1930 to negotiate yet again. The two companies formed another partnership, this time the Joint American Study Company (Jasco) and would be a 50/50 marriage.

Bosch knew the potential for growth, even if it would seem to some he had given away that coveted goose. But better to have half the pie than an empty plate.

This was all based on the rapid decline in oil reserves – many had said at the turn of the decade the world would run out of oil sooner rather than later. The massive oil fields in the Arabian Peninsula had not been discovered yet, and off-shore drilling was a decades-away dream. But six months after Jasco had been formed, huge oil deposits were found in Texas. This coupled with the Depression and lack of demand for automobiles (and oil) sent the price of crude spiralling down. In 1931, the finds were beginning in the Middle East and the price of crude oil tumbled to the equivalent of seven cents a litre. The price of synthetic still stood at fifty-five. The Aufsichtsrat was ready to pass on the synthetic fuel project.

By 1939, the Jasco shares were turned over to Standard, which paid the IG the minute sum of $4,000. But Standard would have the rights to everything Jasco developed in the United States, the British and French Empires and Iraq. The rest of the world went to IG Farben. This was great for Standard, but they still wanted the egg which the IG had promised them – the mythical patent for synthetic rubber. The IG had procrastinated on this for ten years, giving many different excuses as to why they couldn't just yet hand over the information. The two companies met on neutral ground in Basel in 1940. At this meeting, the IG had the best excuse yet – the German government would never allow such important data to fall into the hands of another government, Standard Oil left, disappointed and chagrined. The project was abandoned.

14
Men of Conscience

Twenty years ago the world was introduced to Oskar Schindler, a man who did the best he could with the hand he was dealt. The cry of many Nazis after the war was they were just following orders. For some though, an attack of conscience meant they did not follow orders – they acted as human beings should act.

The story of Schindler is well known now thanks to Steven Spielberg's film *Schindler's List*, which chronicled a flawed man's life from war profiteer to savior of 1,200 Polish Jews. One thing the movie did was introduce many people to the Holocaust and its horrors, an introduction most would not have, save for the writings of Anne Frank before she was abducted by the Gestapo.

While much of this book has presented the German business community in World War II as barbaric, unfeeling and unheroic, there should be one chapter devoted to those who went the extra step to do what they thought was best, even if it did cost them their families, their homes or their lives. Before the war, many of the man presented in the following pages were avaricious, contemptuous businessmen. Schindler himself was "a cynical, greedy exploiter of slave workers during the Second World War, a black-marketeer, gambler, member of the Nazi party eternally on the lookout for profit, an alcoholic playboy and shameless womanizer of the worst sort."[582]

Oskar Schindler was born in 1908, in Zwittau, Moravia. His family's neighbors were a Jewish Rabbi and his family, and the two sons became Oscar's best friends. The Schindlers were one of the richest and most prominent families in Zwittau, but as a result of the Depression, the family firm went bankrupt. Like many other Germans, the great call of Adolf Hitler beckoned – his voice of economic prosperity was musical to Schindler. In 1936, while still in Czechoslovakia, he joined the Abwehr to collect information about ethnic Poles, a great bit of forethought on Schindler's part, considering the contacts he acquired during his time with German Military Intelligence. He joined the Nazi party in 1939.

He followed the Wehrmacht into Poland in October 1939, seeing the opportunity which arose there. He left his wife Emilie in Zwittau and moved to Krakow, where he took over a Jewish family's apartment after the Nazi occupation.

Using bribes of both money and illegal black market goods, Schindler quickly got on good terms with the local Gestapo chiefs. He gained control of the Aryanized and formerly Jewish-owned enameled-goods factory Rekord Ltd. which was renamed *Deutsche Emalwarenfabrik Oskar Schindler* or Emalia. Emalia was close to the Jewish ghetto in Krakow and he principally employed Jewish workers at the plant. Schindler operated two other factories in Krakow, but only at Emalia did he employ Jewish workers who resided in the nearby ghetto. At its peak in 1944, Emalia employed 1,700 workers; at least 1,000 were Jewish forced laborers, whom the Germans had relocated from the Krakow ghetto after its liquidation in March 1943 to the forced labor camp and later concentration camp Krakau-Plaszow.

Although the prisoners deployed at Emalia were still subject to the brutal conditions of the Plaszow concentration camp, Schindler intervened repeatedly on their behalf, through bribes and personal diplomacy, both for the well-being of Jews threatened on an individual basis and to ensure until late 1944 the SS did not deport his Jewish workers. In order to claim the Jewish workers to be essential to the war effort, he added an armaments manufacturing division to Emalia. During the liquidation of the Krakow ghetto in March 1943, Schindler allowed his Jewish workers to stay at the factory overnight.

After the SS re-designated Plaszow as a concentration camp in August 1943, Schindler persuaded the SS to convert Emalia into a subcamp of Plaszow. In addition to the approximately 1,000 Jewish forced laborers registered as factory workers, Schindler permitted 450 Jews working in other nearby factories to live at Emalia as well, saving them from the systematic brutality and arbitrary murder that was part of daily life in Plaszow. Schindler did not act here without risk or cost; his protection of his Jewish workers and some of his shady business dealings led SS and police authorities to suspect him of corruption and of giving unauthorized aid to Jews. German SS and police officials arrested him three times while he owned Emalia, but were unable to charge him.

In October 1944, after the SS transferred the Emalia Jews to Plaszow, Schindler sought and obtained authorization to relocate his plant to Brünnlitz (Brnenec) in Moravia, and reopen it exclusively as an armaments factory. One of his assistants drew several versions of a list of up to 1,200 Jewish prisoners needed to work in the new factory. These lists came to be known collectively as "Schindler's List." Schindler met the specifications required by the SS to classify Brünnlitz as a sub-camp of Gross-Rosen concentration camp and thereby facilitated the survival of around 800 Jewish men whom the SS deported from Plaszow via Gross-Rosen to Brünnlitz and between 300 and 400 Jewish women from Plaszow via Auschwitz.

Though classified as an armaments factory, the Brünnlitz plant produced just one wagonload of live ammunition in eight months of operation. By presenting bogus production figures, Schindler justified the existence of the sub-camp as an armaments factory and thus facilitated the survival of over 1,000 Jews, sparing them the horrors and brutality of conventional camp life. Schindler left Brünnlitz on May 9, 1945, the day that Soviet troops liberated the camp.[583] Oskar Schindler died penniless and alone in October 1974 in Frankfurt.

Berthold Beitz

Berthold Beitz was born in 1913 in Zemmin in the former German Empire. Beitz started his career as a banker and then joined Royal Dutch Shell's Hamburg office as a 27-year-old junior executive. One evening in 1941, his grandfather, a Nazi notable, took him to dinner at the lavish home of German munitions magnate Alfried Krupp. Among the guests was SS Obergruppenführer Reinhard Heydrich, Himmler's number two man. Heydrich proudly told Beitz the Wehrmacht was taking over oil refineries in western Poland. Beitz enthusiastically offered his services and was named a director of *Karpaten Ol* in Boryslaw, Poland.

Beitz soon found that while there was relatively little oil in the mountain region, there were a lot of Jews - almost 50% of the population. Most were in ghetto work camps, a fact that Beitz admits didn't bother him at first. When death trains began running to Auschwitz and Treblinka, though, his conscience was stirred. It was "those children sitting in the station, with those enormous eyes, looking at you."[584]

It was in the oil fields in 1942 that 14-year-old Jurek Rotenberg first encountered Berthold Beitz. At considerable personal risk, Beitz and his wife secured the requisite working papers for Rotenberg and hundreds of Jews like him, saving them from the SS and the gas chambers. More than 70 years later Rotenberg joined 400 leading figures from German business and politics at the palatial Villa Hügel – the former Krupp estate in Essen – on what would have been Beitz's 100th birthday. Rotenberg had a chance to say a personal thank you in April 2013 when he flew from his home in Haifa, Israel, to meet Beitz at a synagogue in Essen.[585] Beitz was a person of deep Protestant principles and convictions, who had never succumbed to Nazi propaganda or joined the party. When he was sent to Eastern Poland he was shocked by the brutality of Germans and Ukrainians. He witnessed, for example, the murder of a child in its mother's arms. Beitz was able to employ Jews for several years because of the German need for oil. He was under constant pressure to surrender them, but Beitz found he could control the local SS officer, Friedrich Hildebrand. During tennis matches or hunting trips he would convince Hildebrand to leave his Jews alone.

Beitz began to save Jews by hiring them. "I should have employed qualified personnel. Instead, I chose tailors, hairdressers and Talmudic scholars and gave them all cards as vital petroleum technicians." Beitz and his young wife also hid a Jewish child in their own home. And like Oskar Schindler, Beitz often went to the train station to pull his Jewish workers off the death trains. "Once I found one of my secretaries and her aged mother," He got them out, but the SS were not fooled. They judged the mother too old, and forced her back on the cattle car. "The daughter turned to me. 'Herr Direktor, may I also return to the car?'" Beitz never saw her again.[586]

When the Nazis finally fell, more than 800 of Beitz's Jews were still alive. At the end of 1953, Beitz and Alfried Krupp crossed paths again. Krupp, recently released from jail, appointed Berthold Beitz as his chief executive. Krupp swore off arms production and embarked on an effort to diversify the company. With Beitz as general manager, it became one of the most powerful businesses in the world. After

Krupp's death in 1967, Berthold Beitz became executor of his will and head of the Krupp Foundation, which still holds 23% of ThyssenKrupp. In 1993, Beitz said "As I look back, I can now say that I did something in my life...I am proud of what I did out of a sense of humanity. ... I passed through that period, as you cross through a dark forest: with self-assurance and with incredible luck."[587]

Berthold Beitz is singular among these men of conscience. Most either died during World War II and did not receive the recognition due to them or died in poverty or with their name stigmatized. Beitz lived a long, impressive life, to the ripe old age of 99. His lack of Nazi Party ties allowed him to prosper after the war – he was able to get a job in the British zone as an insurance administrator, though he had absolutely no experience in the field. As a good manager always does, he surrounded himself with people who knew a lot more than he did, in this case ex-Nazis with insurance knowledge. Within four years, as general manager of the Iduna-Germania-Versicherungsgesellschaft insurance company, he raised the company from sixth to third in the German insurance industry.

His marriage with Alfried Krupp was one of chance and is considered in German business circles as a strange one. In 1952, while Beitz worked as general manager, he was having a sculpture commissioned for the company's new administrative building in Hamburg. While sitting in the studio of Jean Sprenger, Beitz ran into Alfried Krupp's younger brother Berthold. Beitz invited Sprenger and Krupp for dinner. Berthold Krupp asked Berthold Beitz if he would like to meet Alfried.[588] Beitz said yes and the younger Krupp mentioned it to his brother. Sprenger stepped in and told Alfried that Beitz was "an extraordinary self-made man, aged thirty-seven and the Generaldirektor of an insurance firm. You could do something with him."[589]

At this point, Krupp was in the throes of attempting to get back his empire after John J. McCloy had terminated Krupp's prison sentence and the confiscation of his assets. Sprenger, Alfried and Beitz arranged to have drinks at Sprenger's studio then moved on to the Essener Hof for dinner. Beitz and Krupp became great friends, skiing weekly at Saint Moritz. Alfried and his wife Vera had dinner with Berthold and Else Beitz in Hamburg's Hotel Vier Jahreszeiten. Vera and Else chatted at the bar after dinner and Alfried invited Berthold for a walk along the river Alster. Krupp asked Beitz: "Do you want to come to Essen and help me rebuild the Group?"[590] After talking for fifteen minutes, Beitz agreed. The next year he went to Essen as general manager of the Krupp works, where Alfried gave Berthold a free hand.

The board of directors were told they would follow the orders of nobody except Alfried; and if Beitz joined Krupp, they would follow his orders as well. The company could produce anything, except for arms. The coal and steel holdings must be sold, as per the Allied demands, and the company must remain in family hands. Beitz had his own terms as well – he would be paid DM1 million per year, a very high figure in the early 1950s. Both men agreed to the terms and Beitz took control when his contract with the insurance firm ended.

They were an odd couple – Alfried was afraid of people and liked sitting at Villa Hügel smoking American cigarettes; Berthold was socially adept. An extrovert, he would grate on the personalities in the Krupp management – he insisted on being called Beitz and if he liked you or your work, he would call you by your first name or a nickname. He banned heel-clicking when men entered his office to speak and frowned upon monocles. The worst though, was that Berthold Beitz liked to barbecue: "there were rumors that he presided over arcane "bar-b-q's" wearing an apron decorated with coy slogans, cooking the steaks himself on an outdoor grill, and executing a peculiar little soft-shoe dance."[591]

Barbecuing his own steaks on an outdoor grill, wearing an apron? What a horrible, low standing little man! Of course he didn't get along with the starched collars and stuffed shirts, but he did get along with somebody important – Bertha Krupp. In 1953, shortly after he took command of the company, he proposed having a Christian Dior fashion show at Villa Hügel. Alfried asked his mother and if it came from someone else, the answer would have been "no." But for Berthold Beitz, the matriarch acquiesced. As Beitz told William Manchester years later in his book *The Arms of Krupp*: "That was the day that I realized she was *die grosse (great) Bertha*, not *die dicke (fat) Bertha*. Her greatness was illumined by her sense of humor. She was so amused because the reporters came to look at her, not at the good-looking girls in the show."[592]

There were good years and bad at Krupp after the war. Unfortunately for Alfried, the bad ones came when he was close to death. The company was reeling in poor business decisions, but the worst blow was not from bad business, it was from the tax man. A ruling from German courts removed Krupp's exemption from inheritance taxes as well as from sales taxes it had previously avoided. The two major creditor banks – Dresdner and Deutsche Bank – panicked and the company had to reorganize and request federal loans to continue. On April 1 1967 the company became a public corporation. By July 30, Alfried was dead from lung cancer but not before he made some changes to his will.

Berthold Beitz was no longer on the management board, a casualty of the reorganization. Beitz did serve as one of three executors of Alfried Krupp's will, which proved to be Krupp's last laugh. Whether it was a lack of a great heir – his son Arndt despised the business – or if it was an attack of conscience, all of his money, save for a $500,000 a year stipend to his son – went to form the Alfried Krupp von Bohlen und Halbach Foundation. The foundation held all of Krupp's multi-billion-dollar fortune in a charitable trust. Berthold Beitz was named chairman of the foundation, a position he held for over forty years.

Perhaps Beitz's greatest triumph was when the Israeli Yad Vashem organization awarded him the title *Righteous Among the Nations*, its highest honor for saving the Jews from Nazi extermination. From Yad Vashem's website:

> *Beitz's nomination as Righteous Among the Nations, strongly supported by the great majority of survivors from Boryslaw and its environs (many of whom had kept in contact with their rescuer after the war), was hotly contested by a small minority. The opponents argued that the primary motive was to increase the production capacity of the German armaments industry, that he had acted only in order to line his own pockets with money and, finally, that he had not put himself at any substantial risk in rescuing Jewish workers for the German oil industry.*
>
> *Yet none of these allegations appear to be borne out by the facts of the case.*[593]

Robert Bosch and Hans Walz

Robert Bosch was born in 1861 in Albeck, a village to the northeast of Ulm in southern Germany. After his education, Bosch spent seven years working in Germany, for Thomas Edison in New York and for Siemens in Great Britain. In 1886, he opened *die Werkstätte für Feinmechanik und Elektrotechnik Robert Bosch* (Workshop for Precision Mechanics and Electrical Engineering) in Stuttgart. The next year he was asked to improve a magneto device which would become the basis for modern commerce – the sparkplug.

In World War I, the company switched to armaments production as the needs of the Second Reich required. Robert Bosch was singular to other industrialists – he refused to profit from war materials. By the end of World War I, the company had lost all of its facilities in the Allied countries, but this didn't stop Bosch from donating his war profits to charity – which amounted to RM20 million.

The days of hyperinflation in Germany affected the company like any other – the workforce dropped from 13,000 to 8,000 in just a few months, and even the executives were not immune, with the Vorstand shrinking from eleven members to just three. This rationalization showed Bosch the company had to diversify and during the 1920s the company started manufacturing power tools and by 1933 the first Bosch refrigerators. Also during this time Robert Bosch was politically active. As a liberal businessman, he sat on a number of economic committees. He devoted a great deal of energy and money to the cause of bringing about reconciliation between Germany and France. He hoped this reconciliation would bring about lasting peace in Europe, and lead to the creation of a European economic area. The rise of the Nazis ended his attempts at peacekeeping.

As in World War I, the group had to move to armaments production during the Second World War, a fact which grated on Robert Bosch. Something else which grated on Bosch was Nazism. Bosch was virulently anti-Nazi; he hated what they stood for and along with senior Bosch executives, supported resistance against Hitler and provided those facing persecution with money or help with emigration. One of those executives was Aufsichtsrat member Hans Walz, a member of the *Verein zur Abwehr des Antisemitismus* – the Society to

Combat Anti-Semitism. Walz was a member of both the SS and a member of the Keppler Kreis, Himmler's inner circle, but at the same time financed the emigration of Jews from Germany. Bosch himself became a conduit, being the most vocal industrialist dissenter to National Socialism. People were secretly taken into the company, their religious origins hidden from the Gestapo. The most prominent person given employment by Bosch was Carl Gördeler, the former mayor of Leipzig. Gördeler served as a financial adviser to Bosch, where he could conduct covert actions against the Nazis, including helping to plan the failed coup in July 1944.

In the late 1930s, as Walz realized the futility of engaging in open political activity under a totalitarian system that respected no human value, he dedicated himself – in full agreement with Bosch – to clandestine activities on behalf of persecuted Jews. His most important assistant and co-worker in this was Dr. Karl Adler, a Jewish musical instructor, who, after 1938, took charge of the Jewish Mittelstelle in Stuttgart. The Mittelstelle, originally an adult education institute, became an emigration agency. Between 1938 and 1940, Walz advanced hundreds of thousands of Reichsmarks, which were used to ransom Jewish prisoners from concentration camps and send them across the border. One of the most dramatic incidents occurred in August 1939, when a group of 17 Jews from Köln were prevented from crossing the French border by the Gestapo, which insisted on the payment of an exorbitant sum as ransom money. When the Jews could not raise the money, Adler turned in despair to Walz, and he provided the funds at an hour's notice.[594]

Robert Bosch died of complications from an ear infection in 1942 at the age of 80. His lasting legacy was, like Alfried Krupp, made in his will – the bulk of the company went to the formation of the Robert Bosch Foundation, the rest to the Bosch family. Unlike Alfried Krupp, Robert Bosch had a long history of charitable giving. Bosch drew up his will in 1921, deciding to form a wealth management company. The mission he gave it in 1935 was simple:

It is my intention, apart from the alleviation of all kinds of hardship, to promote the moral, physical and intellectual development of the people[595]

Bosch's giving started early. In 1910, he donated one million marks to the Stuttgart University of Applied Sciences. To put that into perspective, the average manufacturing wage in 1910 was about $10 a week. Based on this figure, this would be a $20 million donation today. (All figures following will be based on current figures.) Robert Bosch continued donating to various causes, including World War I relief in his native city of Stuttgart and the building of a war hospital at the factory site ($7.5 million); a homeopathic hospital and affordable housing ($22 million); the Neckar Canal foundation, a program for gifted children and a homeopathic hospital foundation ($314 million) and $9 million to other various charitable concerns – and this was just during World War I. After the war, Bosch established a foundation to build a hospital in Stuttgart ($89 million) as well as funding Hans Walz to help Jews escape Germany.

Today the Robert Bosch Foundation holds 92.5% of Robert Bosch GmbH common stock and funds over 800 projects, including palliative care, education, science and international relations. In 2013 the foundation granted €68 million to various causes, as well as funding the Robert Bosch Hospital in Stuttgart, the Dr. Margarete Fischer-Bosch Institute for Clinical Pharmacology and the UWC Robert Bosch College, which received €40 million from both the foundation and the company. As with Schindler and Beitz, Hans Walz accepted the Yad Vashem Righteous Among the Nations award in 1969.

Fritz Thyssen

Now here's a man you wouldn't expect on a list of men with conscience. The following facts are true:
- Fritz Thyssen did donate at least 200,000 marks to Adolf Hitler in 1923, then helped to secure a loan for another 300,000 in 1931 to purchase a building to act as offices for the Nazi Party
- Fritz Thyssen did organize a meeting for about 300 industrialists at which Hitler would speak
- Fritz Thyssen did dismiss Jewish employees from the Thyssen works, as required by the Nazis.

But here is also what Thyssen did: he denounced the Reich when he felt Hitler went too far. For Fritz Thyssen, the breaking point was the night Nazi mobs rampaged in 1938, looting and burning Jewish businesses and synagogues and killing Jews. By that point Thyssen, who felt his Catholicism was threatened both as a religion and in a spiritual sense, had enough. Elected to the Reichstag, he was alone when he voted against going to war in Poland. So how does this make Thyssen a man of conscience?

Thyssen left his company and his country behind due to his convictions – in return, he was captured in France and sent first to a sanitarium, then to a concentration camp where he and his wife spent most of the remainder of the war. After Thyssen died, his wife and daughter set up the Fritz Thyssen Foundation in 1959 with DM 100 million worth of Thyssen AG stock. In 2012, the foundation donated €18 million to various causes, mainly in history, language and culture. Yes, Fritz Thyssen was not a model citizen, but at least he had the wherewithal to realize the error of his ways and renounce Nazism and Hitler before it was in vogue – it was easy to say you weren't a Nazi after the war; it was very difficult to say it during the war.

John Rabe

There is an interesting term out there thanks to the work of Iris Chang and her book *The Rape of Nanking*. The term is "Good Nazi" and refers to John Rabe. Rabe was born in Hamburg in 1882 and was managing director of the Siemens offices in Nanjing, China. Though he was a member of the Nazi party, he used this to the benefit of the people of Nanjing once Japanese troops moved in and began the Nanjing Massacre in 1937. He was elected chair of the International Committee for the Nanking Safety Zone, which had the goal of saving Chinese nationals from the marauding Japanese. He used his German citizenship and Nazi party affiliation to save Chinese civilians, some of which he sheltered on his property. He wrote to Hitler: "...there is a question of morality here. I cannot bring myself for now to betray the trust these people have put in me, and it is touching to see how they believe in me."[596] It is estimated his actions saved 200,000 Chinese from the Japanese atrocities. His Nazi credentials were only partially helpful – they managed to delay the Japanese and let thousands of refugees escape the city.

Rabe was recalled to Berlin in 1938 and tried to draw attention to the crimes of the Japanese. He showed films and photographs of the atrocities until he was silenced by the Gestapo. When Siemens intervened, Rabe was released, and worked in Kabul in relative safety from the German authorities. He returned to Berlin and worked at Siemens in Berlin until 1945. After the war, he was called out on his Nazi past and had to go through the "denazification" process. He defended himself vigorously, using his family's savings. Destitute, his family lived on wild seeds the children would eat with soup and on dry bread until that was no longer available either. By 1948, the citizens of Nanjing learned of Rabe's situation and would send a food package to the Rabe family every month until the communist takeover in China.[597]

The truly amazing part about Rabe's story is that it was virtually unknown until the 1990s when Chang's book came out. Imagine if you will, between Rabe and the American doctor Robert Wilson they managed to keep a group of people about the size of Shreveport, Louisiana safe from Japanese soldiers running amok. For six weeks, soldiers raped, pillaged and held killing contests, murdering an estimated 200-300,000 people including men, women and children. Rabe and a group of international businessmen and missionaries set up an International Safety Zone to protect as many people as they could, saving upwards of 200,000 of the population of the city.

Rabe died in 1950 of a stroke. His home in Nanjing has been renovated and made into the John Rabe House at Nanjing University thanks to donations from his employer Siemens. There you can view the diary he kept at the time as well as other exhibitions relating to the Nanjing Massacre.

Conclusion

What was at first very troubling about this whole exercise was a nagging question: why did American government officials agree to release these criminals back into the mainstream? After the end of World War II, it became evident to the Western Allies that the Soviet Union was embarking on a communist manifest destiny. With the threat of communism on the horizon in the Far East coming not just from the Soviets, but also Mao Zedong in China, the British and Americans decided it was better to have a buffer in Europe from an encroaching Soviet sphere of influence. The most obvious buffer was the newly-created West Germany, but it would be ineffective if it was a poor, failed economy. Therefore, West Germany had to rise from the ashes of World War II and it couldn't do that without the right people in charge.

When I first started researching this book, I was angered and outraged at what I saw – former Nazis, some of whom sent Jews to the gas chambers at Auschwitz, Birkenau and Sachsenhausen as well as stolen their property, were now free and able to take their old jobs as the heads of large multinationals. Had they paid their debt to society? Of course not, but society needed them, and just like those bad Hollywood movies where the federal agents would go to a prison and extract a notorious villain because he needed to save the world, so did the thinking go in 1951 when the likes of Fritz ter Meer and Hermann Schmitz of IG Farben were released and went on to be the chair of Bayer AG and on the board of Deutsche Bank respectively.

The other reason many of these men made it out of prison so early was the Allies realized the error of the Versailles Treaty, and the damage it did to Germany after the First World War. It would be much easier for these powers to let a couple of penny-ante Nazis out of jail then it would to have an uprising in Germany in 20 years' time, or even worse, for the country to feel the pull of communism and join the Warsaw Pact of countries. Basically, a strong Germany is a safe Germany (at least safe for everyone outside of Germany).

NOTES

[1] John Maynard Keynes. *The Economic Consequences of the Peace*. (New York: Harcourt, Brace and Howe, 1920), Chapter V. Reparation. eBook.
[2] Ibid.
[3] Ibid.
[4] Ibid.
[5] United States Holocaust Memorial Museum. "ADOLF HITLER AND WORLD WAR I: 1913–1919," retrieved August 13, 2014. www.ushmm.org, retrieved August 13, 2014
[6] PBS. "Interview: Ford's Anti-Semitism," retrieved September 24, 2014. www.pbs.org/wgbh/americanexperience/features/interview/henryford-antisemitism.
[7] Martin Luther. *On the Jews and Their Lies*. 1543.
[8] Antony C. Sutton. *Wall Street & the Rise of Hitler*. (Forest Row: Clairview Books, 2012), Chapter 6. eBook.
[9] Bob Carruthers (ed). *I Knew Hitler*. (Coda Books Ltd., Warwickshire, 2011)
[10] Neil Baldwin. *Henry Ford and the Jews: The Mass Production of Hate*. (Cambridge: Public Affairs, 2001), p186.
[11] David Noon. "Happy Birthday, Mr. Ford. Love, Adolf," *The Chronicle of Higher Education*, chronicle.com, July 30, 2008, retrieved May 19, 2014.
[12] Adolf Hitler (translation by John Chamberlain et al.). *Mein Kampf*. (New York: Raynal & Hitchcock, 1941), p654.
[13] Ford Germany. "Ein Auto für alle – von Ford." Zeitleiste. retrieved September 12, 2016 http://www.ford.de/UeberFord/FordinDeutschland/Geschichte.
[14] Michael Dobbs. "Ford and GM Scrutinized for Alleged Nazi Collaboration," *The Washington Post*, November 30, 1998, pA01.
[15] Simon Reich. *Research Findings about Ford Werke under the Nazi Regime*. (Dearborn: Ford Motor Company Archive, 2001), p35.
[16] Elsa Iwanowa, et al v. FORD MOTOR COMPANY and Ford Werke A.G., Defendants. United States District Court, D. New Jersey, October 28, 1999.
[17] Ken Silverstein. "Ford and the Führer." *The Nation*, January 24, 2000, retrieved October 19 2016. https://www.thenation.com/article/ford-and-fuhrer/
[18] Silverstein. "Ford and the Führer."
[19] Silverstein. "Ford and the Führer."
[20] Max Wallace. *The American Axis*. (New York: St. Martin's Press, 2003), p226.
[21] Ibid, p227.
[22] Ibid, p229.
[23] Ibid, p231.
[24] John Cunningham Wood et al. (ed). *Henry Ford: Critical Evaluations in Business and Management, Volume 1*. (London: Routledge, 2003), p131.
[25] Wallace, *American Axis*, p233.
[26] Reich, *about Ford Werke*, p37.
[27] Wallace, *American Axis*, p235.

[28] Reich, *about Ford Werke,* p88.
[29] Ibid.
[30] Wallace, *American Axis,* p237.
[31] Charles Higham. *Trading with the Enemy.* (New York: Delacorte Press, 1983), p156.
[32] Convention relative to the Treatment of Prisoners of War Part III, Section III, Article 31. Geneva: July 27, 1929.
[33] Reich, *about Ford Werke,* piv.
[34] Reich, *about Ford Werke,* p89.
[35] Wallace, *American Axis,* p347.
[36] Edwin Black. "Hitler's Carmaker: The Inside Story of How General Motors Helped Mobilize the Third Reich." *History News Network,* May 14, 2007, retrieved June 15, 2014. http://historynewsnetwork.org/article/37935
[37] John Cunningham Wood (ed). *Alfred P. Sloan: Critical Evaluations in Business and Management.* (London: Routledge, 2003), p354.
[38] *The New York Times.* "Alfred P. Sloan Jr. Dead at 90; G.M. Leader and Philanthropist," February 18, 1966, retrieved August 16, 2014 www.nytimes.com/learning/general/onthisday/bday
[39] Rodney Dutcher. "'Red' Menace Remains, Some Say." *The Tuscaloosa News,* February 27, 1930, p4.
[40] Dobbs. *Ford and GM Scrutinized*
[41] Black. *Hitler's Carmaker*
[42] Anita Kugler et al. *Working for the Enemy.* (New York: Bergahn Books, 2000), p43.
[43] "THIRTY-SECOND ANNUAL REPORT OF General Motors Corporation YEAR ENDED DECEMBER 31, 1940." p14.
[44] Harry Schneiderman. "REVIEW OF THE YEAR 5693." *American Jewish Year Book Vol. 35* (1933-1934), p29.
[45] David Hayward. "Mr. James A Mooney – A Man of Missions." www.gmhistory.chevytalk.org, retrieved August 8, 2014.
[46] Kugler. *Working for the Enemy,* p39.
[47] Dobbs. *Ford and GM Scrutinized*
[48] Hayward. *Mr. James A Mooney*
[49] "Statement of Bradford C. Snell before the United States Senate Subcommittee on Antitrust and Monopoly." February 26, 1974, p4.
[50] Henry Ashby Turner. *General Motors and the Nazis.* London: Yale University Press, 2005), p127.
[51] Turner, *General Motors,* p132.
[52] Turner, *General Motors,* p145.
[53] Yuji Nisimuta. "General Motors Corporation as an Armaments Producer." *The Ritsumeikan Economic Review (Vol. 61, No. 5),* (Kyoto: Kyoto University), p188.
[54] Nisimuta, *General Motors,* p197.
[55] THIRTY-FIRST ANNUAL REPORT OF GENERAL MOTORS CORPORATION, YEAR ENDED DECEMBER 31, 1939, p23.
[56] Nisimuta, *General Motors,* p186.

[57] Turner, *General Motors,* p152.
[58] Wood. *Alfred P. Sloan*, p382.
[59] Beth Hale. "Max Mosley turns on BMW and Mercedes over their role in WWII as 'Nazi orgy' row escalates." *Daily Mail,* www.dailymail.co.uk, April 4, 2008, retrieved September 11, 2016.
[60] Dennis Adler. *Daimler & Benz: The Complete History*. (New York: Harper Collins, 2006), p79.
[61] BMW. "The history of BMW aero engines." www.bmwgroup.com, September 8, 2008, retrieved April 20, 2014.
[62] Bernard Bellon, as quoted by Herbert Mittgang. "Books of The Times: Daimler-Benz and Its Nazi History." *New York Times*, August 23, 1990.
[63] Ibid.
[64] "May 28, 1937: Volkswagen is founded." www.history.com, retrieved May 2, 2014.
[65] Dietmar Hawranek. "Designing Cars for Hitler: Porsche and Volkswagen's Nazi Roots." *Der Spiegel*, www.spiegel.de, July 21, 2009, retrieved May 5, 2014.
[66] Frederic F Clairmont. "Volkswagen's history of forced labour." *Le Monde diplomatique*, www.mondediplo.com January 11, 1998, retrieved May 5, 2014.
[67] Volkswagen Aktien Gesellschaft Corporate History Department. *Place of Remembrance of Forced Labor in the Volkswagen Factory*, (Hildesheim: Quensen Druck + Verlag GmbH, 1999), p37.
[68] "MUNICH-ALLACH: WORKING FOR BMW." www.ausstellung-zwangsarbeit.org, retrieved May 8, 2014.
[69] Volkswagen Aktien Gesellschaft, p42.
[70] Ibid, p45.
[71] Ibid, p72.
[72] Ibid, p54.
[73] Ibid, p109.
[74] "Porsche und die Geheimsache Kirschkern." *Der Speigel*, April 13, 1987, p91.
[75] Volkswagen Aktien Gesellschaft, p59.
[76] Ibid, p84.
[77] Michael J. Neufeld. "Mittelbau: Conditions." www.ushmm.org, retrieved May 16, 2014.
[78] Andrea Hiott. *Thinking Small: The Long, Strange Trip of the Volkswagen Beetle*. (New York: Random House, 2012), p179.
[79] Bellon, quoted by Mittgang. *New York Times*.
[80] BMW. "Milestones – 1942." www.bmwgroup.com, retrieved May 12, 2014.
[81] Daimler. "Daimler-Benz in the Nazi Era (1933-1945)." www.daimler.com, retrieved May 10, 2014.
[82] Mark Pendergrast. *For God, Country & Coca-Cola*. (New York: Basic Books, 2013), Chapter 13 Coca-Cola Uber Alles, e-book
[83] Ibid.
[84] Coca Cola. "Made in Germany – Fanta ist eine Erfindung aus Essen." www.coca-cola-deutschland.de, retrieved September 5, 2014

[85] Brian Palmer. "Why Do Foreigners Like Fanta So Much?" www.slate.com, August 5, 2010, retrieved June 16, 2014.
[86] Barbara Mikkelson. "The Reich Stuff?" www.snopes.com, April 29, 2011, retrieved June 16, 2014.
[87] "Jews in America: The Kashering of Coca-Cola(1935)" www.jewishvirtuallibrary.org, retrieved June 21, 2014.
[88] Pamela E. Swett et al (ed). *Selling Modernity: Advertising in Twentieth-Century Germany*, (Durham, NC: Duke University Press, 2007), p166.
[89] Pendergrast, *For God,* Chapter 13.
[90] Ibid.
[91] Evan Burr Bukey. *Hitler's Austria: Popular Sentiment in the Nazi Era, 1938-1945*. (Chapel Hill, NC: University of North Carolina Press, 2000), p21.
[92] "KRISTALLNACHT: A NATIONWIDE POGROM, NOVEMBER 9–10, 1938." www.ushmm.org, retrieved June 21, 2014.
[93] "Reichenberger Synagoge in Flammen." *Reichenberger Stadtzeitung*, November 11, 1938, p1.
[94] Pendergrast, *For God,* Chapter 13.
[95] Ibid.
[96] Ibid.
[97] Ibid.
[98] Nestle. www.company-histories.com, retrieved June 28, 2014.
[99] Jean-François Bergier et al. *Final Report of the Independent Commission of Experts Switzerland – Second World War*. (Zürich: Pendo Verlag GmbH, 2002), p294.
[100] Ibid, p300.
[101] Ibid, p315.
[102] Ibid, p319.
[103] Ibid, p298.
[104] Ibid, p302.
[105] Ibid, p328.
[106] Ibid, p297.
[107] Ibid, p335.
[108] Nestlé Historical Archives, *Report from the managing director to the board of directors*, meeting held on 8 September 1938, document no. 2511 (original French).
[109] Ben Wubs. "Guns and margarine. Or how the Nazis disliked margarine, but could not afford to attack the Dutch Margarine Trust." (Glasgow: 14th Annual Conference EBHA, August 26-28, 2010), p9.
[110] Ibid, p16.
[111] Ibid, p18.
[112] Ibid, p21.
[113] Ben Wubs. *International Business and National War Interests: Unilever Between Reich and Empire 1939-1945*, (New York: Routledge, 2008), p115.
[114] Christian Ignatzi. "Another German company reveals its Nazi past" *Deutsche Welle*, dw.de, October 22, 2013, retrieved August 21, 2014.
[115] "Was für ein Mann." *Der Spiegel*, September 30, 1968, p80.

[116] David de Jong. "Nazi-Forged Fortune Creates Hidden German Billionaires." *Bloomberg*, Bloomberg.com, Feb 3, 2014, retrieved August 6, 2014.
[117] Tian Kang Go. *American Commercial Banks in Corporate Finance, 1929-1941: A Study in Banking Concentration*. (New York: Routledge, 2011), p88.
[118] "Display Ad 9." New York Times, May 16, 1892, p.7.
[119] "Banks' Stock List Full of Surprises." *New York Times*, September 23, 1914.
[120] Barbara W. Tuchman. *The Zimmermann Telegram*. (New York: NEL Mentor, 1967), p72.
[121] H.R. Balkhage and A.A. Hahling. "The Black Tom Explosion." *The American Legion Magazine*, August 1964.
[122] Michael J. Sulick. *Spying In America: Espionage from the Revolutionary War to the Dawn of the Cold War*. (Washington: Georgetown University Press, 2012), Chapter 13.
[123] Franz von Rintelen. *The Dark Invader: War-Time Reminiscences of a German Naval Intelligence Officer*, (Harmondsworth, UK: Penguin, 1936), e-book.
[124] Letter from Mississippi Valley Trust Co., St. Louis, to L. de la Garza & Co., Inc., New York. 1915, September 16
[125] Antony C. Sutton. *Wall Street and the Bolshevik Revolution: The Remarkable True Story of the American Capitalists who Funded the Russian Communists,* (Cutchogue, NY: Buccaneer Books, 2007), p56
[126] National Archives and Records Administration. *Zimmermann Telegram - Decoded Message*. Record Group 59: General Records of the Department of State, 1756 – 1979.
[127] Sutton. *Bolshevik Revolution*, p56
[128] "TRUE CONDITION OF RUSSIA'S FINANCES." *The Americas (Vol. 3, No. 5*, February, 1916, National City Rank of New York.
[129] Ron Chernow. *The House of Morgan: An American Banking Dynasty and the Rise of Modern Finance*. (New York: Atlantic Monthly Press, 1990), p188.
[130] Ibid, p189.
[131] Ibid, p185.
[132] Ibid, p249.
[133] Ibid.
[134] Ibid, p250.
[135] Ibid, p251.
[136] Ibid, p208.
[137] Ibid, p208.
[138] "The Dawes Plan, the Young Plan, German Reparations, and Inter-allied War Debts." *US Department of State Archive, 2001-2009*.state.gov, retrieved September 25, 2014.
[139] Chernow, p395.
[140] Ibid, p394.
[141] Ibid, p214.
[142] "Guaranty Trust Reopens in Paris." *New York Times*, Mar. 3, 1945

[143] "World: Europe US banks gave Jewish money to Nazis." *BBC World Service*, news.bbc.co.uk, February 3, 1999, retrieved May 30, 2014.
[144] Michael Bazyler. *Holocaust Justice: The Battle for Restitution in America's Courts*, (New York: New York University Press, 2003), p186.
[145] Herbert R. Reginbogin. *Faces of neutrality: a comparative analysis of the neutrality of Switzerland and other neutral nations during WW II*, (New Jersey: Transaction Publishers, 2009), p182.
[146] Bazyler. *Holocaust Justice*, p186.
[147] Chernow, p453.
[148] Ibid.
[149] "Thousands of Intelligence Documents Opened under the Nazi War Crimes Disclosure Act." *US National Archives, Media Release*, www.archives.gov, May 13, 2004, retrieved June 1, 2014.
[150] Richard Breitman et al. *U.S. Intelligence and the Nazis*. (Cambridge: Cambridge University Press, 2005), p182.
[151] "Custodial Detention Headquarters."8-17.
[152] Breitman, p188.
[153] Frank Allan Southard. *American Industry in Europe*. (New York: Routledge, 2000), p87.
[154] Jonathan D. Salant. "Newly Unclassified US Documents: Bush Ancestor's Bank Seized by Gov't." *Associated Press*, October 18, 2003.
[155] "Memo to John Pehle from E. G. May." August 14, 1941.
[156] Fernande Bodner, et al., v. BANQUE PARIBAS, et al., Defendants. Anne Marie Benisti, et al., v. Banque Paribas, et al., Defendants. Nos. 97 CV 7433(SJ), 98 CV 7851(SJ). United States District Court, E.D. New York. August 31, 2000.
[157] Stuart E. Eizenstat. *Imperfect Justice*. (Cambridge MA: Perseus Book Group, 2004), p319.
[158] Yad Vashem. "Vallat, Xavier" www.yadvashem.org/odot_pdf/Microsoft%20Word%20-%206334.pdf, retrieved September 18 2016.
[159] Jean Mattéoli. *Summary of the work by the Study Mission on the spoliation of Jews in France*. (Clinton Presidential Library, www.clintonlibrary.gov, 2000), p10.
[160] Eizenstat, *Imperfect Justice,* p335.
[161] Mattéoli, *Study Mission,* p24.
[162] Antony Barnett. "Holocaust shame of Barclays." *The Guardian*, www.theguardian.com, March 28, 1999, retrieved June 15, 2014.
[163] Ibid.
[164] C. S. Duncan. *Statement of Barclays Bank PLC before the Committee on Banking and Financial Services of the United States House of Representatives*. September 14, 1999, p8.
[165] Duncan, *Barclays Bank,* p13.
[166] Duncan, *Barclays Bank,* p17.
[167] "Business: The Company File: Barclays to compensate Jews.' *BBC Online*, bbc.co.uk, December 17, 1998, retrieved June 8, 2014.

[168] James Calvin Baker. *The Bank for International Settlements: Evolution and Evaluation*. (Westport CT: Quorum Books, 2002), p214.
[169] Ibid.
[170] Bergier et al. *Final Report – Switzerland*, p255.
[171] Scott B. MacDonald, Albert L. Gastmann. *A History of Credit and Power in the Western World*. (New Brunswick, NJ: Transaction Publishers, 2009), p179.
[172] Bergier, *Final Report – Switzerland*, p249.
[173] Ibid, p250.
[174] Ibid, p267.
[175] Ibid, p270.
[176] Ibid.
[177] Ibid, p275.
[178] Ibid, p276.
[179] Ibid, p271.
[180] Ibid, p273.
[181] The International Petroleum Cartel, *Staff Report to the Federal Trade Commission, released through Subcommittee on Monopoly of Select Committee on Small Business*, U.S. Senate, 83d Cong., 2nd sess (Washington, DC, 1952), Chapter 4, "Joint Control Through Common Ownership--The Iraq Petroleum Co., Ltd.," pp. 47-112
[182] Jürgen Fitschen. *A Century of Deutsche Bank in Turkey*, Deutsche Bank, 2009.
[183] Office of the Military Government for Germany (OMGUS). *Report on the Investigation of the Deutsche Bank*. (Washington: National Archives and Records Administration), November 1946, p49.
[184] "Dresdner Bank, The." *The Encyclopedia Americana* (1920), p398.
[185] Prof. Dr. Manfred Pohl. *Bank and History Historical Circular*. (Frankfurt am Main: Historical Association of Deutsche Bank), June 2003, p3.
[186] Office of Military Government for Germany (US), Finance Division. *Report on the Investigation of the Commerzbank*. (Washington: National Archives and Records Administration, September 1947), p6.
[187] OMGUS Commerzbank, p13.
[188] Detlef Krause. "Friedrich Ludwig Reinhart." deutsche-biographie.de, retrieved July 12, 2014.
[189] Frederick L. Schuman. *Hitler and the Nazi Dictatorship*. (London: Robert Hale & Company,1936), p470.
[190] OMGUS Commerzbank, p25.
[191] OMGUS Commerzbank, p71.
[192] Daniel Uziel. *Arming the Luftwaffe: The German Aviation Industry in World War II*, (McFarland & Company, Jefferson, NC, 2012), p264.
[193] OMGUS Commerzbank, p72.
[194] OMGUS Commerzbank, p78.
[195] Office of Military Government for Germany (US), Finance Division. *Report on the Investigation of the Dresdner Bank*, (Washington: National Archives and Records Administration, 1946), p87.
[196] OMGUS Dresdner Bank, p88.

[197] OMGUS Deutsche Bank, p2.
[198] OMGUS Deutsche Bank, p16.
[199] OMGUS Deutsche Bank, p39
[200] Nils Klawitter. "Reemtsmas ZwangsarbeiterTabakrausch im Osten." *Der Speigel*, www.spiegel.de, August 23, 2011, retrieved July 2, 2014.
[201] Office of Strategic Services. *Biographical Report on Albert Pietzsch*. (Washington: National Archives and Records Administration, April 18, 1945), p2.
[202] OMGUS Deutsche Bank, p136.
[203] OMGUS Deutsche Bank, p142.
[204] OMGUS Deutsche Bank, p145.
[205] OMGUS Deutsche Bank, p45.
[206] Harold James. *The Deutsche Bank and the Nazi Economic War against the Jews*. (Cambridge: Cambridge Univesity Press, 2004), p30.
[207] OMGUS Deutsche Bank, p50.
[208] OMGUS Deutsche Bank, p172.
[209] Gian Trepp. "Bankier des Holocaust." *Die Zeit Online*, www.zeit.de, December 31, 1998, retrieved July 7, 2014.
[210] Jonathan Steinberg. *The Deutsche Bank and Its Gold Transactions During the Second World War*. (Munchen: Verlag C. H. Beck, 1999), p61.
[211] OMGUS Deutsche Bank, p63.
[212] OMGUS Deutsche Bank, p80.
[213] OMGUS Deutsche Bank, p99.
[214] OMGUS Deutsche Bank, p133.
[215] OMGUS Deutsche Bank, p136.
[216] 1944 Annual Report, Commerz- und Privat-Bank, p4
[217] OMGUS Deutsche Bank, p118.
[218] OMGUS Deutsche Bank, p122.
[219] OMGUS Deutsche Bank, p125.
[220] OMGUS Commerzbank, p32.
[221] OMGUS Deutsche Bank. p128.
[222] 1934 Annual Report, Commerz- und Privat-Bank, p11
[223] 1936 Annual Report, Commerz- und Privat-Bank, p13.
[224] 1938 Annual Report, Commerz- und Privat-Bank, p9
[225] 1940 Annual Report, Commerz- und Privat-Bank, p11.
[226] 1942 Annual Report, Commerz- und Privat-Bank, p4.
[227] 1944 Annual Report, Commerz- und Privat-Bank, p4.
[228] OMGUS Deutsche Bank, p129.
[229] OMGUS Deutsche Bank, p161.
[230] OMGUS Deutsche Bank, p162.
[231] OMGUS Deutsche Bank, p164.
[232] OMGUS Deutsche Bank, p263.
[233] OMGUS Deutsche Bank, p297.
[234] OMGUS Deutsche Bank, p306.
[235] OMGUS Commerzbank, p19.
[236] OMGUS Commerzbank, p35.

[237] OMGUS Deutsche Bank, p187
[238] "The Central Bank during the Third Reich." *Oesterreichische Nationalbank*, www.oenb.at, retrieved September 10, 2014.
[239] OMGUS Dresdner Bank, p90
[240] OMGUS Deutsche Bank, p196
[241] OMGUS Deutsche Bank, p199.
[242] OMGUS Deutsche Bank, p199.
[243] OMGUS Dresdner Bank, p99
[244] "DRESDNER BANK A.G. - Company Profile, Information, Business Description, History, Background Information." www.referenceforbusiness.com, retrieved July 19, 2014.
[245] OMGUS Deutsche Bank, p236.
[246] OMGUS Deutsche Bank, p237.
[247] Francis R. Nicosia (ed). *Business and Industry in Nazi Germany*. (Vermont: Berghahn Books, 2004), p54
[248] OMGUS Deutsche Bank, p239
[249] OMGUS Dresdner Bank, p116
[250] OMGUS Dresdner Bank, p120.
[251] OMGUS Deutsche Bank, p250.
[252] OMGUS Dresdner Bank, p122
[253] OMGUS Dresdner Bank, p153
[254] OMGUS Dresdner Bank, p126.
[255] OMGUS Dresdner Bank, p154.
[256] OMGUS Dresnder Bank, p17.
[257] OMGUS Dresdner Bank, p156
[258] OMGUS Commerzbank, p58
[259] OMGUS Deutsche Bank, p232
[260] OMGUS Deutsche Bank, p254
[261] OMGUS Deutsche Bank, p222.
[262] OMGUS Dresdner Bank, p128.
[263] OMGUS Dresdner Bank, p128
[264] OMGUS Dresdner Bank, p129
[265] OMGUS Dresdner Bank, p130
[266] Jacob Presser. *Ashes in the Wind: The Destruction of Dutch Jewry*. (Detroit: Wayne State University Press, 1988), p366.
[267] OMGUS Dresdner Bank, p141
[268] OMGUS Dresdner Bank, p143.
[269] OMGUS Dresdner Bank, p145.
[270] OMGUS Dresdner Bank, p146
[271] OMGUS Dresdner Bank, p147
[272] OMGUS Dresdner Bank, p.150
[273] OMGUS Dresdner Bank, p149
[274] OMGUS Finance Division Records, *Investigations of Reichs-Kredits-Gesellschaft*, Reports, Exhibits and Annex, 1945-1949, p129
[275] OMGUS Commerzbank, p57
[276] OMGUS Deutsche Bank, p169

[277] OMGUS Dresdner Bank, p170
[278] OMGUS Dresdner Bank, p163
[279] OMGUS Deutsche Bank, p225
[280] OMGUS Deutsche Bank, p228
[281] Christian Leitz. *Nazi Foreign Policy, 1933-1941: The Road to Global War*. (New York: Routledge, 2004), p118
[282] Götz Aly. *Hitler's Beneficiaries*. (New York: Metropolitan Books, 2005), p49
[283] Aly, *Hitler's Beneficiaries*, p50
[284] OMGUS Dresdner Bank, p78.
[285] Herman G. Kleikamp. United States Third Army Screening Center, re: Georg Eidenschink, No 6-6411, September 21, 1945
[286] OMGUS Dresdner Bank, p80
[287] Ibid.
[288] OMGUS Dresdner Bank, p81
[289] OMGUS Dresdner Bank, p82
[290] OMGUS Dresdner Bank, p104
[291] OMGUS Dresdner Bank, p107
[292] Ibid
[293] OMGUS Dresdner Bank, p111
[294] OMGUS Dresdner Bank, p112
[295] Mario R. Dederichs. *Heydrich: The Face of Evil*. (Drexel Hill, PA: Casemate, 2009), p 92
[296] OMGUS Dresdner Bank, p110
[297] OMGUS Dresdner Bank, p113
[298] OMGUS Dresdner Bank, p131
[299] OMGUS Dresdner Bank, p134
[300] OMGUS Dresdner Bank, p135
[301] OMGUS Dresdner Bank, p136.
[302] OMGUS Deutsche Bank, p151
[303] Ibid
[304] OMGUS Deutsche Bank, p153
[305] OMGUS Reichs-Kredit-Gesellschaft, p14.
[306] OMGUS Commerzbank, p51.
[307] OMGUS Commerzbank, p54
[308] Ibid
[309] OMGUS Commerzbank, p55
[310] Werner M. Loval. *We Were Europeans: A Personal History of a Turbulent Century*. (Jerusalem: Gefen Publishing House, 2010), p167
[311] Brandon Mitchener. "Deutsche Bank Admits It Helped Hitler: Confronting a Dark Past." *New York Times*, nytimes.com, February 22, 1995, retrieved July 13, 2014
[312] Harold James. *The Expropriation of Jewish-Owned Property*, (Cambridge: Cambridge University Press, 2001), p2
[313] OMGUS Dresdner Bank, p84.
[314] OMGUS Dresdner Bank, p85

[315] OMGUS Dresdner Bank, p185
[316] Steinberg, *Deutsche Bank and Its Gold Transactions,* p14
[317] Ibid, p15
[318] Ibid, p18
[319] OMGUS Deutsche Bank, p22
[320] Brian Connell (trans). *Franz von Papen Memoirs*. (New York: E. P. Dutton & Company, 1953), p279
[321] "Nazi Spy Ring in Germany." *The Argus*, Melbourne, August 2, 1944, p16
[322] Dieter Pohl. "Hans Krueger and the Murder of the Jews in the Stanislawow Region (Galicia)." *Yad Vashem*. www.yadvashem.org, retrieved July 18, 2014
[323] OMGUS Deutsche Bank, p233
[324] Allianz. "Allianz During the Nazi Era." 1933-1945.allianz.com, retrieved July 30, 2014.
[325] Gerald D. Feldman. *Allianz and the German Insurance Business, 1933-1945*, (Cambridge, Cambridge University Press, 2001), p191
[326] Hannah Arendt. *Eichmann in Jerusalem: A Report on the Banality of Evil*, (Toronto: Penguin Books, 2006), p227
[327] Feldman, *Allianz,* p193
[328] Ibid, p194
[329] Allianz. "The meeting at the Ministry of Aviation on November 12, 1938.", 1933-1945.allianz.com, retrieved August 10, 2014
[330] Ibid, p204
[331] Ibid, p205
[332] Ibid, p209
[333] Ibid
[334] Ibid, p219
[335] Ibid, p228
[336] Ibid, p237
[337] Ibid, p243
[338] Emil Lang. *Interrogation of Dr. Kurt Schmitt*. NARA, OMGUS Finance Division Records Regarding Investigations and Interrogations, 1945-1949 July 9, 1947, p4
[339] Ibid, p6
[340] Feldman, *Allianz,* p437
[341] Gerald Feldman. *The Allianz Concern and Its Leaders, 1918–1933*. Cambridge University Press Excerpt, p7
[342] Feldman, *Allianz,* p262
[343] Allianz. "The confiscation of life insurance policies." 1933-1945.allianz.com, retrieved August 16, 2014
[344] Allianz. "Jewish employees at Allianz." 1933-1945.allianz.com, retrieved August 16, 2014
[345] Allianz. "Max Beier: Business canvasser and member of the SS." 1933-1945.allianz.com, retrieved August 15 2014.
[346] Von Wiegrefe. "Das Wagnis Auschwitz." *Der Spiegel 23/1997*, June 2, 1997
[347] Feldman, *Allianz,* p393

[348] Allianz. "Herbert Hansmeyer at the Washington Conference on Holocaust-Era Assets 1998," www.allianz.com, Retrieved August 8, 2014
[349] "AEG AG." www.brittanica.com, retrieved March 19, 2014
[350] Josephine Young Case et al. *Owen D. Young and American Enterprise: A Biography.* (Boston: David R. Godine, Publisher Inc., 1982), p838
[351] Hans Pohl (ed). *Competition and Cooperation of Enterprises on National and International Markets.* (Stuttgart: Steiner, 1997), p28
[352] Harm Schröter. "A typical Factor of German International Market Strategy: Agreements between the US and German Electro-technical Industries up to 1939." *Multinational Enterprise in Historical Perspective.* (Cambridge: Cambridge University Press, 1986), p166
[353] M.L. Flaningam. "International Co-operation and Control in the Electrical Industry: The General Electric Company and Germany, 1919–1944," *American Journal of Economics & Sociology 5.1* (Oct. 1945): p7–25
[354] Sutton, *Wall Street and the Rise of Hitler,* p56
[355] Flaningam, *International Co-operation,* p18–22
[356] John A. Miller. *Men and Volts at War: The Story of General Electric in World War II.* (New York: Whittlesey House, 1947), 220–232
[357] *American Bar Association Journal.* September 1952, p797
[358] UNITED STATES v. GENERAL ELECTRIC CO. et al., District Court, S. D. New York, April 18, 1941
[359] Mildred Gwin Andrews. *Tungsten: The Story of an Indispensable Metal.* (Washington: The Tungsten Institute, 1955), p11-14
[360] "Monopoly Problem May Get Airing if US Wins General Electric Case." *The Gazette and Daily,* York, PA. January 28 1947, p28
[361] Benjamin B. Ferencz. *Less Than Slaves: Jewish Forced Labor and the Quest for Compensation.* (Bloomington, IN: Indiana University Press, 1979), p106
[362] Ibid, p107
[363] Ibid
[364] Ibid, p108
[365] Ibid, p109
[366] Ibid, p108
[367] Geoffrey P. Megargee (ed). *The United States Holocaust Memorial Museum Encyclopedia of Camps and Ghettos, 1933-1945.* (Bloomington, IN: Indiana University Press, 2009), p1316
[368] Ibid
[369] Werner von Siemens. *Personal recollections of Werner von Siemens,* (London: Asher & Co., 1893), p20, ebook
[370] "Minutes of conference April 6, 1933." Records of the External Assets Investigation Section of the Property Division, OMGUS, 1945-1949, Reports and Exhibits Relating to Investigations, compiled 1948 - 1948, documenting the period 1931 – 1948, Siemens And Halske AG (Exhibits 71-90)
[371] "Excerpt from letter." Records of the External Assets Investigation Section of the Property Division, OMGUS, 1945-1949, NARA M1922, Siemens and Halske AG (Exhibits 91-117)

[372] "Exhibit 98." Records of the External Assets Investigation Section of the Property Division, OMGUS, 1945-1949, NARA M1922, Siemens and Halske AG (Exhibits 91-117)
[373] Richard S. Levy (ed). *Antisemitism: A Historical Encyclopedia of Prejudice and Persecution, Volume 1*, (Santa Barbara CA: ABC-CLIO Inc., 2005), p258
[374] Aubrey Pomerance (trans). "Letter to Flora Meyer from Carl Friedrich von Siemens." March 17, 1933
[375] Ibid
[376] "Der liebe Gott von Siemens." *Der Spiegel*, www.spiegel.de, March 8, 1947, retrieved August 21, 2014
[377] Tanja von Fransecky. *Zwangsarbeit in der Berliner Metallindustrie 1939 bis 1945: Eine Firmenübersicht*. (Berlin: Otto Brenner Stiftung, 2003), p87
[378] Peter Hohnen et al. *The Wolf: How One German Raider Terrorized the Allies in the Most Epic Voyage of WWI*. (New York: Simon & Schuster, 2010), p296
[379] Siemens. "The National Socialist economy and the war years (1933-1945)." www.siemens.com, retrieved April 15, 2014
[380] Megargee, *Holocaust Memorial Museum*, p398
[381] Rosa Luxemburg Stiftung. "Siemens & Halske im Frauenkonzentrationslager Ravensbrück." www.rosalux.de, May/June 2000, retrieved August 20 2014
[382] "Hermann von Siemens, Director of German Concern for 27 Years." *New York Times*. www.nytimes.com, October 15, 1986, retrieved July 31, 2014
[383] Leonard Dorn. *Guide for Investigation of Siemens & Halske Aktiengesellschaft Berlin, Germany*. (New York: Department of Justice Economic Warfare Section, 1945), p41
[384] Siemens. "The National Socialist economy and the war years (1933-1945)." http://www.siemens.com/history/en/history/1933_1945_the_national_socialist_economy_and_the_war_years.htm, retrieved April 15, 2014
[385] Hermann Langbein. *People in Auschwitz*. (Chapel Hill NC: University of North Carolina Press, 2004), p459
[386] Megargee, *Holocaust Memorial Museum*, p228
[387] Ibid, p229
[388] Ferencz, *Less Than Slaves*, p117
[389] Siemens. The National Socialist economy and the war years (1933 - 1945). http://www.siemens.com/history/en/history/1933_1945_the_national_socialist_economy_and_the_war_years.htm, retrieved October 4, 2016.
[390] Ibid. "Chairmen of the Managing Board." www.siemens.com, retrieved April 15, 2014
[391] Richard J. Evans. *The Third Reich in Power*. (New York: Penguin, 2005), p397
[392] OMGUS Deutsche Bank, p327
[393] Bernhard Menne. *Blood and Steel: The Rise of the House of Krupp*. (New York: Lee Furman Inc., 1938), The first ironworks, ebook
[394] "Krupp, Friedrich." *The New International Encyclopædia*, 1905 edition.

[395] Jay Scriba. "His House Was Built on War." *Milwaukee Journal,* April 19, 1967, p12
[396] Ibid
[397] William Manchester. *The Arms of Krupp*. (Boston: Little, Brown & Company, 1968), p190
[398] Thomas K. McCraw (ed). *Creating Modern Capitalism: How Entrepreneurs, Companies, and Countries Triumphed in Three Industrial Revolutions*. (Cambridge, MA: Harvard University Press, 1998), p193
[399] Scriba, *His House Was Built on War,* p12
[400] Manchester, *The Arms of Krupp* p249
[401] Jeffrey R. Fear. *Organizing Control: August Thyssen and the Construction of German Corporate Management*. Cambridge, MA: Harvard University Press, 2005, p63
[402] Ibid, p61
[403] Ibid, p67
[404] McCraw, *Creating Modern Capitalism,* p.194
[405] Günther Birkenstock. "The Krupp dynasty - glorified and vilified." *Deutsche Welle*, www.dw.de, April 10, 2012, retrieved August 18, 2014
[406] Manchester, *The Arms of Krupp,* p290
[407] Ibid, p301
[408] Fear, *Organizing Control,* p300
[409] Ibid, p445
[410] McCraw, *Creating Modern Capitalism,* p209
[411] David Litchfield. "The killer countess: The dark past of Baron Heinrich Thyssen's daughter." *The Independent*, October 7, 2007. http://www.independent.co.uk/news/people/profiles/the-killer-countess-the-dark-past-of-baron-heinrich-thyssens-daughter-395976.html. Retrieved October 5, 2016
[412] Ibid.
[413] "Letter to John Pehle." Assistant Secretary of the Treasury, August 18, 1941.
[414] "Gustav Krupp von Bohlen und Halbach." brittanica.com, retrieved August 20, 2014
[415] Manchester, *The Arms of Krupp,* p293
[416] International Military Tribunal "Blue Series," Vol. 1, p. 136
[417] "1919: THE SPARTACIST UPRISING." www.weimarandnazigermany.co.uk, retrieved August 6, 2014
[418] Sally Marks. "The Myths of Reparations" *Central European History, Volume 11, Issue # 3*, September 1978, pages 240–241
[419] H.J. Rupieper. *The Cuno Government and Reparations 1922–1923: Politics and Economics*. (The Hague: Martinus Nijhoff, 1979), p16
[420] "Fritz Thyssen's Letters." *Life Magazine*, April 29, 1940, p11
[421] Report #1, *Examination of Dr. Fritz Thyssen*, US Group Control Council (Germany). Office of the Director of Intelligence, September 4, 1945, p15
[422] Ibid.

[423] John M. Ries. "German Big Business and the Rise of Hitler (review)." *The Journal of Historical Review, Fall 1988* (Vol. 8, No. 3), p369-371
[424] Report #1, Examination of Dr. Fritz Thyssen, p1
[425] Ibid, p12
[426] Ibid, p14
[427] Jewish Virtual Library. "The Nazi Party: The Night of the Long Knives." www.jewishvirtuallibrary.com, retrieved June 30, 2014
[428] "Fritz Thyssen's Letters," p12
[429] Ibid, p96
[430] Manchester, *The Arms of Krupp*, p346
[431] Telford Taylor. *Sword and Swastika: Generals and Nazis in the Third Reich.* (New York: Simon & Schuster, 1952), p84
[432] Manchester, *The Arms of Krupp*, p382
[433] Ibid, p369
[434] "Fritz Thyssen's Letters," p96
[435] Ibid
[436] Report #1, Examination of Dr. Fritz Thyssen, p10
[437] THE UNITED NATIONS WAR CRIMES COMMISSION. *LAW REPORTS OF TRIALS OF WAR CRIMINALS, THE I.G. FARBEN AND KRUPP TRIALS.* (HM Stationery Office: London, 1949), Vol X. p82.
[438] Ibid
[439] Ibid, p83
[440] Ibid, p84
[441] Ibid, p85
[442] Ibid, p87
[443] Ibid, p88.
[444] Ibid.
[445] Ibid, p90.
[446] Ibid, p94
[447] Ibid, p99.
[448] Adam Tooze. *The Wages of Destruction: The Making and Breaking of the Nazi Economy.* (London: Penguin Group, 2006), Section III, ebook
[449] Paul Garson. *New Images of Nazi Germany: A Photographic Collection.* (Jefferson, NC: McFarland, 2012), p130
[450] Roman Köster as quoted. "Hugo Boss apology for Nazi past as book is published." *BBC Online.* www.bbc.com, September 21, 2011, retrieved April 6, 2014
[451] Elisabeth Timm. *Hugo Ferdinand Boss (1885-1948) und die Firma Hugo Boss: Eine Dokumentation*, April 18, 1999, p13
[452] Roman Köster. *Hugo Boss, 1924-1945. A Clothing Factory During the Weimar Republic and Third Reich (abridged version)*, Hugo Boss AG, p2
[453] Roman Köster as quoted. "German fashion label Hugo Boss goes public with Nazi past." *Deutsche Welle*, www.dw.de, September 25, 2011, retrieved August 8, 2014
[454] Timm, *Hugo Ferdinand Boss*, p15
[455] Ibid, p17

[456] Ibid, p19
[457] Köster, *Hugo Boss*, p3
[458] Timm, *Hugo Ferdinand Boss*, p23
[459] Ibid, p49
[460] Ibid, p27
[461] Zwangsarbeitern in Metzingen. "Die Firma Hugo Boss." www.metzingen-zwangsarbeit.de, retrieved August 17, 2014
[462] Ibid.
[463] Timm, *Hugo Ferdinand Boss*, p55
[464] Köster, *Hugo Boss*, p6
[465] Siegfried Boss, as quoted. "Hugo Boss Acknowledges Link to Nazi Regime." *New York Times*, www.nytimes.com, August 15, 1997, retrieved July 31, 2014
[466] Barbara Smit. *Pitch Invasion – Three Stripes, Two Brothers, One Feud: Adidas, Puma and the Making of Modern Sport*. (New York: Penguin Adult, 2006,) p4
[467] Ibid, p7
[468] Erik Kirschbaum. "How Adidas and Puma were born." *Reuters*. www.reuters.com, November 08, 2005, retrieved August 9, 2014
[469] Smit, *Pitch Invasion*, p28
[470] Ibid, p25
[471] Robert Kuhn and Thomas Thiel. "Shoes and Nazi Bazookas: The Prehistory of Adidas and Puma." *Der Spiegel*, www.speigel.de, March 4, 2009, retrieved August 9, 2014
[472] "Adidas versus Puma: Origins of a rivalry between brothers." *New York Times*, www.nytimes.com, November 8, 2005, retrieved August 9, 2014
[473] Omar Akhtar. "The hatred and bitterness behind two of the world's most popular brands." *CNN*. www.features.blogs.fortune.cnn.com, March 22, 2013, retrieved August 9, 2014
[474] Ibid.
[475] BASF. "1865 – 1901: The birth of the chemical industry and the era of dyes." www.basf.com, retrieved March 18, 2014
[476] Diarmuid Jeffreys. *Hell's Cartel: IG Farben and the making of Hitler's war machine*. (New York: Macmillan, 2008), p51
[477] Vaclav Smil. "Detonator of the population explosion." *Nature*, July 29, 1999, p415
[478] Nobel Prize. "Carl Bosch – Facts." www.nobelprize.org, retrieved April 19, 2014
[479] Wollheim Memorial. "The Role of the German Chemical Industry in the First World War." www.wollheim-memorial.de, retrieved April 21, 2014
[480] Victor Lefebure. *The Riddle of the Rhine: Chemical Strategy in Peace and War*. (London: Collins, 1922), p27
[481] Charles E. Heller. *Chemical Warfare in World War I: The American Experience, 1917 – 1918*. (Fort Leavenworth, KS: U.S. Army Command and General Staff College, 1984), p7

[482] "PHOSGENE (CG): Lung Damaging Agent." *The Centers for Disease Control and Prevention*, www.cdc.gov, retrieved April 30, 2014
[483] Chris Bowlby. "Fritz Haber: Jewish chemist whose work led to Zyklon B." *BBC Online*. www.bbc.com, April 11 2011, retrieved April 30, 2014
[484] Lydia Mulvany. "Heroin, Nazis, and Agent Orange: Inside the $66 Billion Merger of the Year" *Bloomberg*. http://www.bloomberg.com/news/articles/2016-09-14/the-heroin-laced-history-behind-the-year-s-biggest-deal, September 14, 2016, retrieved October 13, 2016.
[485] Alexander Jung. "Als die Mark vernichtet wurde" *Der Spiegel*. http://www.spiegel.de/einestages/hyperinflation-1923-a-948427.html July 31, 2009, retrieved October 13, 2016
[486] Alexander Jung. "Millions, Billions, Trillions: Germany in the Era of Hyperinflation." *Der Spiegel*, www.spiegel.de, August 14 2009, retrieved April 16 2014
[487] Jeffreys, *Hell's Cartel*, p145
[488] Ibid, p150
[489] Office of the Military Government for Germany (OMGUS). *Report on Investigation of I.G. Farbenindustrie*. (Washington: National Archives and Records Administration, 1945), p98
[490] Jeffreys, *Hell's Cartel*, p168
[491] Georg von Schnitzler on Hitler's Appeal to Leading German Industrialists on February 20, 1933 (Affidavit, November 10, 1945). *United States Chief Counsel for the Prosecution of Axis Criminality, Nazi Conspiracy and Aggression, Volume VII*. (Washington, DC: United States Government Printing Office, 1946), Document 439-EC
[492] OMGUS I. G. Farben, p89
[493] Heinrich Gattineau. Affidavit, March 13, 1947, NI-4833. *Archive of the Fritz Bauer Institute, Subsequent Nuremberg Trials, Case VI, Prosecution Exhibits*, reel 016, pp. 227–232
[494] Hermann Bässler. *Tabulation by the former staff chief of the Central Committee office*, July 30, 1947, NI-9200. Archive of the Stiftung für Sozialgeschichte Bremen, Nuremberg Documents: NI-Series
[495] OMGUS I.G. Farben, p1
[496] James Neal Harvey. *Sharks of the Air: Willy Messerschmitt and How He Built the World's First Operational Jet Fighter*. (Havertown PA: Casemate Publishers, 2011), Chapter 71, ebook
[497] OMGUS I.G. Farben, p2
[498] Ibid, p3
[499] Ibid, p6
[500] Ibid, p3
[501] Ibid, p7
[502] Ibid, p14
[503] OMGUS Deutsche Bank, p235
[504] OMGUS I.G. Farben, p122
[505] Statement of Max Ilgner to OMGUS authorities, August 15, 1945

[506] OMGUS I.G. Farben, p116
[507] Ibid, p114
[508] Ibid, p128
[509] CASE No. 57. THE I.G. FARBEN TRIAL: TRIAL OF CARL KRAUCH AND TWENTY-TWO OTHERS. (Nuremberg: United States Military Tribunal, August 14, 1947), p19
[510] Division of Investigation of Cartels and External Assets Office of Military Government, U.S. (Germany). *Report on the Investigation of I.G. Farbenindustrie A.G.*, November 1945, p109.
[511] Conference at French Ministry of Production, March 6 1941
[512] OMGUS I.G. Farben, p149
[513] Ibid, p143
[514] Statement of von Schnitzler to OMGUS authorities, August 30 1945
[515] OMGUS I.G. Farben, p147
[516] Ibid, p145
[517] Ibid, p119
[518] Wollheim Memorial. "Forced Labor at I.G. Farben." www.wollheim-memorial.de, retrieved April 28, 2014
[519] Ibid, "Wilhelm Rudolf Mann (1894–1992)." www.wollheim-memorial.de, retrieved April 28, 2014
[520] Ernst Klee. *Das Personenlexikon zum Dritten Reich*. (Frankfurt am Main: Fischer, 2007), p455
[521] UNITED NATIONS WAR CRIMES COMMISSION. LAW REPORTS OF TRIALS OF WAR CRIMINALS. Volume I. (HIS MAJESTY'S STATIONERY OFFICE: London, 1948), p95.
[522] Gerald L. Posner, John Ware. *Mengele: The Complete Story.* (New York: Cooper Square Press, 1986), p26
[523] Alan Levy. *Nazi Hunter: The Wiesenthal File*. (London: Constable & Robinson Ltd., 1993), part21
[524] Posner and Ware, *Mengele,* p34
[525] Ibid, p37
[526] Levy, *Nazi Hunter*, part21
[527] Helena Kubica. "The Crimes of Josef Mengele." *Anatomy of the Auschwitz Death Camp.* (Bloomington, IN: Indiana University Press. 1984), p317–337
[528] Jeffreys, *Hell's Cartel*, p328
[529] The Trial of German Major War Criminals. 29 January, 1946, Nuremberg, p253.
[530] Naomi Baumslag. *Murderous Medicine: Nazi Doctors, Human Experimentation, and Typhus*. (Westport, CT: Praeger, 2005), p150.
[531] Wollheim Memorial. Selections and Human Experiments in the Prisoner Infirmary. http://www.wollheim-memorial.de/en/selektionen_und_menschenversuche_im_haeftlingskrankenbau#_edn3, retrieved October 17, 2016
[532] Von Halter, Hans. "Erinnerung an den Teufel." *Der Spiegel*, www.spiegel.de, June 11, 2001, retrieved May 6, 2014

[533] Rolf Winau. "Medizinische Exeperimente in Konzentrationslagern." *Der Ort des Terrors – Geschichte der nationalsozialistischen Konzentrationslager, Vol. 1: Die Organisation des Terrors*. (München: C.H. Beck, 2005), p174
[534] "The Headquarters of the American Forces in Germany in the Former I.G. Farben Building in Frankfurt am Main (1949)." *German History in Documents and Images (GHDI)*, www.germanhistorydocs.ghi-dc.org, retrieved April 17, 2014
[535] The United States of America v. Carl Brauch et al. (Case VI). (Nuremberg: Records of the United States Nuernburg War Crimes Trials, August 14, 1947 – June 30, 1948), p7
[536] Roger Williams. "The Nazis and Thalidomide: The Worst Drug Scandal of All Time." *Newsweek*, www.newsweek.com, September 10, 2012, retrieved April 21, 2014
[537] Wollheim Memorial. Otto Ambros (1901–1990). http://www.wollheim-memorial.de/en/otto_ambros_19011990#_edn3, retrieved October 17, 2016.
[538] Ibid, Wilhelm Rudolf Mann (1894–1992). http://www.wollheim-memorial.de/en/wilhelm_rudolf_mann_18941992, retrieved October 17, 2016.
[539] OMGUS I.G. Farben, p114
[540] Ibid, p115.
[541] Ibid, Introduction p1
[542] Ibid. p2
[543] Ibid, p6
[544] Ibid, preface p4
[545] Ibid, p21
[546] Ibid, p31
[547] Ibid, p25
[548] Robert J. Baptista and Anthony S. Travis, "I.G. Farben in America: The Technologies of General Aniline and Film." http://www.colorantshistory.org/IGFarbenAmerica.html, 2006, p7
[549] "IG Farbenindustrie Aktiengesellschaft 1930, Frankfurt am Main (annual report)."p13,14, 16, 25–6, 38; "General Aniline & Film." Fortune 36, no. 2 (August 1947). p68–73, 148–53
[550] OMGUS I. G. Farben, p45
[551] Ibid, p30
[552] Ibid, p36
[553] Ibid, p39
[554] Walter C. Louchheim, Jr. *Memorandum to Sam Klaus, Foreign Economic Administration*. The United States Securities & Exchange Commission, February 3, 1945
[555] OMGUS I.G. Farben, p41
[556] Ibid, p42
[557] Ibid, p44
[558] Ibid, preface p4
[559] Ibid, p19
[560] Ibid, p17
[561] Ibid, p50a

[562] Ibid, p51
[563] Ibid, p52-53
[564] Ibid, p57
[565] Ibid, p62
[566] Ibid, p70
[567] Ibid
[568] Ibid, p83
[569] Ibid, p72
[570] FEZANDIE & SPERRLE, INC., v. COMMISSIONER OF INTERNAL REVENUE. United States Tax Court. Promulgated December 10, 1945
[571] "CLARENCE OPPER, JUDGE, DIES AT 67." *New York Times*. www.nytimes.com, June 21, 1964, retrieved August 21, 2014
[572] OMGUS I.G. Farben, p.74
[573] Ibid
[574] Ibid, p78
[575] Ibid
[576] Ibid, p91
[577] Ibid, p10
[578] Ibid, p12
[579] Ibid, p85
[580] Jeffreys, Hell's Cartel, p138
[581] Ibid, p140
[582] "Prewar." www.oskarschindler.com, retrieved July 16, 2014
[583] United States Holocaust Memorial Museum. "OSKAR SCHINDLER." www.ushmm.org, retrieved July 16, 2014
[584] "Berthold Beitz." http://auschwitz.dk/rescuers/id16.htm, retrieved October 18, 2016
[585] Chris Bryant. "Germany remembers ThyssenKrupp patriarch Berthold Beitz." *Financial Times*, www.ft.com, September 26, 2013, retrieved September 17, 2014
[586] Emily Langer. "Berthold Beitz, German industrialist who rescued Jews during World War II, dies at 99." *Washington Post*. www.washingtonpost.com, August 1, 2013, retrieved September 16 2014
[587] "Berthold Beitz." www.auschwitz.dk/rescuers, retrieved September 16, 2014
[588] Manchester, *Arms of Krupp*, p704
[589] Ibid, p707
[590] Maria Marquart. "Zum Tode von Berthold Beitz: Der Getreue des letzten Stahlbarons." *Der Spiegel*, http://www.spiegel.de/wirtschaft/unternehmen/thyssenkrupp-berthold-beitz-ist-tot-a-914148.html, July 31, 2013, retrieved October 19, 2016.
[591] Manchester, *Arms of Krupp*, p755
[592] Ibid, p712
[593] Yad Vashem. "Berthold and Elsa Beitz." http://www.yadvashem.org/yv/en/righteous/stories/beitz.asp, retrieved September 17, 2014

[594] Ibid, "Walz Family." www.yadvashem.org, retrieved September 17, 2014
[595] Robert Bosch GMbH. "Mission and Establishment of the Foundation." http://www.bosch-stiftung.de/content/language2/html/3290.asp, retrieved October 19, 2016.
[596] John Rabe. "Letter to Hitler." From Rabe's diary, Nanjing
[597] Iris Chang. *The Rape of Nanking: The Forgotten Holocaust of World War II.* (New York: Penguin, 1998, p191)